Bismarck

PROFILES IN POWER

General Editor: Keith Robbins

LLOYD GEORGE
Martin Pugh

HITLER
Ian Kershaw

RICHELIEU
R.J. Knecht

NAPOLEON III
James McMillan

OLIVER CROMWELL
Barry Coward

NASSER
Peter Woodward

GUSTAVUS ADOLPHUS
(2nd edn)
Michael Roberts

CHURCHILL
Keith Robbins

DE GAULLE
Andrew Shennan

FRANCO
Sheelagh Ellwood

JUÁREZ
Brian Hamnett

ALEXANDER I
Janet M. Hartley

MACMILLAN
John Turner

JOSEPH II
T.C.W. Blanning

ATATÜRK
A.L. Macfie

CAVOUR
Harry Hearder

DISRAELI
Ian Machin

CASTRO (2nd edn)
Sebastian Balfour

PETER THE GREAT
(2nd end)
M.S. Anderson

FRANCIS JOSEPH
Stephen Beller

NAPOLEON
Geoffrey Ellis

KENNEDY
Hugh Brogan

ATTLEE
Robert Pearce

PÉTAIN
Nicholas Atkin

THE ELDER PITT
Marie Peters

CATHERINE DE' MEDICI
R.J. Knecht

GORBACHEV
Martin McCauley

JAMES VI AND I
Roger Lockyer

ELIZABETH I (2nd edn)
Christopher Haigh

MAO
S.G. Breslin

BURGHLEY
Michael A.R. Graves

NEHRU
Judith M. Brown

ROBESPIERRE
John Hardman

LENIN
Beryl Williams

WILLIAM PENN
Mary Geiter

THE YOUNGER PITT
Michael Duffy

KAISER WILHELM II
Christopher Clark

TANAKA
David Babb

PORFIRIO DÍAZ
Paul Garner

CATHERINE THE GREAT
Simon Dixon

ADENAUER
Ronald Irving

GANDHI
David Arnold

JAMES II
W.A. Speck

LINCOLN
Richard J. Cawardine

WOODROW WILSON
John A. Thompson

THE GREAT ELECTOR
Derek Mckay

TALLEYRAND
Philip G. Dwyer

WILLIAM III
A.M. Claydon

IVAN THE TERRIBLE
Andrei Pavlor and
Maureen Perrie

HENRY VIII
Michael A.R. Graves

BISMARCK
Katharine Anne Lerman

Bismarck

Katharine Anne Lerman

Harlow, England • London • New York • Boston • San Francisco • Toronto
Sydney • Singapore • Hong Kong • Tokyo • Seoul • Taipei • New Delhi
Cape Town • Madrid • Mexico City • Amsterdam • Munich • Paris • Milan

PEARSON EDUCATION LIMITED

Edinburgh Gate
Harlow CM20 2JE
Tel: +44 (0)1279 623623
Fax: +44 (0)1279 431059
Website: www.pearsoned.co.uk

First edition published in Great Britain in 2004

ISBN 0 582 03740 9

British Library Cataloguing in Publication Data
A CIP catalogue record for this book can be obtained from the British Library

Library of Congress Cataloging in Publication Data
A CIP catalog record for this book can be obtained from the Library of Congress

10 9 8 7 6 5 4 3 2 1

Set by 35 in 9.5/12pt Celeste
Printed in Malaysia

The Publisher's policy is to use paper manufactured from sustainable forests.

Contents

Acknowledgements

We are grateful to the following for permission to reproduce copyright material:

Map 1 redrawn from *The Origin of the Wars of German Unification*, published by Longman, reprinted by permission of Pearson Education Ltd (Carr, W. 1991); Maps 2 and 3 from *The Formation of the First German Nation-State, 1800–1871*, published by Macmillan, reproduced with permission of Palgrave Macmillan (Breuilly, J. 1996).

In some instances we have been unable to trace the owners of copyright material, and we would appreciate any information that would enable us to do so.

Preface

Otto von Bismarck was one of the most significant and powerful men in modern European history. He was appointed minister-president of Prussia in 1862, a state which had few claims to be included among the first ranking European powers even if it represented Austria's main challenger for influence over German affairs. Nine years later in 1871, after three victorious Prussian wars, the restructuring of central Europe and a fundamental realignment of political forces in Prussia and Germany, he emerged as the leading statesman of a new and powerful German Empire or Reich. For the next nineteen years he enjoyed an authority and dominance at home which defied all challengers, and his stature, prestige and proven diplomatic skill ensured that he eclipsed all his contemporaries on the European stage. For over a quarter of a century he held tightly to the reins of political power, impressing his personality on German and European politics, and tolerating no opposition to his indomitable will. When, two weeks before his seventy-fifth birthday in 1890, he was forced to relinquish control by a superior authority, the young monarch Kaiser Wilhelm II, he made no attempt to conceal his extreme reluctance, and his bitterness over the loss of power never waned. The pursuit and exercise of power are central to an understanding of Bismarck as a man and a statesman. Power shaped Bismarck's personality and its ultimate effect was corrosive: it consumed all his other interests and passions, took precedence over his family and ate away at his basic humanity.

How Bismarck used his political power has long been the subject of controversy. The 'small German' or *kleindeutsch* unification of Germany was once celebrated as the triumphant culmination of nearly two centuries of Prussian history, the embodiment of human progress and vindication of previously disappointed German aspirations for nationhood. But after the experience of two world wars, historians inevitably cast a more critical gaze on Bismarck's creation. They questioned the methods by which unification was achieved and concluded that the enforced conquest of Germany by Prussia had profound implications for the subsequent development of this dynamic new state in the middle of Europe, a state with enormous economic potential but riddled with social and political tensions. The politically volatile Bismarckian Reich engendered and ultimately fell victim to an explosive and virulent form of German nationalism which, in fuelling dreams of conquest and perceptions of superiority, brought unprecedented misery and destruction before it was finally defeated in 1945. Moreover, Prussia's victory in the 'civil war' against Austria in 1866 was seen to have dismembered an older, historic Germany with consequences which were not dissimilar to the division of Germany after the Second World War. Bismarck's 'unification' of Germany was really a partition of the German nation. The Reich he created was not national, liberal and united; it was artificial and unnatural, an entity soldered from a fractured nation rather than a nation-state. Political nationhood was only achieved at the high price of demonising all alternative conceptions of German national identity and seeking to suppress ethnic minorities such as the Poles, the French and the Danes who found themselves included in the new Prusso-German entity.

Bismarck's ability to use political power creatively between 1862 and 1871 to reshape German and European politics cannot fail to impress historians interested in the role of the individual in history. Although Bismarck himself maintained that he could only ride the forces of history or cling on to history's coat-tails, and although there were many factors which clearly favoured the eventual outcome of a Prussian victory over Austria for influence over German affairs, it is impossible to argue that things would have turned out much the same if Bismarck had not been at the helm or that his personality did not make a significant difference. The form which German unification eventually took and, perhaps more importantly, the future political development of the Reich bore the indelible imprint of Bismarck's personality and his exercise of power. His unique contribution to the development of modern Germany raised the question among contemporaries whether the Reich could survive or be ruled at all once the *Reichsgründer* (founder of the Reich) had left the political stage. Furthermore, Bismarck's style of governance as Prussian premier and Reich chancellor set new standards of political leadership in Germany, against which all who followed were measured. As Christopher Clark noted in his volume on Kaiser Wilhelm II in this series, Bismarck defined the meaning of political power for a generation of Germans. His authoritarianism and illiberalism, his domineering will to power, his ruthless and confrontational response to all who dared to cross him, and his marked aversion to consensual politics, were some of Bismarck's qualities which served to shape the contours of German politics well into the twentieth century.

This book is less concerned with analysing Bismarck's political legacy than with investigating how he exercised political power during his twenty-eight years in high office. As a 'Profile in Power', it does not seek to provide a political biography or life and times of Germany's first chancellor, nor can it provide a balanced overview of his main achievements, most of which are amply covered in the wider literature on nineteenth-century German history. It does, however, draw on an extensive Bismarck historiography and, in particular, the detailed research of several pre-eminent Bismarck scholars in its attempt to explore how Bismarck pursued political power, what kind of power he exercised and by what mechanisms he sought to maintain and enhance his power. It offers students an interpretation of Bismarck's rule which eschews the myths and his self-justifying reflections and reminiscences, and focuses on the reality of his position within the Berlin executive and his actual role in German decision-making. It looks at what Bismarck sought to do in office and the extent to which he was able to achieve his objectives. For all the contemporary talk of Bismarck's autocratic rule and his chancellor dictatorship, the constraints on his exercise of power ultimately weighed heavily on him, overshadowing his freedom of action and decision.

A short, interpretative work on Bismarck's power was always going to be a challenge and I am extremely grateful to the series editor, Keith Robbins, and to Heather McCallum at Pearson Education for their patience in bearing with me throughout this project. I should also like to thank the Faculty Research Committee at the University of North London (now London Metropolitan University) for funding visits to the archives in Berlin and Koblenz, as well as to Friedrichsruh. The encouragement and friendship of my colleague, Kathryn Castle, who read a substantial part of the manuscript, was indispensable. John Röhl, too, made time despite a very busy schedule to read and comment on the book. His unparalleled expertise has been a source of great inspiration to me over the years and he knows how highly I value his opinion. Any mistakes are, of course, my own. Finally, I owe a huge debt of gratitude to my husband, Tony, and to my three children, all of whom have grown up surrounded with books, papers and photographs of Bismarck and must have wondered whether their mother would ever have a life 'after Bismarck'. This book is dedicated to Ben, Rachel and Emma in the hope that one day they may have the time or inclination to read it and understand better the fascination of the stern old gentleman.

List of Abbreviations

Engelberg	Ernst Engelberg, *Bismarck*, 2 vols, I: *Urpreuße und Reichsgründer*, II: *Das Reich in der Mitte Europas* (Berlin, 1986–90).
Fuchs	Walther Peter Fuchs (ed.), *Großherzog Friedrich I von Baden und die Reichspolitik 1871–1907*, 4 vols (Stuttgart, 1968–80).
Gall	Lothar Gall, *Bismarck: The White Revolutionary*, 2 vols, I: *1815–1871*, II: *1871–1898* (London, 1986).
Gerlach	Hellmut Diwald (ed.), *Von der Revolution zum Norddeutschen Bund: Politik und Ideengut der preußischen Hochkonservativen 1848–1866: Aus dem Nachlaß von Ernst Ludwig von Gerlach*, 2 vols, I: *Tagebuch 1848–1866* and II: *Briefe, Denkschriften, Aufzeichnungen* (Göttingen, 1970).
Große Politik	J. Lepsius, A. Mendelssohn-Bartholdy and F. Thimme (eds), *Die Große Politik der Europäischen Kabinette, 1871–1914*, 40 vols (Berlin, 1922–27).
GW	Otto von Bismarck, *Die gesammelten Werke (Friedrichsruhe Ausgabe)*, 15 [19] vols (Berlin, 1924–35).
Holstein	Norman Rich and M.H. Fisher (eds), *The Holstein Papers*, 4 vols (Cambridge, 1955–63).
Oncken	Hermann Oncken (ed.), *Großherzog Friedrich I von Baden und die deutsche Politik von 1854 bis 1871: Briefwechsel, Denkschriften, Tagebücher*, 2 vols (Stuttgart, 1927).
Pflanze	Otto Pflanze, *Bismarck and the Development of Germany*, 3 vols, I: *The Period of Unification 1815–1871*, II: *The Period of Consolidation 1871–1880*, III: *The Period of Fortification 1880–1898* (Princeton, NJ, 1990).
Quellensammlung	Karl Erich Born, Hansjoachim Henning and Florian Tennstedt (eds), *Quellensammlung zur Geschichte*

der deutchen Sozialpolitik 1867 bis 1914.
I. Abteilung. Von der Reichsgründungszeit bis zur
Kaiserlichen Sozialbotschaft (1867–1881),
II. Abteilung. Von der Kaiserlichen Sozialbotschaft
bis zu den Februarerlassen Wilhelms II (1881–1890).

Rothfels   Hans Rothfels (ed.), *Bismarck-Briefe* (Göttingen, 1955).

Spitzemberg   Rudolf Vierhaus (ed.), *Das Tagebuch der Baronin Spitzemberg: Aufzeichnungen aus der Hofgesellschaft des Hohenzollernreiches* (Göttingen, 1960).

Steglich   Wolfgang Steglich (ed.), *Quellen zur Geschichte des Weimarer und Berliner Hofes in der Krisen- und Kriegszeit 1865/67*, 2 vols, I: *Der Weimarer Hof*, II: *Der Berliner Hof* (Frankfurt, 1996).

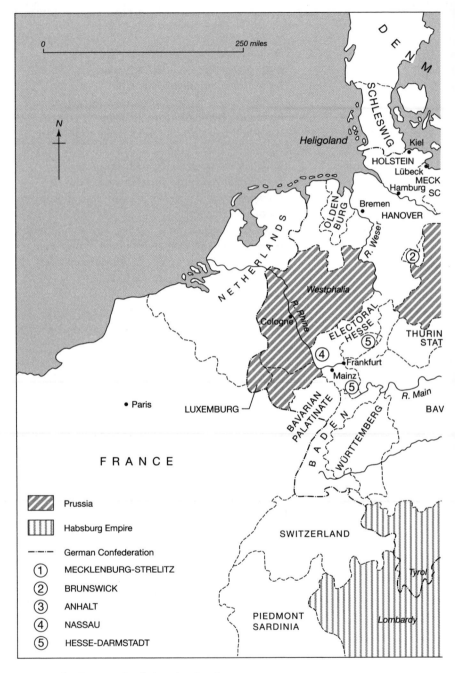

Map 1 The German Confederation in 1815

Source: Redrawn from Carr, W. (1991) *The Origin of the Wars of German Unification*
(pub. Longman), Map 1, p. 222. Reprinted with permission of Pearson Education Ltd.

SWEDEN

BALTIC SEA

A R K

LENBURG
HWERIN

①

Pomerania

Danzig

West Prussia

East Prussia

R U S S I A N

Berlin

R. Oder

Brandenburg

③

R. Elbe

Dresden

SAXONY

Posen

R. Vistula

POLAND

GIAN
ES

Silesia

Prague

ARIA

Bohemia

Olmütz

Munich

A U S T R I A

Moravia

R. Danube

Budapest

Gastein

H U N G A R Y

Venetia

Venice

Carniola

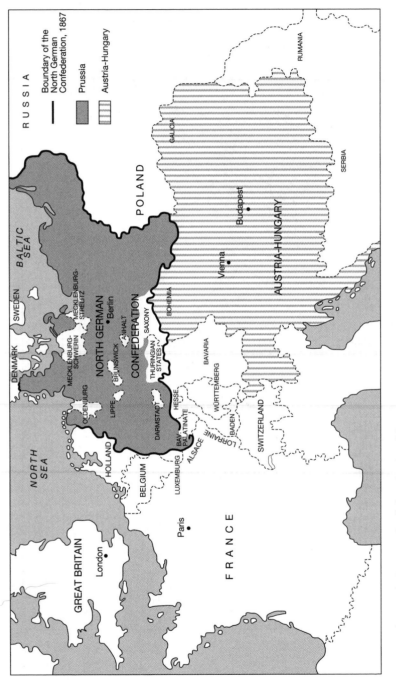

Map 2 The North German Confederation in 1867

Source: Breuilly, J. *The Formation of the First German Nation-State, 1800–1871*, pub. 1996, Macmillan, p. xii, reproduced with permission of Palgrave Macmillan.

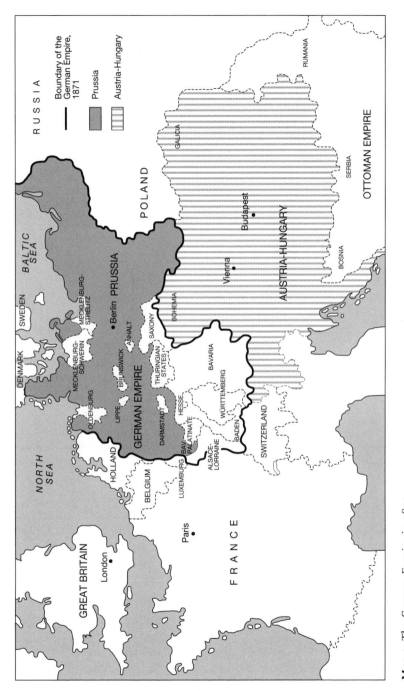

Map 3 The German Empire in 1871

Source: Breuilly, J. *The Formation of the First German Nation-State, 1800–1871*, pub. 1996, Macmillan, p. xiii, reproduced with permission of Palgrave Macmillan.

Chapter 1

Personal Power

What kind of a man was Bismarck and how exceptional was his personality? Modern historians have rightly become reluctant to single out major historical figures for their individuality or their unique blend of qualities and no one today would attempt to argue that Bismarck would have achieved power and prominence irrespective of the historical conditions in which he found himself. Nevertheless, a discussion of Bismarck's personality is important in seeking to explain why he eventually sought political power and how he exercised it. Moreover, Bismarck clearly developed a marked appetite for power and, at some deep psychological level, his will to power sprang from an inner necessity. He did not always seek power, but power became for him a means of self-realisation and self-fulfilment.

'Bismarck's whole person was calculated to impress, and he knew it', the diplomat and later counsellor in the German Foreign Office, Friedrich von Holstein, recalled.[1] Long before he achieved virtually mythical status as the 'Iron Chancellor', represented in both monumental official pictures and satirical cartoons as a towering, forbidding figure wearing thigh-high cuirassier boots, Bismarck compelled notice. An early chalk drawing of Bismarck in 1826 as an 11-year-old boy suggests a mischievous urchin with a penetrating gaze. Philipp Petri's porcelain picture seven years later reveals the brooding, dissatisfied countenance of a young man by no means reconciled to his existence.[2] Standing at an erect 6' 4" high, with reddish blond hair and a rather sallow complexion, Bismarck was quite slender as a youth. In his student days he enjoyed striding around Göttingen in unconventional clothes and accompanied by a large mastiff dog. With maturity he developed a powerful build, fuelled by his voracious consumption of food and drink, and upon his massive frame his head sometimes appeared peculiarly small. Those who heard him speak for the first time were often surprised, too, by his rather thin, high-pitched voice. As a public speaker Bismarck developed a caustic, sarcastic, confrontational style but, publicly and privately, he often spoke haltingly as he searched (usually successfully) for the right words.

Even as a young man Bismarck was supremely self-confident and physically courageous. He was a strong swimmer, singlehandedly rescuing two men and their horses from drowning in a lake in 1842, and an enthusiastic hunter of game. As a student he often lacked self-discipline and indulged in bouts of wild, unrestrained behaviour. He fought countless duels, the last one in 1852 when he already had three children under the age of 5 and risked his life in a shoot-out with the liberal politician Georg von Vincke (they both missed). Even as Prussian minister-president in 1865 he twice challenged another parliamentary opponent, Rudolf Virchow, to a duel, but his adversary, a surgeon, insisted he could only give satisfaction with the pen or the operating knife. Bismarck also attacked his would-be assassin in 1866, Ferdinand Cohen-Blind, seizing him by the neck and right arm as his assailant fired shots from his revolver. Bismarck possessed an explosive and unpredictable temperament, but he complained that most portrait painters gave him too violent an expression and failed to capture his sentimental, pensive nature. Emotional and prone to weeping, he precipitated the death of a favourite dog in 1877 by thrashing him for running away, and then he sobbed inconsolably with remorse. A reader of romantic fiction and professed lover of music, he refused to pay money to go to a concert and believed that music, like love, should be free.

Bismarck always attracted interest and notice, but it is questionable whether he allowed anyone in his life, even his wife and family, to know him intimately. An early female admirer, Marie von Thadden, confessed in 1843: 'His fine carriage, his brilliance, both internal and external, attract me more and more. But when I am with him I always feel that I am skating on thin ice and might go through at any moment.'[3] Friedrich von Holstein, encountering the 45-year-old Bismarck in 1861 when the latter was ambassador to St Petersburg, suggested that Bismarck thrived on constant strife. 'Total impression one of a dissatisfied man, partly a hypochondriac, partly a man insufficiently reconciled to the quiet life led in those days by the Prussian representative in St Petersburg. His every utterance revealed that for him action and existence were one and the same thing.'[4] The Prussian secretary of legation in St Petersburg and later minister at the Vatican, Kurd von Schlözer, came to much the same conclusion. 'Bismarck is politics personified,' he wrote. 'Everything is fermenting within him, pressing to be activated and given form.'[5]

Family, education and early life

Bismarck's childhood and youth offer few indications that he was a man destined to play a role of great historical significance. Especially in later life, he often dwelt on the unhappiness of his childhood and he blamed most of his early misfortunes on his mother whom he accused of coldness and even maternal neglect. But it can scarcely be argued that he encountered any significant degree of adversity in his early life or that his family circumstances nurtured any particular, unusual qualities or talents that proved beneficial to him in later life. For a man of his social class he had a fairly typical upbringing, with the notable exception that he was sent away to school at a relatively young age rather than being educated at home. But he never made the most of his education, at school or university, and by the time he was ready to embark on a career, he displayed little sense of direction or highly developed motivation. Nor is there any real evidence that he had much interest in politics before he was in his thirties.

Otto Eduard Leopold von Bismarck was born on 1 April 1815 on his father's estate at Schönhausen, some 60 miles west of Berlin near the river Elbe in the *Altmark* of Brandenburg. He was born into the Prussian landowning nobility or Junker class whose history is closely intertwined with the rise of monarchical absolutism in Prussia and the growth of the modern state. Traditionally the power and privileges of the Prussian Junkers derived from their control of the land and the economy it supported, but in the course of the eighteenth century they had developed into a confident and cohesive ruling elite, combining their social power and material wealth with a pervasive ethos of state service. The Bismarcks could trace their ancestry back to the thirteenth century and Otto's great-grandfather had excelled as an officer in the army of Frederick the Great.

Both contemporaries and historians have often sought to portray Bismarck as a typical representative of his social class, a man whose first interventions in public life were in defence of aristocratic privilege and who famously remarked during the revolution of 1848–49, 'I am a Junker and mean to have the advantages of being one.'[6] Nevertheless, it is too easy to see Bismarck as a man who expected to enjoy power and privilege by virtue of his birth and whose subsequent political activity and achievements were directed towards the preservation of the traditional Prussian political and social system. The Junkers were a hard-working nobility, neither parasitic nor ostentatiously wealthy, who were integrated into state and local hierarchies and thus peculiarly well placed to defend their interests and traditional way of life against the encroachments of an increasingly centralised and bureaucratic state. But in the fluid and unstable social conditions of the early nineteenth century, noble status could guarantee neither wealth nor power, even if it brought the expectation of social esteem. To survive materially, the Junker landowners had to adapt to new forms of property-ownership, a different kind of social dependency on the land and the growing pressures of a capitalist market economy. To survive politically, the ruling elite had to redefine its role in state politics and confront challenges to its traditional authority, for example the demand for popular representation and participation. That the Junkers as a social class were able to make these adjustments was not a foregone conclusion even by the middle of the nineteenth century.

Bismarck was the second surviving son of a marriage which has received close scrutiny from historians. Ferdinand von Bismarck was a fairly typical Junker of comparatively modest means who had given up his army career in 1795 to farm his estates (thus forfeiting the chance to fight in the wars of liberation against Napoleon) and who in 1816 moved his family from Schönhausen to Kniephof, one of three much smaller estates he had inherited in Pomerania. His wife, Wilhelmine Louise Mencken, appears to have been the dominant partner in the marriage and it has become customary for historians to emphasise her more middle-class origins as well as how her social ambitions and the educational choices she made for her two sons diverged from traditional Junker expectations.

The Menckens were not of noble birth and, despite investing in land, did not enjoy the same ties to the land as the Prussian landed aristocracy. Nevertheless, Ernst Engelberg has questioned Wilhelmine's 'bourgeois' credentials and stressed that her world was not antithetical to that of the Bismarcks.[7] The Menckens were doubtless more cultured and urbane (for there was nothing elegant or luxurious about the life of the average Prussian Junker) but they shared the ethos of monarchism and the tradition of state service. Wilhelmine's father, Ludwig Mencken, came from Leipzig but he made his way to the top of the Prussian state bureaucracy, advising three successive monarchs, Friedrich II, Friedrich Wilhelm II and Friedrich Wilhelm III. Wilhelmine was his only daughter and she enjoyed the company of the royal children at the Prussian court, playing with the future Friedrich Wilhelm IV and his brother, who later became Kaiser Wilhelm I, before she married Ferdinand von Bismarck, then more than twice her age, when she was 17. Hence, despite the obvious differences in social milieu, it can be said that Bismarck's parents came from complementary rather than conflicting backgrounds and that they shared a similar ideological outlook in their commitment to an enlightened monarchical absolutism. The couple were not particularly happy but this can be attributed to disparities in age, education, intelligence and social aspirations.

Bismarck was not really close to either of his parents, both of whom died before he attained high office. He later complained to his wife that his mother had shown him little affection, had mistakenly wanted her children to become intellectuals and, far from enjoying their company, had sent them off in the school holidays to their more congenial Uncle Fritz who lived near Potsdam. With his more lenient and less demanding father he professed a deeper, emotional bond. But here, too, a distance developed as he came to be embarrassed by his father's uncouth behaviour and frequently blunt remarks. The tensions between Bismarck and his parents, complicated by his association of each parent with a different urban or rural environment, cannot be said to have ruined his childhood or made him unduly unhappy. But his later insistence that he felt estranged from his parental home from early childhood indicates anger and regret about his relationship with them. While his mother was alive he never felt he could live up to her exacting expectations; despite his affection for his father, the reality of their relationship always disappointed him. When he eventually married, Bismarck seems to have welcomed the opportunity to adopt his wife's family as his own, while at the same time he left no one in any doubt that he was the head of the household.

Bismarck's education was determined by his mother, who chose to send her sons away to school rather than educate them with the help of private tutors at home. From the age of 6 Bismarck attended the Plamann Institute in Berlin, by his account a very strict and spartan establishment where he felt imprisoned after the freedom of Kniephof and later complained he was always hungry. He then went on to attend two reputable *Gymnasia* or grammar schools in Berlin before studying law, the usual prelude to a career in state service, at the universities of Göttingen (one of the most dynamic academic institutions in central Europe at that time but not the usual choice for a Prussian) and Berlin.

There is little evidence that Bismarck exploited the educational and academic opportunities offered to him by these institutions. At school his best subjects were languages, but he proved to be an intellectually lazy pupil who preferred riding to studying and whose overall performance was well down in the bottom quarter of the class. He also wasted much of his time at university, although he may have gained insights into the relationship between foreign policy and economics from attending the lectures of the historian Arnold Heeren. Not very interested in ideas, he had a retentive memory and, as his letters reveal, considerable literary talent. But he read serious books about philosophy, politics or history only sporadically, culling what he needed from them and discarding the rest, and he much preferred the romantic works of Byron, Scott and Shakespeare. At Göttingen, Bismarck achieved a degree of notoriety on account of his striking appearance and wild lifestyle. Again by his own account he spent his time womanising, fighting duels, playing roulette and drinking his companions under the table, but he passed his exams by doing the bare minimum. He almost joined one of the radical student fraternities but soon gravitated to the *Hanovera*, an aristocratic duelling corps more appropriate to his social background and much less likely to jeopardise a future political career. In January 1833 he wrote to his brother that he had fought fourteen duels since Michaelmas and only once been wounded.[8] Significantly, too, he accumulated a heavy burden of debt, which his father was soon disinclined to alleviate[9] and which oppressed him for some years after he left university.

Bismarck's education brought him into contact with boys and young men who did not share his Junker background. At Göttingen his two closest friends were an American, John Lothrop Motley, later a United States ambassador and historian of the Dutch Republic, and a Baltic German aristocrat, Alexander von Keyserling, both of whom may have helped him to appraise Prussian conditions more critically. These two friendships proved lifelong and exceptional, for throughout his life Bismarck had few close personal friends. Motley's early autobiogaphical novel, *Morton's Hope* (1839), is of interest to historians, who otherwise rely mainly on Bismarck's memoirs and correspondence as sources for his early life, because of its depiction of a young nobleman, Otto von Rabenmark. Rabenmark's public behaviour was wild and unrestrained but at home he stopped play-acting and became serious, rational and intelligent. Despite their insights into Bismarck's character, neither Motley nor Keyserling played any significant role in his subsequent political career. More important were Bismarck's friends from his own social class. Moritz von Blanckenburg, for example, whom Bismarck met at the Gymnasium zum Grauen Kloster, later played an important role in introducing him to the Trieglaff circle of pietists. But the development of Bismarck's political views and his later conduct in office cost him the friendship of many of his erstwhile conservative friends.

The social aspirations and political connections of Wilhelmine von Bismarck were also important influences on her son's decision to embark on a bureaucratic career. Despite parental pressure, Bismarck himself ruled out the main alternative for a younger son of a nobleman, namely an army career.[10] He even later tried to evade the obligatory year of military service by pleading a persistent injury after one of his duelling escapades, but this was discounted. The experience of army discipline in 1838 as a private in the Fusiliers at Potsdam and Greifswald was not agreeable to Bismarck, who already found it very difficult to accept any hierarchical structure of authority which placed him at the bottom. But he did complete his training and he also qualified for a commission in the militia in 1841.

Bismarck's own preference in 1835 was to become a diplomat and travel abroad, but he was advised by no less a person than the Prussian foreign minister, Friedrich Ancillon (who had a rather low opinion of the intellectual abilities of Junker offspring), that he should gain some administrative experience before setting his sights on a less prestigious role within German affairs, perhaps in the newly formed German customs union or *Zollverein*. Bismarck therefore embarked on the lowest, unsalaried rungs of the ladder which led to a career as a Prussian higher civil servant, serving for nearly a year at the Berlin municipal court, and then in the regional administration at Aachen and Potsdam.

But Bismarck's early pursuit of the traditional path to power and influence in Prussia, like his second, much briefer foray into the lower echelons of the Prussian civil service in 1844, ended in disillusionment. Although he successfully passed his exams, he could not discipline himself for long and found the degree of subordination required of him intolerable. He was contemptuous of the men he had to work with and dismissive of the routine administrative tasks he had to perform. Despite his mother's connections and some evidence that his superiors recognised his talent and ability, within the system of limited competition for high office which pertained in Prussia he believed that he lacked sufficient acquaintance with 'the people at the top' and the requisite family and personal ties to rise quickly. He also, yet again, simply could not live within his means. His indulgence in gambling and womanising brought him to the verge of professional disgrace and, after going absent without leave in late 1837 in pursuit of an Englishwoman, Isabella Loraine-Smith, he sought a transfer from Aachen to Potsdam in December 1837, not least to avoid his numerous creditors. Finally, in the late summer of 1838, he resolved to leave state service altogether and return to his father's estates where he could live the life of a country squire.

Bismarck's decision 'to exchange the pen for the plough and the briefcase for the bag of game'[11] at the age of 24 was essentially the result of his lamentable financial situation. He desperately needed to acquire independent means to pay off a mountain of debts, and increasing the efficiency of the family estates appeared to be the best, perhaps only way to do so. The change of lifestyle represented an escape from his predicament in 1838 but it was not a spontaneous decision. Since leaving university in 1835 Bismarck had felt increasingly oppressed by family and professional expectations, and he may have unconsciously wished to take revenge on his disappointed mother, whose illness and death in January 1839 removed a further obstacle. Yet it was typical of Bismarck that in a famous letter to his cousin, Caroline (Lienchen) von Bismarck-Bohlen, in August 1838 he passed quickly over the financial imperative and justified his decision far more histrionically with reference to the suppression of his freedom and individuality.[12] He lamented how 'in order to take part in public life, one must be a salaried and dependent servant of the state, one must belong completely to the bureaucratic caste'. Despite his ambitions, he recognised that he could not persevere under the existing system of bureaucratic absolutism in Prussia and that he could not truckle to a career structure where promotion was determined 'by examinations, connections, examining of files, seniority and the goodwill of my superiors'. He wanted to give orders, not to obey. He went on:

The Prussian civil servant is like one musician in an orchestra; whether he plays first violin or the triangle, he is confined to his own little part which he plays without influence or overview, as it is written, whether he likes it or not. I, however, want to make my own music in my own way or none at all.

Bismarck confessed that he was attracted 'like a moth to a flame' by the idea of being a statesman in a free constitution. But, so long as the only way to enter high politics in Prussia was through the civil service, he was not prepared to suppress any part of his being in pursuit of a political career. Bismarck wanted the same degree of independence and autonomy in public life as he believed his birth and ancestry entitled him to in private life. In short, until the political system in Prussia changed, there was no place for a man of Bismarck's temperament within it. Bismarck's realisation of this reveals as much about the predicament of Prussian bureaucratic absolutism by the 1840s as it does about the nature of his own political drive and lust for power.

The Junker inheritance

Bismarck's social and material base as a Junker landowner remained of deep importance to him throughout his life, but the advantages conferred on him by his birth and ancestry were not the decisive factors in his eventual rise to power. By the time he was reaching maturity, he was already becoming something of an outsider, unable to follow conventional paths and ready to defy tradition if it did not suit him. Similarly, although the eight years Bismarck was to spend from 1839 to 1847 living the life of a typical Prussian Junker were important in confirming his sense of belonging to a privileged social estate or *Stand* and in enabling him to create the material security from which he could launch his subsequent political career, they are probably more significant in revealing what was individual and unique in his character. Confirmed in his contempt of the Prussian bureaucratic mentality, which he inevitably associated with his mother, he was deeply conscious of his Junker inheritance and believed that if he followed his father in making his living on the land, he would find the personal happiness, inner peace and self-fulfilment which had eluded him during the many years he had lived away from home. But in the 1830s Bismarck entertained a very idealised view of Junker existence and underestimated the extent to which his superior education and intellectual capacity would conspire to make him feel bored and alienated in the company of his landed peers. By 1844 loneliness and frustration drove him to undertake a second, even less successful attempt at a career in the state service which he abandoned within a few weeks. Only his introduction and social acceptance into an influential circle of Pomeranian pietists eventually rescued him from isolation and obscurity, not only anchoring his personal life through marriage and religious conversion but also offering new opportunities of political patronage.

Bismarck felt a profound emotional attachment to the land and invariably sought to return to it when he confronted moments of personal or political crisis. As a child he loved the freedom of the countryside, playing with the local children in the wooded and gently undulating hills around the Bismarcks' two-storey farmhouse at Kniephof, and he deeply resented his banishment to the city. As an adult, even when most actively engaged and energised by the political challenge, he always paradoxically yearned for the rural retreat, the quiet company of horses and dogs, and the opportunities for tranquillity and reflection the countryside provided. Bismarck's early letters to his friends and family reveal the extent to which he felt at home on the land and saw himself as part of an organic natural world. They are replete with observations about nature, the weather and landscape, and many commentators have stressed the naturalness of his spoken and written German, suggesting that his whole manner of observation and expression was rooted in his appreciation of nature. After he became Prussian premier Bismarck frequently yearned to be far away from the city of Berlin, a city which changed almost beyond recognition over the time-span of his political career and which he occasionally professed to loathe. Yet he also had a far more urban upbringing than he subsequently made out (he lived in Berlin from the age of 6 and once joked that he had known the city well enough to have become a cabby).[13] As a young man Bismarck soon learnt that he could never feel completely satisfied or fulfilled living on the land. Boredom, frustration and ambition ultimately propelled him towards politics.

Bismarck's emotional attachment to the land was significantly reinforced by his appreciation of the material independence and personal freedom it guaranteed. From 1839 he devoted himself with energy to the management of his father's Pomeranian estates, responding to the growing commercialisation of agriculture by studying soil chemistry and familiarising himself with the intricacies of double-entry bookkeeping. Along with his elder brother Bernhard, who was elected the local *Landrat* in 1841, he was able to improve the agricultural productivity of the three small neighbouring estates of Kniephof, Külz and Jarchelin, thus banishing the major threat of financial insolvency even though he could not as yet pay off all his debts. After the death of his father in late 1845, Bismarck formally inherited both Kniephof and Schönhausen, and he took the decision to move to Schönhausen in 1846 because it was closer both to Berlin and to his new political patron, Ludwig von Gerlach, who was a career official in Magdeburg. Returning to Schönhausen after a short period away in January 1847, he wrote to his future wife that 'On reaching the village I felt more distinctly than ever before how beautiful it is to have a home [*Heimat*], and a home to which one is bound by birth, memory and love.'[14]

His pecuniary difficulties in the late 1830s and the need to safeguard the survival of the family estates in the adverse economic conditions of the 1840s were formative experiences for Bismarck, who in several respects came to represent a more modern breed of Junker, ready to exploit new economic opportunities and adapt to the demands of the market. For all his cherished memories of his childhood home, Bismarck eventually sold Kniephof to his nephew, apparently for the full market price.[15] And long after he had ceased to regard the life of a rural Junker in rosy-coloured hues, he continued to value land above all other investments. As Prussian minister-president and Reich chancellor he accumulated land, devoting much time and attention to his estates and the manufacturing enterprises they sustained. In 1867 he bought the extensive entailed estate of Varzin in Pomerania, an estate which comprised over 14,000 acres, and in 1871 he was presented by the monarch with some 17,000 acres of Sachsenwald woodland and meadowland near Hamburg which became the estate of Friedrichsruh. In 1885 he controversially used the proceeds from a public donation on his seventieth birthday to re-purchase the larger part of the ancestral estate of Schönhausen which his father had sold to a non-noble property-owner in 1830. Bismarck thus eventually became one of the largest landowners in Germany with estates which together comprised about 40,000 acres and represented an investment of between five and six million marks.[16] His active role in their management is not merely evidence of his sentimental attachment to the land but also of the handsome material rewards they provided. Bismarck loved trees and was inspired with a sense of awe by oaks that had existed since the Thirty Years War; but he also had a keen eye for the profits to be made from the sale of timber. Some of the decisions he made with respect to forestry can be criticised from a modern environmentalist standpoint. He experimented with the introduction of exotic foreign species on his estates, and he even expected the Reichstag to provide him with the financial means to plant Douglas firs at Varzin in 1878.[17] Bismarck also ensured that he made his estates pay by setting up alcohol distilleries and paper mills at Varzin, and other industries at Friedrichsruh. In becoming something of a rural industrialist, Bismarck exposed himself to accusations that some of his later policies were directly related to his business interests and calculated to bring him material gains.[18]

Bismarck was completely unyielding and uncompromising when it came to the principle of private property ownership and his rights as a landowner. In 1848 his conservative patrons rebuked him for complaining excessively about a hunting law 'as if private law were holier than the state'.[19] Over forty years later Bismarck raged over the 'completely communist view' of the finance minister, Johannes von Miquel, that woods should not belong to private individuals.[20] Bismarck readily acknowledged his land hunger and how he coveted his neighbours' estates. But as he grew older, possession became a significant part of his appreciation of landscape and he took less and less interest in woods, meadows and views which were not his own. He could not enjoy the scenery at Kissingen, his wife bemoaned in 1877, because it was not called Sachsenwald or Varzin; resisting a health cure there in 1892, he argued 'meadows and trees in Kissingen are not my meadows and trees'.[21]

Bismarck's love of animals was also self-evident, although this may appear paradoxical to modern readers given his great enthusiasm for hunting. He was a keen horseman if not always a very skilled one. In 1870 he admitted to Moritz Busch, his press officer, that he must have experienced at least fifty falls but that they were only bad when the horse fell too and pinned him underneath.[22] At Königgrätz, the crucial battle in the Austro-Prussian war of 1866, he rode his chestnut horse for thirteen hours without feeding him and expressed his admiration and gratitude in a letter to his wife. 'He bore it very well, did not shy at shots or corpses, ate ears of corn and plum tree leaves with zest at the most difficult moments, and went on gaily to the end, when I was more tired than the horse.'[23] The Reich Chancellery chief, Christoph Tiedemann, later attributed the closeness he and Holstein enjoyed with the chancellor not merely to their reliable work but to the fact that they could both ride tolerably well.[24] But even more important to Bismarck than his horses were his dogs, which accompanied him through all stages of his life. The 'Reich dogs', Sultan (whose death Bismarck precipitated[25]) and Tyras, were the most famous, and Bismarck claimed he felt more secure with Tyras than under the protection of the entire Berlin secret police.[26] As a Christian, though, Bismarck reproached himself as sinful for being so attached to Sultan, a mere animal. And even Bismarck became exasperated after his daughter (who already had three children of her own) erected a shrine to one of her favourite guinea-pigs that had been killed by Tyras.[27]

Like many from his milieu, Bismarck was also an eager hunter and he believed that hunting was the natural pursuit of man. From childhood onwards he shot chickens, pheasants, hares, deer, foxes, ducks, wild boar and all manner of other game, always returning reinvigorated from his hunting trips and only renouncing this most serious of pleasures after 1870. In September 1857, during a hunting trip in Sweden, he wrote to his wife that, apart from roebuck and fallow deer, he had slaughtered five elks, including 'a very strong buck' with a 'colossal head' which was 'probably nine or ten feet in the air. He fell like a hare, but, as he was still alive, I put another shot into him out of pity.' In the meantime, however, he lost his chance to shoot an even bigger one which ran by. 'I can't get over my vexation at this, and have to work off some of it to you,' he complained.[28] The high point in Bismarck's hunting career was when he was ambassador in St Petersburg (1859–62) and went hunting for bear. He had no qualms about shooting bears disturbed from their winter sleep, which he acknowledged were a soft target, and he ruled out bear hunting in summer as too dangerous.[29] The Bismarcks subsequently ate the kill: for three months salted bear meat was offered at their breakfast table which, Bismarck told his sister, 'was particularly loved by the children'.[30] Bismarck's enthusiasm for hunting was shared by many in the Prussian ruling elite and facilitated his smooth integration into the aristocratic court culture once he achieved power. Six weeks after he became Prussian minister-president, he joined the royal hunt at Letzlingen. Onlookers were not only impressed by his constant, close proximity to the king and the degree of influence this suggested, but also by his 'self-assurance and certainty of victory'.[31] These qualities doubtless inspired confidence that he could dispatch his liberal opponents in the constitutional conflict as easily as he felled his prey.

Bismarck's attachment to the land and the natural world was part and parcel of a Junker inheritance which also, of course, incorporated a commitment to a particular social and political order. Despite the erosion of seigneurial rights in the first half of the nineteenth century, traditions of *Herrschaft* (authority) and deference retained vitality in a hierarchical society which was still widely regarded as the God-given order. The *gnädigster Herr* (most gracious lord) owed allegiance to the king, the *Allergnädigster Herr* (most supreme gracious lord) and he in turn derived his position from the will of the Lord God, the *Herr Gott*. As a *Gutsherr* (lord of an estate) Bismarck enjoyed a patriarchal authority over his estates as economic and social units, even defending the landowners' police powers and rights of jurisdiction over their peasant workforce. He took pride in the continuity of service from one generation to another, lamenting the death of a childless gardener at the age of 75 at Schönhausen in 1846 because it marked the end of a line.[32] In 1847, faced with the prospect of leasing out Kniephof, he felt 'uneasy in my conscience' at the idea of surrendering his trees and his workmen 'whose defence God entrusted to me' into the hands of strangers.[33] Despite changing rural relationships, Bismarck remained convinced of a fundamental community of interest which bound both aristocracy and peasantry on the land and set them apart from the concerns of rural town-dwellers who still at mid-century constituted a minority of the population as a whole. His confidence in the resilience of the old rural order, and its ability to withstand new, alien, ideological challenges which had no social basis in the countryside, meant that he was to be far less intimidated by the revolutionary upheavals of 1848 than many of his contemporaries.

Even after the revolutions of 1848, however, it may be that Bismarck saw the main threat to his Junker inheritance as external. The social and political order into which he had been born in 1815 had been severely shaken by the impact of the Napoleonic Wars, during which the Prussian army had suffered humiliating defeats and the Prussian state had confronted the prospect of internal disintegration as well as international collapse. Schönhausen itself had been occupied by French troops, and for a period the vicinity assumed the character of a 'frontier territory' when neighbouring settlements on the west bank of the Elbe were ceded by Prussia and incorporated into the new Kingdom of Westphalia ruled by Napoleon's brother, Jerome. The Holy Roman Empire, which for centuries had provided a fragmented German Europe with a reasonably flexible and not too oppressive institutional framework and some measure of international security, had also been swept away in the deluge, a further casualty of France's revolutionary zeal. Despite Napoleon's eventual defeat and Prussia's territorial gains at the Congress of Vienna in 1815, their direct contact with the French revolution cannot have left the Bismarcks or any members of the old Prussian nobility untouched. Three of Bismarck's uncles fought against Napoleon, and the Junkers had appeared vulnerable even in the heartland of Brandenburg. If their traditional way of life was to survive and adapt, this depended crucially on the survival and security of Prussia as a German and European power.

By 1842 Bismarck's idealisation of his father's Junker existence was clearly beginning to pall. He had met the immediate challenges and, more moulded by his mother's aspirations than he cared to admit, he was tiring of the limitations of his Pomeranian existence, above all the relatively low intellectual level of his neighbours. Bored and lonely, especially after his brother moved to Jarchelin, he began to resort to the kind of wild, flamboyant behaviour and pranks which had characterised his student days, gaining a reputation throughout Pomerania as 'the mad Bismarck'. In 1842 he travelled extensively in England, France and Switzerland, toying with the idea of visiting India 'to bring a change of scene to my comedy and to smoke my cigars on the Ganges instead of the Rega'.[34] For a few months in 1843–44 a growing sense of depression was alleviated by the company of his 16-year-old sister, Malwine (or Malle), but she eventually left Kniephof to marry one of Bismarck's former schoolfriends, Oskar von Arnim-Kröchlendorff. In early 1844 he attempted for a second time to embark on a career in the state administration, but he was now even more used to making his own decisions and obeying no one; he abandoned the civil service again after a few weeks. Bismarck summed up his situation ironically to a friend in January 1845. He was 'unmarried, very lonely, 29 years old, physically healthy again but mentally rather unreceptive'. He went about his business diligently but without real engagement, and his social life consisted of dogs, horses and country Junkers who respected him not least because he could read without difficulty.[35]

Women, marriage and domestic life

Patrimonial power was part of Bismarck's inheritance and helped to shape his character. Another important dimension to his personality, albeit one which he shared with the vast majority of men from his social class and background, was the exercise of patriarchal power. Bismarck's decision to marry, his choice of Johanna von Puttkamer and his determined courtship leading to their marriage in July 1847 when he was 32 years old, represented a significant milestone in his personal development and rightly occupies a central place in his early biography. The conventional, undemanding and compliant woman he chose to be his lifelong partner and the kind of relationship he sought to have with her casts a rather different light on his character after the excesses of his student days and years as the crazy Junker. But Bismarck's marriage also needs to be set within a wider discussion of his attitude and conduct towards women more generally and his position in private life as head of the household. Bismarck's pursuit of political power and the standards of absolute authority and obedience to his will which he attempted to enforce in public life had their mirror and counterpart in the patriarchal family life he enjoyed in his home. His wife and children, consciously or unconsciously, suppressed elements of their own individuality under the impact of his personality, and all aspects of the Bismarcks' household revolved around the *paterfamilias*. Challenging Bismarck's will in the domestic environment came to be viewed in the same terms as opposition in the political sphere, construed as insubordination, disloyalty and betrayal.

Bismarck may not have had many lasting male friendships but he moved easily in a man's world, regarded himself as a good judge of men's character, and was manifestly comfortable with his own masculinity. His attitude to women on one level was equally uncomplicated. There is no evidence that he disliked female company; on the contrary, he often sought out congenial, witty and interesting female companions such as Baroness Hildegard von Spitzemberg to sit next to him at official dinners, and he enjoyed their presence on social occasions. The strong affection he always retained for his much younger sister, Malle, also indicates how he valued female intimacy on a non-sexual level. Nevertheless, Bismarck developed a reputation as something of a misogynist and frequently railed against the influence of 'petticoats' on men in public life. All his life he had an aversion to women who, like his mother, exerted the dominant influence in a marriage, and this hostility was compounded by his deep-seated conviction that men and women should occupy completely separate spheres in society. The patronising attitudes and assumptions he displayed towards women were typical of his class and generation. But his prejudices were significantly reinforced by his bitter experience of women's interference (or 'meddling') in politics during his tenure of office. He directed his most vituperative barbs against two royal women, Augusta, the wife of the later Kaiser Wilhelm I, and her daughter-in-law, Vicky, the future Kaiserin Friedrich. Both held liberal political views and were prepared to cross Bismarck in the course of his political career. He also suspected that both women encouraged intrigues against him and forgave neither the influence they exerted over their husbands. Bismarck never abandoned his conviction that a woman's place was in a domestic setting, nurturing the next generation. But after he left office he was so disillusioned with the divisiveness of male party politics that he claimed his confidence in the future ultimately rested on the constancy of German women and their support within the family for the Reich idea.[36]

As well as believing that women should stay out of public life and leave politics to men, Bismarck also sharply distinguished between women from his own social class or background and the rest. His sense of social propriety ensured that as a young man he had very different attitudes to women from his own *Stand* whom he – or his friends – might marry, and women of inferior status from whom he might expect to receive sexual favours. We are mainly reliant on Bismarck's own account of his dissolute student life but there seems little reason to doubt that, apart from duelling and gambling, he spent much of his time whoring. Alexander von Keyserling later wrote that Bismarck followed his natural drive without great scruples when it came to women.[37] This did not mean, however, that he was not looking for a more stable and lasting attachment. In 1835–36 he fell in love with his beautiful second cousin, Caroline von Bismarck-Bohlen (the daughter of Lienchen, to whom he later justified his decision to abandon his political career), who was already engaged to Hermann von Malortie. 'The best thing about it', he confessed to his friend, Gustav Scharlach, in May 1836, 'is that my acquaintances of both sexes always consider me to be a cold-blooded misogynist; how wrong can people be!'[38] In Aachen later in 1836, he developed a passion for a young Englishwoman, Laura Russell, who was allegedly the niece of the duke and duchess of Cleveland, but he broke off the relationship when he suspected she was illegitimate. He wrote to his brother that there would have to be a very important reason for him to marry anyone but the legitimate daughter of a nobleman. After a brief affair with a woman he boasted was fourteen years his senior, he then found himself even more infatuated with another Englishwoman, Isabella Loraine-Smith, with whom he apparently became engaged. He spent months trailing her family across Europe in 1837 before both his passion and his credit were spent.

As Bismarck's correspondence with friends such as Gustav Scharlach reveals, by his late twenties he was very conscious of his single status and personal loneliness and he was keen to acquire a wife with whom he could share his domestic life. In 1841 he fell in love and became engaged to Ottilie von Puttkamer, but his reputation for wildness may have preceded him and within a fortnight he had made an enemy of her disapproving mother. There are no surviving descriptions of Ottilie (who was no relation of Johanna) and historians cannot even speculate about what attracted Bismarck to her. But Bismarck complained to Scharlach that 'after intrigues which went on for nearly a year', Ottilie's mother, 'a woman who, to do her justice, is one of the nastiest I know', induced her to write a very laconic letter, terminating the relationship. 'I considered it beneath my dignity to reveal the offended agitation of my soul and give vent to it with a few shots at the faithless one's brothers and such like,' he added, intimating that the mother's objections to the match had eventually dissolved but that he himself could not suppress his deep feelings of bitterness and betrayal. [39] This experience, as well as his earlier amorous adventures and attempt to marry into the English nobility, ultimately made him cautious and more inclined to value such qualities as loyalty, constancy and devotion. 'I admittedly love female company very much,' he wrote to Ludwig von Klitzing in 1843, 'but marriage is indeed too serious a matter and my experiences have made me reflective.'[40]

Bismarck eventually came to have very traditional expectations when it came to his choice of a wife, and he had no desire to emulate his father by marrying a woman with social ambitions or obvious intellectual interests. After he was rebuffed in his suit of Ottilie von Puttkamer, the woman who attracted him most powerfully was Marie von Thadden, whose father's estate at Trieglaff was a focal point for a circle of Pomeranian pietists who played a crucial role in launching Bismarck's political career. From their first meeting in 1843 Bismarck was impressed by Marie's charm, sensitivity and piety, finding he could talk to her intimately about the boredom and emptiness of his life, and she came to personify Bismarck's ideal partner in life. Yet, as with Caroline von Bismarck-Bohlen, Marie von Thadden was already engaged to one of Bismarck's closest friends, Moritz von Blanckenburg, whom she married in 1844. There seems no doubt, however, that the magnetic attraction was mutual. Marie wrote to her friends, including Johanna von Puttkamer, about her passionate interest in a man she evidently found far more exciting than her worthy but comparatively dull fiancé. But, although Bismarck was clearly deeply in love with Marie and their relationship attracted some adverse comment, there was no question of their overstepping the bounds of social propriety. Bismarck finally extricated himself from a hopeless situation when he moved to Schönhausen in 1846.

The deep, emotional bond Bismarck had felt with Marie undoubtedly encouraged him to seek a similarly close, spiritual union with the woman who would be his partner in life. Bismarck was first introduced to Johanna von Puttkamer in 1844, but he only pursued his suit of her and overcame the reluctance of her doubting father after the untimely death of their mutual friend, Marie von Blanckenburg, from an epidemic in November 1846. The news of Marie's sudden illness so soon after he left Pomerania had a profound impact on Bismarck, not only in determining his resolve to marry her friend but also in precipitating his apparent conversion to Lutheran pietism. 'It is really the first time that I have lost someone close to me through death', he told Malle, and he envied the composure of Marie's husband and relatives and their calm confidence that they would be reunited in the after-life.[41] Marie had tried unsuccessfully in many conversations with her sceptical neighbour to persuade him to embrace her family's Christian faith, which placed emphasis on a direct, unmediated relationship between the individual and God, the experience of conversion and a very personal understanding of the scriptures. But in Bismarck's famous letter to his future father-in-law, he revealed that it was only the news of her imminent death which 'tore the first ardent prayer' from his heart. 'God did not hear my prayer at that time, but neither did he reject it, for I have never since lost the ability to ask things of him, and I feel within myself if not peace, at least a confidence and optimism such as I no longer knew in my ordinary life.'[42] Bismarck's new-found religious faith may not have had a formative impact on his character or significantly affected his conduct. But crucially it liberated him from a debilitating depression about the meaning of his existence. In enabling him in some senses to abdicate responsibility for his actions to a superior power, it may also, as Otto Pflanze has suggested, have 'relieved him of any sense of selfishness in his relentless pursuit of power and domination'.[43] Furthermore, it facilitated his union with Johanna, whose religious belief was fundamental to her character.

Bismarck's choice of Johanna von Puttkamer has clearly disappointed many biographers and historians, and contemporaries, too, were far from complimentary about the match. An unworldly, unassuming and pious woman from his own social background, Johanna was considered rather plain, even by the Schönhausen peasants.[44] Unlike his sister Malle (with whom she did not get on well) and other society women to whom he continued to be attracted, she was also completely lacking in elegance. Bismarck, however, was biased in her favour because she had been Marie's friend and he single-mindedly pursued his suit in the six weeks after Marie's death, eventually almost storming the family home at Reinfeld in

January 1847 and presenting the speechless parents with a *fait accompli*. He claimed he knew what kind of a woman he was marrying, 'a woman of rare intelligence [*Geist*] and rare nobility of mind' who was very kind and would be easy to live with, *'facile à vivre'*.[45] In his letters to his fiancée (which can undoubtedly be seen as some of the most beautiful and poetic love letters in the German language) he insisted to Johanna that they should share all their joys and sorrows, regard themselves as mutual father confessors and become 'one flesh'. 'Make me serviceable, use me for what purpose you will, ill-treat me without and within, if you have the wish to do so. I am there for that purpose, at your disposal; but never be embarrassed in any way with me. Trust me unreservedly, in the conviction that I accept everything that comes from you with profound love, whether it be glad or patient.'[46] After their marriage on 28 July 1847, he continued to appreciate above all her warmth, loyalty and devotion. He wrote to her reassuringly in 1851 before the family moved to Frankfurt:

I did not marry you in order to have a society wife for others, but in order to love you in God and according to the requirements of my own heart, to have a place in this alien world that no barren wind can cool, a place warmed by my own fireplace, to which I can draw near while it storms and freezes outside. And I want to tend my own fire and lay on wood, blow the flames, and protect it and shelter it against all that is evil and foreign.[47]

Bismarck knew that Johanna trusted him blindly[48] and that she would mould herself completely to his wishes. She, for her part, assured him that she would remain faithful to him until death and 'try to *bend* whatever I cannot *break*; – and if that does not work, I will be silent and do – what you want.'[49]

Johanna was natural, warm and welcoming to anyone whom she regarded as a friend of her husband. But she was certainly not an asset to his early political career in social terms. Bismarck had to tactfully encourage her to learn French, insisting it was for her own benefit, and he also sought to persuade her to learn to ride. He later recalled 'how difficult it was for me to make out of Fräulein von Puttkamer a Frau von Bismarck'.[50] For all her compliance, he never really succeeded, however, as Holstein observed:

Bismarck displayed considerable nobility of character in the way he bore with his wife's inept behaviour, which was at times appalling. He never winced at it, but would on occasion gently admonish her. Even though he did not move much in society it seems hardly credible that he can have failed to notice his wife's blunders. It was most probably the conviction that he could never bring his wife to mend her ways, coupled with disdain for mankind, which determined him to let well alone. And it was part of Bismarck's strength of character to remain true to that decision.[51]

Bismarck's choice of Johanna confirmed his profound, emotional need for security, warmth and peace in his private life. His wife, who later acquired a perhaps unjustified reputation for bitchiness because she viewed the world so much through her husband's eyes, remained at his side for forty-eight years, devoting herself wholeheartedly to his needs and those of their three children, Marie (born in 1848), Herbert (born in 1849) and Wilhelm, known as Bill (born in 1852). But she showed no interest or understanding for politics and remained completely separate from his public life, only occasionally serving as a conduit to Bismarck, later in his career, for some of their former conservative and pietist friends. Despite his selfish egoism and sometimes wilful self-indulgence, there seems little doubt that Bismarck sought a deep, emotional and spiritual union with his wife ('I fear I would become nothing that pleases God if I did not have you', he once told her[52]) or that the marriage was essentially a happy one. His marriage to Johanna helped to anchor his private life, and Bismarck enjoyed a stable, loving and harmonious domestic environment, the importance of which should not be under-estimated throughout his stormy political career.

The negative side of Bismarck's domestic life was that it further rein-forced his authoritarianism, for Johanna was quite happy that the house-hold should revolve around his needs and allowed him complete freedom of decision and action. It may also have caused him physical harm, for she indulged all his whims and appetites, especially his gluttony, by encouraging the extraordinary consumption of food and drink which eventually led to obesity and other serious health problems. Visitors to the Bismarck household remarked on the heavy, six- or seven-course meals served at their table, the endless flow of champagne, beer and wine, and constant smoking of Havana cigars (from 1879 he smoked a pipe). Even after his doctor, Ernst Schweninger, prescribed a strict regi-men in the 1880s, Johanna was still inclined to smuggle 'treats' to him. Committing herself to a life of self-sacrifice and service to her husband (for even Herbert later said his mother was 'composed only of a sense of duty and self-denial'[53]), she became so narrow in her concerns and so ready to defer to her husband on all matters, however minor, that she ultimately contributed to robbing Bismarck of the domestic peace and tranquillity he craved.

Moreover, Bismarck's relationship with Johanna, while ensuring that there were few major disturbances in his personal life, could never satisfy him completely because it was too unequal. Especially in the first years of their marriage when they spent protracted periods apart, Johanna knew only the more gentle and tender side of his personality. She never shared in his public life or understood how central political power was to his being. She never understood what motivated him. As early as 1862, when she was merely 37 years old, she wrote to a close friend from St Petersburg that while Bismarck was out hunting wolves and bears and the children were studying or walking, 'I become more and more an old woman, grey-haired, wrinkled, crooked and barren – and live with my interests only in the family and in the friendships of past times.'[54] Life with the 'Iron Chancellor' did little to broaden her horizons, and Bismarck continued to be drawn to beautiful, spirited and sophisticated society women who resembled his mother rather than his maternal wife. There is no evidence that he was ever sexually unfaithful to Johanna, although a scandal almost ensued in 1865 when he allowed himself to be photographed with a famous opera singer as a joke, sent copies to Johanna, and then the photographer began to sell unauthorised prints to the public before he was compelled to destroy the plate.[55] More significantly, in the summer of 1862, he undoubtedly fell in love with the 22-year-old wife of a Russian diplomat, Katharina Orlov, with whom he spent a blissful recuperative holiday at Biarritz. With the benefit of hindsight, this relationship undoubtedly represented a final, carefree fling before he assumed the burden of high office in Berlin. He quite openly wrote to Johanna about his new passion for Kathy, who had 'a little bit of Marie Thadden' about her, and his wife appears to have indulged him his obvious infatuation without resentment, content that he was enjoying the rest and relaxation he needed.[56] Bismarck continued to correspond with Kathy and met up with the Orlovs in Biarritz again in 1864. 'The memory of that time, when I discovered this magic, has accompanied me through the political storms and tribulations like the last reflection of a beautiful day that is no more', he wrote to her husband on Kathy's early death in 1875.[57]

Bismarck's encounter with Kathy Orlov reminded him of his lost youth but it was essentially a transitory aberration. After his marriage his private life revolved around his family and even this domestic world became increasingly circumscribed as his public life encroached more and more. Before he attained high office, Bismarck's personal correspondence recounted the trials and tribulations of parenthood with good-natured humour, even though his ambivalence over the loss of personal autonomy was clearly in evidence. He rejoiced in the birth of his daughter in

August 1848, 'but even if it had been a cat I would have got down on my knees in thanks to God the moment Johanna was liberated from it; it is indeed a terribly desperate business', he told his father-in-law.[58] After the birth of Herbert in 1849, he wrote to Malle of 'The boy screaming in a major key, the girl in a minor one, two singing nannies [and] me as the suffering father of the family between wet nappies and milk bottles.'[59] He found Schönhausen unbearably empty when his family was away and wondered how he could ever have survived there on his own.[60] Yet the prospect of travelling with his family filled him with such dread that he preferred to follow them on separately, having nightmares in 1850 that 'next year I will doubtless have to travel with three cradles, wet nurses, nappies [and] bedding'.[61]

The Bismarcks welcomed friends to their home but eschewed high society. Motley vividly portrayed the domestic chaos in the Bismarck household in Frankfurt in the middle of the 1850s. 'It is one of those houses where everyone does what one likes,' he observed. 'Here there are young and old, grandparents and children and dogs all at once, eating, drinking, smoking, piano-playing, and pistol-firing (in the garden), all going on at the same time.'[62] Robert von Keudell, a Prussian official, musician and family friend, also recalled how the Bismarcks kept two bear cubs as pets in St Petersburg which wreaked havoc in their living rooms. (Bismarck had presumably shot their mother and he subsequently donated them to Frankfurt zoo.[63]) Yet, for all the informality and social anarchy of the Bismarck household, Bismarck himself could be remarkably detached. At the same time as he was writing from Schönhausen to Malle about nappies and breast-feeding, he revealed to a political collaborator, Hermann Wagener, that he was living 'an incredibly lazy life, smoking, reading, going for walks and playing the father of the family . . . I lie in the grass, read poems, listen to music and wait for the cherries to ripen.'[64] Baroness Spitzemberg, too, who became their frequent guest in Berlin, observed of Bismarck that 'There is in him a peculiar aloofness [Fürsichsein] amid wife and children.'[65]

Indeed, the impact Bismarck's career and domestic circumstances had on his children undoubtedly carried its cost. There is no doubt that Bismarck loved his children – his fears for the personal safety of his sons when they fought in the Franco-Prussian War are sufficient testimony of that. He was also sufficiently concerned about his children's development to urge Johanna to get them to correct the letters they wrote to him,[66] and he always wrote apologetically when he missed successive birthdays because political matters kept him away from home.[67] But, however much he valued domestic tranquillity and conjugal love, Bismarck's thoughts,

preoccupations and energies were primarily directed towards his existence outside the home. Politics eventually consumed his other interests
and preoccupations and ensured that even his home became part of the
battleground, a place where he sought reinforcement and support rather
than refuge and solace from the political struggle.

Moreover, as his children grew up, Bismarck could not allow them the
personal autonomy and freedom he himself had craved but instead expected their lives, and in the case of his sons their careers, to revolve
around his own. He trusted his own family more than anyone else so he
came to rely on them more than anyone else, personally and politically.
Both his sons had political careers, served their father as private secretaries and were *Reichspartei* (Free Conservative) members of the Reichstag
for a period. Herbert, the most gifted of Bismarck's children, joined the
diplomatic service in accordance with his father's wishes in 1874 and
advanced rapidly on the basis of both talent and nepotism to become
state secretary of the Foreign Office in 1886 and his father's closest
political adviser. Bill, never as robust as Herbert physically, preferred
provincial service as a *Landrat* in Hanau and was later appointed
Oberpräsident of East Prussia under Kaiser Wilhelm II. Bismarck also
relied heavily on his son-in-law Count Kuno zu Rantzau, a diplomat who
married Marie in 1878 (her first fiancé, Wend zu Eulenburg, had died in
1876) and became another conscientious private secretary. Marie herself
grew into a more indolent and less happy copy of her mother, sharing
none of her father's qualities or aspirations (except perhaps his hypochondria[68]) and, like Johanna, dividing the world into those who were for
Bismarck and those who were against him. It was self-evident that she
and her husband took over the role of caring for Bismarck after Johanna's
death in 1894.

Bismarck's treatment of his children could be brutal and ruthless, as is
demonstrated by the famous episode when he refused to allow Herbert
to marry the woman he loved, Princess Elisabeth von Carolath-Beuthen,
in 1881. Bismarck was prejudiced against the Catholic divorcée, the daughter of a wealthy Silesian magnate and ten years older than Herbert,
because she was related by marriage to Count Alexander von Schleinitz.
Schleinitz had been Prussian foreign minister before Bismarck and, as
minister of the royal household, was suspected by Bismarck of intriguing
against him with Kaiserin Augusta. It was doubtless the mere idea that a
woman with such connections could regularly invade his inner sanctum
that determined Bismarck's tyrannical reaction. In order to prevent the
marriage he brought enormous personal and political pressure to bear on
Herbert, resorting to tears and emotional blackmail, refusing him official

permission to marry (which was required in the diplomatic service) and threatening to disinherit him by inducing Kaiser Wilhelm I to change the primogeniture statutes applying to entailed estates. He threatened suicide and claimed that preventing the marriage was more important to him 'than the entire German Reich'.[69] Herbert eventually abandoned and compromised his lover but the devastating experience left him a very embittered (and alcoholic) man. He eventually married Countess Marguerite Hoyos late in life and delighted Bismarck by producing a son and heir. But by this time he had already sacrificed his own political career for the sake of his father, resigning with him in 1890 even though he could have stayed on in the New Course government as a highly influential mediator. Bill's marriage, incidentally, aroused much less controversy in the Bismarck household: he married his cousin, Sybille von Arnim, the daughter of Malle, and Bismarck did not object to this match even though his dislike of his niece was well known.[70]

Bismarck's private life thus reinforces the view that he was a domineering and authoritarian man with a very strong will. For all the gentleness and emotion he displayed in some of his relationships, especially in his early life, he expected those who were closest to him to organise their lives in accordance with his needs and dictates and to put his interests first. As his political stature grew, so did his sense of his own importance within the home. Yet the growing number of physical ailments which beset him in later life, which included facial neuralgia, migraines, insomnia and all kinds of digestive disorders, were partly the result of hypochondria and an acute hypersensitivity which obviously had psychological origins. At home, the lack of opposition to his will did not ultimately make him any happier than in his public life where he eventually came to feel constrained at every turn. Indeed, as Otto Pflanze has shown, it was only when he finally submitted his body to the regulation and control of his Bavarian doctor, Ernst Schweninger, and accepted his dependence on him that Bismarck's physical and mental condition improved. For the last fifteen years of his life, Schweninger became a kind of surrogate parent who spent long periods resident in the Bismarck household and even put the 'Iron Chancellor' to bed at night, comforting him like a restless child.[71]

Notes

1 Holstein, I, p. 5.

2 Both these pictures as well as many other portraits of Bismarck are reproduced in Lothar Gall and Karl-Heinz Jürgens, *Bismarck: Lebensbilder* (Bergisch Gladbach, 1990).

3 Louis Snyder, *The Blood and Iron Chancellor: A Documentary-Biography of Otto von Bismarck* (Princeton, NJ, 1967), p. 56.

4 Holstein, I, p. 5.

5 Kurd von Schlözer, *Petersburger Briefe 1857–1962*, ed. Leopold von Schlözer (Stuttgart, 1922), p. 127.

6 GW, VII, conversation with Viktor von Unruh, Spring 1848, p. 15.

7 Engelberg, I, pp. 47–8.

8 Rothfels, Bismarck to Bernhard von Bismarck, 27 January 1833, p. 24.

9 See ibid., Bismarck to Gustav Scharlach, 14 November 1833, p. 25.

10 Ibid., Bismarck to Gustav Scharlach, 5 May 1834, p. 28.

11 Ibid., Bismarck to Scharlach, 18 June 1835, p. 30.

12 Ibid., Bismarck to his father, 29 September 1838, pp. 33–40. See also copy in GW, 14/I, pp. 13–17.

13 GW, XIII, speech of 16 July 1894, pp. 536–7.

14 Rothfels, Bismarck to Johanna, 1 February 1847, p. 65.

15 Fritz Stern, *Gold and Iron: Bismarck, Bleichröder and the Building of the German Empire* (London, 1977), p. 101.

16 Ibid., p. 290.

17 See Rolf Hennig, *Bismarck und die Natur* (Suderburg, 1998), pp. 34 ff., 45.

18 See Pflanze, II, pp. 74–85.

19 Gerlach, I, 5 November 1848, p. 135.

20 See Waltraut Engelberg, *Das private Leben der Bismarcks* (Berlin, 1998), p. 147.

21 Ibid., p. 146.

22 Moritz Busch, *Tagebuchblätter*, 3 vols (Leipzig, 1899), I, 9 November 1870, p. 373.

23 Rothfels, Bismarck to Johanna, 11 July 1866, p. 329.

24 See Christoph von Tiedemann, *Sechs Jahre Chef der Reichskanzlei unter dem Fürsten Bismarck: Erinnerungen*, vol. 2 (Leipzig, 1909), 26 October 1877, pp. 205–6.

25 Ibid., pp. 206–7.

26 Hennig, *Bismarck und die Natur*, p. 104. See also Engelberg, *Das private Leben*, pp. 148–54.

27 For this episode, see Rothfels, p. 16, and Bismarck to Rantzau, 7 May 1889, p. 423.

28 Herbert Bismarck (ed.), *The Love Letters of Prince Bismarck*, 2 vols (London, 1901), II, Bismarck to Johanna, 12 September 1857, p. 64.

29 Robert von Keudell, *Fürst und Fürstin Bismarck: Erinnerungen aus den Jahren 1846 bis 1872* (Berlin and Stuttgart, 1901), p. 90.

30 Cited in Hennig, *Bismarck und die Natur*, p. 60.

31 Gerlach, II, Jacob von Gerlach to Gerlach, 9 November 1862, pp. 1125–6. For the Letzlingen hunt, see Isabel Hull, *The Entourage of Kaiser Wilhelm II 1888–1918* (Cambridge, 1982), pp. 38–9.

32 Rothfels, Bismarck to Johanna, 4 March 1847, p. 91.

33 Ibid., Bismarck to Johanna, 28 April 1847, p. 98.

34 Ibid., Bismarck to Ludwig von Klitzing, 10 September 1843, p. 41.

35 Ibid., Bismarck to Scharlach, 9 January 1845, p. 47.

36 GW, XII, speech of 30 March 1894, pp. 523–4.

37 See Waltraut Engelberg, *Otto und Johanna von Bismarck* (Berlin, 1990), p. 11.

38 Rothfels, Bismarck to Scharlach, 4 May 1836, p. 31.

39 Ibid., Bismarck to Scharlach, 9 January 1845, p. 46.

40 Ibid., Bismarck to Klitzing, 10 September 1843, p. 41.

41 Ibid., Bismarck to Malwine, 18 December 1846, p. 55.

42 Ibid., Bismarck to Heinrich von Puttkamer [*c*. 21 December 1846], pp. 58–9.

43 Pflanze, I, p. 56.

44 See Engelberg, *Das private Leben*, p. 29.

45 Rothfels, Bismarck to Bernhard, 31 January 1847, p. 62.

46 Ibid., Bismarck to Johanna, 21 February 1847, p. 76; translation in Herbert Bismarck, *Love Letters*, I, p. 33.

47 GW, XIV/I, Bismarck to Johanna, 14 May 1851, pp. 211–12; cited in Pflanze, II, p. 62.

48 See Rothfels, Bismarck to Johanna, 21 February 1847, p. 75.

49 Cited in Engelberg, *Otto und Johanna*, p. 28.

50 Pflanze, II, p. 62; Engelberg, I, pp. 367–72.

51 Holstein, I, pp. 9–10.

52 Cited in Engelberg, *Otto und Johanna*, p. 46.

53 Walther Bußmann (ed.), *Graf Herbert von Bismarck: Aus seiner politischen Privatkorrespondenz* (Göttingen, 1964), Herbert Bismarck to Rantzau, 2 July 1887, p. 458.

54 Cited in Engelberg, *Otto und Johanna*, p. 60.

55 See Pflanze, II, p. 62.

56 Rothfels, Bismarck to Johanna, 19 August 1862, p. 293.

57 Nikolai Orloff, *Bismarck und Katharina Orloff: Ein Idyll in der hohen Politik* (Munich, 1936), p. 134.

58 Rothfels, Bismarck to Heinrich von Puttkamer, 21 August 1848, p. 116.

59 Ibid., Bismarck to Malwine, 28 June 1850, p. 131.

60 Ibid., Bismarck to Johanna, 1 October 1850, pp. 137–8.

61 Ibid., Bismarck to Malwine, 8 July 1850, pp. 136–7.

62 G.W. Curtis (ed.), *The Correspondence of John Lothrop Motley* (London, 1889), I, Motley to his wife, 30 July 1855, p. 178.

63 Keudell, *Fürst und Fürstin Bismarck*, p. 90.

64 Rothfels, Bismarck to Hermann Wagener, 30 June 1850, pp. 131–2.

65 Spitzemberg, 3 April 1885, p. 218.

66 Herbert Bismarck, *Love Letters*, Bismarck to Johanna, 17 May 1860, pp. 104–5.

67 See for example ibid., Bismarck to Johanna, 1 August 1862, p. 119 and 2 August 1863, p. 139; Rothfels, Bismarck to Wilhelm, 1 August 1859, p. 262 and 1 August 1866, p. 330.

68 See her letters to Schweninger in Bundesarchiv Berlin, Schweninger Papers, 121.

69 See Pflanze, III, pp. 54–6.

70 See Engelberg, *Das private Leben*, p. 122.

71 Pflanze, II, pp. 50–8.

Chapter 2

※

Achieving Power

The politics of conservatism

Bismarck might never have achieved political power if it had not been for the revolution of 1848 and the introduction of a constitution in Prussia. Historians have tended to denigrate the liberal achievement in 1848, conscious that the emasculated parliament which survived the revolutionary upheavals proved unable to win the constitutional struggle against the crown (and Bismarck) in the 1860s and that, even after the unification of Germany, Prussia remained a semi-autocratic state, impervious to demands for reform until defeat in the First World War heralded the collapse of the monarchy in 1918. Nevertheless, the revolution changed the Prussian political landscape and, crucially, offered a man like Bismarck new opportunities for political activity. Although he lacked the temperament to succeed under a system of bureaucratic absolutism, the advent of participatory politics enabled Bismarck to develop and hone new skills as a conservative politician and parliamentarian which served to distinguish him from an older, less flexible generation of conservatives who continued to rely on the more traditional channels of conservative influence. Furthermore, his resolute defence of conservative orthodoxies brought him not merely notoriety but also gratitude and a tangible reward. Despite some misgivings about the independence of his arguments, the monarchy and its supporters were indebted to Bismarck for his services on their behalf and hence ready, once the counter-revolution was assured, to catapult him over the bureaucratic obstacles which had previously impeded his political career.

Bismarck's achievement of political power was to be closely intertwined with the history of Prussian constitutionalism but, despite his earlier claim to be attracted by the career of a statesman under a free constitution, Bismarck launched his political career as a committed opponent of liberal demands for a constitution. Despite the series of reforms inaugurated after 1806 under the impact of the Napoleonic wars, Prussian kings had repeatedly reneged on the promise of a constitution, and in 1823 Friedrich Wilhelm III had chosen to create eight provincial, corporately organised assemblies, composed of members of pre-defined status groups and with very limited competence, rather than accede to liberal demands for a representative, elected parliament. In February 1847, when Friedrich Wilhelm IV sought approval for a loan to build a railway between Berlin and Königsberg in East Prussia, he was reminded of a promise made in 1820 to consult with the estates of the realm, but he preferred to summon a United Landtag, made up of the members of the provincial assemblies and the higher aristocracy, rather than submit to popular pressure for a constitution or concede regular parliamentary sessions. In May 1847 Bismarck took a seat in the United Landtag as an ultra-conservative representative of the Prussian province of Saxony. Deliberately provocative and sarcastic, he intervened against the moderately liberal, albeit aristocratic majority to defend royal authority, corporate institutions and the traditional social hierarchy. Aggressively asserting the legitimacy of seigneurial rights as well as his bitter hostility to Jewish emancipation if it meant that Jews could hold public office in a Christian state, in the few brief weeks before the Landtag's rejection of the loan and its subsequent closure in June 1847, Bismarck appeared as an uncompromising opponent of constitutional reform, a man whose originality derived less from the content of his speeches than from his offensive and combative style. His first experience of Berlin politics also proved intoxicating. 'This whole business [*die Sache*] grips me far more than I thought', he wrote to Johanna, confessing that he was in such a state of permanent excitement that he could scarcely eat or drink.[1]

Bismarck owed his seat in the United Landtag to the patronage of Ernst Ludwig von Gerlach, who presided over the court of appeal in Magdeburg and had a sharp eye for the talents and abilities of younger men.[2] During his time in Pomerania in the 1840s, Bismarck increasingly sought out the company of men who shared his noble background but had other interests apart from agriculture, and without doubt he gravitated towards those who might be able to promote a political career. The initial attraction of the Thaddens for Bismarck probably resided in the prospect of warm, social companionship, the quiet confidence they exuded and their sense of inner peace. But, apart from decisively influencing Bismarck's religious faith and introducing him to his future wife, the Thaddens also performed one other vital service for Bismarck, for their Trieglaff estate was at the centre of an influential circle of conservative Junker pietists who played a crucial role in providing him with a social and political base on the eve of the revolution of 1848. Both Ernst von Bülow-Cummerow, an agrarian politician and publicist who wrote a book on Prussia's role in Germany in 1842, and Ernst von Senfft von Pilsach, a career official and later *Oberpräsident* of Pomerania who was responsible for the Prussian drainage system and had some quite progressive ideas with respect to the economic modernisation of Prussia, were associated with the Thaddens and took some interest in Bismarck. But Ludwig von Gerlach, to whom Bismarck was introduced in 1845, proved to be far more important. A year later, in 1846, he also met Ludwig's brother, Leopold, who was Friedrich Wilhelm IV's *Generaladjutant* (adjutant-general) from 1850 and one of his closest advisers.[3] The opportunities these two men offered Bismarck for political advancement were too good to miss, and Bismarck duly let out Kniephof and moved to Schönhausen in February 1846 in order to exploit his new contacts more effectively.

In the autumn of 1846, while at Schönhausen, Bismarck secured his appointment to his first public office, as a dyke reeve who was responsible for guarding a stretch of the east bank of the Elbe against flooding. It was indicative of the future that he considered this to be such an important position that no other gentleman in the neighbourhood was competent or brave enough to undertake it,[4] and he certainly committed himself to his new task with exceptional energy and dedication. He also began to make regular visits to Magdeburg to work with Gerlach on a plan to revive and reform patrimonial jurisdiction. Convinced like his new mentor of the urgent need to strengthen the police and judicial powers of landed estate-owners at a time of acute economic crisis and social unrest, Bismarck admired Gerlach's knowledge and practical skill as a jurist and clearly impressed him as a very able, enterprising and committed defender of traditional landed interests. In May 1847 it doubtless reflected the influence of Ludwig von Gerlach that the Magdeburg estates had 'a quite unusual degree of confidence' in Bismarck and thus enabled him to leapfrog over the list of substitutes when one of their representatives at the United Landtag fell ill.[5] Bismarck's cultivation of connections within his own *Stand* had paid off, and his performance in the Landtag further ensured that he acquired some influence with 'delegates of the so-called Court party and the other ultra-conservatives from several provinces'.[6]

Bismarck was no longer in Berlin, however, when the European revolutionary contagion reached the Prussian capital in March 1848 and the king capitulated to liberal demands for a new ministry and promised a constitution. It has become commonplace to caricature Bismarck's immediate response to the news of the revolution as the impulsive gesture of an arch-reactionary Junker who, from the outset, never underestimated the potential role of armed force in quelling the disturbances. His hasty departure to Potsdam and his offer to a bemused army command that he march his loyal Schönhausen peasants to Berlin in support of a counter-revolution was certainly ill-considered, for, quite apart from their dubious military utility, the political reliability of the Schönhausen villagers could scarcely be taken for granted in the prevailing circumstances. Much more damaging in the longer term than his conspiratorial discussions with the commanding generals was his willingness in March 1848 to serve as a spokesman of a Junker deputation to Princess Augusta, the wife of the king's brother, Wilhelm, and future Kaiserin. His suggestion that her husband or son might head a reactionary coup to depose the reigning monarch qualifies his much-vaunted royalism and indicates how, for ultra-conservatives, the legitimacy of kings might be contingent upon their preservation of the traditional order. Bismarck's role in the counter-revolutionary plot was otherwise not very great and, indeed, he nearly lost the support of his conservative friends in the early stages of the revolution because he was ready to bury the past and adapt to the new circumstances. But Bismarck succeeded in incurring Augusta's lasting enmity in the course of their interview. Both these incidents highlight his pugnacious, even hot-headed temperament and his prompt recourse to action to reverse the perceived humiliation of the crown in March 1848. They also confirm the failure of his early attempts to shape events via two of the traditional channels of conservative influence, namely through the army and direct access to the monarchy.

More significant, however, than this further evidence of impetuosity and perhaps immaturity in his character was the sustained and energetic work he undertook from the summer of 1848, when the prospects of a counter-revolution improved, to mobilise popular support for the conservative cause and to forge a cohesive conservative movement and programme out of previously quite disparate strands of ideological opinion. Before the revolution, in an era of corporate as opposed to parliamentary representative institutions, there had been no occasion or need to form a conservative party. Along with other young conservative nobles, among them Hans von Kleist-Retzow with whom he shared a room in Berlin, Bismarck now put his practical, agitational and organisational skills to good use in an effort to convince not merely the landed nobility but also quite diverse sections of popular opinion from lower social classes such as the peasantry and artisans that they had certain common interests which had to be defended in the face of the liberal challenge. Bismarck was closely involved in the establishment of a new conservative newspaper, the *Neue Preußische Zeitung* (or *Kreuzeitung* as it came to be called), ensuring that it would have broad popular appeal through the inclusion of advertisements and economic information, and himself writing numerous articles expounding conservative arguments. He helped to found new conservative associations, notably the somewhat conspiratorial Association for King and Fatherland, which endeavoured to maintain links with loyal conservative supporters across the Prussian provinces and encouraged their infiltration into other conservative associations. He also participated in the preparations for the so-called Junker parliament, which met in August 1848 and again served to organise the nobility to defend its common interests.

Bismarck thrived in the new conditions of association politics. Most importantly, too, he built on his début in the United Landtag of 1847 and continued to make his presence felt as an ultra-conservative parliamentarian and speaker whose sharp mind and caustic wit were used with often devastating effect against his opponents. He was a member of the second estate-based United Landtag, which convened in April 1848 with the specific purpose of arranging for national elections to a constituent assembly. Deemed an uncompromising reactionary, he knew he had no chance of winning a seat in the Berlin National Assembly, elected by a democratic but indirect suffrage in May 1848, and he consequently did not stand. But he secured election to the Lower House or Chamber of Deputies of the new parliamentary Landtag elected in early 1849. The growing strength of the counter-revolution, and his apparent acceptance of the relatively liberal constitution imposed by a new conservative ministry under Friedrich Wilhelm von Brandenburg in December 1848, had made his candidacy a feasible undertaking, but, even so, he remained virtually isolated on the extreme right of a predominantly much more moderate conservative grouping in the chamber. The duration of this Landtag was also brief since it was soon dissolved by Friedrich Wilhelm IV and his ministers, but Bismarck had his mandate confirmed in further elections in July 1849, under a revised, indirect and unequal three-class suffrage which heavily favoured the highest taxpayers. Finally, although he had taken little interest in the wider German situation in 1848 and focused his attention almost exclusively on events in Berlin rather than on the simultaneous deliberations of the German national parliament in Frankfurt, Bismarck took a seat in the parliament convened at Erfurt in March 1850 (again elected by three-class suffrage) to debate the plans of the king's confidant, Joseph Maria von Radowitz, for a small German union based on an alliance of the three kingdoms of Prussia, Hanover and Saxony, and excluding Austria. Again Bismarck excelled in the role of opposition spokesman (for paradoxically it now fell to the moderate liberal majority to defend the king) and he coolly castigated this Prussian initiative for its failure to take account of international realities, its implications for Prussia's monarchy and domestic order, and its dilution of Prussian power.[7]

Throughout the political upheavals Bismarck worked closely with the Gerlach brothers and was associated in the public mind with their ultraorthodox, pietistic conservatism and with the 'secret camarilla' around Leopold von Gerlach, which struggled to gain decisive influence over the king. Nevertheless, despite their close collaboration, it would be wrong even at this stage to identify Bismarck as an unreconstructed and wholly intransigent member of the Gerlach faction of conservatism. Indeed, even the Gerlachs had some doubts in the course of the revolution about Bismarck's political loyalty and reliability. Before the revolution Bismarck shared their hostility to bureaucratic absolutism and their wish to restrict its centralising power by strengthening corporately organised institutions which effectively aligned the monarchy with the interests of the aristocracy. He also to a degree shared their romantic and idealised view of traditional society, with its clearly defined status groups enjoying specific liberties and obligations as part of a God-given order. But by 1848 there is already some evidence of the divergence of opinion and approach that became more marked in the 1850s and eventually led to a definitive rift between Bismarck and his former patrons. Bismarck's realism in accepting the permanence of a constitution in December 1848 is but one example of his inability to indulge in the ultra-conservative illusion that, despite all that had happened, the restoration of the past was both desirable and feasible. As early as April 1848, he incurred the Gerlachs' displeasure when he made a manifestly mild speech in the second United Landtag, claiming that he did not wish to make difficulties for the new liberal government. This display of political independence at a time when he still needed the support of his influential patrons and had no kind of power base of his own could have condemned him to permanent obscurity, and he eventually found himself forced to make an uncharacteristic apology in order to regain their confidence.[8]

Bismarck had to proceed cautiously in 1848 but it is evident that he did not always think in the same categories as the Gerlachs and that, in so far as he shared their objectives, he often reached them by a different route and used different kinds of arguments. Far less willing to subscribe to an ideological and religious world view which he recognised would find little echo among popular forces, Bismarck's approach was from the outset more pragmatic and flexible, being focused on issues of power, the need to defend certain interests in society and hence to preserve an appropriate balance between the various social and political forces. For Bismarck, it was important to uphold agrarian material interests, to compensate landowners for any deprivation of their income or rights, and to ensure that the agricultural classes remained the pillars of society. In his view, the state was not an impartial or neutral element in the divine order but a crucial source of power. Consequently those who advocated liberal legislation, the transfer of resources to industry or any other measures which adversely affected the existing distribution of power and the interests of landed property, had to be purged from the state apparatus. If a parliament might usefully serve to neutralise an increasingly powerful bureaucracy, it should not be ruled out as a matter of principle.

Bismarck's ideas were not particularly original or innovative and, while it is perfectly possible to read his speeches and detect the origins of an amoral *Realpolitik*, his preoccupation with power and frequent references to 'material interests' should not be confused with a latent sympathy for a materialist conception of history or encourage the conclusion that he was a particularly perceptive analyst of the social conditions of his day. Conservative discourse was generally becoming broader in response to developments both before and during the revolution and, within the Gerlach circle, Bismarck had personal contact, for example, with the important conservative theorist Friedrich Julius Stahl, who was already addressing questions concerning the role of constitution, parliament and bureaucracy in the monarchical Christian state and hence preparing conservatives for their eventual acceptance of the concept of the *Rechtsstaat*, a state founded on the rule of law. Bismarck reportedly dismissed Stahl in the 1840s as 'only a Jew' but also appreciated his political realism, recognising that he could learn a lot from him even if their ways would probably eventually part (and Stahl died in 1861 before Bismarck achieved high office).[9] A pragmatic and at times eclectic politician, throughout his career Bismarck tended to be influenced by different individuals and different strands of conservative opinion at different times. He adopted and discarded ideas when it suited his immediate purposes, and was also always prone to underestimate the role of principles and convictions in politics. Impatient with those who preferred talk to action, he emphasised his practical skills to the Gerlachs by remarking that if the three of them witnessed an accident from an upstairs window, the president (Ludwig) would make a philosophical remark about man's lack of religious faith and the imperfections of life on earth; the general (Leopold) would give precise instructions about what had to be done below to help but do nothing; 'I would be the only one who went down or called people to help . . .'[10]

While the seeds of the later conflict between Bismarck and Ludwig von Gerlach are apparent, a conflict to which Bismarck attached great significance in his *Reflections and Reminiscences*, it would, however, also be wrong to overplay the extent of disagreement between Bismarck and the Gerlachs at this time. The Gerlachs may never have trusted Bismarck completely, rebuffing his hopes for a ministerial office in late 1848 and sensing perhaps, as Lothar Gall has suggested, that by using Bismarck to fight the revolution, they were somehow playing with fire and inviting revolution through the back door.[11] But these suspicions, rather than differences, were not allowed to interfere with their collaboration during the revolutionary period and, just as Bismarck needed his influential patrons, they, too, found Bismarck extraordinarily useful, above all as a parliamentary spokesman. His speech of 6 September 1849, in which he diplomatically but forcefully pointed out the dangers for Prussia's internal power structure and international position of Radowitz's union scheme, elevated him to new heights as a conservative spokesman on foreign affairs and immeasurably increased his influence and prestige in conservative circles. On 3 December 1850 he made another highly significant speech in which he defended the recently concluded Olmütz agreement, whereby Prussia finally bowed to Austrian and Russian pressure, abandoned the union project and agreed to a face-saving conference to decide on Germany's future. His ability to defend what was widely perceived to be a humiliating outcome for Prussia, managing to appeal to diverse strands of conservative opinion and launch an effective attack on the liberal opposition, was greatly appreciated by Otto von Manteuffel, the Prussian minister-president and foreign minister since November 1850.[12] It proved a landmark in his political career, helping to secure his appointment the following year as Prussian representative to the Federal Diet at Frankfurt once, inevitably, the old German Confederation was restored.

Thus Bismarck served the conservative cause well during the revolution and its aftermath and, despite some tactical errors in 1848, he was launched on his political career. Even if his political allies were occasionally inclined to disown him as too much of a liability, too immature and overly ambitious, his skills and qualities were suddenly at a premium among conservative sympathisers who, all too often, appeared weak, timid and negative. Combative, energetic, an articulate speaker and effective organiser, he also proved he was a skilful negotiator when he helped to persuade Manteuffel to join the counter-revolutionary government in late 1848. He was prepared to devote his whole being to the political fight and even moved his family to Berlin, leasing out Schönhausen and discounting the financial implications, so that he could live the life of a professional party politician. He gained enormously from his efforts, acquiring invaluable political experience, learning how to adapt to rapidly changing circumstances and increasing his understanding of what was attainable and feasible in political life. Attuned to new techniques of popular persuasion, he was also not shaken in his fundamental conviction that, in order to defend monarchical and aristocratic interests, it was imperative to control the means of force and ensure the loyalty of the state apparatus. For all his effectiveness as a parliamentarian, it cannot have been lost on him that, despite the vociferous exchanges of views, none of the representative assemblies of which he was a member was able to achieve much of substance.

Finally, Bismarck emerged as an important figure on the extreme right of a broadly based conservative movement, which had the political initiative after the ebbing of the revolutionary tide. As such he could expect some kind of reward for his services and something better than the position of a *Landrat* or the premiership of the tiny state of Anhalt-Bernburg, both of which were mooted in early 1851. Despite Ludwig von Gerlach's misgivings about 'violent promotions' of men without the usual qualifications or diplomatic experience,[13] Friedrich Wilhelm IV readily agreed to the suggestion, apparently from Leopold von Gerlach,[14] that Bismarck be appointed to the legation at Frankfurt which had been empty for nearly three years; indeed, the king was only reluctantly persuaded of the need for a three-month transition period while an experienced ambassador showed Bismarck the ropes. With most of Prussia's diplomats and bureaucrats disadvantaged by the entrenched positions they found themselves in after the years of upheaval, the appointment favoured an outsider and especially a man who had appeared to espouse the cause of conservative solidarity and Austrian friendship. Bismarck himself exuded self-confidence, convinced it was God's will that he had been given what he judged to be 'at this moment the most important post in our diplomatic service'.[15] It was a remarkable and unprecedented achievement, attesting not merely to Bismarck's exceptional qualities as an individual but also to how his whole political career was founded and built on his successful ability to exploit times of crisis.

The issue of Prussian power

If Bismarck was widely seen as an upstart in German diplomatic circles from 1851, the position of Prussia appeared no less contentious within the German Confederation during the fifteen years which elapsed between the latter's restoration after the Olmütz agreement and its eventual destruction in the Austro-Prussian war of 1866. After the frustration of liberal hopes to achieve the political unification of the German nation (however they might define it) during the revolutions of 1848 and after the subsequent failure of Prussian and Austrian reform plans for central Europe, it was decided at a conference in Dresden in the spring of 1851 to restore the old German Confederation, originally formed in 1815 after Napoleon's restructuring of the German lands, with no concessions either to the revolutionary aspirations of 1848 or to the manifest shift in the distribution of power among the German states in Prussia's favour.

The German Confederation, a federal arrangement of originally thirty-nine states and free cities for their mutual security, had been conceived at a time when the concept of a territorially consolidated, sovereign state was still a relatively new one in central Europe. While accepting the destruction of the Holy Roman Empire, the reduction in the number of German states and the emergence of new, larger, 'middle states', notably in the south, the statesmen of 1815 had looked to the past for guidance with respect to the political and institutional structure of German-speaking Europe and had aimed to restore a political entity which could accommodate diverse sources of authority or 'layers of sovereignty' as well as multiple, if not necessarily conflicting, claims for loyalty and allegiance. The German Confederation which resulted has been negatively judged by many historians who have tended to see it only as a barrier to the eventual political unification of Germany – or, like Bismarck, as an obstacle to Prussian expansionism – but it need not have been devoid of progressive potential. It was perhaps unfortunate in that its birth coincided with the genesis of a new, potent form of state particularism which aimed at safeguarding the states' newly won sovereignty as well as the achievement of bureaucratic and territorial consolidation. Before 1848 the Confederation was also scarred by its identification with the reactionary policies of the presidial power, Austria, and the Austrian chancellor, Metternich. Hence it failed to develop any common institutions and was criticised by liberals for its failure to promote any kind of national identity or allegiance. In 1851 it was only restored because neither Austria nor Prussia could compel the acceptance of their own preferred solutions to the 'German question'.

The willingness of the governments of the so-called middle states to accept a restored and unchanged Confederation under Austria's presidency reflected to a considerable extent their growing concern over Prussia's expansionist ambitions and hegemonial claims in the wake of the revolutions of 1848. There is little doubt that (without subscribing to a *kleindeutsch* interpretation of German history) Prussia appeared the most dynamic state within the Confederation, having augmented its powers considerably in the first half of the nineteenth century. Although Prussia had not been satisfied with its territorial gains after the Napoleonic wars, its acquisition of the Rhineland and Westphalia (in addition to northern Saxony and Swedish Pomerania), and the loss of much of the Polish territory it had acquired at the end of the eighteenth century, had made it a much more German power, intent on consolidating its dominant position in northern Germany and integrating its two new, non-contiguous provinces. The new territories also signified a doubling of Prussia's population, which further increased by a remarkable 87 per cent in the period between 1816 and 1865. Demographic growth was accompanied by significant economic advances within Prussia for, by fortunate accident, Prussian territorial gains of 1814–15 coincided with the location of areas of rich mineral deposits and immense industrial potential.

Symptomatic of the dynamic increase in Prussian power in the first half of the nineteenth century was Prussia's role in the foundation of a German customs union or *Zollverein* in 1834, the administration of which Ancillon, the Prussian foreign minister, had deemed an appropriate vehicle for an aspiring young diplomat like Bismarck at the end of the decade. Both the economic and political significance of the *Zollverein* can easily be exaggerated by historians who seek to interpret German history in this period in the light of the subsequent wars of unification. Nevertheless, the creation and expansion of the Prussian-dominated customs union, from which Austria was to be permanently excluded despite promises and some expectations of its eventual accession, indicates the sense of purpose with which Prussian bureaucrats set about integrating the new territories, eliminating not only internal tariff barriers but also the external impediments to the freedom of movement and commerce between the geographically divided Prussian provinces. While the *Zollverein* signified a common market rather than a national economy, it came to exert a magnetic attraction over the lesser German states, the overwhelming majority of which were members by the mid-1850s, and it encouraged the use of the Prussian thaler as a common currency throughout the union. Again it is important to emphasise that this development in no sense necessarily anticipated the creation of a small Germany, but it did give Prussia some political leverage over the lesser German states and it indicates the offensive nature of Prussian policy. As Prussian envoy at Frankfurt, Bismarck played a minor role in the re-negotiation of the

Zollverein treaties in the early 1850s, which not only once again excluded Austria but also effectively marginalised the German Confederation as a power factor in the negotiations.

In 1851, when Bismarck took over the Prussian legation at Frankfurt, neither the Habsburg monarchy nor the German Confederation under Austrian presidency was prepared to make concessions, even of a formal nature, to Prussia's growing power and influence. The fact that the majority of the delegates at the Frankfurt parliament, representing the German people, had ultimately looked to Prussia for leadership in 1849 and even offered the imperial crown of a lesser Germany to Friedrich Wilhelm IV (which he rejected) only heightened the mistrust of Prussia. The Austrian response to the issue of Austro-Prussian dualism within Germany was to deny the legitimacy of Prussian claims to parity and equality. Insisting on their own primacy and regarding their presidial authority as sacrosanct, successive Austrian representatives were sup- ported by the envoys from the lesser German states in suspecting Prussia's designs. Determined to ensure Prussia's status barely surpassed that of the other individual member states, Austria even abandoned the practice that had applied before 1848 of consulting with Prussia and seeking their common agreement on key issues prior to more general deliberations in the Diet. What began as a latent antagonism became progressively more marked during the period of Bismarck's envoyship, but this conflict would have developed irrespective of personalities. By the late 1850s Austria was openly hostile to Prussian demands for military parity within the Confederation, refusing, for example, to allow Prussia supreme command over German forces north of the Main in 1859 as the price of Prussian support of Austria in the Italian war.

Bismarck owed his appointment in 1851 not least to his advocacy of Austro-Prussian friendship and conservative solidarity after the 1848 revolution, speaking out against the policy of war with Austria, on which Radowitz, during his brief spell as foreign minister in September and October 1850, appeared intent, and supporting Prussia's retreat at Olmütz in November 1850 in the face of Austrian and Russian pressure. Never- theless he had based his arguments on what he conceived to be Prussia's national interest, not wishing to see Prussia pursue a hegemonial posi- tion in Germany if this were achieved at the price of an alliance with the revolutionary forces of liberalism and democracy and hence signified the destruction of the traditional bastions of power within the Prussian state. Thus, in asserting Prussian interests at Frankfurt from 1851 and seeking to undermine the Confederation with its austrophile majority, Bismarck was not inconsistent with his earlier attitude. Guided by his conception of Prussian interests, he interpreted even the relatively petty formalities at Frankfurt, which had their origin in deference to Austria's superior position, as personally and politically humiliating, injurious to his dignity as the envoy of a rival German power.

Bismarck's views on the German question developed in the 1850s under the impact of his experiences as Prussian envoy at Frankfurt and also in response to major shifts in European international relations precipitated by the establishment of a Bonapartist regime in France under Louis Napoleon from 1851, the Crimean War in the middle of the decade and the Italian war of 1859. With no interest in national aspirations for German unity unless they had an instrumental utility, Bismarck was essentially preoccupied with the issue of Prussian power and security, which he viewed in a European context, conscious that Prussia had almost been extinguished as a significant actor on the European stage in 1806 (when it had been reduced to a mere four provinces) and that it remained vulnerable if, as had happened during disturbances in Hesse-Kassel in 1850, Austrian and Confederation troops threatened to occupy a sensitive area located between Prussian territories. Increasingly convinced that if Austria refused to concede Prussia's parity as a German power, it would eventually have to be coerced to accept a Prussian sphere of influence north of the river Main, Bismarck had little regard for the governments of the lesser German states (or the 'Third Germany' as they were sometimes called), seeing only the rivalry between the two dominant powers. Prussia was imprisoned by the majority system in the German Confederation so he sought to obstruct its business as far as possible, challenging its claim to represent 'German' interests and ensuring that any serious negotiations between Austria and Prussia would have to be conducted on a bilateral basis. Bismarck was determined to elevate the Austro-Prussian relationship to a European level. While he came to appreciate that there were interests and forces within Germany – material interests as well as the national liberal movement – which might be harnessed to the service of Prussian foreign policy, he recognised that the problem of Austro-Prussian dualism was essentially an international question and that in any contest between the two states for influence in Germany, the intervention of other European powers could be decisive. Hence it was imperative that Prussia retained the good-will of its neighbours, especially France and Russia, and that its foreign policy did not alienate any potential friend or ally against Austria.

Bismarck became convinced in the 1850s that there was not room for both Prussia and Austria in Germany, that they were breathing each other's breath and that Prussia's fundamental goal had to be the resolution of their rivalry in its own favour. Nevertheless, it would be wrong to conclude that he regarded a future war as inevitable. Bismarck did see a military conflict as increasingly likely, but most historians have also emphasised his 'strategy of alternatives' and desire to preserve as many options as possible. He developed clear views about what Prussia's object-ives should be, but he was flexible about the choice of means to achieve those goals, not wholly ruling out the possibility of a peaceful, organic reform of the Confederation if this was in conformity with Prussia's power interests,[16] and seeking to pressure Austria (and the middle states) into accepting Prussian equality by conjuring up the mere spectre of a Prussian alliance with France.

It was this flexibility and pragmatism in his contemplation of the possible means to secure Prussia's power and security in Germany that ultimately distanced him from other conservative elements in Prussia and heightened the suspicion and mistrust of many of those who had political dealings with Bismarck at this time. For it was scarcely novel in the conditions of the 1850s that a Prussian diplomat was preoccupied with the issue of Prussia's future 'existence' and regarded the attempt to return to the *status quo ante* 1848 as untenable. What disturbed a more ideological conservative like Leopold von Gerlach (for whom the Napoleonic wars had been a formative experience) was Bismarck's ostens-ible willingness to abandon the principle of conservative solidarity at home and abroad and to pursue a foreign policy in opposition to Austria, apparently with the encouragement of a Bonapartist pretender who threat-ened to reawaken the forces of national revolution in Europe. For Bismarck, France was but one chess piece in the political game and, as he declared in the course of his famous correspondence with Gerlach in 1857, 'In this game it is my business to serve only my king and my country.'[17] Prussian national interests overrode other considerations such as the legitimacy of foreign monarchs, whose authority in any case, as Bismarck pointed out, derived originally from some kind of re-volution. If the creation of a united and viable Italian kingdom was advantageous to Prussia as a wedge between Austria and France, or if the aspirations of the national movement for a united Germany could be channelled and controlled into the service of Prussian interests, he saw no reason to lament the implications for the traditional conservative order in Europe.

Bismarck's advocacy of an offensive strategy against Austria, capitalis-ing on the European crises in the 1850s, was seen as irresponsible and reckless by those in Berlin who were charged with the task of adapting Prussian foreign policy to what appeared a rapidly changing and unstable international state system. While Gerlach continued to uphold the value of the conservative Holy Alliance between Austria, Prussia and Russia, which had been at the heart of Restoration Europe since 1815, the Crimean War wrecked this combination, isolating Austria, which alienated all belligerents by pursuing an anti-Russian policy that, however, fell short of war. Bismarck successfully helped to prevent Austria from mobilising the Confederation behind its policy (and Prussia thereby won Russian gratitude), but his persistent advice that Prussia should exploit Austria's weakness and his bitter complaints about the passivity of Prussian foreign policy in the late 1850s fell on deaf ears. A lengthy memorial he wrote in May 1857 on the need for closer relations with France was greeted with scepticism by the Manteuffel government.[18] After October 1857, when Friedrich Wilhelm IV suffered a stroke and his brother, Wilhelm, deputised for him before becoming prince regent in October 1858 and king in January 1861, Bismarck continued to urge policy recommendations on a new, less conservative government but he was unable to overcome Wilhelm's mistrust. In his 'Booklet' of March 1858 he argued that popular opinion and the moral force of German nationalism might usefully be mobilised in support of Prussian interests and against the governments of Austria and the Confederation. For, he explained, 'there is nothing more German than the development of Prussia's particularist interests, properly understood'.[19] In another significant document, his Baden-Baden memorial of October 1861, he argued that some kind of national representative parliament, chosen by the various state *Landtage* rather than directly elected, or a *Zollparlament* (customs parliament) within the *Zollverein* could serve to balance the particularism of the states. Bismarck's proposals in this period can be seen as tactical rather than serious in intention, designed to curry favour with German national opinion and to break up the Confederation. But his views on the German question ultimately counted against him rather than recommended him for high office. Wilhelm distrusted his hostility to Austria. His suggestion that Prussia exploit the opportunity of Austria's involvement in the Italian war of 1859–60 to seize control of northern Germany, consolidate its territory, march south and proclaim Prussia as the kingdom of Germany[20] was viewed by the majority of those in government as wildly at odds with international realities and practical common sense.

Despite the difficulties in interpreting some of Bismarck's enunciations on Prussian foreign policy prior to his accession to power, it is evident that by the late 1850s he had formulated clear, strategic goals aimed at securing Prussian hegemony in a lesser Germany which would be defined neither with reference to the Habsburg monarchy nor the existing Confederation. Flexible about the means employed towards that aim, both with respect to the international constellation of powers and the use of domestic forces (provided they could be channelled and controlled), he was not a mere opportunist, ready to exploit any exigency to further Prussian power. One of his great strengths was his ability to appreciate the multidimensional qualities of the 'chess game' Prussia was engaged in, the process of response and counter-response which could be triggered by each move and the myriad consequences which might ensue. Fundamentally, he had no inside knowledge about what those possible consequences might be, but by 1857 he was thoroughly exasperated with the 'completely passive role of our policy' and apparent dearth of positive aims and ideas in leadership circles in Berlin.[21] Always invigorated by challenges, he preferred to take risks and gamble on the most likely outcome.

Bismarck, however, was eventually to achieve power despite his political views rather than because of them. Moreover, the key issue in looking at Prussia's position in Germany prior to his accession to power is not the development of his ideas and proposals about how best to improve it, relevant though these may be. Rather, it is the widespread dissatisfaction with the existing situation and the largely autonomous forces, irrespective of individuals, pressing for a resolution of the German question. However many alternatives there were to the eventual Bismarckian unification of Germany under Prussia and however fateful the division of the German nation in 1866 may have been, the pressures for some kind of solution at this time were undeniable. Internationally, of course, it was no accident that the political unification of both Italy and Germany occurred during this period and, as one classic study of the German problem in European international relations between 1848 and 1871 concluded, if Bismarck eventually played his hand with great skill, it was a good one to begin with.[22] A later war may not have been inevitable, but the seeds of Austro-Prussian conflict were evident to all by the close of the 1850s and few deluded themselves that the existing arrangements in Germany could be preserved, as it were, in aspic.

International crisis highlighted the limitations and the vulnerability of the Confederation. The creation of the *Nationalverein* (National Association) in 1859, which aimed to act as an influential pressure group in support of a lesser German state, and a rival *Reformverein* in 1862, which favoured a greater Germany including Austria, indicated growing support among middle-class elites for national unity. In the early 1860s there was a succession of schemes for the reform of the Confederation initiated by a liberalising Austrian government and by lesser states such as Baden. Prussia ran the risk that a new structure, determined by Austria and the middle states, would be imposed upon it. Finally recognising that passivity would be akin to defeat, the Prussian government was moving on to the counter-offensive well before Bismarck's accession to power in September 1862. As early as 1857, Prince Wilhelm acknowledged the need for Prussia to make 'moral conquests' in Germany.[23] There were clear political motives as well as sound economic arguments behind Prussia's determination to espouse *laissez-faire* commercial policies by the early 1860s. Under Albrecht von Bernstorff's leadership as foreign minister from 1861, Prussia effectively quashed any remaining Austrian hopes of eventually joining the *Zollverein* by concluding a commercial treaty with France in 1862. The Austrian economy, with its infant manufacturing industries in need of protection, could not go along with such moves towards free trade. In December 1861 Bernstorff revived the small German union policy which had brought Prussia into direct conflict with Austria after the revolutions of 1848. His plan prompted a coalition between Austria and the middle states, which rejected Bernstorff's proposals in February 1862. Finally, the issue of army reform was squarely on the government's agenda by the early 1860s. Just as Bismarck responded to the manifest deficiencies in the size and efficiency of the Prussian army, as revealed by its mobilisation during the Italian campaign, by calling for armaments, so the king, too, was resolved to reorganise the army and ensure its fighting capacity.

In all these ways Prussian policy already anticipated the course later pursued by Bismarck and, despite his later attempt in his memoirs to highlight the significance of his appointment in September 1862, there was a fundamental continuity. Bismarck may have set himself up as the most ruthless advocate of a policy of Prussian interests, but the direction those interests dictated in Germany was clear. The chief difference between Bismarck and his immediate predecessors at this point resided not so much in their assessment of Prussia's foreign policy options as in the extent to which they were prepared to accommodate the aims of the national liberal movement in Prussian domestic politics. For despite his advocacy of often startlingly radical methods to achieve his aims, Bismarck's essential conservatism was never in doubt. And just as he was not prepared to see Prussia merged into a wider German union, so he was not prepared to watch Prussia pursue its hegemonial ambitions in Germany if this signified a simultaneous liberalisation of its political and social system. Any compromise with the national liberal movement would have to be on his terms.

The impotence of office

The years Bismarck spent as a diplomat, first in Frankfurt (1851–59), then in St Petersburg (1859–62) and finally, very briefly, in Paris (1862), were important for his political development in many ways. They enabled him to gain valuable diplomatic experience and some initiation into the official processes of Berlin high politics. He soon became a cynical and self-proclaimed expert in the art of writing diplomatic reports which said nothing.[24] Particularly the Frankfurt years provided him with the opportunity to familiarise himself more thoroughly with aspects of the 'German question', as well as related international issues such as the Schleswig-Holstein problem which, even before the London protocol of 1852 subjected the status of the duchies to international regulation, Bismarck was convinced had to remain beyond the competence of the German Confederation. His diplomatic apprenticeship deepened the understanding he had gained during the revolutions of 1848 of the interconnections between foreign and domestic policies. It also enhanced his appreciation of the role of the press and public opinion in the struggle for influence in Germany and, drawing on his earlier journalistic experience, he sought to turn the Prussian legation at Frankfurt into a centre for the dissemination of Prussian propaganda. Not least, too, Bismarck exploited his new location to visit France privately in 1855 (he returned again in 1857) and meet personally with Napoleon III, who was viewed with uncompromising hostility by virtually all significant political groups in Prussia in the 1850s. As soon as he took up residence in Frankfurt, Bismarck was indicating that Prussia might have to do a deal with Bonapartist France and cede the Rhineland voluntarily in exchange for consolidating Prussian control over north Germany and securing Hanover as compensation.[25]

Clearly, then, Bismarck accumulated valuable knowledge and experience as a diplomat, political capital on which he would draw in the subsequent decades in power. In so far as his political conceptions can be seen to have influenced his future conduct of policy, he may have formed other judgements, too, as a result of his period in Frankfurt. For example, he was impressed by the significance of the confessional divide in German politics and he rapidly became convinced that to profess to be Catholic or 'black' was synonymous with an admission of implacable anti-Prussianism. Lothar Gall has also claimed that Bismarck later erred in judging both liberalism and the commercial middle classes on the basis of his first-hand experience of Frankfurt where social and economic relationships were not typical of conditions prevailing elsewhere in

Germany.[26] Observation of the restrictive practices of the city's guilds also may have led him to revise his attitude to liberal economic doctrine and some social issues so that he came to acknowledge more readily the advantages of *laissez-faire*.

Yet, however formative the years Bismarck spent as a diplomat were with respect to the development of his political views, especially on Prussian foreign policy, it can scarcely be claimed that he made a significant political impact during this period or that he exerted much influence on decision-making in Berlin. Indeed, when his envoyships are viewed from the perspective of his political ambitions, it is evident that they did little to advance his prospects of achieving a ministerial post, let alone a position of power at the centre. Bismarck's dismissive and destructive attitude to the German Confederation doubtless impeded his ability to capitalise on his extraordinary promotion in 1851 and bolster an official position which he recognised from the start gave him little freedom of manoeuvre or scope for personal initiative.[27] But, more significantly, the outspoken independence of his political views, his reluctance to identify himself with any significant political group in Prussia and his frequent refusal to make the compromises necessary to build bridges to other conservatives all militated against him.

In Frankfurt, where Bismarck lived a relatively modest and provincial life with his wife and their three young children in a villa on the outskirts of the city before moving into the city centre, assessments of his political role tended to be couched in personal and predominantly negative terms. His domineering personality irritated not only his early mentor, Theodor von Rochow, who called him a drunken student and soon departed back to St Petersburg, but also many of his diplomatic colleagues who, while often recognising his intelligence and energy, variously found him conceited, arrogant, excessively self-confident, insufferably ambitious, petty, envious and sarcastic.[28] Since he obstructed the business of the Confederation and claimed an equality with his Austrian counterpart, which even ran to asserting his equal right to remove his jacket or smoke cigars during sessions, his relations with successive Austrian representatives were often stormy. Count Friedrich von Thun-Hohenstein regarded him as a coarse and uncouth Junker without diplomatic expertise or finesse; Count Anton von Prokesch-Osten saw him as a fanatical Prussian whose policy was driven by an insatiable hunger for power in Germany; Count Johann Bernhard von Rechberg judged him to be an ambitious careerist who would stop at nothing to oppose Austrian policy. Politically uncooperative and sometimes personally abrasive, Bismarck thwarted any evolutionary potential the Confederation might have had to act as a single German power and he was happy to see the Diet bypassed on all important matters. Consequently there were no fundamental changes in either the organisation of the Confederation or the way it functioned while he was at Frankfurt. Bismarck also had little interest in seeking political allies among the envoys of the lesser German states. He was contemptuous of the south Germans and, with one or two exceptions such as the Danish envoy to the Federal Diet, Bernhard Ernst von Bülow (whom Bismarck appointed state secretary of the Foreign Office in 1873), he did not rate his colleagues at all highly. Moreover, even while Austria and Prussia competed for influence in the rest of Germany, Bismarck refused to woo governments whose legitimacy he scorned and which he eventually would seek to neutralise by appealing over their heads to the German people.

Bismarck had useful diplomatic and negotiating skills and, until Friedrich Wilhelm IV's stroke in October 1857, he enjoyed the confidence of a monarch who was willing to entrust him with special assignments and who appreciated the freedom of manoeuvre created by conflicting advice.[29] But neither his official activities nor his frequent policy recommendations endeared him to his own government in Berlin. Although it was recognised even before he achieved a diplomatic post that 'he has the genuine diplomatic quality of standing on friendly terms with his most bitter opponents',[30] Bismarck was not a born diplomat because he was never inclined to adhere to his diplomatic brief or subordinate himself to directives emanating from his superiors if these in any sense deviated from his own political judgements. Moreover, Bismarck remained suspect in the eyes of the Berlin government because of the circumstances of his appointment, and Manteuffel soon realised that his ambitious subordinate was being groomed by the Gerlachs for the premiership and wished to replace him. Viewed as the candidate of the camarilla, the circle of 'irresponsible' advisers surrounding Friedrich Wilhelm IV which was dominated by the Gerlachs and wielded an intermittent influence over the king, Bismarck's political loyalty could never be assumed in Berlin.

Bismarck was not disposed to cultivate good relations with the higher bureaucracy in Berlin nor did he feel compelled to develop strong links to any significant political grouping in Prussia other than the Gerlachs and the 'old conservatives'. Soon after his appointment to Frankfurt, he also deliberately resigned his seat in the Upper House of the Prussian Landtag (an elected body) so that he could concentrate on his new diplomatic role and keep out of Berlin party politics. However, in July 1854 he was appointed one of twenty-six new members of the advisory *Staatsrat*

(Council of State) which the King convened in Berlin, and in 1855 he became a member of the new House of Lords or *Herrenhaus* (composed of hereditary peers and crown appointees), a chamber he belonged to for the next forty-three years.[31] In the eyes of the opponents of ideological conservatism, Bismarck remained associated with the camarilla and, even as his foreign policy recommendations increasingly diverged from those of his patrons in the 1850s, he still saw his connections with the Gerlachs as most likely to serve his ambitions. Bismarck was told by the Gerlachs that they could make him premier as early as 1851. His candidacy was seriously considered in 1852 and there were rumours of an imminent Bismarck ministry in 1853. In 1854 Ludwig Gerlach again discussed with Bismarck the possibility of his becoming minister-president and exhorted him to couple his ambition with humility. 'He is not completely transparent and hence unreliable', Gerlach concluded in his diary after this conversation, a comment he was to look back on ruefully after the events of 1866.[32] The extent of the rift between Bismarck and the Gerlachs from 1857 has been exaggerated, for, even after the exchange of views with Leopold in 1857–58, it is clear that there were still many political issues that drew them together. Bismarck and Ludwig were united in their determination to secure Prince Wilhelm's regency in 1858 in the face of opposition from many of their conservative associates. Above all, the onset of the constitutional crisis ensured that differences over foreign policy assumed less significance. Moreover, although the 70-year-old Leopold von Gerlach died eight days after his master, Friedrich Wilhelm IV, in January 1861, Bismarck continued to have a relationship with Ludwig and seek out his advice right up to the definitive break between the two men in 1866. Indeed, Gerlach himself may have seen some of Bismarck's foreign policy pronouncements as merely tactical, designed to distance himself from the 'old conservative' stance of the two brothers and the *Kreuzzeitung* and make himself more acceptable to the new prince regent and his government.

But Bismarck's views on foreign policy confirmed his status as a conservative outsider and did not bring him any closer to other strands of conservative opinion. Formerly intimate conservative friends began to adopt a cooler attitude towards him and in 1860 Bismarck wrote to Leopold von Gerlach that 'at least you talk things out with me'.[33] While he increasingly alienated himself from his old friends, he also remained aloof from the so-called *Wochenblatt* party, a group of conservatives who had been in the Association for King and Fatherland in 1848 but had subsequently broken away from the more intransigent and reactionary

Kreuzzeitung party and favoured a more moderate conservatism. These 'liberal conservatives', who enjoyed the sympathy of Prince Wilhelm and his wife in the 1850s, were committed to uphold the constitution and they had objected to Manteuffel's resurrection of the old provincial estates in 1851 as a possible prelude to replacing the elected parliament with a new United Landtag.[34] Their willingness to countenance moderate liberal concessions at home and their instinctive leanings towards an anglophile foreign policy separated them from Bismarck.

Bismarck's political isolation became more apparent after Wilhelm began to deputise for his brother in 1857. He did not enjoy Wilhelm's confidence in the same way that he had found favour with Friedrich Wilhelm IV, and his suspicions about the hostility of Wilhelm's wife, Augusta, were well-founded. Moreover, Wilhelm's accession to power as prince regent in October 1858 was accompanied by expectations of a 'New Era' in Prussian domestic politics. Manteuffel's bureaucratic government was dismissed and Wilhelm, who had always been more in sympathy with the moderate Gotha liberals, had supported Radowitz's union policy and experienced Olmütz as a bitter humiliation of Prussia, turned to the liberal conservatives to form a new ministry. However superficial this apparent liberal shift proved, it nevertheless signified the definitive end of the older, ideological conservatism associated with the Gerlachs, who had not been *persona grata* with Wilhelm since the 1830s. Bismarck, who had owed so much to their patronage and remained closely identified with their circle, had no other significant political support in Berlin. He was soon shunted off as envoy to St Petersburg, technically a more prestigious position but in reality, given the hopes of the new men for better relations with liberal Britain, a less significant post.

Bismarck's frustration at being so far removed from the corridors of power, literally and metaphorically, was intense. Acutely aware of his political isolation, he knew there was no support in Berlin for the kind of policies he advocated and in many respects this period represented the nadir of his political fortunes. It was also perhaps not coincidental that shortly after his transfer he was further debilitated by prolonged physical ill-health. An injury to his left leg, which he had sustained while hunting in 1857 and never had the patience to let heal, became infected in June 1859. Serious complications arose after it was poorly treated by his doctors, and inflammation of the veins became a recurring problem throughout the rest of his life. In addition, a lung infection brought him close to death, rendering him out of action for weeks in the winter of 1859–60 and inducing Johanna to express her dream that he would give up the diplomatic life altogether since it had 'brought him nothing good at all, only illness, annoyance, enmity, disfavour, ingratitude and banishment' and was completely alien to 'his honest, decent, thoroughly noble character'.[35] Bismarck came close to acknowledging his political failure, not merely exuding personal dissatisfaction but also, as in earlier times, allowing his consciousness of personal and political futility to undermine his confidence in his own will-power and effectiveness.

Bismarck's lack of scruple about the implications of his own behaviour for the position of the responsible ministers in Berlin became even more marked in St Petersburg than it had been in Frankfurt. Confronted with a regent and a government that had good grounds to suspect him, he refused to truckle to the new line in foreign policy and, as Ernst Engelberg has pointed out, behaved more like a noble *frondeur* than an official diplomat.[36] He certainly enjoyed better relations with the Russian government during this period than he did with his own. Mistrusted in Prussian court and government circles, he only evaded recall because he enjoyed the confidence of the Russian premier, Alexander Gorchakov, who perceived that Bismarck was more sympathetic to the interests of Russian foreign policy than any likely replacement.

Bismarck undoubtedly deepened his understanding of international affairs in St Petersburg. Yet, at a time when his impatience for high office in Berlin was becoming increasingly evident, he remained politically impotent and excluded from the real centre of Prussian decision-making. His diplomatic career seemed to have turned him even more into a one-man party, a loner and something of a maverick or misfit who could never be completely trusted by anyone he worked with. Still unable to refrain from voicing his political judgements and making alternative policy recommendations, he must have appeared a subversive influence even to his own government and it is remarkable how he managed to remain in office. While Friedrich Wilhelm IV may have appreciated his outspoken political views, they could not further his prospects under the future Wilhelm I whose mistrust intensified. Belatedly Bismarck came to realise that he would gain the new monarch's confidence only if he avoided specific policy recommendations and commitments and sought only to assure him of his general loyalty and devotion. But, as Lothar Gall has indicated, one of the most perplexing features of Bismarck's career is how, at virtually every stage of it, his fall seemed 'an immediate and not even particularly dramatic possibility'.[37] Mere months before his appointment as Prussian minister-president, the likelihood of Bismarck's achieving political power seemed more remote than ever.

The opportunity

In 1851 when Bismarck became Prussian envoy to Frankfurt against all the odds, he clearly hoped to use his new position as a stepping-stone to high ministerial office. But he was able to achieve little as a diplomat, remaining on the periphery of power and largely devoid of political influence. A conservative outsider who continued to be tainted and handicapped by his reputation as an arch-reactionary extremist, he weakened his links with influential circles of conservative opinion and also failed to impress successive monarchs and governments in Berlin with the wisdom of his opinions. In many respects he remained a lone and largely unheeded voice, even while a rapidly changing international environment served objectively to push Prussia's foreign policy onto the kind of course he advocated. Reluctant to relinquish his political ambitions, in the middle of the 1850s Bismarck lamented to his brother that it might well be 'downhill all the way now to the Schönhausen crypt'.[38] And, in 1859, his transfer as Prussian envoy to St Petersburg seemed to underline his political as well as his physical distance from Berlin. For all his hunger for power, his will to decide and to act, Bismarck appeared impotent, unable to capitalise on his rapid promotion and further his career in relatively tranquil times. Bismarck's eventual achievement of political power depended, once again, on exceptional and unforeseen political circumstances. The increasingly bitter Prussian constitutional conflict between crown and parliament from 1860 provided the opportunity, and Bismarck's peculiar position as a conservative outsider enabled him to step into the highest political office after the elimination of all feasible alternatives.

The Prussian constitutional conflict in the 1860s arose over the issue of army reform but its origins are complicated. They involve technical matters relating to the army's organisation and efficiency as well as wider political, social and economic considerations affecting the army's role in the Prussian state and the development of Prussian constitutionalism. The radicalisation of the dispute and the bitterness it engendered are also not readily intelligible given that the need to reorganise and expand the army was never in dispute and that on several occasions, especially in 1861–62, the government and parliamentary majority seemed to be on the verge of an acceptable compromise. Nevertheless, even if the conflict was never quite the decisive struggle between monarchical absolutism and parliamentary government that protagonists on both sides made it out to be, by September 1862 it had led to the resignations of the king's most capable ministers and the possibility of Wilhelm's abdication in favour of his son, Friedrich Wilhelm, who was well known for his liberal sympathies. Prussian politics were once again being conducted in an atmosphere of crisis and Bismarck was finally able to convince the monarch that he owed it to his country to make one last attempt at a political solution by appointing him as premier.

The developing conflict between the monarchy and the Prussian Landtag over the reform of the army needs to be set in the context of the revival of Prussian political life in the late 1850s after several years of political repression. This politicisation reflected the gathering pace of economic change in Prussia in the 1850s, a decade which not only began to lay the basis for Prussia's future industrial prosperity but also strengthened support for liberalism within her burgeoning urban communities. The new interest in politics and resurgence in associational life were also connected to the upheavals in the international state system after the Crimean War and the fresh opportunities created for movement in the German question. The Franco-Austrian war especially, the achievements of Count Camillo di Cavour in unifying most of Italy under Piedmont's leadership, and the potential French threat to the security of the Rhine, could not fail to arouse public interest and debate in educated circles across Germany, even if opinion was very divided. Finally, the changed political climate in Prussia in the late 1850s was also prompted by the high expectations attached to Wilhelm's regency from October 1858, expectations which may have proved largely unfounded but which nevertheless indicated the widespread perception, not just in Prussia, that rifts had opened up within the political establishment. Wilhelm's known sympathy for the *Wochenblatt* party, his dismay over the Olmütz agreement, and his wish for Prussia to play a more assertive role, morally if not militarily, in German affairs all contributed to the impression that there was suddenly new scope for a plurality of views on a wide range of foreign and domestic issues. Manifestly, the reactionary front, which had typified the Manteuffel era, was in the process of dissolution.

In 1858 Wilhelm dismissed the Manteuffel government which had come to stand for the restoration of many of the political privileges of the nobility and which had undeviatingly sought, in the wake of the revolutionary era, to discipline and control all those involved in the political process. In its place the new regent appointed a much less obviously conservative ministry under Prince Karl Anton von Hohenzollern-Sigmaringen, a ministry which included Bethmann Hollweg and Rudolf von Auerswald, men clearly identified with more liberal values. As we have seen, these events heralded a review of Prussian foreign policy and soon signified the removal of Bismarck from his post at Frankfurt and his dispatch to St Petersburg. But they also proved to be the signal for Prussian voters to turn out in much greater numbers in the elections of November 1858 than they had done in the previous elections of 1855, when only one-sixth of those eligible to vote had done so. The easing of governmental pressure on the electoral process also contributed to the return of a new Landtag which was markedly more liberal than its predecessors. The new majority did not reflect a change in the social composition of the parliament, for it continued to be dominated by the same social and professional groups as before, especially aristocratic landowners and state officials, who included not only civil servants but also judges and professors. But it highlighted the growing tensions within what can broadly be described as the 'political class' in Prussia, as well as a generational shift towards liberalism. While liberalism was in no sense a homogeneous or cohesive movement even in the 1860s and the political divisions within the Lower House tended to be fluid, the overwhelming majority of those who took up their seats in 1859 were committed to compromise with the 'New Era' government to achieve moderate reform at home and a more national policy abroad.

The hopes of the new parliamentary majority for a gradual liberalisation of government in Prussia were probably misplaced from the beginning. It must be stressed that the change of monarch did not represent a generational change and Wilhelm soon demonstrated that he was as intent on upholding the traditional pillars of the Prussian monarchy as his brother had been. Moreover, even after the appointment of more sympathetic ministers, there remained many institutional obstacles to a liberal course in Prussia. For example, many of the proposed reforms after 1858 were to stumble at the hurdle of the Prussian *Herrenhaus*, a highly aristocratic body which had replaced the originally more plutocratic Upper House in 1854. The *Herrenhaus* could veto all legislation and it rapidly developed into a powerful bastion of Junker power and interests. Nor was it alone in constituting a major impediment to liberal reform. Conservative elements in the Prussian bureaucracy as well as the king's own political and military prerogatives imposed severe limitations on any prospective liberalisation. Above all, the king's power of command over the army (his *Kommandogewalt*) remained a crucial qualification to Prussian constitutionalism, for, to all intents and purposes, the army remained outside the constitution after 1848, under no obligation to swear an oath of loyalty to it and answerable only to the crown. Only in two respects had the introduction of constitutionalism in Prussia impinged on the army's autonomy within the state. First, as a member of the king's government, the Prussian war minister was now legally bound to defend the constitution and appear before parliament, a requirement which served to make him highly suspect to an army leadership which was intent on ensuring that most military matters remained the exclusive preserve of the king. In December 1859 Eduard von Bonin had to resign (for a second time) as war minister because he was seen as 'too constitutional' by Wilhelm's other influential military advisers, above all the chief of the king's Military Cabinet, Edwin von Manteuffel (who was technically Bonin's subordinate!).[39] Second, the military budget now had to be approved by parliament, and the Landtag was bound to seek to use its budgetary powers as a means of bringing political pressure to bear on the army.

The fears which the issue of army reform engendered and the increasingly acrimonious nature of the struggle between the government and the Prussian parliament after 1860 cannot be understood without reference to the memories of the revolution of 1848, when the army would have been quite prepared to fight the Berlin insurgents if the king had not intervened. The perception on both sides of the political divide was that the limited constitutional settlement of 1850 was but a recent and imperfect compromise that might still be contested and revised to their benefit or detriment. Prussian liberals, on the one hand, wanted a strong army that could underwrite Prussian claims to hegemony in Germany. But they also suspected the political motives of the king's military entourage and feared that a reformed army would be a formidable instrument of domestic repression unless it were securely accountable to parliament. On the other hand, the man who replaced Bonin as war minister in 1859, Bismarck's friend from Pomerania, General Albrecht von Roon, was convinced after the king's submission to his subjects in 1848 that 'The army is now our fatherland, for there alone have the unclean and violent elements who put everything into turmoil failed to penetrate.'[40] The need to preserve the army's independence from parliamentary control was construed as even more urgent by Manteuffel, for whom even the highly circumscribed constitutional responsibility of the war minister was unacceptable. Manteuffel saw no distinction between the liberals in the Landtag and the insurgents in 1848, anticipating at any moment the popular and democratic onslaught and drawing up contingency plans for the army's execution of a *Staatsstreich* or *coup d'état* that would put an end to Prussia's brief experiment in constitutional government. Comparing the king's plight in the constitutional conflict to that of Charles I in England or Louis XVI in France, he was ready, at the merest hint of parliamentary criticism, to take offensive action to restore monarchical absolutism.

Even before he officially became regent in 1858 and before Prussian mobilisation on the Rhine during the Italian war revealed to all the military deficiencies of the Prussian army, Wilhelm was determined to instigate a thorough reorganisation of the army and provide for its expansion in line with Prussia's growing population. Bonin had had sufficient political acumen to recognise that such a reform could not be guided solely by military considerations if the government wanted to avoid conflict with the Landtag; his successor was not so troubled by the attitude of parliamentarians. As chairman of a special military commission set up to draft the reform, Roon was largely responsible for the provisions of the army bill he introduced as war minister to the Lower House in February 1860. The bill aimed to increase the peacetime strength of the army by 60,000 men and to enforce three years' compulsory military service rather than two years, which had usually operated in practice since the 1830s. It also proposed major changes to the structure of the army and its operations in wartime. In particular, the *Landwehr* (the territorial reserve or militia), which had been created in 1813 during the war of liberation and had a special place in liberal mythology, was to be severely weakened and separated from front-line service. The aim was to create a genuinely professional army supported by thoroughly trained line reserves. But Prussian liberals were bound to have misgivings about the political and social implications of three years' compulsory military service as well as the demotion of the 'citizens' army'.

These concerns were at the root of the liberal opposition to the army bill rather than a reluctance to agree to the hefty financial cost of the army reorganisation. Indeed, after the government opted for a tactical withdrawal of the bill (on Roon's advice), the broadly based liberal-conservative majority in the Lower House was twice prepared, in May 1860 and again in 1861, to vote through a provisional military budget pending an eventual agreement on the reform. These gestures of goodwill not only enabled the army to start implementing the reforms the Landtag opposed (notably the creation of new line regiments which proved to be permanent) but also triggered protests among the less compliant liberal deputies within the majority coalition and eventually precipitated the foundation of a new Progressive Party in June 1861. In the elections of December 1861 the new party campaigned on a platform of opposition to the government's military measures and it also placed German unification as well as significant domestic reforms, such as the introduction of full ministerial responsibility to parliament and the reform of the *Herrenhaus*, high on its agenda. The electorate responded by returning the Progressives as the largest political party in the Landtag with 109 seats.

As the conflict deepened in the spring of 1862, the king's commitment to the standpoint of his army and his complete hostility to liberal claims dispelled any remaining illusions that Prussia had embarked on a 'New Era'. Confronted with a Landtag majority even more determined to resist the three-year military service and call the government to account, Wilhelm dissolved the Lower House in March 1862 and removed those of his ministers who still had any sympathy with liberalism. The elections in May, however, only exacerbated the problem for, despite massive government pressure, the voters once again endorsed the programme of the Progressive Party and conservative representation in the Lower House shrank to a mere eleven seats. While some of Wilhelm's key military advisers were indisputably ready to countenance a violent *Staatsstreich* in the spring of 1862 to overthrow the constitution and re-impose royal absolutism in Prussia, whatever the cost in civilian bloodshed, Crown Prince Friedrich Wilhelm and his brother-in-law, Grand Duke Friedrich of Baden, opposed unconstitutional action and reinforced Wilhelm's innate sense of caution. The new conservative state ministry, too, which was headed by the former president of the Prussian *Herrenhaus*, Prince Adolf zu Hohenlohe-Ingelfingen, preferred compromise to confrontation, especially since the Progressive Party, even after May 1862, proved reluctant to flex its political muscles and continued to seek cooperation with the crown on the basis of a mutual recognition of the constitution.

Thus although the dispute served to radicalise both sides and encouraged a discourse of intransigence, it is doubtful whether Prussia really stood on the threshold of a fundamental redistribution of political power in the summer and early autumn of 1862. The state ministry, including Roon, who later reneged on his decision when confronted with Wilhelm's opposition, collectively recommended that the crown abandon the three-year service period and thereby secure parliamentary acceptance of a compromise bill which was proposed by three liberal deputies, Stavenhagen, Sybel and Twesten. But it was Wilhelm who, at a crown council meeting on 17 September, brusquely refused to accept the solution which the government offered and which even a majority of his officers did not believe significantly undermined the army reform. Wilhelm's attitude understandably provoked the Lower House to reject the bill on 19 September and to deny the government a legal budget for the army reorganisation. The ministers thus now faced the prospect of governing in clear defiance of the will of the parliamentary majority, a situation that few could contemplate with equanimity, despite attempts on the right to justify such a course on the basis of there being a 'gap' in the constitution. Yet, confronted with the imminent resignation of his government in September 1862 and with a now glaring constitutional conflict, the king had no stomach for a decisive military confrontation. After the crown council meeting he drafted his abdication, but in subsequent discussions with his son on 19 and 20 September he proved unable to convince the crown prince that the succession in such circumstances would not constitute an intolerable capitulation on the part of the crown.

Bismarck undoubtedly followed the course of the constitutional crisis from afar, taking a keen personal interest in the dispute over the army reform and sensing his opportunity. Roon campaigned unsuccessfully for his candidature as minister-president in the early months of 1862. But at the time of the government reshuffle in March, the queen opposed a man 'who will surely stop at nothing and is the terror of everyone because he has no principles'.[41] Wilhelm then recalled Bismarck from St Petersburg at the end of April and interviewed him in May. But he, too, still entertained doubts both about Bismarck's foreign policy recommendations and about the wisdom of appointing a conservative reactionary who so blatantly signalled that he would not shrink from a collision with the Landtag. So he preferred to send him provisionally as envoy to Paris and wait on events. Thus, to all intents and purposes, Bismarck kept aloof from the deteriorating domestic situation in Berlin. He spent a few weeks in Paris and also visited London (where he had a famous conversation with Disraeli about his plan to unify Germany) before whiling away much of the summer with Kathy Orlov and her husband in the south of France. But in reality Bismarck was increasingly impatient, even if he disclaimed all ambition to his wife. 'I long for work for I don't know what I should do', he wrote to Johanna on 1 June.[42]

In the middle of the great city of Paris I am lonelier than you in Reinfeld and sit here like a rat in a deserted house . . . In eight to ten days I will probably receive a telegraphic summons to Berlin, and then this song and dance will be over. If my enemies only knew what a relief their victory would be for me and how sincerely I wish them it! . . . You cannot dislike the Wilhelmstr[asse]* more than I do, and if I am not convinced that it has to be, I won't go. I consider it cowardice and disloyalty to leave the King in the lurch on the pretext of health reasons.

Bismarck recognised that his best chance of high office lay in the exacerbation of the conflict. But, despite some friends in high places, such as the new but little known and scarcely influential minister of interior,

* The Wilhelmstrasse in Berlin was the German equivalent of Downing Street and in common usage often referred to the Prussian Foreign Ministry.

Gustav von Jagow, he still lacked a significant basis of political support in Berlin. Hence the role of Roon must be seen as crucial in explaining his appointment in September 1862. How far Roon, as the political and military representative of the army and arguably the key voice in the Prussian state ministry, pushed Bismarck forward as the candidate of the military elite remains a matter of some doubt.[43] Nevertheless, the evidence suggests that Roon was the only man in the higher echelons of Berlin decision-making with influence over the king who consistently favoured Bismarck's appointment as minister-president in 1862. Even then, Roon must have recognised that he and Bismarck did not share identical views on all political issues (their divergence over the homage question is a case in point[44]) and he was simultaneously prepared to pursue a compromise solution over the summer until the king blocked it. In September he also discussed contingency plans for a *Staatsstreich* with Manteuffel, if all else failed.

Thus, even though Bismarck's name was frequently discussed as a potential candidate in the first half of 1862, the odds scarcely seemed to favour his promotion and he relied heavily on Roon's trust. And until there really seemed no alternative, Roon on his own proved unable to overcome the obstacles to Bismarck's appointment. As late as 11 September, according to Kleist-Retzow, Wilhelm I was still resisting Bismarck's appointment as minister-president because 'he, Bismarck, is urging an alliance with France which he, the king, could never agree to'.[45] When the crown council meeting of 17 September exposed the rift between the king and his government, Roon was presented with another chance to urge Wilhelm to receive Bismarck. The war minister summoned his friend back to Berlin from France with his famous telegram of 18 September, '*Periculum in mora. Dépêchez-vous.*' However, in telling him to hurry back to Berlin without delay, Roon had foreseen that Bismarck might otherwise miss his opportunity rather than meaning to imply (as Bismarck later suggested) that he was needed urgently to rescue the situation. The 'danger' to which Roon referred was less the predicament of the crown than Bismarck's own uncertain career prospects. If he did not return to Berlin at once, he might well be too late to capitalise on the opportunity.[46]

Roon may have wanted to install Bismarck as minister-president because he no longer felt equal to the complicated political situation or felt worn down in his various capacities as government minister, representative of the army and adviser to the crown. Impressed by his friend's energy, his fearlessness and his appetite for power, he perhaps sought to off-load some of the tensions between his political and military roles onto Bismarck,[47] trusting him not to surrender one iota of the king's prerogatives to parliament. Like Roon, Bismarck was a conservative whose political conceptions could only accommodate a confined and restricted role for constitutional government within the existing power structure; and they both adamantly opposed any compromise with the advocates of parliamentarianism that might undermine the security and unassailability of Prussia's traditional institutions, above all the monarchy and army. Moreover, by 19 September even conservatives, like Kleist, who had doubts about a Bismarck minister-presidency, recognised that 'an energetic minister-president [is] absolutely necessary'. 'There is no better man possible than Bismarck', he wrote to Gerlach. 'It is prescribed [*verschrieben*], may God in his mercy bestow his blessing.'[48]

When Bismarck, who was 'fresh and in good spirits',[49] met Wilhelm at the summer palace of Babelsberg near Potsdam in the afternoon of 22 September 1862, he carefully avoided any discussion of the political programme he might follow and concentrated instead on gaining the monarch's trust. Representing the crisis as a stark choice between monarchical rule and parliamentary government, he successfully convinced Wilhelm both of his loyal devotion to his person and his unqualified commitment to defend the interests of the crown. While Bismarck hoped to bring about a political resolution of the constitutional conflict, he had to elevate it into a clash between incompatible political principles, the product of two rival conceptions of sovereignty, for only in this way could he dissipate Wilhelm's doubts about where he stood and unequivocally declare himself to be on Wilhelm's side. In offering himself to the king as a '*Konfliktminister*' who would continue the fight and shrink from nothing to achieve the army reform, Bismarck absolved Wilhelm of his dilemma over whether he should abdicate and appealed to his sense of duty to try all possible avenues before acknowledging defeat. Even so, Bismarck could not overcome all Wilhelm's misgivings on 22 September. Bismarck desperately wanted to head the Foreign Ministry as well as become minister-president. Only reluctantly, after he had been persuaded that there really was no alternative candidate, did Wilhelm I agree to appoint Bismarck foreign minister on 8 October.

The circumstances of Bismarck's appointment in 1862 make it difficult to accept Ernst Engelberg's interpretation that he was essentially serving the interests of significant and powerful elites in Prussian society – the army, the bureaucracy and the property owners.[50] As stated, there is no evidence that behind Roon there was a consensus of army support in favour of Bismarck's candidacy; indeed, Bismarck was the alternative to the army's preferred course as articulated by Manteuffel. As Lothar Gall has suggested, Bismarck's achievement of power is better explained by the stalemate of political forces in 1862 and the inability of most of the key players to see their way out of a cul-de-sac. Bismarck, the outsider, was able to slip 'between the fronts' and his future position would hinge on whether he could maintain a precarious balancing act, effectively holding the conflicting forces at bay.

Gall has also argued that the circumstances of Bismarck's appointment signified a transfer of political leadership from the king to his new chief minister and instituted a peculiarly German form of constitutional monarchy.[51] It must be said, however, that this was no foregone conclusion in 1862 and that there was certainly no immediate transfer of power or 'blank cheque' issued. Bismarck had to commit himself to Wilhelm's course on the army reform and, moreover, whatever power and authority the king bestowed on him could just as easily be taken away. There was widespread concern, above all in liberal circles, in September 1862 about the political course Prussia would now pursue, and some feared a kind of Bismarck dictatorship. But Wilhelm I's appointment of Bismarck as minister-president and foreign minister in 1862, like Wilhelm II's dismissal of him some twenty-eight years later, confirmed the supreme power of the Prussian monarchy. What position the royal appointee could create for himself in the interim remained very much an open question.

Notes

1 GW 14/I, Bismarck to Johanna, 18 May 1847, p. 89.

2 For Gerlach's career, see Hans-Christof Kraus, *Ernst Ludwig von Gerlach: Politisches Denken und Handeln eines preußischen Altkonservativen*, 2 vols (Göttingen, 1994).

3 Leopold's role is discussed in David E. Barclay, *Frederick William IV and the Prussian Monarchy 1840–1860* (Oxford, 1995), especially pp. 255–8.

4 Rothfels, Bismarck to Johanna, 23 February 1847, p. 78.

5 Herbert Bismarck, *Love Letters*, I, Bismarck to Johanna, 8 May 1847, pp. 67–8.

6 Ibid., Bismarck to Johanna, 21 May 1847, p. 73.

7 GW, X, speeches of 15 April 1850 and 17 April 1850 in the Erfurt parliament, pp. 93–9, and 3 December 1850 in the Prussian Landtag, pp. 101–10. For a discussion of the Prussian revolution of 1848 and the various assemblies, see Wolfram Siemann, *The German Revolution of 1848* (London, 1998).

8 See Rothfels, Bismarck to Ludwig von Gerlach, 7 July 1848, p. 114.

9 Hans-Joachim Schoeps, *Bismarck über Zeitgenossen – Zeitgenossen über Bismarck* (Frankfurt, paperback edition, 1981), p. 155; Bismarck to Johanna, 27 April 1850, in Herbert Bismarck, *Love Letters*, p. 139.

10 Otto von Bismarck, *Gedanken und Erinnerungen: Mit einem Essay von Lothar Gall* (Berlin, 1999), pp. 55–6.

11 See Gall, I, especially pp. 50 ff.

12 GW, X, speeches of 6 September 1849, pp. 35–40, and 3 December 1850, pp. 101–10. See also Schoeps, *Bismarck*, p. 176.

13 Jakob von Gerlach (ed.), *Ernst Ludwig von Gerlach: Aufzeichnungen aus seinem Leben und Wirken 1795–1877*, 2 vols (Schwerin, 1903), II, p. 33. See also Gall, I, p. 85.

14 Leopold noted in his diary that Bismarck's appointment was 'all my work'. See Kraus, *Gerlach*, II, p. 710.

15 Rothfels, Bismarck to Johanna, 3 May 1851, pp. 146–7; Herbert Bismarck, *Love Letters*, I, Bismarck to Johanna, 28 April 1851, p. 203.

16 See Andreas Kaernbach, *Bismarcks Konzept zur Reform des Deutschen Bundes: Zur Kontinuität der Politik Bismarcks und Preußens in der deutschen Frage* (Göttingen, 1991).

17 Rothfels, Bismarck to Gerlach, 2 May 1857, p. 209.

18 GW, II, memorandum for Manteuffel, 18 May 1857, pp. 217–23.

19 GW, II, memorandum for Prince Wilhelm, 30 March 1858, p. 317.

20 Rothfels, Bismarck to Alvensleben, 5 May/23 April 1859, p. 247.

21 Ibid., Bismarck to Leopold von Gerlach, 2 May 1857, p. 213.

22 W.E. Mosse, *The European Powers and the German Question, 1848–1871* (Cambridge, 1958), p. 372.

23 See Pflanze, I, p. 132.

24 Rothfels, Bismarck to Johanna, 18 May 1851, p. 150.

25 Gerlach, I, 5 December 1851, p. 351. See also 12 June 1860.

26 Gall, I, pp. 199–200.

27 Rothfels, Bismarck to Ludwig von Gerlach, 28 June 1851, p. 153.

28 See Schoeps, *Bismarck*, pp. 47–59.

29 The best discussion of Friedrich Wilhelm IV's rule in English is Barclay, *Frederick William IV*.

30 Gerlach, I, 10 May 1851 (quoting Arnim), p. 288.

31 Ibid., p. 351, n. 64. See also Hartwin Spener, '"Regulator und Ballast im Landtagsschiff" – Bismarck und das Preußische Herrenhaus', in Jost Dülffer and Hans Hübner (eds), *Otto von Bismarck: Person – Politik – Mythos* (Berlin, 1993), pp. 203–12.

32 Gerlach, I, 2 June 1864, p. 351. See also Kraus, *Gerlach*, II, pp. 710–11.

33 Rothfels, Bismarck to Leopold von Gerlach, 2/4 May 1860, p. 267.

34 See Engelberg, I, p. 399.

35 See Keudell, *Fürst und Fürstin Bismarck*, p. 75.

36 Engelberg, I, p. 468.

37 Gall, I, p. xviii.

38 GW, XIV, Bismarck to Bernhard von Bismarck, 26 March 1855, p. 396.

39 See Gordon A. Craig, *The Politics of the Prussian Army, 1640–1945* (Oxford, 1955) pp. 142–3.

40 Ibid., p. 107.

41 Gall, I, p. 176.

42 Rothfels, Bismarck to Johanna, 1 June 1862, p. 285.

43 Cf. Engelberg, I, p. 517.

44 See Gall, I, pp. 162–3.

45 Gerlach, I, 11 September 1862, p. 433.

46 See Gall, I, pp. 190–1. Cf. Bismarck, *Gedanken und Erinnerungen*, pp. 216–18.

47 See Engelberg, I, p. 513.

48 Gerlach, II, Kleist-Retzow to Gerlach, 19 September 1862, p. 1115.

49 Ibid., Kleist-Retzow to Gerlach, 22 September 1862, p. 1117.

50 See Engelberg, I, p. 534.

51 See Gall, I, p. 175.

Chapter 3

Precarious Power

Bismarck was appointed Prussian minister-president and foreign minister in 1862 because he gained the confidence of the king. Unlike other senior Prussian officials, he was prepared at Babelsberg to declare his willingness to govern unconstitutionally and defy the will of the Prussian parliament in order to secure the army reform without modification. The obstinacy of a 66-year-old monarch who refused to compromise, the polarisation of political opinion so that the constitutional issue superseded all others, and the elimination of political alternatives all conspired to create the opportunity for a man whose chief recommendations were his determination to defend the king's prerogatives, his pugnacious will and his self-confidence that he could succeed where others had failed. Yet while some historians have emphasised that the circumstances of Bismarck's appointment in 1862 were to give him *plein pouvoir*, unprecedented scope and freedom as a minister, ultimately enabling him to remain in office for twenty-eight years and to create a unique position for himself, this was by no means self-evident in 1862. Rather, as the new premier sought to cobble together a ministry which would be willing to rule without a legal budget, his position appeared highly vulnerable and exposed. Apart from the king, Bismarck could only rely on a few friends such as Roon, Kleist and Blanckenburg and the decimated remnant of the conservative party in the Landtag. Bismarck remained an outsider, isolated and without the support of any significant faction within the ruling elite or parliament. His political survival depended upon his ability to retain the confidence of a monarch who, for all their agreement on the issue of principle, had long entertained doubts about Bismarck's specific policy recommendations and who was surrounded at court by many within his own family and entourage who were implacably hostile to the new minister-president. Finally, Bismarck's eagerness for power in 1862 undoubtedly led him to underestimate the obstacles he faced and overestimate the scope for compromise. Thus his position from September

1862 was precarious and, unless he could deliver some tangible successes, his tenure of office was expected to be short.

The servant of the crown

From 1862 until 1890 Bismarck's political career crucially depended on the support of the Prussian crown. For twenty-six years, until the death of the almost 91-year-old king in March 1888, his relationship with Wilhelm I underpinned his exercise of power. Clearly after his successes in the 1860s Bismarck's authority and prestige no longer derived exclusively or even primarily from the monarch's confidence, nor was it solely the withdrawal of royal support which precipitated his resignation in 1890. Yet he was never more dependent on the sovereign than he was during his first years as Prussian minister-president. Bismarck's interview with Wilhelm at Babelsberg provided him with a unique opportunity, but it also imposed significant constraints upon his freedom of action.

In declaring himself to be wholly on the king's side in the constitutional conflict, Bismarck subscribed without reservation to the ideology of Prussian monarchism. In September 1862 he scorned the idea that he should be a constitutional minister who pledged to uphold the letter and spirit of the constitution. Instead, he won Wilhelm's confidence by insisting that his first duty was to serve his royal master loyally, as a vassal owed allegiance to his lord. Bismarck's recourse to an old-fashioned vocabulary, conjuring up archaic images of royal absolutism, feudal obligations and personal homage, fulfilled its psychological purpose in 1862, convincing Wilhelm that Bismarck was unshakeably committed to defend the monarchy and that he should defer his decision to abdicate. Nevertheless the circumstances of Bismarck's appointment ensured from the outset that there would be a latent tension in his relationship with Wilhelm. Bismarck did not favour absolutism as the ideal form of government, believing that public criticism had a valuable role to play and that, provided royal power was supreme, it could cooperate effectively with a popular representation. Unlike the ultra-conservatives, he had not supported the idea that the new king should receive the traditional hereditary homage from the estates in 1861 and he had been ready to accept a new ceremonial coronation which was more fitting for the monarch of a constitutional state. Moreover, not only had Bismarck been quite prepared to criticise Wilhelm personally in the past, but he also had no desire to subordinate his will to that of another man, however elevated, if they should disagree significantly. Bismarck wanted power in his own right to pursue his own aims, above all in foreign policy. He believed he could assert his will and influence over Wilhelm, even though he was not yet seen by the monarch as indispensable. But he underestimated Wilhelm's stubborn will and the extent to which his own appointment signalled the crown's determination to continue the fight. For while Bismarck was immediately painted as the *Konfliktminister*, a reputation which was amply confirmed over the next four years, his freedom of manoeuvre was circumscribed by the tenacity of the 'conflict king' who was often inclined to heed the advice of members of his military entourage rather than accept the recommendations of his chief political adviser.

Bismarck thus not only underestimated the principled opposition of the liberal parliamentary majority between 1862 and 1866, he also failed to appreciate the extent to which Wilhelm was unwilling to make even the most nominal concessions over the army reform. His first, rather clumsy moves as minister-president suggest that he hoped to achieve a compromise with the liberals. But his celebrated appearance at the Landtag's budget committee on 30 September 1862, when he sought to rally the liberals behind a foreign policy which would resolve the issue of Prussia's role in Germany by means of 'iron and blood', not only failed in its desired effect but also precipitated his first crisis with the king. Wilhelm repeatedly rejected any solutions to the domestic conflict which could be interpreted as signifying an increase in parliamentary power and he remained determined to see the army reform implemented without significant amendment. In October 1862 he refused to accept a revised plan for army reform which both Bismarck and Roon supported but which did not insist categorically on the three-year military service. Consequently it had to be modified in such a way as to make it totally unacceptable to the Landtag, which threw out the proposals in 1863. In 1865 a compromise plan initiated by parliamentary deputies had the support of the entire Prussian government including Bismarck and Roon and might have resolved the conflict, but it was again rejected by the king. Wilhelm's attitude was the source of much frustration for Bismarck, but he could scarcely oppose the king's will over the army reform when he had sworn to defend the monarchy's position. In lesser matters, too, he had to do Wilhelm's bidding. In the early years of his premiership Bismarck frequently admitted that he could not achieve a personnel change or pursue a particular policy option because of the king's opposition; in November 1862 he told Gerlach that the king had made reform of the provincial administration a condition of his appointment as premier.[1] While he sometimes used Wilhelm as a cover for his own political preferences, particularly when defending his political actions to critics such as Gerlach, this was not always the case. At this stage of his career Bismarck could not exert independent authority nor could he threaten to resign in order to achieve his way with the monarch.

The need to retain the king's confidence goes a long way to explain Bismarck's conduct during the constitutional conflict, when cautious and conciliatory overtures might suddenly be drowned in a torrent of verbal abuse, and an intransigent and reactionary posture often belied the persistent search for a settlement. Bismarck had no monopoly of influence over Wilhelm during this period and he had not yet developed the means (for example through the purchase of influence in the press and orchestrated press campaigns) to neutralise the impact of political advice which ran counter to his own. Above all, it was the influence of Manteuffel which effectively scuppered the proposals for compromise over the army reform, and, until 1865, when Bismarck finally succeeded in removing this inconvenient chief of the Military Cabinet from Berlin by having him appointed as governor of Schleswig, he could never be sure that he might not be outflanked on the right. Consequently his defiant behaviour *vis-à-vis* the Lower House and his apparent readiness on occasion to exacerbate the constitutional conflict reflected how imperative it was that he gave the ultra-conservatives around the king no grounds for complaint and allayed any suspicions that he might not be 'ideologically sound' on the constitutional issue. Bismarck sometimes had to intensify the crisis to remind the king that he needed him politically. After conservatives deplored evidence of his political weakness in the autumn of 1862, he re-emerged in the Landtag in January 1863 'like an iron wall', resisting all political concessions.[2] 'The Prussian monarchy', he told the Lower House, 'has not yet fulfilled its mission, it is not yet ready to form merely a decorative ornament on your constitutional edifice'.[3] At such times, until he could deliver tangible results, Bismarck's continuance in office depended on the continuation of the constitutional crisis.

Bismarck not only had to compete with the military entourage for control of the mind of a king who he complained in 1864 was impressionable, weak and unreliable.[4] He also recognised that there was a plethora of other influential individuals in government circles who had access to the king and might make recommendations which differed from those of the minister-president. These included diplomats such as Robert von der Goltz, whom Bismarck sent as Prussian ambassador to Paris in 1863, and the former foreign minister, Bernstorff, now Prussian ambassador in London, who were technically Bismarck's subordinates but were well placed to promote their own foreign policy agenda. Both men were linked to the *Wochenblatt* party; as foreign minister in the early stages of the constitutional crisis, Bernstorff had valiantly tried to navigate between his moderate liberal principles and his loyalty to the king. In December 1863 Bismarck reprimanded Goltz for the conflicting advice he was transmitting to the king during the Schleswig-Holstein crisis and insisted that the king could not have two foreign ministers.[5]

The friction in our state machine, already excessive, cannot be intensified. I will tolerate opposition, if it emanates from a competent source such as yourself; but the advising of the king in this matter I will share officially with no one, and if H.M. were to demand that of me, I should resign from my post. I told H.M. that when reading him one of your latest reports. H.M. found my point of view a natural one, and I can only adhere to it. No one expects reports which reflect only ministerial views; but yours are no longer reports in the usual sense, but assume the nature of ministerial presentations [*Vorträge*], which recommend to the king a completely contradictory policy to the one which he himself decided on in council with the whole ministry and has pursued for the last four weeks. Criticism of this resolution, which I would call sharp if not downright hostile, does not constitute an ambassadorial report, but a quite different ministerial programme. Such conflicting viewpoints can only do harm and no good; for they can arouse hesitation and indecision, and I consider any policy is better than a vacillating one.

Bismarck went on to complain that everyone in his position had to overcome frictions with ministers and advisers, with 'occult influences' at court, with the parliamentary chambers, the press and the foreign courts, but that there was no room for competition between a foreign minister and an ambassador. In writing a very long letter to Goltz on Christmas Eve after all his officials had gone home for the holiday, he had no illusions that he could convince Golz to change his views, but trusted the ambassador's judgement and experience in office sufficiently to believe he would acknowledge that there could be only one policy, namely that agreed by the ministry and the king.

Bismarck could insist on a monopoly of influence over the king when dealing with members of the diplomatic service but, as we will see, it was harder for him to deal with critics in the higher bureaucracy. It was especially difficult for him to counter the influence of opponents who held official positions at court, such as the minister of the royal household, Schleinitz, another former foreign minister, or members of the king's own family who sought to undermine him. Wilhelm's wife, Queen Augusta, his son and daughter-in-law, Crown Prince Friedrich Wilhelm and Vicky, his sister, Alexandrine, the grand duchess of

Mecklenburg-Schwerin, and his son-in-law, Grand Duke Friedrich of Baden, all had reason to oppose Bismarck's policies or even, as in the case of the so-called 'Coburg intrigue' in the spring of 1866, to attempt to engineer his fall.

Bismarck's relationship with the crown prince was a source of particular exasperation and vexation for him from 1862. The liberal attitudes of Friedrich Wilhelm and his wife, Vicky, the eldest daughter of Queen Victoria, were well known, and the heir to the Prussian throne made no secret of his opposition to the policies of Bismarck's government. In June 1863 when the government exploited what it alleged were its emergency powers (since the Landtag had just been dissolved) to issue a draconian press decree aimed at suppressing the opposition press, Friedrich Wilhelm informed Bismarck that he regarded it as 'illegal and dangerous for my House and the future of the state';[6] on 5 June in Danzig he publicly disclaimed any responsibility for the decree and underlined his disapproval of Bismarck's government. The crown prince's Danzig speech was enough to prompt the king to threaten to send his son to the fortress at Spandau,[7] and Bismarck, too, was very outspoken in his hostility to the crown prince in the early years of his premiership. The heir to the throne was widely criticised in government circles because he cut himself off politically, did not involve himself in government business and deferred so much to his wife. Within a few months of becoming minister-president Bismarck complained that Friedrich Wilhelm was 'heartless and bereft of ideas, without any interests, even in the army', and his bitterness intensified when he was repeatedly confronted with the 'audacious opposition' of this 'impudent nonentity' and 'cretin'.[8] After Friedrich Wilhelm complained that he was only informed of events in the newspapers, Wilhelm I ordered Bismarck to give his son *Vorträge* on political matters, but this only led to further aggravation between the two men. After a *Vortrag* in Merseburg on the issue of Lauenburg in 1865, the crown prince rode off from Bismarck, remarking that it had been enough to rob him of his good mood for six weeks; and Bismarck in turn emphasised 'the crown prince's stupidity, narrow-mindedness, insensitivity and inaccessibility in the strongest terms', declaring that if Friedrich Wilhelm came to power, he, Bismarck, would go to the scaffold and the new king would not last long. By 1866 the crown prince refused to let Bismarck give him *Vorträge* and Bismarck told him openly that he neither anticipated nor desired ever serving him as king. The dynasties, he told Gerlach, appeared to be finished.[9] Bismarck's relationship with Friedrich Wilhelm, which was seen by some observers even during the turbulent 1860s as the fundamental problem in Berlin, can only be understood if it is set in the context of the succession and the bitter constitutional conflict. Given that Wilhelm I had been born in 1797, Friedrich Wilhelm's accession to the throne already appeared an immediate possibility and many of the liberal opposition pinned their hopes on the future king. Having attained power, Bismarck was determined to retain it, notwithstanding his heated retorts to the heir to the throne. While he necessarily sought to bolster his position with Wilhelm I, he was already also looking to secure his political future by creating his own power base and strengthening his independent authority.

Despite all the intrigues and counter-influences that he had to contend with, Bismarck succeeded remarkably in winning Wilhelm I's trust in his first years in office. In August 1862 the minister of agriculture, Heinrich von Itzenplitz, had admitted he was looking for a minister-president 'who could handle [*maniieren*] the king, queen and crown prince', and he supported Bismarck's candidacy because he knew of no one else.[10] Clearly when Bismarck assumed the minister-presidency conditions at the Prussian court were in a lamentable state, with insiders railing against 'the complete unreliability of the king, intrigues of the queen and attitude of the crown prince' and Berlin full of gossip over Wilhelm's continuous stream of mistresses, some of whom he was alleged to be seeing at the same time.[11] According to one of Bismarck's principal aides in the Foreign Ministry, from the start the new premier 'treats the king "like his father-confessor", he goes to him with everything and tells him everything'.[12] Bismarck himself revealed to Gerlach that, unlike his predecessors who had pulled 'the poor king' in one direction and then the other and constantly threatened to resign, he sought 'to make the king conscious that he, the king, really rules'. He told Wilhelm, 'if Your Majesty orders me to do something stupid, I will remonstrate but still carry it out on Your responsibility', a stance which Gerlach enthusiastically endorsed.[13] Bismarck aspired to have a monopoly of influence over Wilhelm and deal with him personally as far as possible without intermediaries. In January 1864 he admitted he received five or six letters a day from the king, all of which he replied to in his own hand.[14] Perhaps most important in explaining Wilhelm's growing confidence in Bismarck was the sheer survival of the government and its willingness to tough it out in the constitutional struggle without resorting to such extreme measures that it provoked a civil war. In 1862 Wilhelm had been pessimistic and fearful, convinced that he and Bismarck might eventually both be beheaded in front of the opera house by a hostile populace. As each month passed, he was reassured that the situation was not so critical and that the army reform was being delivered. His confidence and gratitude correspondingly increased even before Bismarck's handling of the Schleswig-Holstein crisis brought more tangible rewards.

The most difficult terrain for Bismarck with the king was foreign policy and it was here that Bismarck had to keep his cards closest to his chest. Privately Bismarck was often critical of the king and, not infrequently, chose to hide behind him. In a conversation with Gerlach in March 1864, he blamed Wilhelm's bigoted, stubborn and weak character for those aspects of his Schleswig-Holstein policy which Gerlach deemed most offensive.[15] It is difficult to know how honest Bismarck was with the king about his foreign policy: he could often speak with remarkable candour but could also dissemble and lie. His belief that he could not be a diplomat if he could not lie was particularly abhorrent to Gerlach who believed kings, states and ministers should be bound by Christian ethics and the ten commandments just like everyone else. At the very least Bismarck was often economical with the truth in his dealings with the monarch.

Bismarck always sought to leave his options open until the final moment of decision, but in some respects the tortuous course of his diplomacy between 1862 and 1866, the deceptions, secrecy and subterfuge, is again intelligible only in the light of his relationship with Wilhelm. The king had long harboured doubts about Bismarck's advocacy of a 'Bonapartist' and anti-Austrian foreign policy, and he was naturally predisposed to sympathise with his minister's critics. It must be seen as Bismarck's supreme achievement (though facilitated by the mistakes of others) that he succeeded in keeping Wilhelm with him throughout the Schleswig-Holstein crisis from 1863, preventing precipitate Prussian military action in its early stages but eventually convincing the king that there was no alternative to war against Austria in 1866. Bismarck later propagated the view that Wilhelm was like a clock which had to be wound up every day,[16] but the mechanism was not so simple as this analogy suggests. The minister-president had demonstrably to exhaust all the possibilities of a peaceful resolution of Austro-Prussian differences between 1862 and 1866, keep Wilhelm focused on Prussian honour and dignity, as well as ensure that the king remained ignorant of some of the deeper purposes behind his diplomacy. When Wilhelm wanted to attend the so-called 'princes' congress' in Frankfurt in the summer of 1863 to discuss Austrian proposals for reform of the German Confederation, the 'conflict minister' was placed in the anomalous position of having to argue that, as a constitutional monarch, Wilhelm could not make decisions independently of his responsible ministers. After the end of a day dealing with 'telegraphic intrigues' and the efforts of the king of Saxony, 'the cleverest of all diplomats', to place 'the Austrian noose' around Wilhelm's head, Bismarck wrote to his daughter that he was exhausted and that the king had suffered a nervous collapse that evening.[17] He had, however, eventually succeeded in getting Wilhelm to decline the invitation to Frankfurt which had been urged by '30 German princes in writing and a few women close to us verbally'. Bismarck frequently despaired of keeping Wilhelm harnessed to his foreign policy, believing that 'the heart of the king is in a different camp' and that too often the monarch failed to recognise the true interests of the crown. In January 1864 he confessed his wretchedness to Roon, convinced that Wilhelm was intent on breaking with the rest of Europe, inflicting 'another Olmütz' on Prussia and supporting the creation of yet another middle state under the duke of Augustenburg in Schleswig-Holstein. 'What is one to say and do [*reden und schimpfen*]? Without God's grace the game is lost and we will be blamed by the world now and in the future. Whatever God wants. He will know how long Prussia is to exist. But I will be very sorry if it ceases to exist, God knows that!'[18] Ultimately, of course, if Bismarck could not impress the king with the wisdom of his diplomacy, his only option was to aggravate the rift between crown and parliament in a way that would convince Wilhelm that this was no time to dispense with his services.

Bismarck's inability to take the king into his confidence with respect to his foreign policy and his wariness of rival influences accentuated his isolation. In the conduct of Prussian foreign policy even more than in the constitutional conflict, where he was at least supported by his conservative friends, he was thrown back on his own resources. While it can be argued that he thereby enjoyed a peculiar freedom to formulate his country's foreign policy, his position nevertheless remained very vulnerable. Moreover, his experience during these early years as foreign minister undoubtedly had a lasting impact on his conduct of foreign policy until 1890. Even when his position and authority were unchallenged, Bismarck was disinclined to initiate colleagues and subordinates into his thinking and he avoided detailed discussion of policy with Wilhelm.

Wilhelm eventually came to appreciate his minister's political skill and on 15 September 1865, not long after the signing of the Gastein convention with Austria apparently brought the resolution of the Schleswig-Holstein problem, he elevated Bismarck to the status of a hereditary count. Emphatically and publicly underlining his confidence in his minister-president, the king extolled Bismarck's achievements for the fatherland. 'In the four [*sic*] years since I appointed you to the head of the state government', he declared, 'Prussia has assumed a position which is worthy of her history and promises to add to that a further happy and glorious future.'[19] Nevertheless, he also had no illusions about his minister's infallibility and was not prepared to concede that Bismarck was anything more than first among equals when it came to influencing the king. After Wilhelm invited his military advisers to a meeting of the crown council on 29 May 1865 without consulting his minister-president, Bismarck deemed it essential to win the internal power struggle against the ultra-conservatives who favoured a domestic *Staatsstreich* (an enforced constitutional change or *coup d'état*) before Prussia risked a war against Austria. Bismarck was largely successful in this, though Manteuffel, as governor of Schleswig, was still present at the crucial crown council meeting of 28 February 1866 when a war against Austria was seen as unavoidable. Bismarck's main rival for the premiership, Goltz, was also at the meeting. In the crucial weeks before the Austro-Prussian campaign began in June 1866 the Bavarian minister in Berlin observed that Bismarck and the 'war party' managed to buttress the king's resolve until 5 o'clock in the afternoon when the monarch dined. From then on Wilhelm vacillated, being exposed to the influence of the 'peace party', namely all the guests invited by Augusta to dine with them and put the case against war.[20] The publication of the correspondence between Wilhelm and Augusta confirms Bismarck's view that the queen did everything she could to counter his influence over her husband and avert a war she believed would have catastrophic consequences for Germany and Europe. 'If I could do what I wanted with the king, if I could always have him by me, if I could sleep with him like the queen, everything would be fine', Bismarck admitted to General Govone, the Italian negotiator, on 2 June 1866.[21]

Bismarck had no basis of political support between 1862 and 1866 other than the king's confidence. Wilhelm was prepared to support him repeatedly against the parliamentary majority during the constitutional conflict, but he was not so easily convinced of the rectitude of his foreign policy. Consequently in the early years of his premiership Bismarck always had to include the potential threat of dismissal in his calculations. By 1866 Bismarck appeared to have complete mastery over Wilhelm to the extent that he could call for a national German parliament elected by universal male suffrage and prepare to instigate revolution among the subject nationalities of the Habsburg empire. But it had taken all Bismarck's skill and ingenuity to persuade Wilhelm by May 1866 that 'it is now no longer a question of Schleswig-Holstein but a war to annihilate Prussia'.[22]

Even so, perhaps his most serious conflict with Wilhelm occurred after the Prussian victory in 1866, over the peace terms with Austria, when the monarch resisted the deposition of legitimate princes and strongly argued for the traditional spoils of victory, namely territorial gains. Bismarck, whose determination to treat Austria leniently was as much the result of necessity as far-sightedness since he wanted to prevent foreign intervention, found unexpected support on this issue from his political opponent, the crown prince. Friedrich Wilhelm also wanted the peace treaty to be shaped with a view to the future rather than the past and had new-found authority as the successful commander of the Prussian Second Army at the battle of Königgrätz.

Altogether it was not easy for Bismarck to manage his royal master during these years and he had to devise all kinds of strategies, not all very subtle, to tie Wilhelm to him. In military matters Wilhelm regarded himself as the expert and resisted political interference; Bismarck could not threaten to resign (as he did with such success later) over the army reform to bring Wilhelm into line. On other issues, too, Bismarck was able to build up Wilhelm's trust only gradually. If he wanted to remain in power, he always had to be prepared to truckle to the king's will, however uncomfortable he might find the role of loyal servant. Ultimately his stance in the constitutional conflict between 1862 and 1866 can be seen as reinforcing an absolutist view of the monarchy, just as his foreign policy enhanced its militaristic ethos. In the longer term though, the annexation of lesser German states and deposition of ruling houses in 1866 undermined the principle of dynastic legitimacy, setting in motion a process of slow decay which facilitated the sweeping away of the monarchies in 1918.

Bismarck's government: first among equals

If Bismarck's relationship with the king raised question marks over his political survival, his position within the Prussian executive also ensured that he could not rely on the unqualified support of the rest of the Prussian government from 1862. As Prussian minister-president Bismarck presided over most meetings of the Prussian ministry of state, a body composed of government ministers (or sometimes their deputies) which met regularly to discuss matters of policy. But his minister-presidency was in several important respects merely nominal, and in no sense was his position comparable to that of a modern British prime minister presiding over his cabinet. The constitution of 1850 (which did not mention the role of the minister-president) had not established parliamentary government in Prussia, and the role and status of the Prussian ministry of state had not changed significantly since it was first established during the reform era before 1815. Technically all the Prussian ministers were equal and the minister-president, as *primus inter pares*, had little power over them. As Bismarck later confirmed in the German Reichstag in 1882, 'the real *de facto* minister-president in Prussia is and remains His Majesty the King'.[23]

Prussian ministers were appointed solely by the king, who could also dismiss them at will, and they owed their allegiance exclusively to him. Although Otto von Manteuffel had sought in 1852 to control the independent access of his colleagues to the king by means of a special Cabinet Order, the system of government in Prussia was basically an autocratic one in which the king had the final decision on all matters. Hence it was virtually impossible for the minister-president to assert real authority within the ministry of state when, regardless of the view of the majority, any minister could appeal over the heads of his colleagues directly to the king. If the king chose to preside over the state ministry himself, the minister-president was but one voice advising the monarch in what was then known as the 'crown council'.

Ministerial selection procedures tended to aggravate further the problem of governmental disunity. Ministers were recruited primarily from the ranks of the higher bureaucracy and were thus civil servants rather than politicians, career officials who had risen to the top through their competence in executing orders in a hierarchical structure, and often found it difficult to transcend a narrow, departmental perspective. In choosing his ministers, the monarch was also under no obligation to consider the overall political complexion of the state ministry. In practice, men were appointed to head the eight Prussian departments at different times for different reasons (such as the resignation of an incumbent) so that, despite a basic similarity in ideological outlook, there was not necessarily any unity in political views. Finally, although the introduction of a constitution after the 1848 revolution had signified that ministers became responsible to parliament in a very confined, legal sense, this was a far cry from the kind of ministerial responsibility and accountability to parliament desired by many liberals. Prussian ministers had no organic relationship to the elected representatives in the Prussian Lower House, let alone the support of a particular political grouping (and organised political parties were only just beginning to emerge in the 1860s). Thus Prussian ministers were not bound together by shared political views, a common commitment to a party or the need to avoid a parliamentary defeat (for such a defeat would not necessitate ministerial resignations). They were under no obligation to offer loyal and constant support to the position of the minister-president. In these circumstances it is very difficult to speak of a genuinely collective government in Prussia, yet it was only by acting collectively that ministers could significantly constrain the king. Unless it was absolutely united, the Prussian executive could not provide Bismarck with any kind of political base or support beyond that already provided by the king's confidence.

The appointment of a new minister-president did not normally signify a simultaneous change of personnel in the top echelons of the Prussian ministerial bureaucracy. In 1862, however, ministerial resignations on account of the constitutional crisis and the prospect of governing illegally forced Bismarck to find several new men willing to serve alongside him. His immediate offer of three ministerial posts to moderate liberals who were known to favour compromise evinced a very negative response, and it ultimately proved difficult to convince even men of determinedly conservative stamp that they should hitch their fortunes to those of a government which was intent on defying parliament and hence might only survive a matter of months. Three conservative ministers remained at their posts throughout the September crisis and were not deterred by the prospect of Bismarck's conflict ministry: Roon, as war minister, Heinrich von Mühler as *Kultusminister* (responsible for ecclesiastical affairs, medicine and education) and Leopold zur Lippe as minister of justice. The minister of interior, Gustav von Jagow, a former police chief of Breslau who had joined the conservative government of Adolf zu Hohenlohe-Ingelfingen in March 1862, was initially prepared to serve alongside Bismarck whom he had first met at university. But he soon baulked at the implications of Bismarck's course for the Prussian bureaucracy and he was replaced by Friedrich zu Eulenburg in December 1862. Heinrich von Itzenplitz, the minister of agriculture under Hohenlohe, became minister of trade, and the agriculture portfolio was given to Werner von Selchow. In October Karl von Bodelschwingh, who had served in Manteuffel's government, became minister of finance. Only at the end of the year was Bismarck finally in a position to announce the composition of his new government.

Bismarck set to work with his usual energy and determination from 1862 but he did not find the transition from diplomat to minister-president an easy one. Fearful for the health and nerves of her husband, who worked fifteen-hour days and was sometimes incapacitated by severe headaches, Johanna painted a vivid picture of the demands on Bismarck's time to Keudell in January 1863.

We never see him at all – in the morning at breakfast for five minutes while he skims through the newspapers – thus complete silence reigns. Then he disappears into his study, after that [he goes] to the king, ministerial council, the monstrous Chamber – until about 5 o'clock when he usually eats with some diplomat or other, until 8 o'clock, when he only says good evening en passant, buries himself again in his dreadful paperwork, until he is called to some soirée at half past 9, after which he works again until getting on for 1 o'clock and then of course sleeps badly. And so it goes on day after day.[24]

Inexperienced in the workings of the Berlin bureaucracy, Bismarck soon complained that his obstructive ministerial colleagues were too influenced by their officials, but even in his own department, he found it difficult to strike the right balance. In October 1863 he complained that the Foreign Ministry was in 'a deplorable state of decay' and that he lacked competent agents upon whom he could rely; a year later his complaint was, rather, that he was overrun with advisers.[25] However much they may have come to admire him, subordinates found Bismarck a hard taskmaster. In St Petersburg Schlözer had called him 'the pasha', a man whose *modus operandi* was 'to squeeze the lemon dry and then throw it away'.[26] Eulenburg, the minister of interior, warned Keudell when he began to work in the state ministry in late 1863 that his position would be very difficult as Bismarck 'is a violent man and tolerates no contradiction', insisting on absolute obedience.[27] Another official, an academic who had worked for several years for Schleinitz and Bernstorff as a press officer, concluded after a few months' experience of Bismarck that the new chief was suffering from a 'serious nervous disorder' and appeared 'sometimes not completely of sound mind'. His thoughts galloped uncontrollably so that it was difficult to follow them 'and from time to time he demanded completely impracticable things'.[28] Such views were also not uncommon among the Berlin diplomatic community in the early years of Bismarck's premiership.

Bismarck complained about how he spent much of his time at work, comparing the life of a minister to that of a helot and freely acknowledging that he found it difficult to remain patient and not vent his anger on those around him.[29] But it is clear that part of the problem arose from his reluctance or inability to delegate. 'He is unfortunately too capable,' Blanckenburg lamented in October 1863, 'so capable that, for example, he writes everything on his own, *no one* can do it right for him, he thereby runs the great risk of achieving *nothing*, despite the enormous amount of work, he is losing contact, speaks to few people . . .'.[30] Bismarck was advised by Gerlach to look around for young men whom he could attract into the service, and he also proved willing to bypass the traditional bureaucratic route and bring in outsiders whom he trusted, a practice which aroused hostility and resentment among many of the career officials. The most notorious of these was the former democrat, Lothar Bucher, whose participation in the revolution of 1848 had led to his exile abroad until an amnesty was declared in 1861. Bucher joined the political department of the Foreign Ministry in 1864 and came to carry out special assignments for Bismarck, who also relied on his legal expertise. But his arrival upset the older advisers, as well as some ministers like Bodelschwingh, and the king, too, was suspicious.[31] By contrast, Hermann von Thile, a counsellor in the Foreign Ministry, claimed that after two years as foreign minister Bismarck scarcely knew the career officials in the department, having to ask who this one or that one was at his ministerial dinners.[32]

Bismarck was highly critical in his memoirs about his ministerial colleagues, and historians, too, have been quick to question their political acumen and independent judgement, citing Bismarck's response to Kleist's criticisms of the new ministry in December 1862: 'We're glad to find and keep eight men.'[33] While it must be conceded that the intellectual calibre of Prussian ministers was not generally very high and that the recruitment pool for such positions was very restricted, it is also apparent that Bismarck's later vindictiveness originated as much from bitterness over their insubordination as from a growing conviction of their mediocrity. Although Bismarck's character and style inevitably focused attention almost exclusively on his person during the constitutional conflict, encouraging liberals to regard him as a kind of 'hate-figure' who had to be toppled, he was not in a position between 1862 and 1866 to dominate the Prussian government as he would have liked or in the way he perfected subsequently. Rather, he became profoundly irritated by what he construed to be the obstructive behaviour of his colleagues and resented the extent to which they were prepared to oppose his will.

As early as November 1862 Bismarck complained to Gerlach that his colleagues were 'long-winded bureaucrats' and 'tiresome impediments'.[34] Bismarck had never had any sympathy for the bureaucratic mentality and he resented having to sit through state ministry meetings where each session eight men made eight speeches, making a total of sixty-four.[35] During no other period of Bismarck's political career was he so obliged to cooperate and collaborate with other ministers and, indeed, to give way even when it did not suit him. While some of Bismarck's ministerial colleagues may have been relatively unknown men in 1862, they were certainly not nonentities who had no political views of their own or who wished to cling to office at any price. Frequently ready to oppose Bismarck, they resented any interference in the work of their departments. Bismarck did not yet have sufficient prestige or authority to assume a directing role in domestic policy and all too often his ministerial colleagues had views about foreign policy. Bismarck complained that the entire ministry had opposed his handling of the Polish question in 1863, though it had ultimately been very satisfied with the result.[36] With the exception of Roon, the ministers collectively overruled him when he wanted to prorogue the Landtag after it criticised the Alvensleben convention with Russia (which will be discussed below);[37] and it was the ministers who insisted on a dissolution of the Landtag in the summer of 1863. Many of them were also opposed to the pro-Russian course which Bismarck had chosen to steer, and he complained to Gerlach that he could neither educate his colleagues nor get rid of them.

From 1862 the Prussian government was denied parliamentary and popular support, and all the ministers who served alongside Bismarck had to show considerable courage in being prepared to govern independently. On the face of it, they accepted ultra-conservative justifications of a period of dictatorship, supporting an authoritarian interpretation of the constitution which had been canvassed since the summer of 1862 and which Bismarck immediately adopted. This so-called 'gap theory' suggested that, since there was no provision in the constitution for the eventuality that crown and parliament could not agree, power returned to the former if the deadlock could not be overcome. The crown's ministers thus continued to collect taxes and to authorise departmental expenditure even though their actions were illegal under the terms of the constitution, because the budget had not had parliamentary approval. They all ran the real risk that, especially in the event of a change of monarch, they would be held personally liable for the unauthorised expenditure (and Bismarck, indeed, took steps to protect his private wealth).[38] Bismarck tried to take Gerlach's advice from 1862 and curtail the need for legislation as far as possible, starving the parliament of political issues and limiting the scope for conflict. But this did not always suit the wishes of the king or his ministerial colleagues, some of whom, like Itzenplitz, saw no value in not presenting bills to the Landtag.

Bismarck soon concluded that the support of his ministerial colleagues was wanting, that most of them were prisoners of their departments, and that a priority was the restoration of 'discipline' throughout the Prussian bureaucracy to ensure that all state officials supported the crown. Despite some individual misgivings, all the ministers ultimately acquiesced in Bismarck's determination to remove or punish those liberals who refused to toe the government line. On assuming office Bismarck said he wanted to go on a hunt where all the game to be killed were *Oberpräsidenten* and

Geheimräte.[39] He particularly wanted to deal with officials such as Heinrich von Bockum-Dolffs, who led the left-centre grouping of moderate liberals in the Lower House, chaired the budget committee and advocated joining forces with the Progressives to force the 'Junker cabinet' out of office.[40] Bockum-Dolffs was duly transferred from his official post in Koblenz to a much less desirable one in East Prussia. The drive to instill political reliability into the bureaucracy was not merely confined to those officials who were simultaneously parliamentary deputies. As many as one thousand officials may have suffered from reprisals under Bismarck's new regimen, among whom twenty were deputies and nine were judges.[41] Bismarck was also keen to reform recruitment and selection procedures in the bureaucracy. He was hostile to promotion on the basis of seniority, keen to open careers to talent and favoured streamlining the examination system; and he hoped (unsuccessfully) to make political reliability a criterion for promotion even within the judiciary. Eulenburg, the minister of interior, cooperated more readily in these aims than Lippe, the minister of justice, but Bismarck described even Eulenburg as unreliable and fearful with a ministry full of 'reds'.[42] In 1865 Lippe threatened to resign if salaries were no longer related to seniority and, despite having the agreement of the king and other ministers, Bismarck let the matter drop.[43] Bodelschwingh opposed Bismarck's proposed appointment criteria (above all, the introduction of a single, major exam) and mobilised the king to support him on the issue.

The attitude of the Prussian ministers contributed to Bismarck's insecurity during this period for he could never be sure that he could carry them with him. The ministers did not protest, for example, when he sought to curb the freedom of the press, issuing the press decree on 1 June 1863 with the intention of silencing the opposition press before the autumn elections. But, with respect to foreign and commercial policy, they tended to be even less willing to compromise with Austria than Bismarck himself, insisting for example on Austria's continued exclusion from the *Zollverein* and refusing to reopen negotiations with Austria when the treaties were renewed. There was a consensus within those ministries concerned that Prussia should move in the direction of free trade in the 1860s (the Cobden Treaty concluded between France and Britain in 1860 highlighted the way and encouraged a more western orientation) and even if Bismarck had been more prepared to become involved in domestic issues, he could not have reversed this course which was rooted in political as well as economic considerations. This is important as it indicates that, in this area at least, Bismarck was not deliberately and self-interestedly pursuing a policy to confuse and divide the Prussian liberals (though it cannot have escaped him in March 1862 that the Prussian Lower House, despite its stance in the constitutional conflict, voted by 264 votes to 12 in support of Prussia's trade treaty with France). Rather, he continued the policies of his predecessors who had already recognised the significance of this course in the context of Austro-Prussian dualism and the struggle for future control over Germany. Bismarck's powers of manipulation have frequently been exaggerated and all aspects of domestic policy should not be judged exclusively in the light of the ongoing constitutional struggle. As foreign minister as well as minister-president, Bismarck had more freedom to formulate Prussian foreign policy, but here too the Prussian executive could circumscribe his freedom of manoeuvre. Some of the ministers criticised the pro-Russian course Bismarck steered after assuming office; and in 1865 he had difficulty reining back some of his ministerial colleagues who were far bolder than he and wanted to break with Austria. Bureaucratic pressures ultimately helped to convince him that there was even less basis for cooperation between Austria and Prussia than he may have originally thought.

Bismarck took some interest in domestic issues in the early years of his premiership but he was not yet able to stamp his authority on the Prussian executive. His most notable foray into the social question took the form of secret discussions with Ferdinand Lassalle, the leader of the new General German Workers' Association, in 1863–64. The conversations between the two men focused on the problem of integrating the growing number of industrial workers into the state and the potential benefits of introducing a universal, equal and direct suffrage in Prussia. Even if Bismarck was less concerned about social justice than with finding another weapon with which to divide the liberal opposition (for it was their mutual hostility to liberalism which brought Bismarck and Lassalle together) and securing a more popular basis for the monarchy, it is important to stress that the adoption of any policies which smacked of 'state socialism' was not a feasible option from a government perspective at this time. Economic and social policy remained in the hands of ministers and counsellors who, however conservative politically, favoured liberal *laissez-faire* policies and the deregulation of industry which they believed would promote capitalist expansion. Bismarck had no ascendancy over his colleagues and, while he was able to exert some pressure on them to tackle social reforms (such as legalising trade unions, though this took six years to reach the statute book), his ideas frequently met with hostility or bureaucratic procrastination. Meetings of the Prussian ministry of state were genuinely collegial affairs during these years, with ministers of equal status engaging in real discussion and debate. Bismarck was still a long way from exercising his dominance in internal affairs and, not least, was far too busy with other matters.

In one area in particular, the raising of finance, Bismarck needed the cooperation of his ministerial colleagues and found their wilful independence especially irksome. The finance minister, Karl von Bodelschwingh, and Itzenplitz, the minister of trade, were treated with particular ire in his memoirs, doubtless because they refused to resort to further irregular and unconstitutional methods of raising government money which was urgently required for the military campaigns. Bismarck, however, attributed their objections to more base motives: 'I could not expect any support for my policy from these two ministers – because they neither had any understanding for my policy nor a measure of good will for me as a premier younger than themselves, who had originally not belonged to the service.'[44] Bodelschwingh seems to have been able to persuade a majority of his colleagues in the Prussian state ministry in June 1864 that they should not meet the costs of the Danish war by accepting state loans which had not been approved by the parliament. His concern for legal and constitutional niceties continually irritated Bismarck who believed that their duty was to maintain the monarchy rather than the constitution. Fritz Stern has argued that Bismarck's impatience with Bodelschwingh and the persistent need of his conflict ministry for money increased the minister-president's reliance on his Jewish banker, Gerson Bleichröder, who proved more able and willing to mobilise Prussian funds, above all by brokering a deal between the government and the Cologne–Minden Railway in July 1865.[45] As late as May 1866 Bodelschwingh was advising Bismarck he did not have enough money for a war, and he finally suffered a nervous collapse at the end of the month, unable to reconcile Bismarck's policy with his conservative conscience. His resignation was apparently greeted by Bismarck with glee and he claimed in his memoirs that he had been working for it for over a year. The king, on the other hand, confessed to his wife, 'I am completely beside myself, and now to have to find a successor at this moment.'[46] Bodelschwingh was immediately replaced by August von der Heydt, who had resigned as finance minister in 1862 over the constitutional conflict but proved better able to raise the funds for the impending war. He only accepted the office on condition that after the war the Landtag be asked for an indemnity for all unauthorised expenses of the government (although this was also in line with what Bismarck and Roon had been advocating in September 1862).

The ministers may have caused Bismarck considerable aggravation between 1862 and 1866 but, when the moment for decision came, most of them acquiesced in the war against Austria. Bodelschwingh, most obviously, complained bitterly about Bismarck's policy, as did Hermann von Thile, his deputy in the Foreign Ministry. Itzenplitz also favoured peace but remained passive in the face of what appeared like an irreversible shift within the executive in favour of war. Roon told Gerlach that it was no longer about what the king and government wanted but about hard and difficult necessity.[47] The majority of the ministers were thus fatalistic, and even Bismarck, particularly concerned about the possibility of foreign intervention, was tense and nervous, as was evident during his final, unpleasant encounter with Gerlach on 18 May 1866. Conscious that Gerlach regarded a war between Austria and Prussia with absolute horror, Bismarck appeared to his former paternal friend and patron as 'strikingly serious, pale and agitated'. He was brusque and unfriendly, vehemently denying any aggressive behaviour towards Austria and refusing even to agree to remain on personal terms with Gerlach in the future.[48]

The ministers had some scruples about Bismarck's readiness to dispense with the law during the constitutional crisis but their essentially authoritarian outlook was never in doubt. Indeed, perhaps their most serious display of opposition only came after the Prussian victory in the war against Austria when Bismarck sought to lay the constitutional conflict to rest and they resisted the solution. Bismarck recognised the value of holding out an olive branch to the liberals, and he was willing to admit that he had governed unconstitutionally for four years if the parliament approved the government's unauthorised expenditure retrospectively. But most of his ministerial colleagues, with the exception of Heydt, believed that Prussia's victory in the war against Austria now gave the government the initiative and that there should be no concessions of substance to the parliamentary opposition. A major crisis thus erupted in the ministry of state over the indemnity bill in 1866. Bismarck was able to resist the demands of Prussian ministers that they exploit the new situation to restructure domestic relationships in a reactionary sense, chiefly because he had the support of the king. But Bismarck felt betrayed and deserted by his conservative colleagues in 1866 and the controversy further convinced him of the disadvantages of a collegial executive. His experiences may well have encouraged him to dispense with such an arrangement in the North German Confederation and later Reich.

Defying parliament: the constitutional conflict

From 1862 until 1866 Bismarck was locked in conflict with the liberal majority in the Prussian Lower House. What began as a dispute over the army reform intensified into an acrimonious struggle which struck at the heart of the constitution and the relationship between executive and legislature. Bismarck owed his appointment to the confrontation between crown and parliament, and at times after 1862 his political survival seemed to depend on the continuation of the domestic deadlock. He was prepared to ignore the parliament's budgetary rights and energetically defend the powers of a military monarchy. Yet, as already explained, Bismarck was no believer in monarchical absolutism and, provided the rights of the crown were assured, he wanted to end the conflict in a way which secured the collaboration between government and legislature in the future. There is little doubt that he underestimated the obstacles to such a solution in 1862. A year after assuming office Bismarck was still seen by many in government circles as a foolhardy politician harnessed to a hopeless cause.[49] He still appeared to have his back right up against the wall and confessed to Keudell in October 1863 that he felt he had aged fifteen years since becoming minister-president, for 'The people are indeed much stupider than I thought.'[50] In the end, only the revolution in popular and political attitudes prompted by Prussia's resounding military defeat of Austria and its German allies in 1866 could create the conditions in which a compromise solution became feasible.

An eventual victory for either side in the struggle seemed to imply a massive shift in the distribution of power within the Prussian state, yet in the event neither Bismarck nor the liberal opposition was prepared to espouse the kind of high-risk strategy which might have won them the constitutional conflict. Unlike his ultra-conservative rivals, Bismarck did not believe that a conclusive defeat of liberalism was either possible or desirable, and he had never aspired to power in order to steer Prussia away from the path of constitutional government or implement a *Staatsstreich*. Before 1862 all his efforts had been focused on clarifying Prussian goals in foreign policy, and the constitutional struggle not only represented a distraction from what he conceived to be Prussia's primary political purpose, namely the pursuit of hegemony in Germany, but it also denied him political support which might have reduced his dependence on the king. For Bismarck it was extremely galling that the men in the Prussian parliament who condemned the government's blatant contempt for the rule of law were precisely the same men from whom he might have expected the most enthusiastic support if he embarked on a foreign policy aimed at securing Prussian leadership of a united Germany excluding Austria. In his remarks to the Landtag's budget committee on 30 September 1862, Bismarck candidly but crudely attempted to denigrate the significance of the domestic power struggle by elevating the common national goal. 'Germany does not look to Prussia's liberalism but to her power', he asserted.

Bavaria, Württemberg, Baden can indulge in liberalism, but no one will expect them to undertake Prussia's role; Prussia must gather and consolidate her strength in readiness for the favourable moment which has already been missed several times; Prussia's boundaries according to the Vienna treaties are not favourable to a healthy political life; not by means of speeches and majority verdicts will the great decisions of the time be made – that was the great mistake of 1848 and 1849 – but by iron and blood.[51]

Taken in context Bismarck's famous 'blood and iron' speech scarcely signified a declaration of war on the liberals since he wanted to emphasise their common ground, reminding them why the army reform was necessary and how it could serve the goal of national unification. But his first parliamentary appearance as minister-president alarmed conservatives and provoked an enraged incredulity among his liberal opponents, who concluded Bismarck intended to establish a repressive and reactionary system at home and pursue war abroad. Not for the first time, his clear and often cynical appreciation of liberal interests led him to ignore the role of conviction in liberal politics and to underestimate the obstacles to a compromise. After his experience in September 1862 Bismarck tried to restrict himself to short government declarations in parliament and avoided delivering big speeches as far as possible. But if he hoped that by neglecting parliament he might reduce public interest in the constitutional conflict, he was disappointed.

Until 1866 Bismarck largely followed a 'battle plan' recommended by Gerlach in an article, 'A Hostile Lower House', which appeared in the *Kreuzzeitung* in May 1862. Gerlach had argued that the king should continue to rule as was his right even if there was no approved budget. As far as possible he should try to rule on the basis of the existing taxes, as authorised in the last legal budget, and not attempt to raise new taxes or loans. Avoiding undue provocation of the Lower House, the king's government should act 'without the law' rather than 'against the law'.[52] Bismarck believed he could solve the constitutional conflict without transgressing the main provisions of the constitution,[53] and thus his government endeavoured to steer a middle course between a *Staatsstreich* on the one hand (which could mean anything from the imposition of a new electoral law to getting rid of the constitution and a period of military dictatorship) and capitulation by the throne to the parliamentary majority on the other. But while conservatives like Kleist and Gerlach were agreed that it might take several years before harmony could be restored between government and parliament,[54] Bismarck was much less patient from the start, recognising that his own position and power ultimately depended on his finding a settlement. The new minister-president hoped and expected that he could divide the liberal opposition and win over a section of the more moderate elements to support his policies. But after his blood and iron speech and apparent willingness to make concessions, he was bombarded with advice from his conservative friends who feared he appeared weak. Not merely ultra-conservatives like Manteuffel but also the conservative journalist Hermann Wagener advised Bismarck to institute a period of royal dictatorship in April 1863. Bismarck certainly did not rule this possibility out in the critical months after he assumed power. But in the event he never attempted it, hoping to find a different solution to the conflict.

From 1862 Bismarck did all he could to break the liberal opposition, but instead he found that he was only driving the formerly quite heterogeneous liberal groupings together, forging a more cohesive bloc and increasing his dependence on the king. His determination to rule without a legal budget united the liberals in their defence of parliament's budgetary powers, the juridical responsibility of government ministers and the freedom of the press. On 22 May 1863, after subjecting a government bill to a crushing defeat by 295 votes to 5, the liberal majority delivered an address to the king in which they confirmed:

The House of Deputies has no means of reaching an understanding with this ministry any more; it refuses to cooperate with the present policy of the government. All further negotiations only strengthen our conviction that a chasm exists between the advisers of the Crown and the country which will only be bridged by a change of personnel and, even more, by a change of system.[55]

Despite the press decree of 1863 which enabled the government to intimidate hostile newspapers and despite marked government interference in the elections in the autumn of 1863, the liberals maintained a solid majority and showed no signs of weakening. The newly elected Landtag soon repealed the press edict, even if the government took little notice. The liberals remained singularly unimpressed by what they saw as the manifestly cynical proposals put forward by the Bismarck government in August and September 1863 to reform the German Confederation and provide for an elected national parliament which would counterbalance the dynastic particularism of the states. Even Bismarck's handling of the Schleswig-Holstein question from 1863, widely regarded by historians as his diplomatic *tour de force* from which his other suc- cesses in the 1860s emanated, did not break the opposition or make his domestic position any more secure. Ultra-conservatives were reassured by Bismarck's willingness to cooperate with Austria and defy liberal opin- ion, but most liberals (as well as not a few at the king's court) sympath- ised with the claims of the prince of Augustenburg to the two duchies. In January 1864 the liberals stubbornly refused to vote for the war credits the government claimed it needed to fight the war against Denmark, even though they thereby risked being branded as unpatriotic. Bismarck was beside himself, not least because he was unsure how the king would respond.[56] In fact, however, as Bismarck himself admitted a year later, the government had not desperately needed the money and could have fought the Danish war twice more, having benefited from the steadily rising economic prosperity in the 1860s which led to a surplus in 1863– 64. But Bismarck wanted this information kept a secret from the Lower House in order to encourage dissension within the parliamentary opposi- tion.[57] Even Bismarck's success in wresting the duchies of Schleswig and Holstein from Denmark by the summer of 1864 could not break the liberal opposition, although it revealed the first traces of the fault-lines along which the division occurred two years later, with right-wing liberals such as Heinrich von Treitschke delighting in the victory. The creation of a navy was also a popular liberal cause which Bismarck hoped to exploit by proposing to develop Prussian naval installations in Kiel. But again the liberal majority felt bound to reject the naval construction bill in 1865 on account of the government's flagrant violation of constitutional principles.

Bismarck's efforts to divide the liberals before 1866 were thus unsuc- cessful, even if his policies produced considerable confusion and embar- rassment. The liberals maintained their principled opposition and were only prepared to vote through measures which served their commercial interests. In continuing the economic course of his predecessors and encouraging the *Zollverein* to adopt free trade, Bismarck's government clearly counted on liberal support. The *Zollverein* treaties and the shift towards free trade were readily accepted by the Prussian Landtag. But these policies also conformed to conservative and agricultural interests in the 1860s so they were not politically controversial (though Bismarck sarcastically told Motley that even when all the parliamentarians were in agreement with a treaty, they still argued furiously with each other over the motives for their agreement[58]). They did, however, have longer-term

political consequences since the growing industrial prosperity thus stimulated played into the hands of the government and eventually contributed
to undermining the parliamentary cause. The refusal of the liberal majority
to approve the budget also opened up new opportunities for financiers,
especially Bismarck's banker, Gerson Bleichröder, to do business with the
government. Economic self-interest clearly mattered to the liberals, but
they were generally not prepared to be bought off from their opposition
in principle by other means.

Yet ultimately the liberals, like Bismarck, shied away from a decisive
power contest. They repeatedly voiced their opposition to the government's arbitrary rule but, in the face of the king's repeated expressions of
confidence in his government, they were reluctant to step outside the
legal boundaries. They continued to support uncontroversial legislation
and they never attempted to boycott the Lower House. Faced with a
government which collected taxes illegally, they shied away from a direct
appeal to their constituents to institute a taxpayers' strike. To a certain
extent this reflected an insecurity about the extent to which they enjoyed
mass support. The Prussian three-class suffrage was plutocratic and
unequal, and a majority of those eligible to vote in the second and especially the third classes did not go to the polls in the elections of 1863.
Liberals remained committed to an elitist style of politics based on the
influence of local notables (*Honoratiorenpolitik*) and, especially after their
experiences in 1848, they were deeply ambivalent about mobilising
social forces which they could not control. Only a very small minority on
the most radical fringes of liberalism were democrats. But their reluctance to enter into a real trial of strength with Bismarck and the monarchy was also symptomatic of a frame of mind which was more focused
on achieving a return to the constitutional status quo than in testing
the political boundaries and augmenting parliamentary power. Just as
Bismarck resisted demands on the right for a *Staatsstreich*, so the overwhelming majority of Prussian liberals in the 1860s did not go so far as
to urge the introduction of ministerial responsibility to parliament or
parliamentary sovereignty. Historians may be forgiven for looking back
on the constitutional struggle and concluding that both sides were
engaged in a form of shadow boxing. But it must also be remembered
that the liberals had reasonable grounds to expect that sooner or later,
especially given Wilhelm's age and the political inclinations of his son,
the *Konfliktminister* would have to give way to a new, liberal ministry.

Bismarck thus ignored the Prussian parliament with impunity during
the constitutional conflict, but at the same time he was sufficiently realistic to recognise that the monarchy would eventually have to reach some

kind of accommodation with the liberal opposition. The political vitality of Prussian and German liberalism in the 1860s, confirmed repeatedly in free elections as well as outside parliament in chambers of commerce, voluntary associations, clubs and societies, convinced him that there could be no question of suppressing or defeating liberalism permanently. Sooner or later the government had to compromise with a movement supported by the most dynamic and articulate sections of society. Although emphasis is often placed on the weaknesses of Prussian liberalism, from its apparent failure in 1848 to its 'capitulation' to Bismarck in 1866, this trajectory is misleading as it distorts the potentialities of the 1860s. For after the revolutions of 1848 and the introduction of constitutional government in Prussia, few doubted that liberalism would eventually regain the political initiative. The lack of a mass base was scarcely seen as a fundamental weakness in the conditions of the 1860s, at a time when socialism was still in its infancy and politics remained overwhelmingly the business of notables. Just as Bismarck's talks with Lassalle about state socialism were primarily tactical, searching for ways to bring pressure to bear on the liberals, so there was no question that Bismarck saw in liberalism, representing the educated and propertied bourgeoisie, a more powerful and necessary ally for the monarchy than the inarticulate masses. Theories that Bismarck practised a form of 'Bonapartism', trying to play off the different social forces against one another in order to strengthen his own rule and place himself at the fulcrum, overestimate the importance of the working class in the 1860s and 1870s.[59] Some conservatives such as Wagener were arguing for a 'social monarchy' from March 1864, believing that only by espousing social welfare policies could the government win majorities for itself and secure the future of the monarchy. But this was not an option for Bismarck politically in the 1860s and, in any case, his focus was on liberalism.[60] Whatever the weapons Bismarck chose to use against the liberals, he ultimately wanted to do a deal with them. He wanted to persuade or force a section of the liberal bourgeoisie to align itself with the government. From 1862 until the spring of 1866, however, Bismarck's leadership had the effect of welding together the parliamentary liberals.

In the short term Bismarck also rallied a divided and weakened right, even if in the longer term his policies split both liberal and conservative factions asunder. The constitutional struggle performed a service in demoting other differences among conservatives, for example over foreign policy or the social question, and in some ways Bismarck appears to have exerted an almost charismatic appeal to the monarchy's natural supporters on the right. His forcefulness, energy, determination, even calmness all inspired a new confidence that the current difficulties could be overcome; indeed, there was a perception that he was a leader of superior quality to his predecessors and that his government contrasted favourably to the weak governments which had held sway since the revolution of 1848. Among the conservatives there were also frequent references to Bismarck's manliness which rendered him a cut above any other contenders for the leadership. For all their differences, Gerlach was particularly susceptible to Bismarck's magnetism in this respect. After meeting Bismarck in March 1863, he noted in his diary (with his own emphasis) that 'Bismarck is above everything else a *human being*, a *man*'; and he told Kleist that at such a time he thanked God that they had unexpectedly been given 'such a man ... For he is a *man* first and foremost and not – as Thadden expresses it – a gutted herring.' Bismarck was, in addition, 'a fresh, strong, brave man' with 'calm determination', 'Have we ever seen such a *man* at the top before?'[61] In the elections of September 1863 the conservative party tripled their vote, and both Moritz von Blanckenburg and Hermann Wagener were among those returned to the Lower House. Bismarck also secured a loyal conservative majority in the *Herrenhaus* at the end of November 1863 by creating a large number of new peers to balance the liberal appointments of the previous years. He was unable, however, to have Gerlach included among them since Wilhelm I still associated him with the reactionary camarilla. The *Herrenhaus*, with its right of veto, proved an important bastion of conservative power during the constitutional conflict, even exceeding its authority in its determination to antagonise the Lower House. After Bismarck's compromise with the liberals in 1866, it shifted uncomfortably to a more oppositional role.

By the middle of 1864 Bismarck had his first major diplomatic success behind him and seemed to have accepted that the only way he would be able to break the constitutional deadlock was by presenting the Prussian parliament with a tangible success in the national question. He had always recognised that he shared certain goals in foreign policy with the Progressive Party, hence his rather crass attempt to rally them behind an 'iron and blood' policy in 1862. In 1863–64 his apparent determination to ignore nationalist claims to the duchies of Schleswig and Holstein had enraged national liberal opinion throughout Germany, yet liberal hostility became more muted as the prospect of Prussian territorial gain loomed larger. Bismarck's foreign policy presented the Prussian liberal opposition with a dilemma, as some began to recognise that Prussian annexation of the duchies would better serve the goal of national unification than the creation of yet another sovereign middle state. Indeed, some Prussian liberals were already beginning to argue that Prussian self-interest alone justified such a policy.

As Bismarck candidly remarked in a crown council meeting on 28 February 1866, 'domestic considerations do not make a war a necessity though they are additional reasons to make it look opportune'.[62] The constitutional conflict never determined the course Bismarck took in foreign policy between 1862 and 1866 and German unification was not the result of an audacious attempt to resolve the monarchy's internal problems, as some interpretations have suggested.[63] Otto Pflanze has rightly insisted that Bismarck himself would have sneered at the idea that he adopted the national programme of the Prussian liberals because of their strength in parliament.[64] His ideas about the direction Prussian foreign policy should take pre-dated the constitutional conflict and he would have pursued his foreign policy whatever the constellation of domestic forces at home.

Bismarck, of course, would ideally have liked to enter the decisive military contest with Austria for influence in Germany with the Prussian parliament and people united behind his policy. In 1865 he made a renewed attempt to reach a compromise over the army reform but it again failed on account of the irreconcilability of crown and parliament with respect to the three-year military service. But even as he sought to win national liberal opinion for Prussia's cause in Germany, Bismarck continued his illiberal policies at home, seeking to remove parliamentary immunity from Landtag deputies so that their leaders could be prosecuted for sedition. He was ultimately prepared to pursue his policy even in defiance of liberal and nationalist opinion. For the first time in the constitutional conflict, the Prussian liberals seemed to be heading a popular movement in the spring of 1866 which extended well beyond Prussia's borders. German liberals protested at Bismarck's cynical pursuit of Prussian interests, his apparent denial of any principles in domestic and international conduct, and his willingness to pit Germans against Germans in a fratricidal war. Ultra-conservatives, too, could not fail to see the apparent inconsistency, confusion and immorality in Bismarck's policy: he treated the Landtag with contempt while he propagated parliamentary ideas in Germany, he elevated Prussian interests and simultaneously appealed to the German nation, he colluded with elements he apparently despised, exploiting them as he sought to frustrate them, and 'all this from a *soi disant* conservative statesman!'[65]

Nevertheless, by 1866 Bismarck had learnt to live with the domestic conflict and, just as many liberals were beginning to tire of their impotent exclusion from any role in decision-making, so he no longer saw the parliamentary opposition as a serious threat either to his personal position or to his diplomatic freedom of manoeuvre. The longer he survived in power, and the more secure he felt his position became with the king, the less irksome the constitutional conflict became. This is not to say that he was not very aggrieved personally by the continued opposition of the parliamentary deputies, and it was a source of enormous bitterness and frustration for him that even as the Prussian army moved into Saxony and Bohemia, the domestic carping continued. But the Landtag ultimately had no power to circumscribe his political activities in any significant way and he could afford to ignore it. It was the international struggle which preoccupied him most.

Defying the nation: the Schleswig-Holstein crisis and the gamble on Prussian power

Bismarck's reputation as an extraordinarily skilful diplomat and statesman is largely founded on his foreign policy successes between 1862 and 1871. An older generation of historians encouraged the view that he had pursued clear and consistent aims from becoming minister-president and foreign minister of Prussia which eventually resulted in the unification of Germany.[66] Moreover, his domestic isolation and the aggressive hostility of his critics during the constitutional conflict only served to highlight the impression that he almost singlehandedly achieved what all the liberal hopes and revolutionary fervour of 1848 had proved unable to accomplish, namely the creation of a lesser German national state with Prussia at its head. Through the assertion of Prussian military power and the victories against Denmark, Austria and France, Bismarck appeared to end centuries of political fragmentation in central Europe and precipitated a fundamental restructuring of the international state system in Prussia's favour. At the same time his style of governance and leadership, rooted in his determination to defy and overcome all his internal and external opponents, captured the imagination of a generation of Germans, whether they lauded or loathed his achievements. Bismarck came to personify something essential to the Prussian spirit; he was not merely the architect of German unity but the very embodiment of the new Prusso-German nation, forged with blood and iron.

Bismarck's dramatic foreign policy successes between 1862 and 1871 were momentous events for those who lived through them but they should not blind us to a more realistic and critical appraisal of his role. Self-evidently, no man is ever in a position to shape events entirely according to his own choosing. And even if Bismarck had certain aims which he sought to fulfil as Prussian premier, the role of contingency and opportunity as well as the reactions and mistakes of his opponents must all be seen as significant in determining specific outcomes. Neither Bismarck's intentions nor Prussian interests on their own suffice to explain how Prussia succeeded in augmenting its power immeasurably in the course of a single decade. The wider context in which Bismarck operated – the emergence of Bonapartist France, the impact of the Crimean and Italian Wars, the dissolution of the alliance between the three conservative monarchical powers, the growing impetus of the national idea, the constraints on Austrian policy and so on – facilitated Bismarck's policy. The emergence of the Bismarckian Reich was by no means a foregone conclusion in 1862 but, as we have seen, the convergence of circumstances by the 1860s undoubtedly contributed to make a definitive solution of the German problem more likely. Bismarck's role was crucial in determining the form which Prussian expansion in Germany eventually took and also in helping to shape the institutional framework within which Prussia could exercise its new hegemony. Without Bismarck, the outcome may well have been very different. But by 1865 there were few experienced political observers who did not recognise the way the wind was blowing. Ideological, social and economic forces were pressing for some kind of political consolidation, and the existing system of Austro-Prussian dualism in Germany appeared increasingly provisional and untenable.

Bismarck basically inherited his foreign policy in 1862, for his predecessors, too, had sought a redistribution of influence over German affairs in Prussia's favour and had been prepared to exploit the opportunities presented, for example by Prussian commercial policy, to undermine Austria's political leadership of the lesser German states. Bismarck's experience at Frankfurt probably convinced him to a greater degree than his diplomatic colleagues that the German Confederation served essentially as an instrument of Austrian policy, that its interests were not synonymous with those of Prussia and Germany and that, if Austria refused to accept Prussian parity within it, it would have to be destroyed. He also understood better than most how the future of Germany hinged on the international state system and how any attempt to resolve Austro-Prussian dualism which did not take into account international realities would be doomed to failure. But Bismarck himself had never claimed to know 'what will or should become of Germany'[67] and, for all his self-confidence in his ability to survive in stormy seas better than most, he harboured an essentially modest conception of his role as an individual in history. The tide of history was essentially driven by impersonal and anonymous forces and ultimately subject to an inscrutable divine plan. All one could do was watch out 'and when one sees God striding through history, leap in and catch hold of his coat-tail and be dragged along as far as may be'.[68]

Bismarck knew the broad direction in which he wished to go, and by the 1860s the idea that Prussian foreign policy should be based solely on Prussian interests, without showing any particular hostility or partiality to any one power, fell on much more fertile ground in Berlin political circles than it had in the 1850s. Perhaps more importantly, he also knew what he wished to prevent, an insight which was particularly valuable when one considers that many of Bismarck's most startling diplomatic strokes were essentially reactive, responding to sudden changes of circumstance that he could not pretend to control. But Bismarck was too pragmatic in his approach to believe he could adhere to a premeditated plan or that he could calculate for all eventualities. He always envisaged alternative solutions to the German question from that which eventually emerged, and he was most successful in foreign policy when he accepted the essential fluidity of international relations. Serving his diplomatic apprenticeship in the years after the 1848 revolutions, he had ample experience of how rapidly the international situation could shift and change; and while he often insisted it was important to have a clear conception of foreign policy goals, he was willing to pursue different strategies, adapting them and settling for less, if by these means he brought the attainment of his immediate objectives a little closer. Another of his strengths was an innate sense of caution, the 'ability to wait while conditions develop' until the moment for decisive action struck.[69] 'As a statesman I am not nearly ruthless enough, to my mind [I am] rather cowardly', he wrote in 1869, 'and that is because, in the questions that confront me, it is not always easy to gain the clarity which engenders faith in God.'[70]

As Prussian foreign minister and minister-president from 1862, Bismarck enjoyed a much greater degree of autonomy in formulating Prussian foreign policy than he could claim in other areas of decision-making. Nevertheless he had had no experience of high office before 1862 and, just as he misjudged the impact of his words to liberal deputies in September 1862, so he was something of a novice when it came to putting his foreign policy ideas into practice. One of his first moves in international affairs was to sign the so-called Alvensleben convention with Russia in February 1863, an agreement between the two powers to coordinate their security arrangements during the Polish rebellion of 1863.

Bismarck's hostility to the Poles was unequivocal and his remarks about the need to suppress Polish nationalism make grim reading, especially after the experience of the twentieth century. In 1861 he wrote to his sister, Malwine, that for all his sympathy with the situation of the Poles, 'we can do nothing other than exterminate them if we want to exist; the wolf also cannot help the fact that he is created by God as he is and yet we shoot him dead when we can.'[71] Despite Bismarck's later effort to represent the Alvensleben convention as a successful means of defeating Pan-Slav tendencies within the Russian government and winning the friendship of Russia which served Prussia well in the storms ahead, the move was widely construed to be an unnecessary mistake. The convention was never implemented (Russia dealt with the rebellion on its own) but it rebounded to Prussia's disadvantage by alienating Britain and France (not to mention liberal opinion throughout the German states). Even the Tsar, Alexander II, admitted that 'our dear Bismarck is a terrible blunderer'.[72] In the longer term, however, Bismarck's clumsy diplomacy may well have served Prussian interests since the mistake helped to convince the chancelleries of Europe that Bismarck was a much less dangerous diplomatist than the French emperor, Napoleon III, and it meant that Prussian diplomacy was consistently underrated throughout the 1860s. It also probably served as a useful lesson to Bismarck, whose response to the re-emergence of the Schleswig-Holstein crisis later in the same year was to be much more cautious.

Bismarck was more successful in 1863 in thwarting Austrian proposals to reform the German Confederation, defeating the idea of a conference of delegates from the German state parliaments in January 1863 and ensuring that Prussia played no part in the princes' congress convened at Frankfurt in August 1863.[73] Austria's plans included the creation of a federal executive, the establishment of an indirectly elected assembly and a reformed federal council or Bundesrat, representing the individual states, but the proposals very much conformed to Habsburg interests, also strengthening the role of the small and middle German states so that Prussia could easily be outvoted. It was perhaps fortunate for Bismarck and Prussia that the Austrian plan not only ignored Prussian interests but also largely disregarded the aims and aspirations of the liberal national movement. Prussian public opinion, whether liberal or conservative, was inclined to approve of Bismarck's policy of non-cooperation with Austria, even if there was more dissension over the form of Bismarck's refusal. Bismarck's counter-proposals included an insistence on Prussian parity with Austria, a right of veto for the two largest German states if the Confederation declared war and also the alarmingly novel proposal of a national parliament directly elected by the people. Bismarck defended the proposal to Gerlach. He clearly regarded the indirect and unequal suffrage that existed in Prussia and had produced such an obstreperous parliament as an evil and he expected direct election by the German people to produce a conservative chamber.[74] But this was the first time that he publicly indicated that in the pursuit of its power interests Prussia could ally with the national liberal movement. The Austrians suspected that his proposals were merely a tactical manoeuvre, designed to bring pressure to bear on the other German governments, but there was no doubt that Prussia could make more extensive concessions to national liberalism than the multinational Habsburg empire.

It was the Schleswig-Holstein crisis, however, which can with good justification be seen as a major turning point in Bismarck's political career. It led directly to Prussia's first military success in the war waged by Austria and Prussia against Denmark in 1864 (which the army used to vindicate the army reform) and it also provided the seeds of the antagonism out of which the Austro-Prussian conflict of 1866 eventually grew. Historians who have studied the twists and turns of Prussian diplomacy between 1863 and 1865 often do not conceal their admiration of Bismarck's adept manipulation of the European powers, the political acumen and tactical skill he deployed at each stage of the crisis and the way in which he led his Austrian counterparts to the point where Austria found itself confronted with the prospect of a war with no major allies. Otto Pflanze has called Bismarck's policy over Schleswig-Holstein 'one of the amazing feats in the history of politics'. Beguiled by Bismarck's successes in the 1860s, he further writes: 'Here is one of those moments in the processes of history where a single personality, by his capacity to manipulate the forces within his grasp, influenced the course of history and the lives of millions.'[75] Bismarck's successful diplomacy appears even more significant because it revealed the first cracks in the parliamentary opposition at home, the first traces of the fissure that would rend the liberal nationalist movement in two in 1866 and ensure that a majority of Prussian liberals would rally behind Bismarck's proffered compromise to end the constitutional conflict. Bismarck's handling of the Schleswig-Holstein crisis was of crucial importance in stabilising his power position at home, a diplomatic success which led his domestic critics to falter and furnished the first real proof that his ministry might not prove so ephemeral after all.

The successful outcome of the crisis and its significance for the political future of Bismarck and Prussia should not obscure the fact, however, that Bismarck, in its early stages, played a relatively modest role. He did not create or resurrect this complicated problem in 1863, just as he did not manufacture the struggle against Austria in the Confederation. The two duchies of Schleswig and Holstein (along with the small duchy of Lauenburg which Prussia had ceded to Denmark in 1815 and which had a population of less than 50,000 inhabitants) were personal possessions of the Danish crown but enjoyed their own distinctive political and social structures. Their controversial status had excited liberal nationalist opinion throughout Germany in 1848 when a Danish attempt to incorporate Schleswig into the monarchy had prompted the German population (which constituted the overwhelming majority, although there was a sizeable Danish minority in northern Schleswig) to declare independence. After the intervention of the powers, the personal union of the duchies with the Danish crown had been confirmed by the Treaty of London of 1852 whereby the Danish king also undertook not to seek any further integration of Schleswig into the monarchy. In 1863, however, preparations for a new Danish constitution and a renewed attempt to separate Schleswig from Holstein inflamed German and Danish nationalism again. The death of the Danish king, Frederick VII, on 15 November 1863 with no direct heir further reopened the complicated problem of the succession since, although Prince Christian of Glücksburg's claims to both the duchies and the kingdom of Denmark had been recognised by the Treaty of London, a rival claim to the duchies was made by the German prince, Friedrich von Augustenburg, whose father had renounced his claims in 1852. Holstein, but not Schleswig, belonged to the German Confederation and the creation of an independent German state under a German prince had the overwhelming support of liberal nationalist opinion in Germany in 1863, whether *großdeutsch* (favouring a greater Germany including Austria) or *kleindeutsch* (favouring a lesser Germany centred on Prussia), as well as the approval of the lesser German states in the Confederation and the national independence movement in Schleswig-Holstein itself. In Prussia, too, both Wilhelm I and the crown prince were sympathetic to the German cause. The crown prince had enjoyed a close friendship with Augustenburg since their student days in Bonn; and the king may well have seen the Schleswig-Holstein crisis as an excellent opportunity to placate the parliamentary opposition by promoting the claims of the German prince.

The course Bismarck steered from the outset of the Schleswig-Holstein crisis appears devious both in the light of the eventual outcome, namely Prussian annexation of the duchies, and when Bismarck is judged with the benefit of hindsight, above all with the knowledge that he was not in any sense a typical conservative statesman. However, his attitude in 1863 was not so surprising given that he had recently burned his fingers in the Polish crisis, and indeed seemed entirely in character to the Prussian opposition. Bismarck's position was that international law had to be respected, that Prussia had no quarrel with Denmark and that Prussia would consequently stand by the Treaty of London. Bismarck thus drew a sharp distinction between the policy of Prussia and the wishes of the German Confederation (which had not been a party to the Treaty of London). This was entirely consistent with his conviction that Prussia was a European great power rather than a German federal state and with his determination to undermine the Austrian-led Confederation. As he insisted to Goltz:

The chase after the phantom of popularity 'in Germany', which we have been pursuing since the forties, has cost us our position in Germany and in Europe, and we shall not regain it if we let ourselves be driven by the current in the belief that we are guiding it, but only if we stand firmly on our own feet and are first and foremost a great power, and only then a federal state. Austria, to our detriment, has always recognised that as the correct course for herself, and she will not allow herself to be wrested from her European alliances, if she has any, by the farce she is playing with German sympathies.[76]

In refusing to recognise and support the claims of the German prince, Augustenburg, Bismarck showed a keen appreciation of international realities. The Schleswig-Holstein question was an international issue, subject to international agreement, and Prussia would gain nothing by acting independently in defiance of the other powers. He saw more clearly than most how Prussian interests did not conform to those of the Confederation since Prussia had nothing to gain from the creation of yet another German middle state on its northern boundary which would be bound to look to Austria for support against its powerful neighbour. He quite openly reassured France, already mindful of an extension of Prussian or German influence without commensurate compensation, that he saw no point in squandering Prussian arms on behalf of Augustenburg (as had happened in 1848 when Friedrich Wilhelm IV had sanctioned a military campaign against Denmark). Bismarck was not prepared to place Prussia at the head of the German national movement in 1863–64 and subject it to rule by 'professors, district judges and provincial gossips' in accordance with the 'majority verdicts' he had so disdained in September 1862. As he reminded Goltz, Prussia should not waste its energy in support of Augustenburg or let the 'in itself mediocre question' of the Elbe duchies blind it to the more important issue.

If we now turn our backs on the great powers in order to throw ourselves into the arms of the policy of the small states, which is caught in the net of the democracy of associations, that would be the most wretched situation in which one could bring the monarchy internally and abroad. We would be pushed instead of push; we would support ourselves on elements which we do not control and which are necessarily hostile to us, to which we would have to surrender ourselves unconditionally. You believe that there is something in 'German public opinion', in the parliaments, newspapers, etc. which could support or help us in a policy aimed at union or hegemony. I consider that a radical error, a fantasy. Our strength cannot emanate from parliamentary and press politics but only from armed [*waffenmäßiger*] great power politics . . . If the beerhall enthusiasm makes an impression in London and Paris, I will be delighted as it suits our purposes; but for that reason it has not yet impressed me and has delivered no shots and few dividends [*Groschen*] in the struggle.[77]

He thus consistently opposed the Augustenburg solution to the problem unless (as he spelled out in June 1864) the German prince was prepared to accept humiliating conditions which rendered him dependent on Prussia. Prussian policy had to be guided by Prussian ambition rather than by a fickle public opinion which concerned itself one moment with the two-year military service, another with the Poles and currently with Schleswig-Holstein.[78]

Nor was it so difficult for Bismarck to harness Austrian policy to his course from 1863, for, as a major European power and a multinational monarchy, Austria clearly had good reason to uphold the sanctity of international treaties and resist popular demands for national self-determination. Bismarck rightly calculated that Austria's European interests, as opposed to its German interests, would dictate that it support the policy of its main rival in Germany. Indeed, the Austrian foreign minister, Rechberg, must have been pleasantly surprised and relieved when he learnt that Bismarck was ostensibly committed to maintaining the status quo in the duchies, especially when, just weeks before, the Prussian premier had sought to scupper Austria's plans to reform the Confederation by calling for a national parliament. Rechberg's decision to cooperate with Prussia was entirely logical given Austria's wider interests and the pressure it was under from France in Italy and Russia in eastern Europe. Only later, when the likelihood of Prussian annexation loomed larger, did Austrian policy become more nationalist and pro-Augustenburg in tone. But by this time Austrian policy had already alienated the middle states which were its main supporters in Germany and it had effectively committed itself to a policy of cooperation with

Prussia in an area geographically remote from its traditional sphere of influence.

Initially, then, when the Scheswig-Holstein crisis erupted again in late 1863, Bismarck could afford to do nothing and it was precisely his refusal to let Prussia make the running over the issue which so inflamed liberal nationalist opinion. While the middle German states in the Confederation were anxious to challenge King Christian IX's claims to the duchies and facilitate the succession of Augustenburg, the position of Prussia and Austria was that they recognised the dynastic claims of King Christian but insisted that he abide by the provisions of the 1852 treaty and withdraw the new constitution. Their attitude incensed national liberal opinion throughout Germany (which had already made up its mind about Bismarck but was sorely disappointed by Austrian policy) but it also made it very difficult for the other signatories of the Treaty of London, above all Britain and Russia, to intervene on behalf of the Danes (which they probably would have done if the German Confederation had attempted to place Augustenburg on the throne). The gathering momentum of the Augustenburg cause in late 1863, which stimulated German nationalism even more than the Italian crisis of 1859–60, alarmed Bismarck not least because of its implications for his position within Prussia. Neither Prussia nor Austria could afford to give a fillip to the perceived 'forces of revolution' in Europe by supporting the Augustenburg succession. After the German Confederation voted to institute a 'federal execution' (i.e. resort to military action) against King Christian as duke of Holstein for violating the Treaty of London (a decision which Austria and Prussia pushed through with a majority of one vote in the face of middle state support for Augustenburg), Saxon and Hanoverian troops entered Holstein and Lauenburg on 24 December 1863 without encountering Danish resistance. A few days later Friedrich von Augustenburg, who had proclaimed himself Duke Friedrich VIII of Schleswig-Holstein and enjoyed widespread support in Prussia as well as the middle states, illegally established his court at Kiel, a detail which was ignored by the confederal authorities in Holstein but which must have made Bismarck even more determined to find a pretext for Prussian military intervention.

Once Prussia and Austria were working in tandem in the crisis from late 1863, it was much easier for Bismarck to contemplate an eventual separation of the duchies from Denmark and their possible annexation by Prussia. Nevertheless, there is scant evidence that he was actively pursuing such an option before February 1864[79] and in the early weeks of the crisis he was mainly concerned to resist internal as well as external pressures to intervene on Augustenburg's behalf. In late 1863 even the king and Roon were inclined to support Augustenburg and take military action,[80] and Bismarck appeared more isolated than ever. Blanckenburg confirmed that 'Bismarck is *unfortunately the only, completely clear, completely* firm man in the government. All the others are more or less intoxicated and are urging war, the worst is the *furor militaris* which goes up to the *highest* circles . . .'[81] By the end of January 1864 Kleist could report that Bismarck had a united ministry behind his policy.[82]

Even after he intimated that the annexation of the duchies might be his preferred solution in a Prussian crown council meeting on 3–4 February 1864, Bismarck's approach was essentially a pragmatic one, allowing the decisions of others to determine how far Prussian policy could go and always ready to settle for less, at least temporarily, if circumstances dictated it. Far from creating favourable opportunities or cunningly exploiting the situation, Bismarck's behaviour during the protracted crisis was characterised by considerable restraint punctuated by moments of almost baffling honesty. Bismarck knew what he wanted to prevent and was adept at concealing from others what he ideally wanted. Given Denmark's intransigent insistence on incorporating Schleswig under the new constitution, Bismarck could pose as the moderate seeking to restore the Treaty of London and allow others to block or eliminate the undesirable alternatives. Rechberg was taken in by Bismarck's official pronouncements, never questioned his determination to stand by international treaty obligations, and found himself drawn into a form of old-style cabinet power politics which was ultimately extremely damaging to Austria's real interests. But Bismarck's powers of cynical manipulation are also often overstated. It was precisely his willingness to envisage several possible solutions to a problem and always keep open lines of retreat which gave him his freedom of manoeuvre.

In January 1864 the Danish government rejected an Austro-Prussian ultimatum requiring it to cancel its new constitution, and Austrian and Prussian troops subsequently occupied Holstein, superseding (and ignoring) the confederal forces which were already there. In early February they in effect launched an undeclared war against Denmark by crossing the Eider and moving into Schleswig, which was beyond the competence of the German Confederation. Bismarck succeeded in securing Austria's agreement that after their victory the two powers would jointly decide on the future of the duchies, thus signifying their abandonment of the London Treaty, but he could not prevent a British initiative to convene an international conference to clarify the status of the two duchies. In the event, the London conference did not open until 20 April, two days after Prussian and Austrian troops stormed the Danish fortifications at Düppel, a victory which met with patriotic jubilation throughout Germany and prompted even Gerlach to say that not only the Danes had been defeated but also 'the internal opponents of our army'.[83] With Austria and Prussia in effective control of the two duchies (and Bismarck sanctioning policies designed to facilitate annexation), the conference dragged on for several weeks without reaching an agreement. The Danes, both stubborn and indecisive, were willing to let the conference fail in the misplaced hope that Britain would stand by them militarily; and Bismarck further confused his liberal opponents at home by calling for a plebiscite in the disputed territory of Schleswig, a proposal which was criticised by his conservative friends. When the conference ended on 25 June there was clearly no question of a return to the Treaty of London. One day later Austria and Prussia resumed their war against Denmark, a war which the Danes had no chance of winning. In a preliminary peace signed on 1 August, the Danish king renounced his claims to the three duchies in favour of the Austrian emperor and the Prussian king. These terms were confirmed in the Treaty of Vienna signed on 30 October. The Schleswig-Holstein problem was thus no longer an international issue but one requiring resolution by the two major German powers. Viewed within the context of Austro-Prussian dualism by the 1860s, the chances of a lasting Austro-Prussian condominium over the duchies on the basis of conservative cooperation and solidarity were remote.

In successfully harnessing Austrian policy to Prussian policy and luring Austria to become directly involved in distant territories in northern Germany, Bismarck undermined Austria's prestige with the middle states in the Confederation and disappointed all *großdeutsch* nationalists who were dismayed by its unprincipled complicity with Prussia. With hindsight he contributed to knot 'the Prussian noose' around Austria's neck which would eventually hang it in 1866. Nevertheless, it would also be wrong to see a straight path from 1864 to 1866, for Bismarck never ruled out cooperation with Austria to achieve Prussian dominance in north Germany. Bismarck's flexibility is evident at every stage, not least because he never saw the duchies themselves as the key issue. In June 1864 he wrote to a friend that 'for me Prussian annexation is not the prime or necessary purpose but probably the most pleasing result if it were to arise from circumstances, without us falling out with Austria over the issue'.[84] Andreas Kaernbach has argued that Bismarck's 'real political achievement consisted in keeping this less significant conflict [over Schleswig-Holstein] hanging in the balance for so long until it could be linked to the more important problem of the reform of the Confederation'.[85]

In the summer of 1864 Bismarck conducted wide-ranging negoti-ations with Rechberg in Schönbrunn. The future of the duchies consti-tuted only part of their discussions and they also reached agreement on an astonishing draft treaty whereby Prussia, in return for receiving Aus-tria's share of the newly acquired territory in northern Germany, would help Austria win back Lombardy and restore Habsburg rule in Tuscany (which could only have been achieved by destroying the newly founded Italian kingdom and launching a war against France). It appears that Rechberg would have preferred territorial compensation in Germany (for example in Prussian Silesia) but that this was blocked by Wilhelm I. Indeed, it was the two monarchs, Wilhelm and Franz Joseph, who even-tually scuppered the treaty that had most likely been drafted by Rechberg. Historians have viewed the Schönbrunn convention with some scep-ticism. Otto Pflanze has argued that Bismarck deliberately used the king and that he had merely wanted to dangle the possibility of a deal in front of the Austrians in order to gauge their thinking. Others, too, have argued that the convention was an illusion and that Bismarck, the *Realpolitiker*, would never have waged war to help Austria regain north-ern Italy.[86] The episode, however, can be seen as an interesting reflection of Bismarck's thinking, showing his consistent willingness to devise and pursue alternatives, as well as his cynical attitude to nationalism and federalism, both of which he saw as merely instrumental in the pursuit of Prussian aggrandisement.

From the summer of 1864 the question of the future of the two duch-ies was submerged in the wider contest between Prussia and Austria for influence in Germany. Bismarck clearly now aimed to resolve the issue by Prussian annexation but, despite some signs of growing support for such a solution within Prussia, he was all too aware that such an aim on its own could not justify a war against Austria to secure Prussian hegemony in northern Germany. Thus for the next eighteen months he continued to demonstrate his willingness to work in partnership with Austria (which was necessary in any case to retain the confidence of the king) while at the same time he sought to extract the maximum conces-sions from Austria short of war by encouraging all kinds of frictions between them. There was no question that Austria would voluntarily surrender its rights over the duchies to Prussia without comparable ter-ritorial compensation. But Bismarck did not rule out a peaceful solution to the problem of Austro-Prussian dualism that might have divided Ger-many into spheres of influence. The fact that there was no such outcome resulted as much from Austrian diplomacy as from Prussian power pol-itics. The policy of the Austrian leadership ultimately exposed the gulf between the Habsburg monarchy's ambitions and its resources. By cooperating with Prussia from 1863, Austria forfeited a considerable amount of prestige with the lesser German states, a process which continued as successive bilateral arrangements between the two powers undermined the Confederation. Yet, despite the obvious strategic importance of the duchies for Prussia and their geographical location, Austria continued to believed that it could not afford to leave Prussia a free hand in the duchies and that it could retain its leadership role in Germany.

Faced with the growing prospect of Prussian annexation as a solution, the Austrians, no longer constrained by international considerations and now represented by Count Alexander Mensdorff-Pouilly as foreign minister after Rechberg had to resign in the autumn of 1864, sought to retrieve their position in the Confederation by supporting the Augustenburg succession and the inclusion of Schleswig-Holstein as a new member. Nevertheless, Austria was increasingly confronted with the choice between supporting the wishes of the German middle states and adhering to the Prussian alliance. By 1865 tensions between Austria and Prussia reached a level sufficient to prompt widespread fears of a military confrontation. But, in the Gastein convention of August 1865, Austria again opted to preserve the alliance with Prussia and Bismarck was willing to settle for less if it furthered his aims. Austria agreed to sell the small duchy of Lauenburg outright to Prussia for two and a half million thalers (the purchase was condemned by the liberal majority in the Prussian Landtag in January 1866 as constitutionally it should have been approved by parliament) and, while the two powers in theory retained joint sovereignty over the remaining two duchies, in practice Austria assumed the *de facto* administration of Holstein while Prussia enjoyed a similar status in Schleswig. There were compelling reasons for Austria to avoid a conflict with Prussia in 1865 but, once again, its prestige with the lesser German states plummeted (they expected nothing better from Prussia). Moreover, in securing Austria's agreement to some significant concessions, namely that the two duchies should be included in the *Zollverein* and that Prussia should have lines of communication to Schleswig through Holstein, Bismarck further consolidated Prussia's grip on the duchies. He deferred a war but the diplomacy of attrition continued, and the new arrangements ensured that there would be plenty of seeds for a future conflict.[87]

From the summer of 1865 Bismarck stepped up the pressure to force Austria out of Holstein and the Austrians, still essentially wishing to cooperate with Prussia, began to retaliate by pursuing policies which were antithetical to Prussian interests. Otto Pflanze has highlighted the futility and frustration experienced in Vienna as a result of Bismarck's manoeuvrings during this period. 'Constantly aggressive, he invariably depicted himself as on the defensive; always injuring, he continually assumed the role of the injured; ever working for the upset of the status quo, he steadily posed as a genuine conservative.'[88] But recent research has also indicated that, even as he threatened and postured, Bismarck never completely ruled out a peaceful solution and that he always pursued a multi-track policy. In early 1866, for example, Bismarck negotiated with Bavaria in the hope of reaching an agreement on confederal reform. The proposals might have led to a *kleindeutsch* Bavarian–Prussian dualism (with south Germany under Bavarian leadership) or to a triadic arrangement which included Austria as the third power but allowed for concentric circles or different layers of influence. The negotiations failed not least because Bavaria wanted Austria to be included in the discussions.[89] Their failure ensured that Prussia would go ahead with its reform proposals on its own in the spring of 1866.

In January 1866 Bismarck vigorously protested against Austria's toleration of pro-Augustenburg activities in Holstein, above all a popular meeting in Altona on 23 January. Prussia officially accused Austria of allying itself with the forces of democracy and revolution and threatened that if Austria did not desist from this course, Prussia would regard their alliance as over and claim full freedom of decision. In the developing crisis with Vienna from February 1866 Bismarck saw war as increasingly likely and a key issue was whether he could carry the king with him. There is some evidence that Bismarck convinced Wilhelm I of the necessity of preparing for war in a conversation with the monarch which took place in the Foreign Ministry on 26 February 1866. Thus the crown council meeting two days later, which some historians have seen as the crucial meeting at which the decision for war was made, was for the purpose of informing others within the German political and military leadership.[90] In the crown council meeting on 28 February 1866 Bismarck argued that Prussia was the single viable creation to come out of the ruins of the old Reich and that it had a mission to lead Germany. Austria had always fought against Prussia's natural and legitimate aspirations and refused to grant Prussia the leadership of Germany even though it was incapable of it itself.[91] The crown prince counselled against a 'civil war' but Wilhelm was sufficiently indignant about Austria's behaviour to give his conditional agreement that Prussia should prepare for war in case 'the attempt [to reach] a desirable understanding with Austria should fail'. Historians are divided over how sincerely Bismarck explored the avenues for peace. Heinrich Lutz has argued that Bismarck never seriously pursued an understanding with Austria and that 'It is astonishing how Bismarck disregarded this condition of the king'.[92] Yet Bismarck never contemplated war lightly if it could be avoided, nor do his detailed reform proposals for the Confederation make much sense in 1866 if he was wholly determined on war.[93]

As the prospect of war loomed closer in early 1866, the situation involved numerous risks for Prussia as well as for Bismarck personally. The contemplation of a war against a major European power was a very different undertaking from a war against a small country like Denmark in alliance with Austria. Prussia had not participated in a major war for over fifty years and, certainly without allies, there was no guarantee that Prussia would be successful. Since the 1850s Bismarck had been prepared to consider all the major European powers, including the French Second Empire, as potential Prussian allies in a confrontation with Austria but, in the event, he was only successful in securing an alliance with Italy in April 1866. This offensive–defensive alliance was important since it meant Austria could not concentrate its forces against Prussia; it also gave Prussia a 'blank cheque' in promising Italian support if a war were launched at any time within three months and it usefully put pressure on Wilhelm and other waverers at court who were presented with an unrepeatable opportunity. Although it was a secret treaty, Bismarck expected that Austria would find out about it (as was indeed the case) and it has also been interpreted as adding to the diplomatic pressure on the Habsburg monarchy, a means of intimidating it into making concessions or re-entering negotiations rather than a definite decision for war.[94] Apart from the Italian alliance, Bismarck was forced to launch the war in June 1866 counting only on the benevolent neutrality of the other European powers and very conscious that Russia or France might seek to intervene. The Russians were rapidly losing their illusions that Bismarck was a conservative statesman of a traditional kind; and in June 1866 France concluded a secret alliance with Austria which envisaged the creation of an independent Rhineland state, carved from Prussian territory, within the German Confederation, and which also secured Venetia for Italy even if Austria won the war. Bismarck was thus only likely to achieve his objectives if the war was short and victorious and presented the powers of Europe with a *fait accompli.*

Bismarck's awareness that the French would expect compensation for any adjustments made in Germany further encouraged him to exploit the national card as a means of legitimising Prussian expansionism and holding Napoleon III at bay. But this policy, too, was fraught with dangers.

The lesser German states were singularly unimpressed by Bismarck's diplomacy in 1866 and Prussia eventually embarked on the war against Austria with no significant German allies. Moreover, the proposal delivered by the Prussian envoy, Karl Friedrich von Savigny, on 9 April to the Federal Diet at Frankfurt, that a national parliament elected by direct and equal universal male suffrage should consider the reform of the German Confederation, was met with disbelief and incredulity throughout Germany, coming as it did from what was universally perceived to be a most reactionary ministry. No German state had adopted the electoral law of the revolutionary Frankfurt Parliament of 1848, nor did many German liberals favour a genuinely democratic, equal and direct suffrage without any wealth or property qualifications. Even Bismarck at this stage assumed the voting would be oral (as was the practice in East Elbia) rather than by means of a secret ballot, a further guarantee that the suffrage would produce a conservative parliament.[95] Moreover, he also envisaged that the parliament would only have an advisory function and that its mere existence would suffice to pressurise the particularist governments to agree to a reform from which nationalist and democratic forces would thus be effectively excluded.[96] The proposal, however, seemed to confirm prevailing opinions of Bismarck's unprincipled and cynical duplicity, enraging Prussian ultra-conservatives as well as liberal opinion throughout Germany and contributing to split the conservative party by the end of May. Gerlach tried to argue, as he had done in 1863, that the gesture might be merely tactical, but he was soon corrected by Blanckenburg who revealed that it was by no means 'a mere diplomatic chess move' but rather 'it is deadly serious'.[97] Wagener and other conservatives emphatically defended universal suffrage in a series of articles, and the moderate, younger majority rallied to Bismarck's cause around Wilhelm von Kardorff, taking the *Kreuzzeitung* with them. Gerlach, however, felt compelled to write his highly critical article, 'War and Reform', which marked his definitive break with Bismarck and appeared in the *Kreuzzeitung* on 8 May 1866.[98]

Bismarck was never so exposed, personally and politically, as he was in the weeks before the Austro-Prussian war. In the late afternoon of 7 May, walking back along Unter den Linden from a *Vortrag* with Wilhelm I at the palace, he was bruised in the chest by two bullets shot from a revolver by Ferdinand Cohen-Blind, a 22-year-old model student and patriot.[99] Blind directed five shots at the minister-president, two of them with the pistol pressed against his body, before he was overpowered by Bismarck and some military and civilian onlookers. In a letter written the previous day he claimed that he intended to kill Bismarck, the 'betrayer of Germany', to prevent the impending war and carnage, and he succeeded in committing suicide within hours of his arrest. Bismarck owed his life to his thick clothing but he saw his deliverance as a sign of divine intervention (and his silk undershirt was subsequently preserved by Johanna as a relic). He soon became convinced that the assassination attempt was the result of a conspiracy hatched in Bradford or St John's Wood by the student's stepfather, the exiled 1848 revolutionary, Karl Blind. And he hounded the Berlin police officials charged with investigating the case, eventually instituting disciplinary proceedings against them because he was dissatisfied with their findings and suspected their political sympathies. Bismarck thus took the incident very seriously and there is no doubt that, despite his initial composure, he was severely shaken after the attempted assassination. But he nevertheless soon had word sent to Gerlach that his article 'had injured him badly and wounded him more than the assassination attempt of the same day [sic]'.[100]

Bismarck thus faced real personal and political dangers in 1866. It was one thing to defy German public opinion when allied to Austria, as during the Schleswig-Holstein crisis, but quite another to embark on an unpopular 'civil war' between Germans without any significant domestic basis of support within Prussia or Germany. After four years of internal strife Bismarck was inevitably the main focus and target of public hostility. He depended more than ever on his king, who had daily to be convinced that Austria's behaviour was provocative and aggressive and that it was to blame for the failure of mediation attempts. Even the Austrian ambassador in Berlin, Count Alois von Károlyi, suspected that what was at stake was Bismarck's political future rather than the expansion of Prussian power. 'Bismarck regards the annexation of the duchies or a result which approximates to that as a vital matter for his political existence, and he is intent on making it appear as such for Prussia too', he warned his government in February. 'After such a success, especially if it were to be achieved through a propitious war, the government would more easily become master of the internal dissension . . . Bismarckian policy is led by such considerations.'[101] But the Austrian leadership in Vienna, beset with difficulties throughout the empire and shifting its attention from Schleswig-Holstein one minute to the Tyrol, Croatia, Budapest or Venice the next, never understood whom it was dealing with in 1866 or formulated a realistic response. In February 1866 Mensdorff still feared the fall of Bismarck because he believed that a liberal Prussian government would be much more dangerous for Austria and its German policy.[102]

No one was more conscious of the risks than Bismarck, who suffered from nervous tension and stomach problems in the weeks leading up to the outbreak of war. His realism helps to explain why, as late as May 1866, he was still prepared to give serious consideration to proposals for what amounted to a peaceful division of Germany into two spheres of influence along the Main. Anton von Gablenz, a Prussian Landtag deputy and brother of the Austrian governor of Holstein, sought on his own initiative to mediate between Prussia and Austria and devised a scheme that would also have left Schleswig-Holstein formally independent but under a Hohenzollern prince. Both Wilhelm I and Bismarck agreed to the Gablenz proposals. The king still had doubts about the consequences of war for the legitimacy of the monarchical order throughout Europe and Bismarck, too, was willing to entertain a further stage of compromise that might provide an escape route if the prospects for war became too risky. Yet ultimately the scheme was rejected by the Austrians. And there is no doubt that Bismarck, too, despite his readiness to consider alternatives, was convinced that a satisfactory solution to the problem of Austro-Prussian dualism could only be attained through war.

On 1 June 1866 Austria, frustrated in her efforts to reach an accommodation with Prussia, handed over the problem of resolving the future of the duchies to the Confederation and revealed that the Austrian governor of Holstein, Ludwig von Gablenz, had called a meeting of the Holstein estates. The Holstein estates had decided in 1460 that the two duchies should be eternally united and ruled by the Danish king, and they undoubtedly now would have voted to install Augustenburg as ruler. Austria's action was interpreted by Prussia as provocation. On 9 June Prussian troops invaded Holstein and prevented the estates from meeting. In the Federal Diet Savigny complained that Austria had broken the Gastein convention and that the Schleswig-Holstein issue should be resolved in a nationally elected parliament rather than a body which served the interests of dynastic particularism.[103] On 14 June an Austrian motion mobilising all non-Prussian confederal forces was carried by eight votes (nine once Baden acceded under the pressure of public opinion) to five. Prussia retaliated by declaring that it regarded the old Confederation as dissolved since it could not guarantee its security and proposing a new confederation from which Austria would be excluded. The small states bordering Prussia had little option but to profess support for their powerful neighbour but the most significant middle states – Bavaria, Saxony, Württemberg, Baden, Hanover, Electoral Hesse and Hesse-Darmstadt – all sided with Austria, taking the view that by declaring it was leaving the indissoluble Confederation, Prussia was in breach of confederal law. On 15 June Prussia sent ultimatums to the neighbouring states of Saxony, Hanover and Electoral Hesse, demanding they join the new Prussian-led confederation, and when these expired Prussia declared war and invaded at midnight. Prussia never officially declared war on Austria but Austrian military support of any state invaded by Prussia was not in doubt.

At midnight on 15 June, as Prussian troops crossed the border, Bismarck confided to the British ambassador, Lord Loftus, 'If we are beaten, I shall not return here. I shall fall in the last charge. One can but die once: and if we are beaten it is better to die.'[104] Isolated and defiant, Bismarck knew that his political future now depended on the success of Prussian arms and (as the Austrian victory over Italy on 24 June at Custozza and the initial Hanoverian success at Langensalza on 27 June soon indicated) that a successful military outcome was far from self-evident. The impression that Bismarck took the supreme gamble of his career in 1866 is further confirmed not only by his proposal for a national parliament (for there was no guarantee that when called upon to vote the German people would support a reorganization of Germany on Prussian conservative and expansionist foundations) but also by his willingness to contact the leaders of ethnic minorities, above all the Hungarians, within the Habsburg Empire with a view to encouraging revolution from within. Even the threat of such an eventuality carried major risks for the Prussian monarchy with its significant Polish population, quite apart from the implications for European stability. Bismarck has been compared to the 'sorcerer's apprentice', willing to unleash revolutionary forces in 1866 that he could not possibly control.[105] But, buoyed up by a fatalistic trust in God's will and grace, which became even more marked after his miraculous survival on 7 May, Bismarck consciously submitted his fortunes and those of Prussia to the turbulence of a war which might have been disastrous for both.

Notes

1 Gerlach, I, 11 November 1862, p. 437.

2 Ibid., II, Kleist-Retzow to Gerlach, 28 January 1863, p. 1133.

3 GW, X, speech of 27 January 1863, p. 157. See also Keudell, *Fürst und Fürstin Bismarck*, p. 116.

4 Gerlach, 13 January 1864, p. 448.

5 Rothfels, Bismarck to Goltz, 24 December 1863, p. 307.

6 See Bismarck, *Gedanken und Erinnerungen*, p. 259. Cited in Christian von Krockow, *Bismarck: Eine Biographie* (Stuttgart, 1997), p. 166.

7 Gerlach, II, Friedrich von Gerlach to Gerlach, 7 June 1863, p. 1145.

8 Ibid., I, 4 March 1863, p. 441, and 22 October 1863, p. 444.

9 Ibid., 26 September 1865, p. 471; 29 December 1865, p. 472; 24 January 1866, p. 475.

10 Ibid., 14 August 1862, p. 432.

11 Ibid., 9 September 1862, p. 433, and 10 December 1862, p. 438.

12 Ibid., 23 October 1863, p. 444.

13 Ibid., 25 October 1863, p. 445.

14 Ibid., 4, 4/5 June 1866, p. 123.

15 Ibid., 28 March 1864, p. 453.

16 GW, VII, conversation with Vilbort, 4/5 June 1866, p. 123.

17 Rothfels, Bismarck to Marie, 24 August 1863, p. 305.

18 Ibid., Bismarck to Roon, 21 January 1864, p. 312.

19 Bismarck, *Gedanken und Erinnerungen*, p. 312.

20 Steglich, II, Montgelas to Ludwig II, 13 April 1866, pp. 87–8.

21 Cited ibid., I, p. xl.

22 Ibid., II, Wilhelm I to his sister, Princess Luise of the Netherlands, 14 May 1866, p. 108.

23 GW, XII, speech of 24 January 1882, p. 329.

24 Keudell, *Fürst und Fürstin Bismarck*, p. 117. See too Rothfels, Bismarck to Malwine, 10 October 1862, pp. 299–300.

25 Gerlach, I, 22 October 1863, p. 444, and 17 August 1864, p. 458.

26 Leopold von Schlözer (ed.), *Kurd von Schlözer: Petersburger Briefe 1857–1862* (Stuttgart and Berlin, 1922), p. 127.

27 Keudell, *Fürst und Fürstin Bismarck*, pp. 127–8.

28 Ibid., p. 124.

29 Rothfels, Bismarck to Motley, 17 April 1863, p. 300, and Bismarck to Magdalena Borcke, 2 May 1863, p. 302.

30 Gerlach, II, Blanckenburg to Gerlach, 3 October 1863, pp. 1151–2.

31 See Christoph Studt, *Lothar Bucher (1871–1892): Ein politisches Leben zwischen Revolution und Staatsdienst* (Göttingen, 1992), especially pp. 245–56; Arthur von Brauer, *Im Dienste Bismarcks*, ed. Helmuth Rogge (Berlin, 1936), p. 116.

32 Gerlach, I, 23 December 1864 and 29 December 1864, pp. 462–3.

33 Cited in Gall, I, p. 202.

34 Gerlach, I, 11 November 1862, pp. 436–7.

35 Ibid., 22 October 1863, p. 444.

36 Keudell, *Fürst und Fürstin Bismarck*, pp. 135–6.

37 See Stern, *Gold and Iron*, p. 30.

38 See Keudell, *Fürst und Fürstin Bismarck*, pp. 124–5, and Stern, *Gold and Iron*, p. 31.

39 Gerlach, I, 19 March 1863 p. 442.

40 Ibid., 27 October 1862, p. 436. See also Pflanze, I, pp. 179, 207.

41 Pflanze, I, p. 208.

42 Gerlach, I, 4 March 1863, p. 441.

43 Ibid., 26 March 1865, p. 466.

44 Bismarck, *Gedanken und Erinnerungen*, p. 244.

45 Stern, *Gold and Iron*, pp. 62–80.

46 Steglich, II, Wilhelm I to Augusta, 1 June 1866, p. 177.

47 Kraus, *Gerlach*, II, p. 808.

48 Gerlach, I, 18 May 1866, pp. 479–80, and Kraus, *Gerlach*, pp. 808–9.

49 See for example Keudell, *Fürst und Fürstin Bismarck*, p. 122.

50 Ibid., p. 126.

51 GW, X, speech of 30 September 1862, p. 140.

52 Kraus, *Gerlach*, II, pp. 757–8.

53 See Rothfels, Bismarck to Friedrich von Beust, 10 October 1862, p. 299.

54 See Kraus, *Gerlach*, II, p. 763 .

55 Ernst Rudolf Huber (ed.), *Dokumente zur deutschen Verfassungsgeschichte. Bd. II: Deutsche Verfassungsdokumente 1851–1900* (Stuttgart, 3rd edn, 1986), p. 70.

56 See Rothfels, Bismarck to Roon, 21 January 1864, pp. 311–12.

57 See ibid., Bismarck to Karl von Savigny, 24 March 1865, p. 317.

58 Ibid., Bismarck to John Lothrop Motley, 17 April 1863, pp. 300–1.

59 See Hans-Ulrich Wehler, *The German Empire 1871–1918* (Leamington Spa, 1985), pp. 55–62, and Engelberg, I, p. 760. Cf. Lothar Gall, 'Bismarck und der Bonapartismus', *Historische Zeitschrift*, 223 (1976), pp. 618 ff.; Otto Pflanze, 'Bismarcks Herrschaftstechnik als Problem der gegenwärtigen Historiographie', *Historische Zeitschrift*, 234 (1982), pp. 561–99.

60 Kraus, *Gerlach*, II, p. 788.

61 Ibid., p. 765.

62 *Die auswärtige Politik Preußens*, 6, no. 449, crown council minutes, 28 February 1866. Cited in William Carr, *The Origins of the Wars of German Unification* (London, 1991), p. 127.

63 See especially Wehler, *German Empire*, pp. 24–31.

64 Pflanze, I, p. 190.

65 Gerlach, II, J. Bindewald to Gerlach, 2 May 1866, p. 1271.

66 See for example Erich Marcks, *Der Aufstieg des Reiches: Deutsche Geschichte von 1807–1878*, 2 vols (Stuttgart, 1936–43). For a useful discussion of the German historiography, see Hans Fenske, 'Das Bismarckbild der Deutschen', in Hans Fenske, *Preußentum und Liberalismus: Aufsätze zur preußischen und deutschen Geschichte des 19. und 20. Jahrhunderts*, ed. Hermann Hiery (Dettelbach, 2002), pp. 505–58.

67 Rothfels, Bismarck to Johanna, 18 May 1851, p. 150.

68 Cited in Gall, I, p. 28.

69 Cited in Andreas Kaernbach, *Bismarcks Konzept zur Reform des Deutschen Bundes* (Göttingen, 1991), p. 242.

70 Rothfels, Bismarck to Alexander Andrae-Roman, 26 December 1895, p. 323.

71 Rothfels, Bismarck to Malwine, 26/14 March 1861, p. 276.
72 Cited in Mosse, *European Powers*, p. 115.
73 For a detailed discussion of these initiatives and Bismarck's policy, see Kaernbach, *Bismarcks Konzept*, especially pp. 169–78 and 187–97.
74 Gerlach, I, 22 October 1863, p. 444.
75 Pflanze, I, pp. 242, 258.
76 Rothfels, Bismarck to Goltz, 24 December 1863, pp. 307–8.
77 Ibid., pp. 308–10.
78 Ibid., p. 309, and Bismarck to Below-Hohendorf, 16 May 1864, p. 313.
79 Cf. his apparent comments on New Year's Eve 1863 to a small group of guests. See Keudell, *Fürst und Fürstin Bismarck*, p. 140.
80 Gerlach, I, Friedrich von Gerlach to Gerlach, 25 November 1863, p. 1165.
81 Ibid., Blanckenburg to Gerlach, 26 November 1863, p. 1166.
82 Ibid., Hans von Kleist-Retzow to Gerlach, 31 January 1864, p. 1176.
83 Kraus, *Gerlach*, II, p. 778.
84 Rothfels, Bismarck to Below-Hohendorf, 16 May 1864, p. 313.
85 Kaernbach, *Bismarcks Konzept*, p. 242.
86 Pflanze, I, pp. 254–5; Carr, *Wars of German Unification*, p. 120.
87 For different views of the Gastein convention, see Otto Becker, *Bismarcks Ringen um Deutschlands Gestaltung* (Heidelberg, 1958), p. 117; cf. Kurt Jürgensen, 'Die preußische Lösung der Schleswig-Holstein-Frage 1863–1867', in Johannes Kunisch (ed.), *Bismarck und seine Zeit* (Berlin, 1992), pp. 66–7.
88 Pflanze, I, p. 267.
89 See Kaernbach, *Bismarcks Konzept*, pp. 211–14.
90 Frank Zimmer, *Bismarcks Kampf gegen Franz Joseph: Königgrätz und seine Folgen* (Graz, 1996), p. 37. See also Gall, I, pp. 280–1, and Carr, *Wars of German Unification*, pp. 127–8.
91 Heinrich Lutz, *Zwischen Habsburg und Preußen: Deutschland 1815–1866* (Berlin, 1998), p. 453.
92 Ibid., p. 454.
93 See Kaernbach, *Bismarcks Konzept*, pp. 224–5.
94 See Eberhard Kolb, 'Großpreußen oder Kleindeutschland: Zu Bismarcks deutscher Politik in Reichsgründungsjahrzehnt', in Kunisch, *Bismarck und seine Zeit*, pp. 30–1.
95 See Heide Barmeyer, 'Bismarck zwischen preußischer und nationaldeutscher Politik', ibid., pp. 47–8.
96 See Kaernbach, *Bismarcks Konzept*, p. 221.
97 Blanckenburg to Gerlach, 15 April 1866, cited in Kraus, *Gerlach*, p. 802.
98 See Kraus, *Gerlach*, II, p. 805.
99 See especially Julius H. Schoeps, *Bismarck und sein Attentäter* (Berlin, 1984) for the following.

100 Kraus, *Gerlach*, II, p. 806.
101 Cited in Zimmer, *Bismarcks Kampf*, p. 33.
102 Cited in Lutz, *Zwischen Habsburg und Preußen*, p. 456.
103 See Carr, *Wars of German Unification*, p. 132.
104 GW, VII, conversation with Lord Loftus, 15 June 1866, p. 127.
105 See Gall, I, p. 376.

Chapter 4

❀

Creative Power

Between 1866 and 1871 Bismarck achieved his major successes. He steered Prussia through two victorious wars against Austria and France, secured Prussia's predominance in Germany and re-drew the political map of Europe with the foundation of the German Reich in 1871. At the same time he transformed his own political career. Almost overnight, as a result of Prussia's dramatic defeat of Austria in 1866, perceptions of his personality and leadership were radically changed. No longer the maverick outsider who clung to power despite all the odds, his political stature grew in proportion to the scale of his achievements. In government circles Bismarck was viewed with awe and regarded as all-powerful. A bemused emissary who was permitted into Bismarck's inner sanctum to drink evening tea with him in August 1866 was told by his closest aides that this was 'now considered to be one of the rarest and most envied attestations of favour'.[1]

Bismarck was undoubtedly at his most innovative and creative during the period of German unification. He used political power to change existing political relationships: the creation of modern Germany bore his imprint at each and every stage. At the height of his mental powers, he consistently found solutions to the problems he encountered and he devised imaginative and flexible arrangements which he hoped could be adapted as necessary in the future. Moreover, although Bismarck reaped personal honours and property as well as political rewards, his moment of triumphalism was fleeting. Bismarck may have been conscious, like everyone else, that he was living through a momentous period in history, but he continued to have an essentially modest conception of his own role in shaping events and had no illusions about the inevitability or permanence of what he was creating. After 1871 Bismarck's efforts would be focused on preserving what he, perhaps more than anyone, regarded as an artificial and precarious construct. But his subsequent political career never gave him the same degree of satisfaction and fulfilment that he experienced during the heady period of German unification. Having achieved more than he had ever anticipated between 1866 and 1871,[2] he could only contemplate a worse future, one in which he would never again have the same freedom to create and act and one in which there was a real danger that his edifice could come crashing down around him.

The Austro-Prussian war and settlement

'To beat the Austrians was no art', Bismarck is reported to have remarked shortly after the Austro-Prussian war. 'I knew that they were not militarily prepared and that I could count on the Prussian army. The difficulty was getting my king to take the plunge. That I succeeded in this is my service, and for that I may claim the thanks of the fatherland.'[3] Nevertheless, despite this retrospective confidence, it was not a foregone conclusion in 1866 that Prussia would win the war. As a result of the army reform, the Prussian army was able to mobilise some 355,000 men (out of a total population of 18 million), which was more than a match for the Austrians whose population was almost double that of Prussia. The Prussian infantry had at its disposal modern breech-loading needle guns, which meant that even smaller units had considerable firepower. In addition, most of the Prussian forces were relatively educated and literate in comparison to their Austrian opponents, many of whom had difficulties with the German language of command. But the Prussian cavalry and artillery were inferior to their Austrian counterparts, and one recent study of the war has maintained that 'Seen overall, neither of the two opposing armies was considerably worse or weaker than the other'.[4] Indeed, most observers in 1866 were inclined to rate the chances of Austria, the well-established great power, more highly than the 'upstart' Prussian state.

Austria admittedly faced a war on two fronts, its inept diplomacy ensuring that it fought Italy as well as Prussia in 1866 even though Austria had promised France it would concede Venetia to Italy even if it won. But Prussia, too, appeared to face something similar, with the possibility of a western front against the larger German middle states. Most of the small states of northern and central Germany were tied militarily to Prussia but a few smaller members of the Confederation also opted to support Austria. However, neither side had coordinated their military plans. Frank Zimmer has claimed that the biggest unknown was the military strength of the middle states and how zealously their troops would fight in what was in effect a German civil war.[5] At the battle of Langensalza on 27 June the well-defended Hanoverian army inflicted a humiliating defeat on Prussian *Landwehr* troops before the arrival of regular reinforcements forced its capitulation the following day; and, although fragmented and uncoordinated, the south German forces were numerically superior to the Prussian forces south of the river Main under Manteuffel. Certainly no one, not least the other powers of Europe, expected that the war would be over so quickly and that the results would be so dramatic.

A crucial difference between the two sides, however, proved to be the quality of Prussia's military leadership and professionalism. Prussia's victory appeared to vindicate not merely the military benefits of the army reform but also its political implications. As Geoffrey Wawro has highlighted, the Prussian general staff, reformed by Helmuth von Moltke in the early 1860s, was unique in Europe because it focused military planning, mobilisation, deployment and operations in a single agency that was free of political and administrative interference. Subordinated only to the Prussian crown, it 'attained a level of military efficiency that other European armies – obstructed by courtiers, ministers and parliaments – could only dream of'.[6]

Moltke had played a major role in the strategic planning of the war against Denmark and now had direct command for the first time. Something of an intellectual, he wrote books (including a novel and travel literature as well as works of history and military history) and had translated a twelve-volume work of history from English into German. He also famously studied maps, appeared to know the terrain of Bohemia better than the Austrian military men on the spot in 1866, and grasped the new relationship between technology and warfare. From 1857, when he became chief of the general staff, he enthusiastically promoted the expansion of the north German railway network for military purposes and ensured that, by means of the telegraph system, separate army divisions could be coordinated and led in accordance with a single plan of operations. Although he had had virtually no practical experience, he devised an effective operations plan in 1866 which involved dividing and transporting Prussia's forces by rail to the frontiers of Saxony and Bohemia, deploying them in three armies over a distance of 500 kilometres (the Second Army under the command of the crown prince was the largest with 115,000 men), concentrating them only on enemy territory during the battle itself and thus enveloping the enemy forces. As Wolfgang Venohr has commented, 'The intellectual superiority was so depressing for the enemy that he ended the war.'[7] By contrast, Ludwig August von Benedek, commander of Austria's North Army, was a popular and experienced commander but an inferior strategist whose mistakes have been blamed for the defeat by recent historians.[8] Conscious of the threat of encirclement, he sent a telegram to the Austrian Kaiser Franz Joseph on 30 June, 'Request Your Majesty urgently to conclude peace at any price. Catastrophe of Army unavoidable.'[9] It was typical of the Austrian emperor, Franz Joseph, that he was to insist on a battle to salve Habsburg honour. Steven Beller, in a sister volume in this series, has seen the deficiencies of the Austrian leadership and the misguided policies of the military establishment as symptomatic of deeper problems which beset the Austrian state, for which Franz Joseph must bear ultimate responsibility.[10]

Bismarck's behaviour in the weeks immediately preceding the outbreak of hostilities indicated that he was very much living on his nerves at this time. On 29 June, the day before he departed for Bohemia, he wrote to Kathy Orlov that if he continued to lead the life he had been living for the past three months, he would fall ill. 'The more the crisis develops, the more matters fall on me [*les affaires se concentrent sur moi*]; I am not allowed to sleep any more and I nevertheless need a lot of sleep; my energies are being exhausted physically as well as mentally. After days of hard work without a break, I'm always being summoned to the king at 1 or 3 o'clock in the night.' He was encouraged, however, by the news of the Prussian troops' advance into Bohemia. 'I see in these first successes evidence of the assistance of God who will conduct us along the right road.'[11]

Bismarck travelled with Moltke, Roon and Wilhelm I to the front and, for the first time, he experienced the reality of war. On 2 July he confessed to Johanna that he had thus far seen more Austrian prisoners than Prussian soldiers; and he urged her to send cigars by the thousand for the wounded, copies of the *Kreuzzeitung* for the military hospitals, as well as a revolver, saddle pistol and a French novel for him personally.[12] Dressed in the uniform of a *Landwehr* major (a practice which had attracted adverse comment in peacetime), he witnessed the decisive battle at Königgrätz (or Sadowa) on 3 July 1866 at first hand. At Königgrätz Prussia lost over 9,000 men and the Austrian casualties – dead, wounded or taken prisoner – totalled over 44,000 men. Filled with emotion, Bismarck had nothing but praise for the Prussian soldiers, 'every man so completely fearless, calm, obedient, well-behaved, despite empty stomach, wet clothes, wet bed, little sleep, boot soles falling off, kind to everyone, no pillaging and burning, pay what they can and eat mouldy bread. There must indeed be a deep fear of God in our common man, otherwise all that could not be.'[13] Bismarck further maintained that his presence on the battlefield had protected Wilhelm I, for no one else present would have dared to speak so sternly to the king when he allowed himself to be dangerously exposed to grenades. Indelibly impressed by his experiences, Bismarck bedded down for the night with only a carriage cushion in a street surrounded by wounded men until he was rescued from the rain by the grand duke of Mecklenburg who let him and three others share his room.

Bismarck claimed that if the battle had not gone Prussia's way, he was resolved to die on the battlefield, but his sincerity was never put to the test. As Fritz Stern has shown, he ensured through Bleichröder that he had plenty of foreign currency in his hand luggage, though exactly what fate he envisaged might befall him remains a matter of speculation.[14] Nevertheless, if the crown prince's army had arrived too late at the battle of Königgrätz, Bismarck's political career would have been over, and there is no doubt that the Prussian premier was the supreme victor of the war. 'But I have defeated everyone! Everyone!' he exulted on 8 July.[15] In the longer term, however, the legacy of Königgrätz was more ambiguous. The presence of Wilhelm I and Bismarck at the battlefield seemed to symbolise a new symbiosis of the monarchical, political and military leadership of the Prussian state. Wilhelm I embraced and honoured his son, the crown prince, on the battlefield. Heinrich Lutz has argued that other conceptions of Prussian and German statehood were defeated as a new kind of military monarchy emerged.[16]

The Prussian victory at Königgrätz on 3 July 1866 proved to be the decisive battle in the war but, just as the victory could have gone the other way, so the battle need not have been decisive in determining the war's outcome. The Austrian army was not obliterated and, with reinforcements from its successful campaign in Italy, might have continued the war. Wilhelm I also wanted to continue the fight and occupy Vienna. Here, though, Bismarck played a key role, prevailing upon his king to conclude a hasty armistice and all too aware that the risk of foreign intervention, above all by Napoleon III, was very real. As he told Johanna, at a time when the intoxication of victory was beginning to encourage dreams of world conquest, it was his thankless task 'to pour water into the foaming wine and to insist that we do not live alone in Europe but with three other powers which hate and envy us'.[17]

Bismarck's insistence on a moderate settlement with Austria in 1866 has been applauded by historians who have seen him as concerned to ensure stability in Europe and perhaps even keep the possibility open of an eventual alliance with Austria, as was concluded in 1879. It can also be argued, however, that the international situation gave him little choice. France was keen to broker a rapid peace, Austria was by no means beyond resisting the imposition of harsh terms, Prussia's ally, Italy, had been defeated and Russia was also threatening to intervene. Moreover, cholera was spreading rapidly among the Prussian troops and, indeed, eventually claimed more victims than the battle of Königgrätz. Bismarck may have later encouraged the view that he displayed considerable foresight in 1866 in seeking to preserve the multinational Habsburg empire, but even while he was conducting the negotiations for the preliminary peace at Nikolsburg, concluded on 26 July, he continued to bolster Prussia's position by all means at his disposal and irrespective of the consequences for the peace and stability of Europe. Not least, he continued to maintain links with key elements among the Habsburg empire's ethnic minorities – Italians, Czechs, Rumanians and above all Hungarians – whom he was prepared to encourage to foment revolution. Moreover, the lenient peace which he eventually concluded with Austria was not matched by a similar magnanimity towards Austria's allies. South of the Main, each Prussian victory was a further nail in the coffin of the old German Confederation, whose non-Prussian representatives beat a hasty retreat from Frankfurt to Augsburg before its fate was finally sealed. The Prussian occupation of Frankfurt on 16 July was particularly brutal. Bismarck encouraged Manteuffel to extract all he could from his former domicile, making exorbitant demands which eventually drove the mayor, Karl Fellner, to commit suicide. Wilhelm I was perhaps reflecting Bismarck's influence when he wrote to the queen that Frankfurt was 'the seat of all intrigues against Prussia'.[18] The outcry on behalf of Frankfurt's citizens eventually led Bismarck to reverse what he recognised was an indefensible policy and endeavour to do what he could to ameliorate the situation in a city 'where I spent such happy times and knew so many kind people'.[19] Money procured from Frankfurt was paid back with interest, but the city was annexed.

Bismarck successfully ensured that neither Italy nor Austria's German allies were represented at the negotiations at Nikolsburg, even though the substantive issues which concerned them were decided there, and that they would have to conclude their own peace treaties later. Königgrätz, however, ensured that more than ever the German question was an international one. Alarmed by the speed of the Prussian victory, Napoleon III was especially keen to mediate in a conflict, the results of which were clearly going to impinge on French interests. From 5 July Bismarck was forced to listen to the mediation proposals and peace plans of the French and he had to conduct highly complex diplomatic negotiations with France, Austria and Italy which were not without their dangers for Prussia. While Bismarck dealt directly in Nikolsburg with the Austrian peace delegation under Alois von Károlyi and with the French ambassador to Berlin,

Vincent de Benedetti, it fell to the Prussian ambassador in Paris, Goltz, to placate the wishes of Napoleon III. By securing Napoleon III's broad agreement to Prussia's programme before the detailed discussions began on 23 July, he successfully outmanoeuvred him and ensured that the French emperor's prestige as a peacemaker would depend on a successful outcome to the negotiations.

Bismarck was primarily interested in securing the north of Germany for a new Confederation led by Prussia, annexing the Elbe duchies, and excluding Austria from German affairs. Goltz confirmed on 22 July that Napoleon III would agree to the annexation of approximately four million people in the north but that (in accordance with the wishes of Franz Joseph) he insisted on the territorial integrity of Saxony and Austria, conditions that were eventually incorporated into the preliminary peace of Nikolsburg on 26 July. Prussia agreed to withdraw its troops from Austrian soil in return for compensation (ultimately the considerable sum of 20 million thalers) and Austria lost no territory except its rights in Schleswig-Holstein and Venetia. The formal independence of the south German states was confirmed (after a sudden proposal by Bismarck to create a wider German Confederation between the North German Confederation and the south was abandoned) and it was anticipated – at least by Napoleon – that they would form some kind of South German Confederation or *Südbund* for their mutual security (though this never materialised and relations between the former coalition partners were tense). The reorganisation of north Germany was to be in accordance with Prussian wishes, which effectively meant that Prussia could annex Schleswig-Holstein, electoral Hesse, Hanover, Nassau and the city of Frankfurt, connecting its eastern and western provinces for the first time, and form a new Prussian-dominated North German Confederation with the addition of the small client states in the north, the northern province of Hesse-Darmstadt (since Napoleon only agreed to Prussian control down to the Main river) and Saxony (which Bismarck would also have annexed if he had got his way and which Austria had wished to be part of the *Südbund*). The old German Confederation was declared dissolved and with it every legal connection between Austria and the rest of Germany. As Károlyi said to Wilhelm I, Austria thus renounced 800 years of history.[20] The Prussian elite was startled at how rapidly and easily Austria agreed to sever its ties with Germany in 1866, but in Austrian ruling circles the mood was one of bitter recriminations and resentment against their German allies, with the notable exception of Saxony. Throughout the negotiations Bismarck kept focused on what for him was the ultimate prize. 'What we need is north Germany', he wrote to his son, Bill, on his fourteenth birthday on 1 August, 'and there we want to make ourselves at home.'[21]

These terms of Nikolsburg, which largely accorded with Bismarck's wishes, were confirmed in the final Peace of Prague of 23 August 1866. However, Bismarck had quite a struggle to convince his monarch that this was a just outcome. Wilhelm's military outlook not only led him to urge taking the fight to Vienna but also to insist that the victor was entitled to territorial compensations. On 20 July he wrote to his wife that he had to take some territory from all the defeated German powers, 'for without such annexations to Prussia we would have no material gains for our unbelievable victories, sacrifice of men, resources [Gut] and blood'.[22] In the Prussian officer corps there was even talk of installing Prince Friedrich Karl of Prussia (the commander of the First Army) as king of Hungary. In the effort to rein back excessive aspirations, Bismarck suffered a nervous collapse and later claimed he even considered taking his own life by throwing himself out of a fourth-floor window.[23] As we have seen, the crown prince, bolstered by his newly won authority as a successful military commander, eventually played a key role in persuading his father to give way to Bismarck. Augusta, too, urged that Prussia had to be 'not merely firm and energetic but also clever and moderate'.[24] But Wilhelm particularly found the concession to respect the territorial integrity of Saxony, 'our most bitter enemy', very difficult to make.[25] Unlike Bismarck, Wilhelm wanted to deprive all his enemies of some of their territory but not depose any legitimate princes, even in north Germany, by annexing all of their territory. As had long been evident, Bismarck had no respect for other dynasties if they got in the way of consolidating Prussia's territory and he urged total annexation where it was practicable. He was thus highly satisfied with Austria's commitment to vacate its place in 'Germany', which, under the terms of the Peace of Prague, took on a new meaning as an entity which excluded the German-speaking lands of Austria (which incorporated some ten million Germans). As Heinrich Lutz has argued, the legal and semantic implications of the settlement in 1866 were of fundamental importance as a prerequisite to the founding of the German Reich in 1870–71. Bismarck effectively got a blank cheque from Austria in 1866 when it came to reorganising non-Austrian Germany.[26]

The south German states, which had largely conducted their own war, now also had to end it themselves, and Bismarck skilfully played them off against each other and against France. In his previous discussions with Napoleon III, Bismarck had often hinted at the possibility of France receiving compensation in return for its neutrality in an Austro-Prussian war and acquiescence in a restructuring of the German lands. But the French ambassador to Berlin, Benedetti, only came forward with a list of France's territorial demands rather belatedly on 5 August, after the negotiations at Nikolsburg were concluded and there was no need for Napoleon's good offices any more. France consequently achieved nothing concrete in the Peace of Prague except the vague promise of a sovereign *Südbund* (which it hoped would be under French influence) and the expectation of self-determination for the Danish population of north Schleswig, a commitment which Bismarck was never inclined to honour. Moreover, since the territory France coveted – a strip of the Saar, the Palatinate and part of Rheinhessen including the federal fortress of Mainz – all lay in south Germany, it was not difficult for Bismarck to persuade Baden, Württemberg and Bavaria (with whom he negotiated separately) to conclude a secret military alliance with Prussia. His negotiations with the remaining duchy of Hesse indicated the scant regard Bismarck attached to the river Main as the new boundary of the North German Confederation, although Austria and France were to seek to maintain this demarcation line right up to the war of 1870. The duchy kept its territory north of the Main for the most part and pledged that this part of the state should be part of the new Confederation. But the duchy's entire postal and telegraph service was taken over by Prussia, as was control over the territory around the fortress of Mainz in the south. All the duchy's forces, north and south, also came under Prussian military command. While ostensibly Germany thus appeared to have been divided into three separate blocs in the wake of the war of 1866 – the north, the south and Austria – Bismarck had in fact ensured that Prussia would dominate the south militarily as well as economically through the *Zollverein*. The military treaties concluded with the south German states were for an indefinite period and could not be abrogated.

In his conduct of the peace negotiations after the war of 1866 Bismarck manifestly demonstrated his sovereign skills in what amounted to an exercise in old-fashioned cabinet diplomacy. But he also revealed his sensitivity to the impact on diplomacy of new forces, most notably 'public opinion' which he repeatedly used to advance Prussian interests. For example, he never personally rebuffed the French demands for territorial compensation in exchange for Prussia's expansion into north Germany; indeed, he positively encouraged the French to think in these terms, especially with regard to Belgium and Luxemburg. But in practice he sought to keep French ambitions in check by threatening to unleash German nationalism. At the height of the compensation crisis in August 1866, Bismarck and Moltke even discussed the possibility of an immediate war against France; they took it for granted that Prussia would have the support of their erstwhile adversaries, the south German states, and that they could fight 'if necessary even with Austria'.[27] Bismarck already understood how a national war against France could serve the cause of German unification, but his flexibility, pragmatism and caution ultimately disappointed those German liberal nationalists in 1866 who wished him to go further. Heinrich von Treitschke, for example, advocated a 'national annexation policy' and many now wished to see the election of a national parliament representing the whole of Germany rather than one confined to the north. Bismarck wanted to ensure that Prussia remained in the driving seat and controlled the 'revolution from above' he was instigating; hence he saw the importance of proceeding step by step for internal German reasons as well as because of the foreign policy constraints. Thus Bismarck combined the skills of traditional diplomacy with what can be seen as a manipulative use of the new national idea to serve his political purposes. Never committed to the idea of German national unity for its own sake, he made functional use of German nationalism in 1866 to promote Prussian interests and he was willing to work with the support of the lesser German national movement to cement the new-style military monarchy in Berlin.

The end of the Prussian constitutional conflict

In 1866 Bismarck pursued a foreign policy which accorded in its essentials with what lesser German liberals had been demanding since 1848. He had clearly hoped to resolve the constitutional conflict before the decisive confrontation with Austria over the future of Germany, but he failed. Instead, in the months leading up to the war, he conducted his policy in the face of widespread popular opposition and disapproval in Prussia, and opinion throughout Germany was also predominantly anti-war and anti-Bismarck. However, even before the military campaign was fully under way, there was a perceptible change of attitude in Prussia to the monarchy, the constitutional conflict and to Bismarck's government. For all the dread of war, few families were unaffected by the general mobilisation, and a concern for loved ones as well as an instinctive Prussian patriotism helped to create a groundswell of public support which cut the ground from beneath the liberal opposition in parliament. As the royal party travelled by rail to the front in Bohemia, thousands of ordinary Prussians turned out at every stop to witness the spectacle and greet the train which bore six carriages of courtiers, officials and foreign attachés. One of Moltke's colleagues described the journey as 'a real triumphal procession for the king and Bismarck',[28] the moral and psychological effect of which was exactly what Bismarck wanted. The Prussian representatives in the Landtag suddenly no longer appeared in tune with the people or the 'people's army' created by the army reforms. With war imminent, the constitutional conflict no longer seemed sufficient grounds to deny the government patriotic support. The new elections to the Prussian parliament, held coincidentally on 3 July, the day of the battle of Königgrätz, changed the political landscape of Prussia. The liberals' representation was virtually halved and the conservatives made massive gains, increasing their representation by more than one hundred seats. Bismarck immediately put out feelers to right-wing liberals and moderate conservatives, eschewing the opportunity to exploit Prussia's victory to implement a *Staatsstreich* and instead seeking a compromise which would give the liberals a share in power but secure the prerogatives of the crown.

The Prussian victory and its consequences in the summer of 1866 proved to be a watershed in Prussian political history and simultaneously transformed prevailing opinions of Bismarck, his leadership and his use of political power. Many liberals, already weary of the protracted conflict with the government, were seduced by the results of Bismarck's policy and intoxicated by the Prussian military success. Men who had been intransigent opponents of the premier's course since 1862 now wavered in their stance and were ready to give him the benefit of the doubt, impressed above all by the fruits of strong and determined leadership. The prominent jurist Rudolf von Ihering, who in May 1866 had condemned the war as an act of 'terrible frivolity', now felt humbled by Bismarck's genius and claimed a 'man of action', such as he, was worth a hundred men of liberal persuasion, of powerless integrity.[29] The historian Theodor Mommsen commented that it was 'a marvellous feeling to be there when history turns a corner'.[30] The implications of a fratricidal war, the claims of Augustenburg to the duchies of Schleswig-Holstein and the rights and wrongs of territorial annexations suddenly paled into insignificance when set beside what Bismarck had achieved for Prussia and Germany. Almost overnight Bismarck was recognised to be an exceptional figure in world history whose successes confirmed the advantages of an amoral *Realpolitik* rather than adherence to dogmatic ideological principles. Only the most committed constitutional liberals clung to the notion that freedom or constitutional liberty was more important than a unity achieved by blood and iron. Even the liberal crown prince could not remain immune from the contagion. 'Without letting myself be in the least blinded or deceived by Bismarck, I cannot deny that I am astonished at the reasonable liberal views which the man is now putting forward and wants to implement', Friedrich Wilhelm wrote to his mother from army headquarters on 29 July, though two weeks later he still admitted to having 'enormous mistrust' of Bismarck and doubts about his good-will.[31]

Bismarck did everything he could to encourage the liberals to bury the hatchet in 1866, introducing a series of bills into the Landtag, each designed to placate elements of the former opposition, and relishing the opportunity to appear personally in the parliamentary committees to defend them and demonstrate his reasonableness.[32] The measure which finally laid the constitutional conflict to rest was the indemnity bill, announced in the crown speech on 5 August 1866 and passed on 3 September by a majority of 230 votes to 75 votes. The government acknowledged it had acted unconstitutionally for the past four years and in return the Landtag retrospectively granted its approval of its illegal expenditure since 1862. The issue, however, produced cleavages in both the liberal and conservative parties. The majority of the Prussian liberals were won over by the prospect of working with the government and nationalist liberals from the other north German states and annexed territories to create a new nation-state. Even the liberal deputy Karl Twesten, against whom the minister of justice was still intent on instituting criminal proceedings, voted for the indemnity bill in September 1866. Only a minority of the Prussian Progressive Party around Virchow and Hoverbeck remained mistrustful of Bismarck and sceptical about the chances of his new creation developing into a liberal, constitutional state.

The indemnity bill did not signify a renunciation of the gap theory or entail a promise that the government might not act arbitrarily again in the future if it deemed it necessary. But, in conceding that the government had governed illegally since 1862, it secured a majority in the Lower House and it was a necessary compromise to achieve liberal collaboration in the future. Bismarck supported a measure which ultra-conservatives such as Gerlach had opposed since 1862 and viewed as akin to introducing parliamentarism or furthering revolution. But even after Königgrätz, the indemnity bill was the minimum precondition for a settlement with right-wing liberals such as Treitschke who were now rapidly forming themselves into a National Liberal Party. These men were disposed to break with the cycle of negative opposition, put the past behind them, share in the national tasks ahead and demonstrate that German unity was the best way to achieve free institutions and overcome particularism.

Perhaps as significant as the cleavage within liberalism in 1866 were the fault-lines within the conservative party. Moderate conservatives were encouraged to see in Prussia's success evidence of God's work and, like moderate liberals, prepared to bury any scruples they may have harboured over the methods Bismarck had used to secure his aims. But ultra-conservatives were appalled at Bismarck's policies – the deposing of legitimate princes in the annexed states, the dilution of Prussia in a larger German entity, the harnessing of nationalism (still seen as a revolutionary doctrine in 1866 and not yet divorced from liberalism) and his commitment to establish a parliament or Reichstag in the new Confederation which would be elected by universal male suffrage. Confronted with the annexation bill, which was introduced into the Landtag on 17 August 1866, many Prussian conservatives could not understand how their former ally could show such a blatant disregard for divine right, the monarchical principle and, indeed, international law. Sovereign states were extinguished, their rulers forced to flee into exile and even contemporaries talked of Bismarck's 'revolution from above'. Their loyalty and proximity to the monarchy made it difficult for them initially to oppose the government, especially when principles such as the power of Prussia, the glory of the Prussian army and the authority of the Prussian king were simultaneously being exalted. But they soon made their hostility to the new settlement felt in the Prussian *Herrenhaus* where their strength of numbers allowed them to indulge their Prussian particularism more readily and Bismarck found their criticisms particularly irksome. Only a small number of conservatives chose to support Bismarck actively and form a new party, the Free Conservative Party (later called the *Reichspartei* in the imperial Reichstag), and these were mainly higher civil servants, diplomats and members of the Silesian nobility. As we have seen, Ernst Ludwig von Gerlach finally broke with his former protégé in 1866 and, notwithstanding his devout Protestantism, eventually found his political home in the Catholic Centre Party in the 1870s, which also mobilised its support on behalf of the ethnic minorities and disgruntled particularists.

Bismarck, however, could afford to be well satisfied with the ending of the Prussian constitutional conflict in 1866 for most of the former liberal opposition gave their support to the government. Moreover, the Landtag also exceptionally granted him an endowment of 400,000 thalers (about £60,000) for his services to Prussia, a welcome windfall with which he bought the Pomeranian estate of Varzin and secured his material independence. The events of 1866 proved far more of a watershed in Prussian and German political history than the subsequent foundation of the German Empire four and a half years later, and after 1945 there was much historical criticism of liberal 'capitulation' to Bismarck in the wake of Königgrätz. Domestic developments in Prussia in the summer of 1866 were likened to 'the first German *Gleichschaltung*', a reference to the Nazis' takeover of the German state in the early months of the Third Reich.[33] However, this view was exaggerated, for nothing was predetermined in 1866 and in reality much remained to be decided. National Liberals and Progressives continued to share similar liberal and national aims after 1866, albeit with differing emphasis, and the cleavage within liberalism was not yet so deep or unbridgeable as it later became. Moreover, the indemnity bill in effect accepted the liberal interpretation of the constitutional conflict and can be seen as evidence of Bismarck's readiness to compromise. It did not resolve or fully clarify the power issue, deferring that for the future. But in the circumstances of 1866 this was probably the most either side could attain.

The North German Confederation

Prussia's prize for victory in the Austro-Prussian war was the establishment of the North German Confederation, a new political entity which was agreed in principle between Prussia and the German states north of the river Main on 18 August 1866 and which secured Prussian hegemony in Germany. Historians have understandably shown a great deal of interest in the subsequent drafting of the constitution of the North German Confederation and in the detailed debates about its provisions in the new German constituent Reichstag, elected by univeral male suffrage, in February 1867. The constitution of the North German Confederation formed the basis of the constitutional arrangements of the German Reich, founded in 1870–71, for the later accession of the south German states was achieved with remarkably few modifications to the formulations agreed in 1866–67. Indeed, the decisions taken in the crucial months from the summer of 1866 through to the acceptance of the new constitution by a big majority in the constituent Reichstag on 16 April 1867 significantly shaped the political development of the Reich until the all-too-belated reforms of October 1918 signalled its imminent demise. Considered from this perspective, too, Bismarck's contribution to the creation of a unified Germany must be seen as unique and extraordinary. His central role in decision-making by the autumn of 1866 is not in doubt. As an individual he enjoyed exceptional authority and influence in late 1866, enabling him to devise and mould the political structures of a new state which by 1914 was to embrace over 65 million Germans.

The constitutional arrangements of the North German Confederation are significant not only with a view to the future but also because they provide unparalleled insights into Bismarck's political thinking. Here we can see concrete evidence of the extent of his conservatism and his liberalism, how far he could look to the future and how far he was rooted in the past, the areas in which he felt he could afford to be flexible and those where his outlook was more rigid. Although some of the implications of the new structures were only evident over time, the relative importance attached by Bismarck to issues of power is also manifest. The constitution sought to secure Prussian power in Germany and stabilise German power in Europe. But not least it was also designed to augment and consolidate his own power within the new state. Bismarck sought to give himself the maximum scope for manoeuvre and was wary of any initiatives which might curb his own freedom of decision.

Bismarck was largely responsible for devising the new constitution, dictating its main provisions to Lothar Bucher, but it was not dreamed up by him in a couple of days, as legend would have it.[34] Rather, it had its origins in the reform proposals Prussia had placed before the old German Confederation in the spring of 1866 (which had been drafted by a subordinate, Rudolf Hepke) and Bismarck incorporated in his final version ideas put forward by Hermann Wagener, Max Duncker, the liberal parliamentarian, and especially Karl Friedrich von Savigny, the conservative and Catholic former Prussian envoy to the Federal Diet who was commissioned by the king to draw up a constitution while Bismarck was on extended leave in the autumn of 1866. The exertions of the spring and summer had taken their toll on Bismarck physically, and he was away from Berlin for two months in late 1866 and then took further leave on account of being 'much more ill than is publicly known'.[35] But, tended to by his solicitous wife and conscientious subordinates, he exploited his absence and outlined the framework of the new constitution while on a recuperative holiday on the Baltic Sea island of Rügen in late 1866. He formulated his thoughts in two key documents known as the 'Putbus dictates'. Although he subsequently passed on the documentation to subordinates for redrafting and although there were undercurrents of complaint among officials, both about his cavalier treatment of some aspects of the constitution and about the number of decisions which had to be made in his absence, the substance of the constitution remained essentially unchanged when it was placed before delegates from the state governments in December 1866. Bismarck's prestige and authority within the Berlin executive now ensured that very few men were inclined to question his guidelines.

Bismarck was concerned to preserve a degree of continuity with the past, at least with respect to institutional forms. He wanted to keep the impression that Germany, as now defined by the North German Confederation, remained a loose *Staatenbund* (federation of states) rather than a *Bundesstaat* (federal state); and he was at pains to maintain at least a façade of federalism even if a mere glance at the map indicated the extent to which an expanded Prussia now dominated Germany north of the Main. From the start one of his main concerns was to make the new structures attractive to the south German states which were eventually expected to join. Hence he dismissed some of Savigny's proposals which would have strengthened the central executive. Indeed, the provisions of the new constitution would disappoint all those liberals who hoped to see the creation of a more centralised and unitary nation-state in 1866, as well as a group of thirteen nationalist states led by Oldenburg. Most liberals, however, reconciled themselves to the idea that the new Confederation might over time develop in a more unitary direction. In December 1866 the states, too, were far from happy with the constitutional draft of the new Confederation, but there was immense pressure on them to reach an agreement before the constituent Reichstag met. Bismarck claimed he wanted 'to overthrow parliamentarianism with parliamentarianism' and that he wanted a Confederation based on the support of the dynasties. But how far these reassurances were persuasive is debatable. It was the threat of an alliance between Prussia and revolutionary liberal nationalism which very much served to concentrate minds.

The key elements in the constitutional arrangements of the North German Confederation can be briefly summarised, although some of the provisions were left deliberately opaque and some important issues were left unresolved, postponed for future discussions. The Confederation was an alliance of German princes and senates, and the constitutions of its member states and free cities remained unchanged. Most crucially this meant that Prussia emerged from its conquests in 1866 with its constitution of 1850 intact; its military system, too, would now be extended over Germany north of the Main. If one of Bismarck's main motivations had been to secure the power of the Prussian state, the North German Confederation was a highly effective vehicle to that end. Apart from Prussia, the only other German state of any significant size in the Confederation was Saxony, which had only narrowly escaped annexation by Prussia in 1866. The Confederation was, as the foreign minister of Baden, Franz von Roggenbach, suggested, 'an alliance of the dog with the fleas'.[36] Even after the inclusion of the south German states in 1871 the new Germany's status as a federal nation-state remained deeply ambiguous.

Especially in the light of how the new system worked in practice, contemporaries and historians have been inclined to regard Bismarck's creation as a Greater Prussia rather than a truly German national state. The duality of Prussia and the Confederation underpinned the whole edifice.

Sovereignty in the Confederation theoretically resided in a federal council or Bundesrat which consisted of delegates appointed by the governments of the federal states. As in the old Confederation the number of votes a delegate disposed of depended on the size of the state; Prussia had the most votes, augmented now by those of the annexed states, and was guaranteed a hegemonic position. (This remained the case after 1871 too, even though it apparently wielded only 17 votes out of 43, because Prussia dominated most of its small neighbours and it was agreed that any constitutional change would require a two-thirds majority in the Bundesrat.) Along with its executive function, the Bundesrat also enjoyed some of the legislative rights of an upper chamber and had to approve all legislation. The only other national institution provided for in the constitution was the parliament or Reichstag elected by universal male suffrage, which Bismarck had always hoped would prove attractive to national forces and expected to have an integrative function. The Reichstag, however, as originally conceived, had fewer parliamentary powers than those enjoyed by the Prussian Landtag which had proved impotent to change government policy during the constitutional conflict. In the constituent Reichstag of the North German Confederation, the National Liberals (who were the largest party) gained the important concession from Bismarck that the Reichstag should have powers to scrutinise and approve the budget. But they were unable to secure any remuneration for Reichstag deputies and the issue of parliamentary control over the military budget – over 90 per cent of the total federal budget – was postponed rather than resolved. These debates occurred at a time when France's claim to Luxemburg as compensation for its 'good-will' in 1866 was creating considerable tension, and Bismarck exploited the international crisis in order to secure a speedy settlement of the constitutional issues.

Bismarck consolidated the power of the Prussian monarchy, reinforcing the fact that it had emerged from the constitutional conflict unscathed. The king of Prussia was to be president of the Confederation and as such he was to enjoy particular rights and privileges which were not even granted to him as king of Prussia. His new powers were, however, cloaked, in the language of the old *Bund* and Bismarck rejected the substitution of 'Kaiser' for 'presidency' because of its likely impact on the French, the south Germans and the Prussian government itself. The

Bundespräsidium (federal presidency) was charged with the conduct of German foreign policy and given the right to declare war and conclude peace. It had control over all personnel appointments in the administration, the right to call and dissolve parliament, and military prerogatives which smacked of absolutism. As Bismarck stated in a letter to Roon in 1869, he attached very little importance to the external form according to which the Prussian king exercised his rule in Germany but every importance to the fact of his rule. Specifically, it did not matter whether the navy was called Prussian, German or North German so long as it was the king's navy.[37] Bismarck's relationship with Wilhelm I was such that he had few hesitations in vesting so much power in the king. Nor did he appear unduly troubled by the issue of the succession. In the longer term he undoubtedly came to regret that so much potential power was concentrated in the hereditary ruler. Moreover, from the outset there was an ambivalence if not a confusion of powers between the sovereign monarch as president of the Confederation and the sovereignty of the united governments represented in the Bundesrat. This too was perpetuated after 1871 when the Reich remained a federation rather than a monarchy and the relationship between the Kaiser (a creation of the constitution) and the sovereign princes remained deeply ambiguous.

There was no provision for a central German executive or government in the Confederation. This was a bitter disappointment to National Liberals who wanted to see the creation of federal ministries headed by men who would be responsible to parliament. The eventual emergence of the federal chancellor or *Bundeskanzler* (later called the Reich chancellor) as the single, responsible, German minister in the new Confederation was not something that Bismarck originally envisaged. In his draft constitution Bismarck had anticipated that the chancellor would have a minor diplomatic role analogous to the one that he himself had enjoyed as Prussian envoy to Frankfurt. The chancellor was thus to be a subordinate of the Prussian foreign minister and instruct the Prussian votes in the Bundesrat. Bismarck may well have initially envisaged that Savigny could fulfil this role, just as he had in the former Federal Diet. However, the National Liberals secured another important concession in the parliamentary debates on the constitution, namely that the chancellor should have the sole right to countersign the decrees and ordinances issued by the president of the Confederation (the Prussian king) and that (according to Article 17) he should thereby assume responsibility for them (a formulation which was open to diverse interpretation but did not signify that the chancellor had to resign if he failed to have the confidence of the parliament). This clearly made the position of chancellor a far more central and important one, and Bismarck immediately recognised this, choosing to assume the role himself alongside his responsibilities as Prussian minister-president and foreign minister. As he told Savigny (though his words indicate that he, too, did not quite understand how the role would evolve in practice):

Through the responsibility clause the chancellor has become to a degree – if not legally, yet actually – the superior of the Prussian cabinet . . . You are too well acquainted with constitutional law not to realize that the chancellor thereby receives the power of final decision in the affairs of the Prussian ministries of trade, war, and naval affairs, of the more important parts of the Finance Ministry, and, if the confederate constitution develops correctly, the Ministry of Foreign Affairs . . . He receives this authority due to the circumstance that he influences the Reichstag by granting or withholding his countersignature. Because of this amendment therefore the chancellor must be simultaneously president of the Prussian cabinet if the new machine is to function at all.[38]

Bismarck's concentration of powers from 1867 was undoubtedly an unambiguous triumph for him, but it is important to bear in mind that in these early days he was still thinking in quite modest terms and that he certainly did not anticipate the development of a federal or Reich administration in Berlin parallel to the Prussian government. Bismarck set up a special chancellor's office, the *Bundeskanzleramt* (later called the *Reichskanzleramt*) from August 1867, which had administrative and supervisory functions and whose chief, Rudolf von Delbrück, was permitted to deputise for the chancellor. Its role was to expand quite dramatically in the years after 1867 with the creation of subordinate offices, the drafting of 'presidential bills' outside the relevant Prussian ministries and the growing volume of business to be tackled at a national level. As we will see, Bismarck modified this system later in the 1870s, dismantling Delbrück's office and fostering the creation of a series of Reich offices each under a state secretary. By the turn of the century, the 'Reich leadership' (as the chancellor and Reich offices were technically called) was increasingly referred to as the 'Reich government' even though the constitutional arrangements had not fundamentally altered. The chancellor remained the sole responsible Reich minister and all the other trappings of the 'imperial German government', including the state secretaries who could deputise for him, remained subordinated to him. In recognising the significance of the new position in 1867, however, Bismarck undoubtedly grasped the chancellor's role as the fulcrum within the new system. Coordinating the activities of the king, eight Prussian ministers, three parliaments (the Reichstag, Prussian Landtag and a newly created customs parliament, which will be discussed below, each with a radically different composition) and 22 federal governments, as well as conducting foreign affairs, was not something he could safely leave to others. But in the accumulation of offices – the chancellorship, the Prussian minister-presidency and the Prussian foreign ministry – Bismarck could also satisfy his own lust for power. The constitution of the North German Confederation can thus be seen as not only tailored to Prussian hegemonial claims but also to Bismarck's personal power ambitions.

From its inception the constitution of the North German Confederation has been seen as an inventive but flawed creation which inevitably failed to satisfy all those – perhaps the overwhelming majority – who had a different conception of the national ideal. Liberals wanted a more centralised state with ministerial responsibility to parliament, and they were severely criticised by a generation of historians for 'capitulating' to Bismarck in 1866–67 and failing to achieve other significant concessions such as a bill of rights, remuneration for Reichstag deputies and political control over the army. Conservatives wanted a two-chamber parliament with an upper House of Lords akin to that in Prussia. However, the arrangements were clearly very complex, having to take into account German political traditions as well as existing power realities. The result was inevitably a compromise. Most participants in the debates of 1867 were prepared to accept the new constitution as being a step nearer to their ideal and there was every expectation that the new constitutional machinery could gradually evolve in the direction of greater consolidation. Bismarck, too, was prepared to compromise in order to secure the necessary liberal support. He eventually conceded the right of parliament to co-decide the military budget (the so-called 'iron budget'), an issue which threatened the entire constitutional settlement in the spring of 1867. And he also had to placate all those Prussian particularists who feared the dilution or submergence of Prussia in a wider German entity. Bismarck can be seen as trying to play off a variety of interests in order to achieve what he regarded as the optimum solution. The Confederation had to incorporate features to placate particularists as well as nationalists, dynastic interests as well as national ideals, and a wide range of viewpoints – the Prussian state ministry, the German princes, the governments of the free cities, the Prussian Landtag and the constituent Reichstag – all sought to have some some input. As Otto Pflanze has argued, 'None desired the solution he devised', and few had sufficient time to digest its real significance.[39] But, in deliberately seeking to use 'elastic, inoffensive but far-reaching expressions'[40] in the draft constitution, Bismarck revealed his pragmatism and his realism rather than a manipulative cynicism. He could no more anticipate the direction the political development of the Confederation would take than his parliamentary collaborators in 1867. He seized the opportunity to create something new while simultaneously preserving what he could salvage from the past. Flexible and willing to compromise, he clearly hoped that what he had created would have the potential to grow and develop without being too prescriptive in advance about the form it should take.

Perhaps the most significant aspect of the constitutional arrangements where Bismarck (and the constituent Reichstag) manifestly failed to exercise sufficient foresight concerned civil–military authority in the new political entity. The North German constitution vested control of the military in the Prussian king personally and the army became in effect his personal weapon, with all troops swearing an oath of loyalty to him. The new arrangement effectively ensured that military matters were outside the constitutional reach of the chancellor and that there was no place in the new Confederation for a federal (later Reich) war minister. By implication it also enhanced the power of the king's military cabinet and contributed to the progressive emasculation of the position of the Prussian war minister (who, being subject to interpellation by the Prussian Landtag, was increasingly seen as suspect and unreliable by the military chiefs). Given the growing ascendancy, too, of the Prussian general staff under Moltke, which also emancipated itself from its subordination to the Prussian war minister in the 1860s, military decision-making was increasingly the preserve of two agencies which were not accountable to parliament or the civil executive and whose chiefs had the right of direct access to the king. Thus the monarch controlled a powerful institution which can be seen as 'outside the constitution' or 'a state within the state'. Bismarck mainly ensured that this system operated in his favour before 1890, contributing when it suited him to weakening the war ministry but never allowing the military to interfere in his political leadership.[11] His successors found they wielded far less power in a system which never resolved the dualism of political and military authority.

After approval by the constituent Reichstag and the Prussian Landtag, the constitution of the North German Confederation came into operation on 1 July 1867 and the first legislative Reichstag was elected in August 1867. Thereafter began a protracted period of intense legislative activity as the Prussian ministerial bureaucracy and the newly appointed president of the *Bundeskanzleramt* worked closely with the liberal majority in the legislature to achieve the economic and legal unification of the new state and to establish the basic liberties of its citizens. In helping to draft a series of new laws establishing, for example, the freedom of migration and settlement (1867), a uniform system of weights and measures (1868), an industrial code guaranteeing free enterprise (1869), and a common currency based on the mark (1871), the Prussian state revealed what Ernst Engelberg has described as its 'Janus face', pursuing a course of economic liberalism despite its obvious authoritarian political features.[42] Many of the reforms were bitterly contested and the liberal parliamentary majority had to argue its case, paragraph by paragraph, in the face of determined resistance from the Prussian bureaucracy. But the results seemed to confirm the advantages of a single-chamber parliament (although the Bundesrat was able to block some initiatives, such as the complete abolition of the death penalty). Klaus Pollmann has argued that reform legislation developed a dynamism seldom seen outside of revolutionary situations.[43] Indeed, since most of the participants were convinced that standing still would be synonymous with going backwards, the North German Confederation rapidly developed its own momentum, becoming much more than simply Bismarck's creation. Bismarck obviously could not be personally involved in all the details of the domestic legislation agreed upon at this time and he was prepared to leave many matters to Delbrück. He interfered most when the interests of landowners, artisans and small businessmen were affected, the traditional social groups upon whom his conception of Prussia rested. He also always regretted how the fiscal arrangements made during this period gave a powerful weapon to the Reichstag, thus linking new taxation to further constitutional changes, but he was never able to reverse these decisions.

Nevertheless, Bismarck worked so hard during this period that he frequently suffered from exhaustion and ill-health. 'I am "used up",' he complained to Kathy Orlov in May 1868; 'I spend 12 hours in bed without resting and the work which formerly gripped me from time to time is repugnant to me, exercise as well.'[44] He had to take protracted periods of leave – more than five months in each of the years 1868 and 1869 – and his usual symptoms (migraines, neuralgia, rheumatism, gout and digestive disorders) were aggravated by breaking three ribs after a fall from his horse in 1868. Such absences often fell at very awkward times for his subordinates, and they were also frequently exploited by his ministerial colleagues to their own advantage.

Bismarck's relations with the Prussian ministers deteriorated again from 1867, not least because his collaboration with the liberals in parliament indicated how out of tune he really was with men whose political convictions had largely been conditioned by the constitutional conflict.

Bismarck continued to resent and despise many of the ministers who had worked with him from 1862, especially when they opposed him in the ministry of state, did not want to see Prussia merged into Germany and felt their influence was being 'completely paralysed by the chancellor's office'.[45] In particular, he clashed with his conservative colleagues over the methods by which the newly annexed territories should be integrated into Prussia. Bismarck advocated a more flexible and decentralised system of administration than the ministers were intent on putting into effect, and he saw no advantage in alienating the new provinces (or the south Germans) by pursuing determined policies of Prussianisation.[46] He also clashed with the ministers (and conservative parliamentarians) over their opposition to allowing the province of Hanover control over its deposed government's financial assets. But he could not easily remove recalcitrant ministers, being stymied by the king's control of personnel appointments as well as his recognition that it would be 'a farce' to threaten resignation over such issues when he had no intention of surrendering power and could name no suitable successor.[47]

One advantage of his new basis of parliamentary support, however, was that he was now more able and willing to exploit parliamentary pressure to effect the fall of an inconvenient colleague. In 1867 Bismarck managed to secure the resignation of Lippe, the minister of justice, who had hounded Twesten and thus been on the receiving end of liberal parliamentary attacks. He was replaced by the former Hanoverian minister and president of the Prussian superior court of appeals, Gerhard Leonhardt. In October 1869 Bismarck succeeded again in using parliament to remove Heydt as minister of finance as a result of his handling of a financial crisis in Prussia. Heydt had continued to enjoy the king's confidence and had even been featuring in Bismarck's dreams in September 1869.[48] Bismarck welcomed his liberal successor, Otto Camphausen, but he also wanted to ensure that the new minister occupied a less powerful position than his predecessor. Otherwise, however, the composition of the Prussian government survived the upheavals of 1866–67 unscathed. Bismarck continued to live with uncongenial ministers and, exacting and mistrustful, he often preferred to shoulder most of the responsibility alone. Only after the creation of the Reich was Bismarck able to remove other conservative ministers he despised, namely Mühler, Selchow and Itzenplitz, replacing them with men who were much more ready to work with the liberals in parliament. Roon survived in office until 1873 but even he had his differences with Bismarck, for example threatening to resign over the new federal status to be accorded to the Prussian navy in 1869.[49] Eulenburg, too, managed to remain as minister of interior until 1878, by which time he was the only member of the government apart from Bismarck who had served during the constitutional conflict. In 1869 Bismarck wrote that he had no political need to remove Eulenburg because he was as soft as wax. But he also complained that he was a poor worker with no organisational ability whose presence undermined the government, and he implied that it was his freemasonry which kept him in royal favour.[50]

Bismarck was out of tune with his colleagues because he was more ready than they were to embrace change. He has been seen as a 'reluctant reformer' from 1867, but this is to underestimate his supreme creativity during this period and the extent to which he personally had a vested interest in making the new mechanisms work. He sought to mobilise support from the most dynamic and articulate sections of society for the monarchy and ensure its survival rested on a broader social basis; he also wanted to safeguard Prussia's security in perpetuity by ensuring that the relationships he forged with the lesser German states would strengthen rather than undermine it. In that sense he can be seen as using radical means to achieve conservative ends or being a 'white revolutionary' as Lothar Gall has called him. In August 1866 Bismarck himself famously told Manteuffel, 'If there is to be revolution, we would prefer to make it than to suffer it.'[51] But the idea of a controlled 'revolution from above' need not detract from what was innovative and even progressive in Bismarck's policy. Bismarck was never the arch-conservative reactionary his liberal opponents made him out to be.

Recent work has, in particular, highlighted the significance of the great leap he took into the unknown by supporting a national parliament elected by universal male suffrage.[52] By the standards of the time, an equal, direct and democratic franchise was a very bold, indeed revolutionary step and few countries in Europe could boast the kind of free and fair elections the German public came to expect. For all the weaknesses of the Reichstag in its relationship with the executive before 1914, the impact of a national parliament and regular elections – held every three years until the 1890s – was immense. If judged in terms of outcomes rather than motives, Bismarck's achievements (as later his social policies) were scarcely less progressive than if they had been implemented by his adversaries; indeed, it is hard to imagine that a liberal government would have been ready in 1866 to accept a franchise for a national parliament without any property or wealth qualifications. Moderate liberals could not always say so openly, but they were never keen on direct and equal universal suffrage and, in securing the secret ballot, they were concerned to forestall the manipulation of the masses for conservative purposes as evidenced by Napoleon III. Margaret Lavinia Anderson's research has confirmed that 'Bismarck's democratic franchise, however improbable its Minerva-like birth, did not preclude democratization but encouraged it.'[53] If imperial Germany became a 'partly democratic country'[54] before 1914, Bismarck's role must be acknowledged.

The goal of national unity: relations with the south

From 1866, when he exploited the national idea to legitimise the expansion of Prussia into northern Germany, Bismarck was committed to completing the unification of a lesser Germany under Prussian leadership which excluded Austria. For diplomatic reasons the river Main had to represent the limit of Prussian ambitions in 1866. Yet as early as August 1866, back in Berlin, Bismarck openly told a confidant of the grand duke of Baden (who was married to Wilhelm I's daughter) that the union of the north and south was merely 'a matter of time' and that in the meantime Prussia was ready to take any step which might prepare the way for unification without provoking its French neighbour. 'In the event of war against France the Main barrier will immediately be broken through and the whole of Germany will be drawn into the struggle, if national opinion in the south wants to make this possible.' When Württemberg's war minister asked him how long the period of transition for the south might be, Bismarck replied 'Perhaps six weeks, perhaps three years'.[55] In asserting that unification might come about in six weeks, Bismarck was clearly still mindful of the possibility of a war against France in 1866. By the end of the year he was more cautious about the prospects of unification in the near future. As one observer remarked, the difficulties in establishing the North German Confederation and in incorporating the annexed territories in Prussia had left no time for anything else, and in Berlin one met only impatient, overworked and ill-tempered individuals who were happy that they did not have yet more issues to deal with.[56]

Once the North German Confederation was established, with constitutional arrangements which anticipated the eventual accession of the south German states, Bismarck hoped that the elected Reichstag would serve to have an integrative function and provide a focus for national life north and south of the river Main. Bismarck did not suddenly become a German nationalist in 1866, but his new alliance with those forces in society which supported the goal of national unification lent a degree of urgency to forging closer links between the North German Confederation and the south German states. Even so, he could not foresee that the political incorporation of the south would be achieved by 1871. In 1868 he remarked that it would be great if Germany were to achieve its national goal in the nineteenth century and it would be extraordinary, an unexpected gift from God, if that could be achieved within ten or even five years.[57]

Without the protection of the old German Confederation, the south German states were inevitably forced to cooperate with their powerful neighbour to the north. Baden actively sought entry into the North German Confederation after 1866, only to be rebuffed by Bismarck who did not wish to alienate France and believed the pro-Prussian state might render greater services to the national cause if it remained outside for the time being. In January 1867, Prince Wilhelm of Baden exploited the opportunity of a hunt to discuss military and political matters with Wilhelm I, Roon and Bismarck and he was told that they saw Baden as the bridge to a rapprochement with the south, especially with Bavaria.[58] Yet although Bismarck gave the impression that he wanted a united Germany in the future, he also indicated, much to the disappointment of the grand duke, that he did not intend to spearhead a nationalist offensive to achieve unification against the south. Without a resolute lead from Prussia, the grand duke did not believe that south Germany would be ready voluntarily to make the sacrifices necessary for unity.[59] Baden thus faced an uncertain future, keen to see German unification under Prussian leadership but receiving little public support from Prussia and also denied stable, friendly relations with its southern neighbours.

While long aware of the utility a war against the traditional enemy, France, might have in cementing relations between the German states, Bismarck hoped in 1867 that there could be a peaceful evolution towards a united Germany and that a nationalist war could be avoided. Napoleon III, having done so much to promote the national cause in Italy, could scarcely pit himself against the national principle if unity was clearly willed by the German people. However, in working to complete national unification under Prussian leadership, Bismarck did not only have to contend with the European powers but also with perhaps his most determined opponents, south German particularists and democrats. He was very quickly to be disabused of the idea that there could be a peaceful evolution towards unification, for south Germans revealed themselves to be hostile to any form of 'takeover' by the North German Confederation and bitter critics of what they described as the new system of Prussian 'militarism'.

Even before the war of 1866 Prussia's economic domination of the southern German states through the *Zollverein* had tended to make them even more determined to defend their political independence against all forms of 'Prussification'. Political hegemony was not a necessary consequence of economic hegemony, and the revelation during the Luxemburg crisis in March 1867 that the south German governments had concluded irrevocable or 'eternal' offensive–defensive treaties with the north, placing them under Prussian command in the event of war, only bolstered the determination of the south Germans, especially in Bavaria and Württemberg, to safeguard their political independence. Conditions in the south German states were highly complex in the aftermath of their defeat in 1866. Economic problems and the need to institute higher taxation (since the states had no financial reserves) were blamed on Prussia by the wider population. Much-needed internal reforms which were introduced between 1866 and 1870 were also seen as Prussian-inspired, especially since they required compromises between governments and liberal parliamentary majorities (until 1868), also now tainted by being 'pro-Prussian'. Heterogeneous groupings of south German democrats, particularists and supporters of political Catholicism (now mobilising to the north of the Main too) were forged into a more cohesive oppositional movement on the basis of anti-Prussianism and played on the economic insecurities of a largely agrarian population which came to believe that any form of union with the north would do lasting damage to their economic interests. In 1869 Landtag elections in Bavaria and Württemberg produced majorities opposed to liberalism and a small German unification. The North German Confederation was seen as synonymous with increased taxation, militarism and a repressive authoritarianism.

Bismarck, however, was able to bring considerable pressure to bear on the south German states after 1866 and, while he could not remain indifferent to the anti-Prussian drift of their domestic politics (with the exception of Baden), he exploited both the international situation after 1866 and the disunity between the south German states themselves to further his aims. He understood how to play off Baden's fears of being dominated by Bavaria and Württemberg to scupper plans for greater cooperation between them. He also benefited from his personal acquaintance with south German leaders, some of whom he had known since his Frankfurt days, and he knew how to exploit their strengths and weaknesses. He intervened in south German politics through the press and by means of paid agents and journalists in order to get his voice heard and emphasise Prussia's new role as the champion of the nation. And, above all, he heightened their fears of French ambitions, using the threat of French territorial compensation, military negotiations between

France and Austria or, indeed, the prospect of war to provide Prussia with leverage over them.

It was never inevitable, however, that at some stage the south German states would join the North German Confederation, and it has been pointed out that Bismarck the *Realpolitiker*, whose reputation has since become so closely associated with his role in founding the '*Bismarckreich*', would have been satisfied with a different organisational framework if the result had been to bring the south into a wider, looser association with the North German Confederation.[60] Bismarck was not completely averse to the formation of a southern union or *Südbund*, such as had been mooted at Nikolsburg in 1866. But, although it has been claimed that such a union was realisable, ultimately, without the benefit of force, there was no way the south German states could agree on a *Südbund* with a common parliament after 1866, especially since both Baden and Württemberg feared that it would be dominated by Bavaria. Thus in his attempt to achieve 'the removal of the existing', which he saw as the hardest part of national reconstruction,[61] Bismarck placed his hopes in reforming the *Zollverein*. He aimed to give it an institutional structure which would not only create an 'economic community' for the whole of Germany but could also further political cooperation between the north and the south.

Before 1866 the *Zollverein* had been unable to develop any political ambitions because of the existence of the German Confederation. In seeking now to push it in a new direction, Bismarck was able to bring Prussian pressure to bear on its member states, not least because many of them had fought against Prussia in the war of 1866 and there was now a need to incorporate new territory, above all Schleswig-Holstein. He supported the creation of a *Zollparlament* (customs parliament) and *Zollbundesrat* (council of government delegates), both of which met in Berlin and were composed of the same membership as the Reichstag and Bundesrat of the new North German Confederation but with added representation from the south German states. By such means he hoped to foster a more organic grafting of south Germany with its new northern neighbour.

The elections to the *Zollparlament* were conducted in February and March 1868 on the basis of direct and equal male suffrage, but the results in south Germany proved highly disappointing for Bismarck. Even in Baden, where the government and liberal parliamentary majority favoured political unification, the population chose to use the elections to express its political hostility to incorporation into the North German Confederation and the particularists gained six of the fourteen seats.

Only in Hesse-Darmstadt, peculiarly straddling the Main line, was there clear support for the national cause. The majority of new south German deputies who travelled to Berlin for the first meeting of the new parliament in April 1868 were thus committed to opposing any political ambitions the *Zollverein* might have – only 35 out of 85 southern deputies were pro-Prussian national liberals[62] – and, for Bismarck, whose policy depended on the great powers accepting the popular legitimacy of German unification, the elections were manifestly counter-productive. He never again put the issue to the vote in the south of Germany. Nor was the *Zollparlament* amenable to his wishes, for Prussian conservatives joined with south German democrats and particularists to block any attempt to extend the competence of the *Zollverein*. Bismarck soon lost interest in the parliament (which was liquidated in 1871 when its legislative powers were taken over by the Reichstag) and he returned to more traditional diplomatic channels to seek the fulfilment of his aims.

Although progress was made in reforming the armed forces of the southern states in accordance with the Prussian model and developing a coordinated plan of mobilisation in the event of war, Bismarck met with few tangible successes in his efforts to achieve the peaceful political integration of the south into a Prussian-led Germany before 1870 and his policy offered little comfort to disappointed German nationalists whose hopes had been raised by the events of 1866. The grand duke of Baden repeatedly expressed his disillusionment with Bismarck's policy, writing in September 1867 that he could see no political leadership in the German question, 'only a hesitant groping and feeling of one's way'. Berlin, he claimed in December, was not sufficiently serious about the issue. 'They would indeed like to rule, but do not want to do the work which is necessary to lead a nation benevolently.'[63] Exasperation mounted in Baden in 1868, with complaints in leadership circles about Prussian pusillanimity and indecisiveness in Berlin. Roggenbach complained about Bismarck's 'distance from affairs'. He believed Bismarck 'has the feeling that he has embarked on something that is impossible to execute and yet does not want to admit this'.[64] By April 1869 Grand Duke Friedrich was bemoaning the fate of Germany, concerned that time was running out for them and that they had no control of events. He suggested that Bismarck had lost the heroic feeling of certainty which he had derived from his earlier successes and which had facilitated his domination of the king. Now Bismarck no longer instilled confidence in his skill and resolve 'for instead of the calm, determined will there is an irritable sensitivity which expresses its force only in a nervous agitation which sets in the moment everything does not go according to [his] wishes. Now people are saying that if something is to be achieved, then Bismarck must resign for he cannot endure such agitation and hence there is only the choice of doing his bidding or letting him go to Varzin.'[65] This situation also troubled Wilhelm I who privately complained to his confidants about his difficulties in dealing with the chancellor. Characteristic of Bismarck's behaviour was his insistence on the dismissal of the diplomat Guido von Usedom who, as minister in Florence in 1866, had contravened his instructions, and his threat to resign in February 1869 if Wilhelm continued to accept advice from others.[66] Wilhelm told his daughter that Bismarck no longer tolerated any contradiction and that many matters could not even be discussed.[67]

From 1869 the situation in the south German states became critical, calling their constitutions into question and indicating that there was virtually no popular basis for Bismarck's policy in the south. The danger existed that the governments in the south would be forced by the changed relationships in their parliaments to repeal some of the reform legislation they had introduced since 1866. In Baden, too, the pro-Prussian outlook of the government left the state apparently exposed and isolated; its future looked bleak after Bismarck rebuffed an interpellation by the National Liberal politician, Eduard Lasker, in the Reichstag in February 1870 about the prospects of Baden joining the North German Confederation. Liberals in the North German Confederation were becoming increasingly impatient at the slow progress made towards unification and Bismarck resented their interference in foreign policy in this way, fearing too that by being forced to speak publicly on the issue, he might lose the support of pro-Prussian elements in Baden. In Bavaria and Württemberg, parliamentary opposition crystallised around the issues of the military constitution and military budget, and the deterioration in Franco-Prussian relations from the spring of 1870 lent a new urgency to discussions about the nature of the military treaties with the north, branded by the particularist Patriotic Party in Bavaria (which had an absolute majority in parliament by the end of 1869) as 'subjugation treaties'.[68] Bismarck, alive to the dangers of the debate in the Bavarian Landtag, used the semi-official newspaper, the *Norddeutsche Allgemeine Zeitung*, as well as the usual diplomatic channels to bring pressure to bear on Bavaria. He indicated that Prussia would accept the dissolution of the military alliance if an ultramontane Bavarian government insisted upon this; but at the same time he suggested that, in the event of a conflict threatening Bavaria's security, Prussia would then be able to dictate its terms. Moreover, as the military treaty and the customs treaty had been ratified together by the North German Confederation, Bismarck intimated that the customs treaty would also be dissolved if Bavaria went down this path.

Ultimately the south German states were only brought into a political union with the North German Confederation by the outbreak of war against the traditional enemy, France. Bavaria and Württemberg especially went to war in 1870 out of self-interest rather than because they believed in the national cause. If they remained neutral they believed they would be sacrificed in the peace negotiations with France. Honouring their treaty obligations may also have been construed as a way of escaping from their domestic difficulties. Either way, political calculation was to the fore rather than a sense of obligation to the German nation, and their governments underestimated the emotional consequences of war and victory, and failed to allow for the impact of popular demands for unification in 1870. By contrast, Bismarck had a clear conception of what he wanted to achieve and, in negotiating with the representatives of the south German states in Versailles in October and November 1870 about the shape of the future national union, he once again demonstrated his tactical skill and flexibility, as well as a willingness to resort to intrigue and bribery if it served his political purpose. The south German states lost their final chance to form a *Südbund*, and Bismarck effectively played them off against each other, negotiating with them individually. Only Baden joined the North German Confederation with any real national enthusiasm. Bavaria and Württemberg once again calculated that only through cooperating with Prussia could they preserve a maximum degree of autonomy.

The Franco-Prussian war

Bismarck's hopes that German unity might evolve over time were thwarted by developments in the south German states between 1866 and 1870, but there is no evidence that he planned a war of aggression against France. In February 1869 he called German unity an 'unripe fruit'[69] and it is clear that from 1866 he pursued several paths, keeping his options open and always ensuring that alternative courses of action were possible. He was aware that a war against the traditional enemy would be the most effective means of igniting German nationalism (or universal fear of France) but he may well have hoped that mere friction with France would further the cause of national unification, as was evident in the Luxemburg crisis of 1867. Even in 1870 his interest in the Hohenzollern candidacy for the Spanish throne, the issue which eventually led to the

Franco-Prussian war, was motivated by its potential to cause complications with France. Bismarck may have come to see a war against France as an unavoidable necessity by 1870 but at no stage was he prepared to launch a war in which Prussia would be seen as the aggressor. Nor could he have calculated for the blunders in French diplomacy which eventually led to the declaration of war.

Bismarck had raised the temperature very high during the Luxemburg crisis in the spring of 1867 but it is unlikely that he wished to precipitate a war. Prussian control over northern Germany in 1866 had signified the limits of what could be achieved without French intervention, and Napoleon III was subsequently keen to secure territorial compensation for a restructuring of central Europe which, whatever the reality, was perceived as inimical to French interests. His hopes to acquire Luxemburg, a member of the former, now defunct German Confederation, met with an outcry of public hostility when Bismarck let the matter become known. Bismarck had done little to dissuade Napoleon from pursuing his designs on Luxemburg and had encouraged him to negotiate directly with King Wilhelm III of the Netherlands, with which the duchy was bound in a personal union. But at the height of the crisis he deliberately posed as a statesman driven by the will of the nation which was outraged by French ambitions to annex this 'German' territory. As well as publishing the texts of the treaties with the south German states as a warning to Napoleon III, he stirred up anti-French sentiment in the press and in the Reichstag. Eventually the Luxemburg crisis was resolved at an international conference in London where the duchy was granted independent status and it was agreed that Prussia should withdraw its troops from the former federal fortress there. But even if Bismarck did not deliberately seek a war, there was a real possibility that war could have broken out over the issue. In May 1867 Bismarck wrote to Kathy Orlov in Brussels that he was convinced he would see her again in the summer: 'if God wants us to have war, it must at least start near the Belgian frontiers and I will pay you a visit in order to enjoy for a moment the benefit of Belgian neutrality'. But he hoped with all his heart that peace would be preserved and that he could spend a day in Brussels on a different pretext, albeit one that would mystify the public and cause him as much internal merriment as his 'political trips to Biarritz'.[70]

As in 1866, however, Bismarck could not have failed to be aware of the favourable military and diplomatic situation in 1870 which ensured that France was likely to be isolated in any confrontation. The fact that the three wars of German unification occurred within a single decade says as much about the European context as it does about Bismarck's personal diplomacy. Just as Bismarck was able to forestall a European peace congress to determine the new arrangements after the Austro-Prussian war in 1866, so he was able to exploit successfully the disunity among the European powers between 1866 and 1870 to prevent the formation of an anti-Prussian coalition and ensure that France would eventually go to war without allies. Napoleon III's diplomacy, which was often muddled and inconsistent and never proved a match for Bismarck's, became more anti-Prussian after 1867 as he sought to block any further expansion of Prussian power. He explored the possibilities of an Austro-French alliance with Baron Friedrich Ferdinand von Beust, the former Saxon minister who had become Austrian foreign minister after 1866 and was bitterly anti-Prussian. But German liberals in Austria were unenthusiastic about a rapprochement with France and, although a treaty was drafted in 1869, it was never signed. Austria, hampered by its internal problems, preferred to remain neutral and wait on events in 1870. Similarly Britain did not regard the issue of German unity as necessitating intervention in 1870 and was only belatedly concerned over the peace terms imposed on France by Prussia; and Italy was not prepared to assist France while French troops still occupied the papal city of Rome. Bismarck had for a long time held out to the Russians the prospect of Prussian support for the repeal of the Black Sea clauses of the Treaty of Paris which had ended the Crimean War in 1856. Russia in due course exploited the Franco-Prussian war to denounce the demilitarisation clauses, causing Bismarck some anxiety about foreign intervention before the matter was regulated at a conference in London in early 1871. Nevertheless, Gorchakov proved he was a loyal friend in 1870 and effectively scuppered British proposals for international mediation in favour of a more lenient peace at the end of the Franco-Prussian war. In effect, then, the breakdown of the international state system after the Crimean War continued to favour the resolution of the German question by means of war. The disunity of the European powers ensured that they were eventually confronted with a *fait accompli* in 1870–71, even if few of their leaders anticipated how rapidly a united Germany would develop into the foremost military and economic power on the continent. Moreover, even if nationalism did not play the role in German unification once ascribed to it, the desire to create a German nation-state was increasingly seen as a legitimate cause even outside Germany. French foreign policy continued to arouse far greater mistrust and suspicion among the other powers of Europe than Bismarck's wish to consolidate Prussia's hold over southern Germany, which was seen as a limited and acceptable aim.

The origins of the war of 1870 can be traced to the issue of the succession to the Spanish throne and whether the French could tolerate a Hohenzollern prince as king of Spain. In 1868 the Spanish military had deposed the Spanish Queen Isabella, and Prince Leopold of Hohenzollern-Sigmaringen, who was married to a Portuguese princess, was seen as a suitable candidate to fill the vacancy. Even at this early stage in October 1868 Bismarck had recognised the value of 'the Spanish question' in causing friction with France and had told the Foreign Ministry that 'a solution acceptable to Napoleon III would scarcely be the useful one for us'.[71] From February 1870 Bismarck was eager to support the candidacy of Prince Leopold and exploit its potential for conflict with France, even though Wilhelm I was opposed to his claim and made his views clear in a crown council meeting in March. Nevertheless Bismarck worked quietly behind the scenes to advance Leopold's cause, recognising the potential to humiliate France, and eventually achieved the consent of both Leopold (whose father had also objected to his candidacy) and Wilhelm in June 1870. Throughout his manoeuvres Bismarck insisted that the issue was purely a dynastic one which had no significance for international relations and in which he himself had played no role. But the French never believed Bismarck's official stance of non-involvement and immediately blamed Berlin when news of Leopold's acceptance became known.

Much controversy has surrounded the issue of Bismarck's role and intentions in 1870, but the issue of war guilt has ultimately been seen as something of a red herring.[72] Although Bismarck clearly wanted to extract the maximum capital from the Spanish question for his national policy and regarded a war in the near future against France as 'an unavoidable necessity' by the spring of 1870,[73] he was never rigid in his approach to problems and he certainly did not want war under any circumstances. Indeed, it was imperative that if such a war arose, Prussia should not be seen as the aggressor, both from the point of view of securing the participation in the war of the south German states and in order to deter foreign powers from intervention. In the July crisis which erupted when news of the candidature became known, Bismarck deliberately acted with restraint, allowing a new and inexperienced French government to make a catalogue of errors, committing itself in public to securing overambitious goals. On 6 July Antoine Agénor, Duc de Gramont, the new French foreign minister, spoke threateningly in the French parliament, pledging the government to prevent Leopold's accession to 'the throne of Charles V' and thereby exposing it to the possibility of public humiliation. He also instructed the French ambassador, Benedetti, to speak to Wilhelm I about the matter at Bad Ems. Bismarck, consistent in his official view that the succession was a dynastic issue, allowed the French to deal directly with the Prussian king; and Wilhelm acted independently in the crisis, adopting a conciliatory line and eventually agreeing that Leopold should renounce the Spanish throne. This was clearly a diplomatic victory for the French, but they then famously overreached themselves. In demanding that the Prussian king should agree never again to support the candidature, the French presented Bismarck with the opportunity to rebuff them publicly. Bismarck received the famous 'Ems dispatch' informing him of the king's conversation with Benedetti and he immediately published an edited version on 13 July, implying that the king had snubbed France's unreasonable demands. France promptly issued the order for mobilisation on 14 July. Returning to Berlin from Bad Ems five days later, Wilhelm I was greeted by patriotic crowds at every station. He discussed the situation *en route* with his son, Bismarck, Roon and Moltke, and he called a council meeting for the next day. But they had scarcely set foot in the royal palace in Berlin when Bismarck opened a telegram informing him that the French had declared war.[74]

Thus, as one detailed study concluded, the war was not the product of reasoned long-term policy and the decision to take up arms was made by the French government.[75] But ultimately neither side held back in 1870 and Bismarck, who felt under increasing pressure to act on the national question, recognised the favourable diplomatic and military situation. The French appeared the aggressors, even the south Germans had been outraged by Gramont's speech and the subsequent treatment of the Prussian king, and the Prussian army was ready with coordinated plans worked out with its south German allies in accordance with their military obligations. On 14 July the Bavarian *chargé d'affaires* in Berlin reported that all initiated circles regarded war as unavoidable and that there was a strange mood of satisfaction not only in the officer corps, which was confident of victory, but also in the Foreign Office. 'Especially Bismarck, as Herr von Thile himself indicated to me, is said to feel "completely in his element".'[76]

Prussia's victory over France in 1870 was dramatic, although Geoffrey Wawro has recently asserted that, as in the previous wars of unification, its opponents had 'splendid opportunities' and only lost because of the 'bitter resistance of companies of Prussian infantry with their guns'.[77] The Germans won a series of opening battles and France's main army was surrounded in the fortress of Metz. The army of Patrice Maurice de MacMahon, which was sent to relieve Metz, was resoundingly defeated by the armies of Crown Prince Friedrich of Prussia and Crown Prince

Albert of Saxony on 1 September at Sedan. Falling back to the fortress of Sedan, it was surrounded and capitulated on 2 September. Napoleon III, and his army of 104,000 men, became prisoners of war, and Sedan entered the popular memory in Germany as the day when not merely the German military had triumphed over the traditional enemy but also German civilisation and the German spirit had proved their worth on a world stage. But despite the defeat of the French army and the capture of Napoleon III, the war dragged on for many more weeks before peace could finally be signed with a new republican government and the people of France were finally defeated. After taking Strassbourg and Metz, the Prussian army found itself confronted with a long siege of Paris, now controlled by a 'government of national defence'; and the struggle assumed the character of an increasingly brutal *Volkskrieg* as French *francs-tireurs* were responsible for a growing number of casualties among the German occupying forces. Eberhard Kolb has emphasised Bismarck's skill and determination in extricating Prussia from a new and unprecedented kind of warfare in 1871. Focused on achieving a political settlement, he seized a sudden opportunity to end the war at the end of January 1871 and did everything he could in a highly complex situation to facilitate the difficult task of Adolphe Thiers and the French negotiators.[78] After some hard bargaining, a provisional peace was signed at the end of February 1871 which stipulated the main terms of a settlement. The final treaty of Frankfurt was only concluded in May 1871 after the French government's forces had crushed the revolutionary Paris commune and restored order throughout the country.

For Bismarck, too, the war was of a different character from that of 1866. First and foremost, it involved his two sons, endangering both their lives. Bill's horse was shot from under him and a bullet went through Herbert's left leg, requiring a long period of convalescence. Bismarck instructed his sons to telegraph him at the king's headquarters immediately if either of them was wounded and on no account to let their mother know first.[79] But at one point he was wrongly informed that Herbert had been killed and Bill was mortally injured and he took off to find them.[80] But even without his family's involvement and the anxieties that this entailed, the Franco-Prussian war aroused different emotions in Bismarck from the fratricidal war against Austria. Already in July 1870, the views he expressed to Moritz Busch, his press officer in the Foreign Office, were vitriolic about the French, and Bismarck stated them in all consciousness that they were intended for publication. He told Busch, 'The French are not the fine people they are usually considered to be. As a nation they resemble certain people in our lower classes. They are narrow-minded and brutal – physically strong and loud-mouthed and impudent and especially through their bold, violent behaviour [*Auftreten*] they gain the admiration of people like them.' He complained about France's boastful politicians, who wanted to control everybody, and about the French nation's bigoted political views. 'They have no idea how things look outside France, learn nothing about it in their schools. Hence also their conceit and overestimation of their own abilities.' Gramont, Bismarck retorted, was no better than 'a blockhead' and Napoleon III's policy had always been stupid. 'The Italian people are much more gifted than the French, only weaker in numbers.'[81] Bismarck's hatred and contempt for 'such a stupid nation as the French'[82] surfaced repeatedly, especially as his exasperation and fury increased over the duration of the war. However, immediately after Sedan and a 'difficult' conversation with Napoleon III in a poor workman's house by the roadside before the former emperor was dispatched to Wilhelmshöhe near Kassel, his tone was more sober. 'It is a great event in world history, a triumph for which we will thank God the Lord in humility, and which decides the war even if we also still have to continue the latter against France without her emperor',[83] he wrote to Johanna on 3 September.

Bismarck also encountered more difficulties during the Franco-Prussian war in working with the military, and although he eventually emerged as the victor in the struggle, the underlying problem of the dualism between military and civilian authority in Prussia and the new Germany remained unresolved. Bismarck increasingly found his authority challenged by Prussia's military leaders (the 'demi-gods' as he called them in his memoirs[84]) who enjoyed growing popularity and prestige in their own right and who sought to prevent him from interfering in military decision-making. Bismarck had accompanied the invasion of France with a small staff of colleagues from the Foreign Office. This staff (which included Keudell, Busch and another valued subordinate, Heinrich Abeken, who had drafted the original Ems dispatch) was at the centre of political decision-making in the autumn of 1870, dealing with all issues relating to the accession of the south German states to the North German Confederation and the founding of the German Reich. But Bismarck soon found he had to rely on military communiqués in the press for information about the progress of the war. He also complained that the king listened to the generals too much in political matters; this invariably meant that Wilhelm could not come to a speedy decision and opportunities were lost.[85] Frictions with Moltke and the military leadership were inevitable as Bismarck resented and resisted his exclusion from such a vital area of decision-making. He clashed with the army leaders over how

Napoleon III was to be treated after his capture, insisting that 'a well-treated Napoleon is useful to us and that is my sole concern'.[86] On 12 September he also wrote to Johanna about 'the unbelievable pig-headedness and departmental jealousy of the military', maintaining that if he had had to work with such a confusion of departments in the civil administration, he would have exploded like a grenade long ago.[87] Particularly after witnessing the heroism and bravery of the German infantry despite its appalling losses and the senselessness of cavalry attacks, he complained about the military leadership's readiness to squander 'the best soldiers in Europe', although he exempted Moltke from this criticism.[88] After Sedan he was increasingly critical of the military's conduct of the war even if his consciousness of his civilian status sometimes made him uncharacteristically reticent about voicing his opinions.[89] Bismarck favoured a brutal intensification of the war in late 1870, urging that fewer French prisoners be taken and that the enemy should be annihilated on the battlefield. When there was no speedy military resolution, he suspected 'an intrigue spun by women, archbishops and scholars' and wrote to Johanna that everyone was blaming anonymous impediments.[90] He sought to avoid the protracted 'war of extermination' advocated by Moltke, who wanted to occupy the whole of France and starve the Parisians into submission.[91] His insistence on the priority of a political settlement with Paris in January 1871 to forestall foreign intervention thus represented a significant victory. Although the two men settled their personal differences, it was probably not accidental that Moltke later wrote a popular history of the Franco-Prussian war which did not mention Bismarck even once.[92]

If Bismarck's authority was ultimately not undermined by these conflicts, it was generally because he was supported, albeit sometimes grudgingly, by Wilhelm I. But from the moment he arrived in Mainz on 2 August 1870, Bismarck complained how difficult it was for him to keep in close proximity to the king. He and his officials found they often had to give way to German princes and their entourages who had come along as spectators, and Bismarck had difficulty maintaining contact even with his own staff if they were quartered some distance away. In November 1870 he expressed his belief that the king was being deceived. He mistrusted the entire general staff 'apart from the good and clever old Moltke' whose name was used as a cover for others, and he insisted it was the regiments which had won the war, not the generals.[93] Bismarck felt politically and emotionally isolated during the war. He was only able to confide in Roon and was away from home for virtually six months, based for the most part at Versailles until he finally departed on 6 March 1871.

Musing about how even political success brought envy and hate in its wake and how one made no new friends to replace those who died or distanced themselves, he became increasingly conscious of the loneliness of high office. 'In short I am freezing emotionally and I long to be with you, alone together in the country', he wrote to Johanna. 'No one can bear this courtly life for any length of time.'[94] After the Franco-Prussian war, Bismarck was never again enticed by foreign travel. He preferred to remain on German soil and the furthest he travelled was to Bad Gastein and Vienna.

Bismarck's concern to avoid foreign intervention in the war became even more urgent in the light of the controversial Prussian decision to annex the two French provinces of Alsace and Lorraine in the wake of Prussia's victory. No longer did Prussia's aims appear so limited and acceptable, and much controversy has surrounded Bismarck's role in supporting a move which not only served to prolong the war but also led to implacable French resentment in the years leading up to the First World War. The evidence suggests that the decision was taken in principle at a 'war council', a meeting between Wilhelm I and his military leaders at which Bismarck exceptionally was present, in the village of Herny in Lorraine on 14 August 1870.[95] Although no irrevocable decision was made, Bismarck made an oral presentation to the king and a consensus was reached that Alsace would be kept after the war was over and that it would not be annexed to Prussia or divided between the south German states. Bismarck appears to have supported this policy freely and independently and was not unduly influenced by the military or by the growing clamour for annexation in the nationalist press. Rather, he emphasised strategic considerations, wishing to enhance Germany's security by incorporating the fortresses of Metz and Strassburg, and he reckoned on French enmity in any case. In August 1870 he wrote that the French had been bitter after the Prussian victory at Sadowa and would be even more bitter after their own defeat. 'In these circumstances the only correct policy is to make an enemy who one cannot turn into an honest friend at least a little more harmless and secure ourselves more against him.'[96] Bismarck perhaps could not have foreseen the future strength of the new German Reich or the relative decline of its previously powerful neighbour, and he undoubtedly wished to weaken France and forestall France's resurgence. He disregarded the French nationality of the majority of the inhabitants of Lorraine and, since this new war aim led to a change of attitude among the foreign powers, he sought to emphasise the vulnerability of south Germany to French attack and to mobilise public opinion to support the 'national' cause of annexation. He also told Crown Prince Albert of Saxony that the annexation of the two provinces, which would become a 'Reichsland', owned by the whole of Germany, would help to forge a closer relationship between north and south.[97] Perhaps as important as all these rational calculations, however, was a more antiquated code of honour, according to which Prussia, as the wounded party, was entitled to compensation for the sacrifices it had made. Bismarck had only with difficulty dissuaded Wilhelm I from this course in 1866 and he probably knew he would have little chance of success in the circumstances of 1870–71 even if he had wanted France to suffer no territorial losses.[98] The annexation was thus decided upon by the middle of August 1870 and, along with the indemnity of 5,000 million gold marks France had to pay, it prolonged the war and soured Franco-German relations for a generation. Placed under a civilian governor-general, the new Reich territory of Alsace-Lorraine was to be entitled to elect fifteen deputies to the new national Reichstag but it had no constitution until 1911 and no full representative in the Bundesrat. Volker Ullrich has described the decision to annex the French provinces as 'a severe mistake, perhaps the severest in Bismarck's career overall'.[99]

The most dramatic result of the Franco-Prussian war, however, was of course the proclamation of the new German Empire or Reich from Versailles on 18 January 1871, the anniversary of the day on which the first Prussian king had been crowned in 1701. From the moment the war against France was launched it was clear that the south German states, bound to honour their treaty obligations, could not continue to enjoy the independent status that had been left to them since 1866. The issue for them was, rather, whether they could gain any special concessions in return for agreeing to accede to the North German Confederation. Once again, Bismarck negotiated with their representatives separately at Versailles in October and November 1870 and, through a potent cocktail of diplomatic intrigue, superficial concessions and corruption – he notoriously bribed the Bavarian king, Ludwig II, with 300,000 marks a year from the secret Hanoverian Guelph fund until 1886 – he managed to achieve their accession with a minimum of constitutional changes. Baden and the southern part of Hesse-Darmstadt were first to agree to become part of the North German Confederation; Württemberg and Bavaria agreed to join the political union by the end of November 1870. Clearly it was deemed important to negotiate the entry of the southern states at the theatre of war in a climate of enthusiasm and euphoria over the victorious outcome. Bismarck was also aided by National Liberal politicians who had an interest in monitoring the mood in the southern states, and he called key party leaders in the Reichstag (Bennigsen, Blanckenburg and Rudolf Friedenthal of the Free Conservatives) to Versailles to reach an understanding with them prior to the negotiations with the states.

Bismarck was pragmatic in his negotiations with the south German states and reassured them with concessions to federalism and particularism, many of which, however, proved subsequently to be illusory. The Bundesrat's powers were strengthened and it was given the right to approve a declaration of war in the event that the new Reich was not attacked. It was agreed that fourteen votes in the Bundesrat would be sufficient to block constitutional changes, ensuring that the southern states together could veto proposals which would strengthen the unitary or parliamentary features of the new Reich. Special rights and privileges were granted to Baden, Württemberg and, above all, Bavaria with respect to the organisation of their military contingents, their tax rights and communications. Bavaria was also to preside over a special diplomatic committee in the Bundesrat. Bismarck was happy to strengthen federal arrangements in the new Reich, especially if these proved a counterweight to the centralising ambitions of the liberal majority in the Reichstag. He did not, however, agree to the territorial changes sought by Bavaria, which coveted the Baden Palatinate. Bismarck found it hardest to negotiate with Bavaria and he complained to the grand duke of Baden that they sent three ministers to Versailles, each of whom spoke differently, so that he could never ascertain the definitive view of its government.[100] But his approach was generally gentle and persuasive rather than demanding and coercive, much to the chagrin of the crown prince who believed Bismarck should have been less yielding.[101] Other liberal nationalists, too, were critical of what they saw as his unduly negative approach.[102] But Bismarck was cautious and reserved in the negotiations in late 1870, often prepared to let others make the running and avoid what could be construed as overt pressure on the southern states. Unity was to appear as a gift bestowed by the south rather than imposed by Prussia even if the actual power relationships told a different story.

The new Reich was essentially a union of princes rather than a state formed according to the will of the German people, as had been envisaged in 1848. The Reichstag of the North German Confederation, which would have preferred a new, all-German parliament to revise the constitution in late 1870, accepted the changes Bismarck had negotiated on 9 December 1870. Legally the German Reich came into being on 1 January 1871, although it was some weeks before the Reich constitution was formally approved by the newly constituted Bundesrat and national Reichstag (elected in March 1871) in April 1871. The Bavarian king, in a letter which Bismarck had drafted, was induced to 'offer' the imperial title to the Prussian king on behalf of the princes of Germany. Wilhelm I bitterly resisted assuming the title of Kaiser or emperor, sensing that it would somehow sever his links with the old Prussia. But Bismarck, who had raised the Kaiser question with the crown prince as early as January 1870 in connection with a change in the designation of the Prussian Foreign Ministry to that of Foreign Office, insisted upon it. The resurrection of the old nomenclature 'Kaiser and Reich' had the support of the crown prince, and Wilhelm, little suspecting Bismarck's hand in it, could not refuse such an offer made by the Bavarian king. The old and venerated imperial title was seen as a symbol of integration and national unity which would also underline the significance of the new political edifice as a confederation of sovereign monarchs rather than a Greater Prussia. As early as August 1870 it was recognised that Bavaria 'will probably subordinate herself to the Kaiser of Germany but not to the king of Prussia as head of the federation'.[103] Even so, the Prussian king would have preferred to have been called 'Kaiser of Germany', a title which was deemed by Bismarck to be unacceptable because of its implied territorial claim, rather than 'German Kaiser', the formulation which was eventually proclaimed. Uncertainty remained over the Kaiser title right up to the proclamation of the new Reich before an audience of princes, diplomats, courtiers and military men (but, significantly, no delegation from the Reichstag of the North German Confederation) in a very cold Hall of Mirrors at Versailles on 18 January 1871. The mood at the ceremony was depressed rather than elated and Bismarck, himself in an irritable mood, wrote to Johanna that the Kaiser had had a difficult birth. 'As the *accoucheur* I felt several times an urgent need to be a bomb and to explode so that the whole edifice would be blown to pieces.'[104]

The arrangements for the new Reich were largely in accordance with what Bismarck wanted and the 'Iron Chancellor' could now reasonably claim yet another new appellation as the *Reichsgründer* or 'founder of the Reich'. His position and authority were secured in the new power structure, but in theory if not in practice under Wilhelm I, he remained dependent on a king whose power he had immeasurably increased. Bismarck had now reached the height of his achievements and received formal recognition of his services to the Prussian monarchy and the cause of German unity through his elevation to the status of a prince and a royal gift in the form of the Sachsenwald near Hamburg. Once again, however, the experience of war in 1870 had chastened Bismarck and he never chose to savour his moment of triumph. Admonishing Johanna from Versailles in October 1870 for her petty complaints about minor matters, he insisted that he had seen too many corpses and cripples, too much unacknowledged heroism, to feel anything other than relief that they had emerged from the war with both their sons alive and in possession of all four limbs.[105] While his subordinates extolled his indefatigable creativity and his superhuman ability to find the right solutions during this period, Bismarck knew that his hardest work was still to come.

Notes

1 See Oncken, II, Gelzer to Grand Duke Friedrich, 20 August 1866, p. 23.

2 See GW, XII, speech of 3 December 1884, p. 519.

3 Cited in Steglich, I, p. xli.

4 Zimmer, *Bismarcks Kampf*, p. 65.

5 Ibid., p. 66.

6 Geoffrey Wawro, *The Austro-Prussian War: Austria's War with Prussia and Italy in 1866* (Cambridge, 1996), p. 284.

7 Wolfgang Venohr, 'Helmuth von Moltke', in S. Haffner and W. Venohr (eds), *Preußische Profile* (Berlin, 1998), p. 131.

8 See especially Wawro, *The Austro-Prussian War*, pp. 57–65.

9 Lutz, *Zwischen Habsburg und Preußen*, p. 460.

10 Steven Beller, *Francis Joseph* (London, 1996), pp. 89–91.

11 Rothfels, Bismarck to Katharina Orlov, 29 June 1866, pp. 326–7.

12 Ibid., Bismarck to Johanna, 2 July 1866, p. 327.

13 Ibid., Bismarck to Johanna, 11 July 1866, p. 328.

14 Stern, *Gold and Iron*, pp. 87–8.

15 GW, VII, conversation with Count Seherr-Thoss, 8 July 1866, p. 140.

16 See Lutz, *Zwischen Habsburg und Preußen*, p. 462.

17 Rothfels, Bismarck to Johanna, 9 July 1866, p. 328.

18 Steglich, II, Wilhelm I to Augusta, 24 July 1866, p. 324.

19 Rothfels, Bismarck to Emma Metzler, 7 March 1867, pp. 331–2.

20 Steglich, II, Wilhelm I to Augusta, 24 July 1866, p. 323.

21 Rothfels, Bismarck to Bill Bismarck, 1 August 1866, p. 330.

22 Steglich, II, Wilhelm I to Augusta, 20 July 1866, p. 310.

23 Bismarck, *Gedanken und Erinnerungen*, p. 332.

24 Steglich, II, Augusta to Wilhelm I, 23 July 1866, p. 321.

25 Ibid., Wilhelm I to Augusta, 24 July 1866, p. 324.

26 Lutz, *Zwischen Habsburg und Preußen*, p. 471.

27 GW, VI, Bismarck to Goltz, 10 August 1866, p. 117.

28 Hermann von Wartensleben-Carow, *Ein Lebensbild 1826–1921* (Berlin, 1923), p. 32. Cited in Zimmer, *Bismarcks Kampf*, p. 126.

29 Cited in Volker Ullrich, *Otto von Bismarck* (Reinbek bei Hamburg, 1998), p. 78.

30 Cited in Gall, I, p. 309.

31 Steglich, II, Friedrich Wilhelm to Augusta, 29 July 1866, p. 34; Oncken, II, Gelzer to Grand Duke Friedrich, 14 August 1866, p. 20.

32 See Pflanze, I, pp. 332–4.

33 See Hans-Joachim Schoeps, *Der Weg ins deutsche Kaiserreich* (Frankfurt, 1970), p. 127.

34 On the origins of the constitution, see especially Becker, *Bismarcks Ringen*, pp. 211 ff.; Kaernbach, *Bismarcks Konzept*, pp. 215–37. See also Studt, *Lothar Bucher*, pp. 261–4.

35 Oncken, II, Gelzer to Grand Duke Friedrich, 23 December 1866, p. 31.

36 Cited in Franz Herre, *Bismarck: Der Preußische Deutsche* (Munich, 1998), p. 237.

37 Rothfels, Bismarck to Roon, 27 August 1869, p. 347.

38 Cited in Pflanze, II, p. 131.

39 Ibid., I, p. 350.

40 GW, VI, Putbus *Diktat*, 30 October 1866, p. 167.

41 See Pflanze, I, pp. 362–3 and Craig, *Politics of the Prussian Army*, p. 226.

42 Engelberg, I, p. 675.

43 Klaus Erich Pollmann, 'Modernisierung als kontrolliertes Risiko: Bismarcks Verfassungspolitik 1866–1871', in Kunisch, *Bismarck und seine Zeit*, p. 111.

44 Rothfels, Bismarck to Katharina Orlov, 11 May 1868, p. 338.

45 Cited in Pflanze, II, p. 140.

46 See Heide Barmeyer, 'Bismarck zwischen preußischer und nationaldeutscher Politik', in Kunisch, *Bismarck und seine Zeit*, pp. 38–55.

47 Rothfels, Bismarck to Alexander von Below-Hohendorff, 25 February 1869, p. 342.

48 Ibid., Bismarck to Josephine von Seydewitz, 4 September 1869, p. 351; see Pflanze, I, pp. 418–22, and II, pp. 142–3.

49 Rothfels, Bismarck to Roon, 27 August 1869, pp. 346–9.

50 Rothfels, Bismarck to Alexander von Below-Hohendorf, 25 February 1869, p. 343.

51 GW, VI, Bismarck to Manteuffel, 11 August 1866, p. 120.

52 See Margaret Lavinia Anderson, *Practicing Democracy: Elections and Political Culture in Imperial Germany* (Princeton, NJ, 2000). See also Stanley Suval, *Electoral Politics in Wilhelmine Germany* (Chapel Hill, 1985) and Jonathan Sperber, *The Kaiser's Voters: Electors and Elections in Imperial Germany* (Cambridge, 1997).

53 Anderson, *Practicing Democracy*, p. 21.

54 H.A. Winkler, *Weimar 1918–1933: Die Geschichte der ersten deutschen Demokratie* (Munich, 1993), p. 601. See also Anderson, *Practicing Democracy*, p. 400.

55 Oncken, II, Gelzer to Grand Duke Friedrich, 20 August 1866, p. 25.

56 Ibid., Grand Duke Friedrich to Gelzer, 23 December 1866, p. 32.

57 GW, VII, conversation with Suckow, 11 May 1868, p. 259.

58 Oncken, II, Prince Wilhelm to Grand Duke Friedrich, 21 January 1867, p. 41.

59 See ibid., Grand Duke Friedrich to Prince Wilhelm of Baden, 10 February 1867, p. 36.

60 Wolf D. Gruner, 'Bismarck, die Süddeutschen Staaten, das Ende des Deutschen Bundes und die Gründung des preußisch-kleindeutschen Reiches 1862–1871', in Dülffer and Hübner, *Otto von Bismarck*, p. 81.

61 See Pflanze, I, p. 400.

62 See Engelberg, I, p. 704.

63 Oncken, II, Grand Duke Friedrich to Gelzer, 2 September 1867, p. 101, and 21 December 1867, p. 109.

64 Ibid., Grand Duke Friedrich to Gelzer, 1 November 1868, p. 116.

65 Ibid., Grand Duke Friedrich to Gelzer, 4 April 1869, p. 119.

66 See Pflanze, I, p. 428.

67 Oncken, II, Grand Duke Friedrich to Gelzer, 4 April 1869, p. 120.

68 Gruner, 'Bismarck', p. 66, also for following.

69 GW, VI/II, Bismarck to Werther, 26 February 1869, p. 2.

70 Rothfels, Bismarck to Katharina Orlov, 1 May 1867, p. 333.

71 GW, VI/I, Bismarck to Foreign Office, 3 October 1868, p. 412.

72 For a useful discussion of the historiography, see Carr, *Wars of German Unification*, pp. 178–83.

73 Cited in J. Becker, 'Zum Problem der Bismarckschen Politik in der spanischen Thronfrage 1870', *Historische Zeitschrift*, 212 (1970), p. 591.

74 See Ernst Deuerlein (ed.), *Die Gründung des deutschen Reiches 1870/71 in Augenzeugenberichten* (Munich, paperback edition, 1977), p. 41.

75 Lawrence D. Steefel, *Bismarck, the Hohenzollern Candidacy, and the Origins of the Franco-German War of 1870* (Cambridge, Mass., 1962), p. 221.

76 Rudolf von Tautphoeus to Otto von Bray-Steinburg, 14 July 1870, cited in Deuerlein, *Die Gründung des deutschen Reiches*, p. 40.

77 See Wawro's review of Arden Bucholz, *Moltke and the German Wars 1864–1871* (Basingstoke, 2001) in *German History*, vol. 20, no. 4 (2002), pp. 532–3.

78 See Eberhard Kolb, *Der Weg aus dem Krieg: Bismarcks Politik im Krieg und die Friedensanbahnung 1870/71* (Munich, 1989), especially pp. 358–64.

79 Herbert Bismarck, *Love Letters*, Bismarck to Herbert, 6 August 1870, p. 185.

80 Rothfels, Bismarck to Johanna, 17 August 1870, pp. 358–9.

81 Busch, *Tagebuchblätter*, I, 24 July 1870, pp. 50–1.

82 Herbert Bismarck, *Love Letters*, Bismarck to Johanna, 30 August 1870, p. 188.

83 Rothfels, Bismarck to Johanna, 3 September 1870, p. 360.

84 Bismarck, *Gedanken und Erinnerungen*, p. 369.

85 Oncken, II, *Tagebuch von Versailles*, 9 [November 1870], p. 160.

86 Rothfels, Bismarck to Herbert, 23 September 1870, p. 361.

87 GW, XIV, Bismarck to Johanna, 12 September 1870, p. 792.

88 Rothfels, Bismarck to Johanna, 17 August 1870, p. 359.

89 Ibid., Bismarck to Johanna, 7 December 1870, p. 367

90 Ibid., Bismarck to Johanna, 28/9 October 1870, p. 364.

91 See Stig Förster, 'The Prussian Triangle of Leadership in the Face of a People's War: A Reassessment of the Conflict between Bismarck and Moltke 1870–71', in S. Förster and J. Nagler (eds), *On the Road to Total War: The American Civil War and the German Wars of Unification 1861–71* (Cambridge, 1997), pp. 115–40.

92 See Schoeps, *Bismarck*, p. 130; Helmut von Moltke, *Geschichte des deutsch-französischen Krieges von 1870/71* (Berlin, 1890–91).

93 Rothfels, Bismarck to Johanna, 22 November 1870, p. 366.

94 Ibid., Bismarck to Johanna, 7 December 1870, p. 368.

95 See Eberhard Kolb, 'Der Kriegsrat zu Herny am 14 August 1870', in E. Kolb, *Umbrüche deutscher Geschichte, 1866/7 1918/9 1929/33: Ausgewählte Aufsätze*, ed. D. Langewiesche and K. Schönhoren (Munich 1993), pp. 95–105.

96 Cited in Eberhard Kolb, *Der Weg aus dem Krieg: Bismarcks Politik im Krieg*, p. 160.

97 See Deuerlein, *Gründung des deutschen Reiches*, p. 85.

98 See Wilhelm's remarks to Augusta, 29 August 1870, and Bismarck's *Erlaß* of 25 August ibid., pp. 88–9.

99 Ullrich, *Bismarck*, p. 93.

100 Oncken, II, *Tagebuch von Versailles*, 13 [November] 1870, p. 174.

101 Ibid., 17 November 1870, p. 182. See also Patricia Kollander, *Frederick III: Germany's Liberal Emperor* (Westport, Conn., 1995), p. 95.

102 Oncken II, Grand Duke Friedrich to Jolly, 16 August 1870, p. 133.

103 Ibid., Grand Duke Friedrich to Jolly, 29 August 1870, p. 130.

104 Rothfels, Bismarck to Johanna, 21 January 1871, p. 369.

105 Ibid., Bismarck to Johanna, 8 October 1870, p. 362.

Chapter 5

Consolidating Power

From 1871 Bismarck had to work within a very different political environment from that which had existed prior to Prussia's unification of Germany. As the *Reichsgründer*, he now carried a major burden of responsibility for the consolidation of the new Reich's institutions. Indeed, throughout the nineteen years he remained in power, the main thrust of his domestic and foreign policy was to preserve what he had achieved in his first years in office. Yet his new role did not come easily to him and in many ways the task that confronted him ill-suited his personality. Not a consensual politician, he chafed against the numerous, new restrictions on his freedom to decide and act. Constrained by the Prussian and imperial constitutions, he was now obliged to work with parliamentary majorities as well as serve the interests of the crown. Bismarck increasingly found that he was a prisoner of the institutional system he had devised and his frustration manifested itself in prolonged absences from Berlin and a deleterious effect on his health. No longer able to take swift and decisive action to shape events and create new possibilities, Bismarck often saw no way forward other than to fortify his own position.

In a wider sense, too, the world in which Bismarck had to operate after 1871 was a very different and increasingly alien place. The process of unification helped to release powerful new forces in Germany and Europe which gathered a momentum of their own and proved well beyond Bismarck's capacity to dominate and control. Internally the early 1870s or '*Gründerjahre*' (founding years) were a period of intense economic activity culminating in the collapse of the boom in the so-called 'Great Crash' of 1873. After 1873 the pace slowed but Germany nevertheless experienced sustained economic growth right up to 1914. The rapid industrialisation of a united Germany was perhaps the most significant development in the era before the First World War and had dramatic implications for German society even in the Bismarckian era. Germany's startling demographic and urban growth, the emergence of new social classes and decline of older, more traditional ways of life, and the rise of new political challenges to the established order all impinged on Bismarck's position at the fulcrum of the new political system. The chancellor's diplomatic freedom of manoeuvre was also curtailed. No longer the minister-president of a relatively junior state in the international system, Bismarck now presided over a powerful and dynamic empire in the centre of Europe. Bismarck's Reich was widely perceived to have the most efficient army on the continent and to constitute, if it so chose, a significant threat to its neighbours.

Controlling the executive

'I demand very little,' Bismarck insisted in 1874. 'I require only two things: that I am understood and obeyed!'[1] Bismarck's essential author-itarianism is not in doubt nor is his aspiration to enjoy the prerogatives of autocratic power. Contemporaries and some historians have claimed that he wielded so much power during his period in office that he came to exercise a 'chancellor dictatorship'. He ensured that his iron grip extended over all aspects of foreign and domestic policy and that no colleagues or subordinates placed any significant obstacles in the way of his indomitable will. Recent historiography has also highlighted the allegedly 'Bonapartist' or 'charismatic' features of his rule and how these underpinned what Hans-Ulrich Wehler called 'the neo-absolutist, pseudo-constitutional dictatorship of the chancellor'.[2] It has been argued that Bismarck not only utilised power in the service of outmoded social forces but that he also incorporated pseudo-democratic, populist and plebiscitary elements into his system of government, anticipating more modern forms of political rule and manipulation.[3]

Yet did Bismarck really enjoy dictatorial power between 1871 and 1890? Bismarck's prestige and authority were so great after 1871 that they have tended to obscure many of the theoretical and practical limita-tions to his position within the political system. He himself clearly felt constrained by all kinds of factors. His dependence on the monarch's confidence, the theoretical sovereignty of the states, the need to secure parliamentary majorities, the collegial nature of the Prussian govern-ment, the political independence of the army and the significance of the court as a centre for political intrigue all imposed limits on his freedom of action. Certainly, too, the notion that he was some kind of dictator would have surprised a man who repeatedly expressed his frustration that his will was thwarted, who never appeared satisfied with the balance of institutions he had created and who persistently sought to improvise and experiment with new ones. Bismarck frequently threatened to resign in order to get his way, bitterly complained about his political isolation and, throughout his long incumbency, often found himself unable to achieve his immediate political objectives. Indeed, his main aims, the internal consolidation of the Reich and its security within a stable international system, were never satisfactorily achieved. The wisdom of his policies was always contested, in the ruling elite (where the crown prince served as a focus for opposition for most of Bismarck's chancellorship) as well as in the parliaments, and Bismarck was eventually forced against his will to surrender power.

From 1871 Bismarck faced a task of enormous political complexity. He had to devote his energies to consolidating the political institutions of the new Reich, while at the same time charting its political course in internal and international politics and simultaneously fostering a new conception of German nationhood. Moreover, already in the 1870s the pivotal role of the chancellor appeared to require superhuman skills and talents. Bismarck was simultaneously Reich chancellor, Prussian minister-president, Prussian foreign minister and president of the Bundesrat. He had to coordinate the affairs of the Reich and Prussian executives, work with two diversely constituted parliaments, retain the confidence of the Kaiser and German princes, ensure the smooth functioning of the Bundesrat and oversee Germany's diplomatic relations with the other European powers. Yet, as early as 1872, doubts were being expressed in Berlin political circles about whether Bismarck as chancellor had the requisite political skills and personal qualities to foster the successful evolution of the new state's political institutions. Impatient, demanding and energetic, Bismarck had never taken much interest in the routine work of the Berlin bureaucracy or even in many aspects of domestic policy unless they ran counter to his political or material interests. Moreover, as the minister-president of Baden, Julius Jolly, observed, Bismarck was a pragmatic, intuitive politician whose methods were unfamiliar to the majority of politicised Germans who adhered to a particular ideological outlook and sought to perfect a system.[4] Bismarck preferred to act in accordance with the needs of the moment and advance whatever arguments and policies best suited his immediate purposes. Thus it was not always obvious even to Bismarck himself where he was heading. The inconsistencies in Bismarck's public pronouncements and the shifting nature of his politics have also widened the scope for diverse historical interpretations.

What is clear, however, is that, whatever the difficulties he faced, Bismarck instinctively sought to buttress his own power. His preferred policies and solutions were always simultaneously calculated to reinforce his own position. The evolution of imperial Germany's political system and the extent to which it proved capable of adapting to the dramatic social and economic transformation of Germany in the decades after unification were thus closely connected to Bismarck's pursuit of his own power interests. While the problems Germany encountered on the path to political modernisation cannot all be blamed on Bismarck's personality, he certainly bears much of the responsibility for the defective government machine that his successors inherited after 1890.

Bismarck's potential to exercise autocratic rule after 1871 was far more marked in the Reich than in Prussia. In the Reich, as in the North German Confederation, Bismarck was the only federal or German minister. Appointed by the Kaiser and legally responsible to the Reichstag, his position was not constrained by the presence of cabinet colleagues. Moreover, as early as 1871, the theoretical sovereignty of the Bundesrat – its claim to be the centre of decision-making in imperial Germany – was recognised to be a farce.[5] Its legislative role was problematical enough, with a deluge of bills, carefully prepared in the Prussian ministries, piling up for approval towards the end of the Reichstag sessions. Individual plenipotentiaries to the Bundesrat had not the time, information or expertise to comment on legislation and they were often instructed by their governments to 'vote with the majority' since there could be no real discussion and it was rarely expedient to oppose Prussia's power. Yet the claim that the Bundesrat was the real centre of decision-making in imperial Germany was even more risible. Denied access to information and lacking an executive, it could be no more than a fig-leaf for Prussian domination despite its ostentatious ceremony. How far Bismarck connived in this situation is questionable. He was sensitive to the power realities in the new Reich, masterful in his handling of the individual states and often mindful not to injure the vanity of even the smallest member of the federation. Moreover, he always recognised the crucial importance of the Bundesrat's position in protecting the rights of the states (above all Prussia's) and blocking liberal ambitions to centralise and parliamentarise the Reich. Not indifferent to its fate, Bismarck threatened to resign in order to achieve a reform of the Bundesrat's procedures in 1880, which he believed would enhance its effectiveness as well as protect his own position.[6] In 1884 he again tried to increase the power of the Bundesrat and devise a more collective leadership of Reich affairs, motivated by the need to safeguard his authority at a time when the monarchical succession appeared imminent. However, the institution was flawed from its inception and lacked any real potential to develop.

It was the *Reichskanzleramt* or Reich Chancellor's Office which, in the first years of the Reich, appeared to accrue the most power. But in the 1870s Bismarck was prepared in practice to delegate much of imperial German domestic policy to Rudolf Delbrück, who headed the *Reichskanzleramt* and was in effect vice-chancellor. Delbrück had previously directed a department in the Prussian Ministry of Trade and been an expert on the *Zollverein* before he became president of the *Bundeskanzleramt* in 1867. Bismarck later admitted in the Reichstag how much he had depended on Delbrück to oversee domestic policy between 1867 and 1876 when he himself had been more preoccupied with foreign policy.[7] Delbrück's willingness to assume much of the responsibility for domestic policy facilitated the chancellor's frequent absences from Berlin. Bismarck took extensive periods of leave at Varzin, a practice which became a habit and increased his reliance on a handful of trusted subordinates and officials to carry out his instructions. He stayed away from the capital between May and December in 1872, in the second half of 1875 and for ten months from April 1877. However, Bismarck was frequently confronted on his return to Berlin with unwelcome *faits accomplis*, for his control in the 1870s was far from perfect. Tellingly, too, Bismarck came to believe that Delbrück was wielding too much power and that he demonstrated too great a propensity for initiative and independence. Bismarck eventually viewed Delbrück as a rival whose personality was imprinted on all the affairs of his office. The president of the *Reichskanzleramt* was also closely associated with a liberal course in imperial domestic politics and, by the middle of the 1870s, Bismarck wanted to reduce the administration's dependence on parliamentary liberalism.

Bismarck thus manoeuvred Delbrück out of office in 1876, replacing him with Karl von Hofmann and instituting a more decentralised administration of Reich affairs under his personal leadership. His aim was to consolidate his personal control over the Reich executive and in 1877–78 a series of Reich offices was created in conformity with Bismarck's wishes, each under a state secretary who was subordinate to the Reich chancellor. Unlike the Foreign Office, which enjoyed a separate status, the new Reich offices communicated with him through a small personal secretariat, the Reich Chancellery, which was situated in Bismarck's official residence in the Wilhelmstrasse. The Reich Chancellery was headed from 1878 by Christoph von Tiedemann and initially comprised merely three officials. This system ensured that there would be a minimum of consultation and discussion between the different Reich departments, and that Bismarck personally would retain overall control. (It also, however, exposed the fiction that one man could be responsible for all imperial affairs – as suggested by Article 17 of the constitution – and ensured that the Reich chancellor's right of countersignature could be delegated to individual state secretaries or to a single deputy or vice-chancellor.) At his parliamentary soirées Bismarck misleadingly referred to the new Reich offices as 'ministries', undoubtedly to confuse liberals who wished to see this innovation. But his real motive was clear. As he told the Württemberg ambassador, Hermann von Mittnacht, as early as August 1875, the machine had become too powerful and too much had been concentrated in the *Reichskanzleramt* rather than in the Reich chancellor, 'who must remain the solely responsible top leader'.[8]

By the close of the 1870s Bismarck's leadership over the Reich executive was effectively unchallenged. As well as the Foreign Office, there were now seven Reich agencies which dealt with imperial domestic affairs (the Reich Office of Interior, the Reich Office of Justice, the Reich Treasury, the Reich Railway Office, the Reich Post and Telegraph Office, the Admiralty and the Reich Chancellery for Alsace-Lorraine). But there was no collective government, a minimum of political discussion and consultation, and all final decisions rested with Bismarck. Only with respect to personnel matters was the chancellor's will sometimes thwarted because of the Kaiser's prerogative in this sphere. Bismarck was extremely unhappy that Albrecht von Stosch remained chief of the Reich Admiralty from its creation in 1872 until 1883. Stosch, who was also a Prussian minister without portfolio, was directly responsible to the Kaiser with respect to naval command matters but responsible to the chancellor in his administrative functions. He also enjoyed close relations with the crown prince and his wife, and was suspected by Bismarck of intriguing to head a future liberal 'Gladstonian cabinet'. Yet despite his best efforts, including a public attack on Stosch in the Reichstag on 10 March 1877 (when he accused him of a dereliction of duty as Admiralty chief),[9] Bismarck failed to oust him because of Wilhelm I's consistent personal support.

Bismarck's power and authority as German Reich chancellor depended crucially on his position as Prussian minister-president and Prussian foreign minister. Technically it was only in his capacity as Prussian foreign minister that he could instruct the Prussian votes in the Bundesrat. Moreover the confidence of the states and the Reichstag in his leadership largely derived from the recognition that he also spoke for Prussia, the largest and most significant state in the union. Bismarck, however, did not enjoy any of the trappings of autocratic rule in Prussia, where the constitution had been left untouched by the process of unification. And in the 1870s he continued to grapple with the task of asserting his authority over the Prussian ministers, some of whom had fought alongside him in the constitutional struggle while others were more liberal, supporting his collaboration with the National Liberals in the parliaments since 1867.

Bismarck found himself at odds with conservative ministers in the 1870s over his campaign to reconstruct the relationship between Church and state in the *Kulturkampf* (which will be discussed below), as well as over reforms aimed at streamlining local government and transforming the *Herrenhaus*. In early 1872 he proved able to remove the *Kultusminister*, Heinrich von Mühler, who had defended clerical influence in schools. But his hopes of removing the minister of interior, Friedrich zu Eulenburg, after the defeat of the local government bill in the *Herrenhaus* in October 1872 were frustrated. Ultra-conservatives in the *Herrenhaus* had opposed the bill because it involved the abolition of landowners' remaining police powers.[10] Eulenburg, however, who had been in post since 1862, secured the subsequent approval of the Prussian state ministry and Wilhelm I to an amended version of the reform while Bismarck was in Varzin. He also persuaded the king to agree to create twenty-four reliable new peers and thus got the reform through both houses of the Prussian Landtag in December 1872. He remained in office until 1878.

The issue of social reform was another area where Bismarck found himself out of tune with some of his colleagues, conservatives as well as those of a more liberal orientation, who opposed state intervention in the economy. The minister of trade, Itzenplitz, another minister he had 'inherited' in 1862, eventually truckled to Bismarck's will and drew up proposals for social welfare legislation in March 1873, but this did not prevent him from being forced to resign three months later. His successor, Heinrich von Achenbach, was more sympathetic to Bismarck's ideas on the social question, but he too incurred Bismarck's wrath after he drafted a factory act with Delbrück's successor, Hofmann, in 1877. An outraged Bismarck called a halt to the proceedings from Varzin, claiming he had found out about the initiative 'by accident', that there had been no discussion in the Prussian ministry of state and that the bill constituted an intolerable interference in private enterprise. As Otto Pflanze has shown, his bitterness arose from the fact that his own paper factories at Varzin were inspected for the first time in July 1877 in accordance with instructions issued by Achenbach's ministry and a number of deficiencies were found.[11]

Bismarck also had his political disagreements with his old friend, the war minister, Roon. From 1867 until his resignation in November 1873 Roon supported the idea of creating a Reich war minister with the right of countersignature, analogous to his position as Prussian war minister. Bismarck successfully resisted Roon's pressure, refusing to surrender his personal authority in this area, even though the existing system of military administration was very imperfect. Thus Prussian military matters were handled by the Prussian war minister directly with the king while imperial military matters went through the Reich chancellor to the Kaiser as Supreme War Lord. Bismarck refused to support a change that might have led to the creation of a collegial Reich cabinet and would have reduced his own power. Roon was also among the ministers who opposed the local government reform and, outvoted in the Prussian ministry of state in 1872, both he and the minister of agriculture, Selchow, expressed their intention to resign. Bismarck was content to see Selchow go (although his proposal of Blanckenburg as his successor was blocked by the king). But he was extremely reluctant to agree to the departure of Roon. Instead, he announced his intention to concentrate on Reich affairs and stepped down as Prussian minister-president in December 1872 so that Roon could become his successor as premier.

Bismarck's willingness to experiment with a division of powers proved an interesting but short-lived episode in 1872–73. Roon, who was twelve years older than Bismarck, was an undistinguished minister-president who was no match for liberal attacks in the Prussian Landtag and resigned in October 1873. Bismarck recalled in 1892, 'Roon was the most capable of my colleagues. But he could not work with others. He treated them like a regiment under his command. They complained about this and I had to take over the state ministry again.'[12] More significantly, Bismarck's justification for his decision to give up the minister-presidency clearly demonstrated that he did not yet fully appreciate how the new political system worked or his own place within it. He dismissed the Prussian minister-presidency as an 'honorific' position, believed that by separating the office from his role as Reich chancellor he might relieve his burden of work, and argued that he would thereby accentuate the German character of the chancellorship.[13] As he later acknowledged, he thereby underestimated the extent to which his influence as chancellor was rooted in the power he wielded in Prussia. He also experienced no reduction in his workload since he continued to be Prussian foreign minister, and was thus still obliged to participate in meetings of the state ministry and be bound by the collegial nature of its decisions.

Bismarck's relations with the Prussian ministers in the 1870s were thus complicated by his multiple roles and also strained by the need to harmonise Prussian policy with the needs of the Reich. Never an easy man to work with, Bismarck became more critical and intolerant of his ministerial colleagues after 1871. By 1875 he was looking for ways to remove several ministers, including Achenbach, the minister of trade, Adalbert Falk, the *Kultusminister*, and Otto Camphausen, the minister of finance. Bismarck had supported Camphausen's promotion to vice-president of the state ministry in 1873 (another experiment in reducing the burdens of office) but he soon saw him as exerting too dominant an influence in the Prussian ministry of state. In addition, Bismarck complained that the ministers had no creative ideas, although this did not stop him from meddling in their departments and quashing their initiatives. He charged each of them in turn with contradictory offences which usually included lassitude, independence, perfidy, cowardice, incompetence and obstructionism. He also talked spitefully to others about them and displayed contempt for them on a number of occasions in the parliaments. In March 1877 he even told the Reichstag that he was the only Prussian minister who supported the interests of the Reich and that if no progress was made, this was because his ministerial colleagues could not agree. 'Friction behind the scenes ... takes up three quarters of my time', he asserted, not without a measure of self-pity.[14] Such revelations were often greeted with disbelief and dismay in the parliaments. They reinforced the impression that the chancellor did not have the temperament to engage positively and constructively in domestic affairs.

Bismarck frequently looked for ways of easing the burden of high office in the early 1870s. But none of his attempts to do so were successful, and their failure reinforced his belief in his own indispensability. The only occasion when he appears to have seriously considered resigning from all his offices was in May 1875 after a series of political misjudgements. Beset by health problems, Bismarck was most humiliated by the 'War in Sight crisis', which damaged his hitherto unshaken reputation for diplomatic competence. After a protracted period of political indecision in early 1875, he offered his resignation to Wilhelm I in May. There is some evidence that the proposal was sincere (unlike his later, successive threats) and, if it had been carried out, it would undoubtedly have changed dramatically historical assessments of his political career. But instead Bismarck withdrew to Varzin for six months where he ruminated over how he could best organise the administration of the Reich, tame the Reichstag and consolidate his personal power.

From 1875 Bismarck's response to political difficulties was invariably to seek methods of buttressing his personal position. He made several attempts to increase his personal control over the Prussian ministry of state in the late 1870s, but it was not until after 1881 that his authority within the executive was unquestioned. Despite protests from colleagues such as Camphausen, he tried appointing state secretaries, who were his subordinates in the Reich administration, to the state ministry as ministers without portfolio as a way of securing his dominance. Both Hofmann and Bernhard Ernst von Bülow, the state secretary of the Foreign Office from 1873, were appointed Prussian ministers in the late 1870s, an initiative which attracted notice not least because neither man was from Prussia (Hofmann came from Hesse and Bülow from Mecklenburg). It was clearly impossible for such men to vote against Bismarck in the Prussian ministry of state and simultaneously carry out his will in the Reich executive. But even with their support Bismarck still found his proposals could be rejected in the state ministry. Bismarck also considered the far more radical course of appointing heads of Reich offices as ministers *with* portfolio, unifying the Reich and Prussian executives and subordinating both to the chancellor. If the Prussian ministers were more involved in Reich affairs, he calculated, this might overcome their Prussian particularism and secure a new degree of cooperation and subordination.[15]

The coordination of two separate yet parallel and connected executives in Berlin was bound to be a major challenge even to Bismarck's ingenuity. The Reich was still in its infancy and its constitutional arrangements could never facilitate a streamlined system of government. Bismarck always anticipated that the political system would have to evolve over time. Yet in altering the balance between them, first in one direction and then in another, he was clearly experimenting with his new creation, seeking the solution most likely to maximise his own power without jeopardising Prussia's relations with the lesser German states or furthering the unitary ambitions of the Reichstag. By 1879 Bismarck had changed his mind again and was no longer convinced that the best solution was to create 'personal unions' between the Prussian ministries and Reich offices. Opposed by the Prussian Landtag and the federal states, he once again sought to strengthen the Reich executive at the expense of Prussia.

Never consistent in his arguments and explanations, he shifted uncomfortably from one experiment to the next, unable to find a satisfactory and durable structure and ultimately appearing only consistent in his drive to increase his own power and authority. As Roggenbach observed in January 1878, the changes in the power structure were designed to satisfy the chancellor's changing power instincts.[16] Yet at times Bismarck appeared baffled by the complexity of his own creation and his apparent impotence within it. In March 1878 he complained to the Prussian Lower House about his inability to make progress in nationalising the German railways, a measure he had supported since 1875 and which he hoped would provide a new source of income for the Reich. 'I had the agreement in principle of my colleagues; I had the agreement in principle of the entire Landtag; and yet, although minister-president I found myself absolutely unable to bring the matter one step further along,' he confessed. 'Agreement does not help me at all when passive resistance – from what direction in this complicated machine is impossible to learn – is conducted with such success that I am scarcely in a position after two to three years to answer even the most basic questions.'[17]

Bismarck's belief that his orders were being sabotaged 'from within' encouraged him to take further measures to discipline the bureaucracy in the 1870s, a policy that was reinforced by the *Kulturkampf* which led to the targeting of Catholic officials who were branded by liberals as Jesuits and 'ultramontanes'. While this policy affected the provincial administration more than the Berlin administration (for discrimination ensured that few Catholics progressed to the highest echelons of state service), it also meant that Bismarck encountered entrenched resistance within the bureaucracy when he sought to re-establish confessional peace in the 1880s. Bismarck demanded high standards of discipline and subordination from his officials, no longer merely selecting men according to talent but also in accordance with their responsiveness to his will. At ministerial level this meant that it became progressively more difficult to find suitable candidates for high office who were prepared to work alongside him, a situation which was compounded by the narrowness of the bureaucratic recruitment pool and the growing recognition that ministers also required parliamentary skills. Bismarck was prepared to consider competent men from outside the usual bureaucratic channels. In 1877 he offered the Prussian Ministry of Interior and vice-chancellorship to Rudolf von Bennigsen, the National Liberal leader, a move which he calculated would secure National Liberal support and strengthen the executive. But the further demands of the National Liberal leadership as well as the doubts of Wilhelm I ensured that the parliamentarian never attained high office.

Between 1878 and 1881 Bismarck presided over a succession of ministerial changes in the executive, changes which affected all the Prussian ministries with the exception of the War Ministry (where Roon's successor, General Georg von Kameke, survived in office from 1873 until 1883). Indeed, Bismarck's anti-socialist offensive from 1878 and his break with the National Liberal party (which are discussed below) can be seen as partly motivated by his desire to subordinate the Prussian ministers. In March 1878 he removed the ministers of finance, trade and interior (Camphausen, Achenbach and Friedrich zu Eulenburg) and he installed men in their place (Arthur Hobrecht, Albert Maybach and Botho zu Eulenburg) who were widely perceived to be inferior. But Bismarck was still not satisfied with the composition of the Prussian state ministry and in June 1878 he brought in the capable and experienced Otto zu Stolberg-Wernigerode as vice-president of the state ministry and deputy chancellor. When in the same month a majority of the ministers opposed the dissolution of the Reichstag after the rejection of a new anti-socialist law, he suspected that they were intriguing with parliamentarians against him. Bismarck turned the issue into one of confidence in his leadership, forcing the dissolution of the Reichstag on 11 June. He made further ministerial changes in 1879 and 1880, all with a view to establishing the docility of the state ministry. The tenure of some of the new men appointed during this period was short. Hobrecht, for example, who had only been prevailed upon to accept the finance portfolio after at least nine candidates had rejected it,[18] survived in office for a mere fifteen months. Bismarck expected the ministers to follow his leadership irrespective of their own political convictions and without questioning his aims or consistency. In September 1880 he personally took over the Prussian Ministry of Trade, further bolstering his position through the accumulation of offices and ensuring that he was strategically well placed to spearhead new social insurance legislation. He also appointed Karl von Boetticher simultaneously as state secretary of the Reich Office of Interior, a Prussian minister without portfolio and his deputy in the Ministry of Trade. As Otto Pflanze has argued, Bismarck thereby 'completed his conquest of the Prussian cabinet and its constituent ministries'.[19] Moreover, the new system may well have violated the Reich constitution since Prussian officials from several ministries now began to work on the technicalities of social insurance legislation under Boetticher's leadership in the Reich Office of Interior.

By the early 1880s Bismarck had successfully asserted his authority over the Prussian ministerial bureaucracy, just as his control over the Reich executive was assured. Significantly, Botho zu Eulenburg resigned in February 1881 after he was suspected by Bismarck of 'wanting to govern';[20] and in the summer Stolberg, too, gave up his offices, disillusioned that his dual role had brought him only minimal authority and influence. The Prussian ministry was now largely composed of commoners and its collegial structure was effectively destroyed. The Prussian ministers had been conditioned to accept a role that was not appreciably different to that of the state secretaries in the Reich. Bismarck now found it easy to work with men like the servile Adolf Scholz, the finance minister from 1882 to 1890. In 1884 he praised him as 'the first finance minister in twenty-two years with whom I have been privileged to work together in mutual understanding'.[21]

Bismarck took some satisfaction from his new omnipotence within the executive but there seems little doubt that the scope for creativity and initiative in the government declined. Moreover, no longer anticipating rebellion, Bismarck reduced his contact with his colleagues to a minimum in the first half of the 1880s and he effectively withdrew. 'He receives almost no one and usually transmits his decisions and directives through Rottenburg', the minister of agriculture, Lucius von Ballhausen, noted in February 1883.[22] Three months later Bismarck presided over a state ministry meeting for the first time in almost a year and his colleagues were shocked by his physical deterioration. Bloated and pale, he complained about constant stomach pains and confessed he had been taking opium for six months on medical advice.[23] Bismarck may have rejoiced that the government machine was now free of conflicts, but neither physically nor mentally could he thrive in a climate of political stagnation. He even found the multiplicity of his political roles confusing, on one occasion approving a measure as Prussian minister of trade only to object to it a few days later as Prussian minister-president.[24]

Ultimately, of course, control of the executive could not satisfy Bismarck's power aspirations. His relief over the absence of frictions in the executive was premature for he continued to be trapped by the complex constitutional arrangements he had devised. The targets of his resentment merely shifted – to the parliaments, Bundesrat, army, the crown prince and his supporters and, by the late 1880s, the Kaiser's court. Bismarck tightened his grip over the Berlin administration, removed inconvenient colleagues and reduced decision-making to a diminishing circle of confidants. But his manifest reluctance to work with others on a basis of compromise and consensus ensured that he remained isolated and often frustrated.

Finally, if Bismarck came to enjoy a dictatorial position in the administration, he also knew that he owed this to the Kaiser's support. In the 1870s he had blamed his problems with the Prussian ministers on 'the power-mania of the king', who would not tolerate a real prime minister who appointed his own cabinet and 'wants to have the last word about everything'.[25] In December 1883, however, he emphatically underlined the role of the monarch's prerogative of appointment in securing his autocracy within the executive. 'Since everyone in the Prussian cabinet came to understand the probability that any minister will be dismissed on my request, a discipline has predominated within the government that never before existed', he revealed to the Württemberg minister-president, Hermann von Mittnacht, at Varzin.[26] As in the 1860s Bismarck's position was dependent on the monarch who had appointed him. Yet, given the Kaiser's age and the presence of the crown prince in the wings, Bismarck could scarcely feel his power was secure. Indeed, Wilhelm I appeared increasingly frail by the mid-1880s. After a series of fainting fits, his military entourage did not believe the 88-year-old monarch could survive the autumn of 1885.[27]

At the very time when he seemed to have achieved his 'chancellor dictatorship' within the executive, Bismarck's position was thus still under intense pressure. The imminence of the monarchical succession called into question his political future. Moreover, a strong left liberal opposition in the parliaments campaigned to institute a more unitary and parliamentary system of government, confidently expecting the future Kaiser to sympathise with its aspirations. These pressures undoubtedly prompted Bismarck's otherwise inexplicable efforts to achieve further constitutional reforms in 1883–84. In March 1884 he announced to his surprised and compliant Prussian colleagues that he intended to resign his Prussian offices and concentrate on his role as Reich chancellor. Justifying his decision on grounds of health, he was apparently willing to disengage from Prussian affairs (where the future king could indulge his liberalism), to strengthen the Bundesrat as a collective government and to see the Prussian government reduced to 'a position no different from that of other governments'.[28] Wilhelm I, however, blocked the move since he had serious doubts about the practicality of the new arrangement, and Bismarck eventually acquiesced (although he angrily boycotted Prussian business for nine days in April 1884). Bismarck also revived the Prussian consultative *Staatsrat* in 1884, ostensibly to relieve the Prussian ministry and advise on legislation. In securing Friedrich Wilhelm's agreement to preside over this conservative body, Bismarck probably hoped to constrain the future Kaiser and also, since he was its vice-president, to ensure that he still had an influence over Prussian domestic policy. But the resurrection of the *Staatsrat* merely complicated further the structure of government and he never realised his idea of creating a parallel *Reichsrat* to advise on national affairs. Axel Riehl has interpreted Bismarck's efforts at constitutional reform in 1883–84 as part of a sweeping strategy to secure his personal position against the threat of a 'revolution from above' under the new Kaiser. Bismarck, he argued,

embarked on these schemes for selfish, egotistical reasons, but he ultimately found colonial policy a more effective weapon against the crown
prince than constitutional reform.[29]

Despite his strong will, Bismarck's authority thus rested on fragile
foundations and he was never likely to be satisfied with the extent of
his personal power. His political decisions were frequently intertwined
with considerations about what would best serve his own interests, but
his tenure of office always appeared provisional and finite. Bismarck
could no more secure his power in perpetuity than he could control
singlehandedly the development of Germany after 1871, a country characterised by the dynamism of its economy, diversity of its social structure and its potential military power. Real power as he had known and
understood it for a brief and exceptional period in the 1860s – the ability
to decide, act and shape events – seemed to elude him after 1871. Indeed,
it was only during periods of crisis that he could be really conscious that
he wielded it.

The policies of national consolidation

During his first nine years in power, Bismarck's efforts were primarily
devoted to securing the future of Prussia within Germany. The achievement of German unification in 1871 in many ways exceeded his political
expectations, resulting from the skilful exploitation of favourable opportunities as much as from deliberate design. Yet Bismarck wielded political power for nearly twenty years after the foundation of the German
Reich, and his historical reputation as one of the towering figures in
European political history is inevitably coloured by assessments of his
role and legacy during this protracted period. What political aims did
Bismarck have after 1871 and how far was he able to achieve them? And
what impact did his policies have on the development of the Reich and
on German society?

Bismarck's role in the domestic politics of the Reich was far more
contentious than his role in foreign policy, which he continued to see as
his particular area of expertise and where his proven diplomatic skill was
much more readily acknowledged.[30] Bismarck's contemporary critics,
and a whole school of liberal historiography which has drawn on their
negative critique, saw him as having little consistency of aim beyond a
cynical and manipulative desire to maintain himself in high office and to
buttress the social and political interests of his own class. Some historical
assessments of his political career as Reich chancellor have also tended to

elevate his parliamentary strategies into a political system, focusing on the almost bewildering series of manipulative devices he used to tame the political parties and ensure the pliancy of the parliaments.[31] To an extent, this negative view of Bismarck's domestic policies reflects his pragmatism as a political leader, his intuitive rejection of political dogma and his willingness to improvise or tack with the wind when it was expedient to do so. Bismarck once remarked that he always tested the ice first to see if it would bear his weight before he launched himself out upon it. As with his efforts to dominate the executive, he thus often appeared to espouse one course of action, only to change his mind when he encountered difficulties and apparently reverse direction.

Yet negative assessments of Bismarck's policies also indicate what one cogent analysis drew attention to over twenty years ago, namely 'the degree to which we perceive the German Empire, even today, through nineteenth century liberal eyes'.[32] It has become almost obligatory to divide Bismarckian domestic politics into two distinct eras, the liberal 1870s and the conservative 1880s, a periodisation which this volume has sought to avoid and which largely derives from liberal perceptions that he deliberately destroyed his political partnership with them in 1878–79. But this division distorts many aspects of Bismarckian domestic politics, not least what continued to unite Bismarck and the liberals and what separated them in the 1880s. And while the party political constellation influenced Bismarck's thinking and imposed constraints on what he was able to achieve in the domestic arena, Bismarck was never driven by parliamentary or party political considerations alone. He always reacted to the changing economic, political and ideological climate around him, but he also pursued certain key objectives far more consistently throughout his chancellorship than is often assumed.

In 1881 Bismarck outlined the aims of his domestic policy in a speech to the Reichstag. 'From the beginning of my [ministerial] activity, I have often acted hastily and without reflection,' he admitted, 'but when I had time to reflect I have always asked: what is useful, effective, right for my fatherland, for my dynasty – so long as I was only in Prussia – and now for the German nation?' He claimed he had never been doctrinaire and that liberalism and conservatism seemed to him to be luxuries, furnishings to be added later to a strong German state. His aim had always been the unity and consolidation of Germany. 'And if you can show a single moment when I deviated from that compass needle, you may perhaps prove that I erred, but never that I lost sight for one moment of the national goal.'[33] Bismarck's fixation on consolidating the national state was also recognised by National Liberals such as Rudolf Haym who, for all his criticism of Bismarck's methods and the 'confusing and even corrupting effect' of his political strategies, reminded himself in 1881 'that nobody else has such a lively regard for the idea of making the young empire vital, permanent, and resilient'. 'All his twists and turns and inconsistencies can be explained by the power of this idea', Haym believed, and he saw Bismarck as 'representing for me the incarnation of the national state'.[34]

The Reich Bismarck created in 1870–71 was in many respects an artificial creation, forged in an atmosphere of militarism and war and not the result of an organic or evolutionary process of unification. As a nation-state it can be seen as defective, excluding the six million Austrian Germans but including a significant number of national minorities – French, Danes, Walloons and, above all, Prussia's two and a half million Polish subjects, who bitterly resented their incorporation into the German Reich. Moreover, although the majority in the constituent Reichstag in 1867 had been prepared to give the new arrangements the benefit of the doubt and support the new confederation, it was also clear that the support of many Germans was conditional upon the future development of the Reich. Political and religious minorities, especially Germany's Catholics who comprised about a third of the total population and who, in the south and west, had traditionally looked to Austria for leadership, were at best lukewarm about Bismarck's new Germany dominated by Protestant Prussia. Conservatives, liberals and socialists all had reason to criticise the new Reich's constitutional arrangements, and disgruntled particularists were also keen to protect and enhance the Reich's federal character. Together these groups represented a significant degree of dissatisfaction with Bismarck's creation.

Bismarck was as aware as anyone that political unification did not signify national unity. He was particularly concerned about all those Germans in the new Reich who had fought against Prussia in the war of 1866. From 1871 he saw his new creation as potentially threatened from within by centrifugal forces or 'internal enemies' (*Reichsfeinde*) who, if given free rein, might undo his work of national unification. Apart from consolidating his own power, his main political aim from 1871 until his dismissal in 1890 was thus to secure and fortify the Reich and ensure its survival in the future. Despite effects to the contrary, he sought to counter the pull of confessional, regional and ethnic loyalties, denigrate political and ideological differences, and consolidate a nation-state that could serve as the focus of the German majority's national loyalty. Ready to compromise with the liberal majority in the early years of his chancellorship to facilitate the economic and legal unification of Germany, his main policy initiatives also stemmed from his overriding preoccupation with stabilising the Reich.

It is in this context that some of Bismarck's most controversial political initiatives must be seen, for, especially in the 1870s, Bismarck's domestic policy can only be understood in relation to the events of the previous decade. Above all, the so-called *Kulturkampf* (or 'struggle for civilisation'), which was waged in Prussia against the Catholic Church and its political representative, the Centre Party, was really a continuation of the struggle to achieve the national state. The methods used were different from those used in the military campaigns of 1864–71, but the battle appeared no less urgent to Bismarck and supporters of the national idea. The fear was very real that what had been achieved so suddenly and dramatically could just as easily collapse or be destroyed by centrifugal pressures, perhaps aided and abetted by a hostile coalition of foreign powers. The *Kulturkampf* can also be seen in a wider European context as a liberal campaign against clerical obscurantism that was partly triggered by the Papacy's efforts to reinforce its spiritual authority through the *Syllabus Errorum* of 1864 and the pronouncement of the doctrine of Papal infallibility in 1870. It was undeniably, too, a stage in the progress of the secular state. But these perspectives, which indicate that some degree of conflict between Church and state might well have ensued irrespective of whether Bismarck was in power, do little to illuminate Bismarck's role or preoccupations in the struggle. The emergence of political Catholicism as a new force simultaneously with the creation of the Reich was bound to impress Bismarck as a singularly unwelcome development. His experience of 'black', Catholic and *großdeutsch* anti-Prussianism in Frankfurt and the problems he had encountered between 1867 and 1870 with democrats and particularists in the south coloured his view of this new threat to the work of national construction. In June 1871 he confidentially told an astonished Schlözer, the designated new minister to the United States, that 'The Centre Party could become as dangerous as the Paris Commune.'[35] A month later he hinted that a victory over Rome to add to those over Austria and France would ensure that the epoch could not be compared with any other.[36]

The German Centre Party that emerged in 1870–71 had its origins in Prussia but was undoubtedly shaped in response to Bismarck's policies of unification (as well as the taking of Rome by the Italian government in 1870). Although primarily a party of German Catholics (from a wide spectrum of social backgrounds), it sought to mobilise support from all those elements in the new Reich that resented their inclusion in a lesser German state dominated by Prussia. Under the leadership of

Ludwig Windthorst, a former Hanoverian minister, it also hoped to attract conservative Protestants into the party. While it was not very successful in this latter aim, it did enrol some Poles, Hanoverian Guelphs, socialists and individual Protestants such as Bismarck's former patron, Ernst Ludwig von Gerlach, who had come to regard Bismarck's policies as unchristian and godless. Undoubtedly, though, the Centre served to focus and lead opposition to government policy in the 1870s and its support grew rapidly as Bismarck, in alliance with national liberalism, worked to forge a new German national, and largely Protestant, culture. In the Reichstag elections of 1871 it gained 61 seats, three more than it had gained in the Prussian Lower House the previous year, and it became the second largest party in the national parliament. Thus it was seen by Bismarck as a new, strong, well-organised, conservative grouping which was bound to attract all those hostile to his creation. Its stance on confessional issues, defence of federalism and protection of minority rights often won it the support of Prussian particularists and Poles in the parliaments, and in February 1872 the Baden minister in Berlin reported that Bismarck wanted to prevent a highly threatening Conservative–Centre coalition.[37] Prone at this juncture to almost paranoic fears about a Catholic conspiracy to undo German unification (a spectre behind which all manner of enemies from Queen Augusta to Polish separatists might lurk), Bismarck was also alienated by the Centre's opposition to Italian unification in 1871. This suggested that the party might have ultramontane tendencies and look to Rome for guidance, though the subsequent course of the struggle indicated that this was generally not the case.

The *Kulturkampf* was primarily waged in Prussia by the Prussian *Kultusministerium* (which was responsible for ecclesiastical affairs, education and medicine) and its origins can be traced back to the abolition of the special Catholic section in the ministry in June 1871. Early measures included the pulpit article in November 1871, which forbade clergymen from making political pronouncements, a school inspection bill and the expulsion of the Jesuit order from Germany in 1872. In 1873 the May laws sought to establish state control over education and the appointment of the clergy, and in 1874 compulsory civil marriage was introduced. Bismarck clearly wanted to establish the authority of the state over the Catholic Church although he may not have approved of all the excesses that followed as the campaign intensified. Many priests were expelled or imprisoned, eventually leaving many parishes without clergymen, and Church property was confiscated and administered by state commissioners.

The man most closely identified with the *Kulturkampf* was Adalbert Falk, the liberal *Kultusminister* who replaced Heinrich von Mühler in January 1872, the latter having opposed the reconstruction of the relationship between Church and state in Prussia. Bismarck, however, was certainly responsible for the renewed legislative offensive in 1874–75 after the early laws failed to achieve satisfactory results. On 13 July 1874 a 21-year-old Catholic cooper's journeyman called Eduard Kullmann attempted to assassinate Bismarck with a pistol in Bad Kissingen but he merely grazed Bismarck's hand. Kullmann's action was undertaken in protest against the May laws, but Bismarck retorted later that evening, 'The blow aimed at me was directed not at me personally but at the cause for which I have dedicated my life: the unity, independence and freedom of Germany.'[38] In December 1874 Bismarck caused outrage in the Reichstag when he identified Kullmann as a member of the Centre Party. 'Try to free yourselves from this murderer as you wish, he clings firmly to your coat-tails', he taunted, reaching for his pistol in his pocket and relishing the uproar.[39]

The *Kulturkampf* was an integral part of Bismarck's bid to consolidate the national state but its failure was never really in doubt, even if the campaign did help to break down opposition to a more interventionist state. The struggle proved immensely damaging, both for relations between Catholics and Protestants in imperial Germany and for Bismarck personally. The anti-Catholic legislation, enthusiastically supported by the chancellor's National Liberal allies, provoked a furious reaction among the Catholic minority who rapidly mobilised to defend its rights and became far more cohesive as a result. The Centre Party too, adroitly led by Windthorst, became stronger under Bismarck's onslaught. Windthorst, a formidable parliamentary speaker and tactician, successfully represented the chancellor as dependent on the liberal majority and he also skilfully exploited conservative mistrust of Bismarck's aims and methods. Bismarck soon found himself in conflict not only with some of his former conservative friends over the issue but also with significant elements at the Kaiser's court, not least Augusta who was deeply disturbed by the assault on confessional peace. Even Wilhelm himself was dismayed. Bismarck underestimated the task he had embarked on and the resistance that would ensue. By the late 1870s it was glaringly apparent that, far from defeating political Catholicism, he had boosted its support. Bismarck effected a very limited rapprochement with Windthorst and the Centre when they supported his shift to a protectionist economic policy in 1879, and aspects of the *Kulturkampf* legislation which had most alienated Catholics began to be slowly dismantled from the mid-1880s. But

Bismarck was unwilling to surrender the state's new powers of control or abandon the campaign altogether. Some of the laws, for example concerning the expulsion of the Jesuits, still remained politically contentious after the turn of the century, and Bismarck's hopes that the easing of the struggle would lead to the decay of the Centre proved illusory. There is thus no doubt that, despite his later attempts to justify it, the campaign represented a serious misjudgement on Bismarck's part. Far from consolidating the Reich, it proved extremely divisive and helped to arouse a lasting mistrust of Catholics in Germany that was only dissipated after the Second World War.

The *Kulturkampf* was indicative of Bismarck's methods in domestic policy. Even when his aim was essentially defensive, the preservation of his creation, his preferred strategy was offensive. Bismarck regarded attack as the best form of defence and he eschewed all compromise. Conscious of a threat, he sought to defeat his enemies by destroying their ability to mobilise against him. Bismarck was instinctively drawn to political repression as a method of resolving domestic conflicts, not least because he was always inclined to believe in conspiracy theories. By the end of the 1870s he no longer saw political Catholicism as the main danger and he renewed his offensive against left liberalism. Convinced that political agitators seduced people who were otherwise loyal to the monarchical state, he also waged war on the Social Democratic party; and he exploited the changing economic and ideological climate to campaign against the national minorities, above all the Poles.

The anti-socialist legislation that Bismarck introduced into the German Reichstag in 1878 was first and foremost a tactical weapon against democratic liberalism. Bismarck had not fundamentally changed his attitude to left liberals since the constitutional conflict in the 1860s, and in 1884 he even suggested that Russian nihilism owed more to progressive liberalism than to socialism. Nevertheless, Bismarck was not complacent about the growth of social democracy. He claimed in 1878 that he was first alerted to its dangers when the anti-Prussian and *großdeutsch* socialist deputy, August Bebel, made a speech extolling the Paris commune as a political model in May 1871.[40] He was also outraged when all six socialist deputies in the Reichstag of the North German Confederation advertised their pacifism by voting against further war credits in November 1870. The emergence of a united Social Democratic workers' party from the Lassallean and Eisenach (Marxist) wings of the socialist movement at Gotha in 1875 further served to focus his attention on the nascent conflict between the state and organised labour. Nine per cent of the electorate voted for the Social Democrats in the Reichstag elections of January

1877 and its representation increased from 9 to 12 seats, prompting even the liberal grand duke of Baden to call for a modification of the Reichstag election suffrage.[41]

While Bismarck may well have been quite ignorant about socialist theory (he claimed in 1886 that he had never heard of Karl Marx) and was quite happy later to appropriate the concept of socialism for his own use, he had few doubts that the Social Democrats (whose party was called the Social Democratic Party or SPD from 1891) were hostile to the Reich he had created. Nor did he fail to recognise the potential political implications if the new party allied with the Centre and left liberals in the Reichstag. For Bismarck the Social Democrats could not be treated like a political party; after he left office he likened them to robbers and thieves or 'rats in the country', which infected the people and had to be exterminated.[42] Since he equated their leaders with terrorists, agitators and enemies of the state, he was convinced that an exceptional law, which suppressed the party's public activities and its press, could reverse its electoral success. German workers, newly conceded the right to vote and the right to strike, clearly represented the most significant opposition to the authoritarianism of the German Reich in the future. But in the 1870s and even the 1880s their numbers remained relatively small and Bismarck did not see them as implacably hostile or revolutionary. Instead, he believed that professional political agitators seduced men who would otherwise remain loyal to the monarchical state. Otto Pflanze has argued that Bismarck 'misconceived the primary problem facing his government in internal affairs' in the 1870s and that 'By the time he reversed priorities in the 1880s the chance to prevent the alienation of labor, either through suppression or reform, had passed.'[43] However, whether Bismarck ever understood the problems of an emergent industrial society, let alone was in a position to solve them, is a very moot point.

Bismarck thus launched a 'war of annihilation' against social democracy in 1878 in the mistaken belief that this might restore social peace. He blamed the socialists for two assassination attempts on the life of Wilhelm I in May and June 1878 and, although there was no evidence of their involvement, the socialists were branded as murderous criminals. The anti-socialist law effectively outlawed the Social Democratic party, seeking to suppress its press, forbid its meetings and exile its leaders from the urban centres. It was renewed in the 1880s even though it proved powerless to prevent the election of a growing number of Social Democrat deputies to the Reichstag. (Only in the elections of 1887 was Social Democratic representation significantly reduced.) In 1884 Bismarck claimed that he did not personally want the law to be extended, arguing that if it lapsed this would scare the urban bourgeoisie who benefited most from it.[44] Nevertheless, the exceptional legislation against social democracy remained in force until Bismarck left office.

Coupled to political repression, however, Bismarck also pursued social insurance legislation in the 1880s which was designed to give German workers a stake in the authoritarian state. As his early talks with Lassalle indicated, Bismarck had long been interested in improving the relationship between workers and the state in so far as this was compatible with the existing political and social order. In the early 1870s a group of 'academic socialists' around Adolph Wagner and Gustav Schmoller began to criticise liberal, *laissez-faire* economic policy and recommend specific social reforms such as the prohibition of child labour and the need to create mechanisms for arbitration in the event of industrial disputes. Some ministers and officials, too, were ready to countenance limited social reform legislation in the 1870s, and their initiatives secured the support of the Reichstag in 1876 and 1878. Bismarck's conservative friends, notably Blanckenburg and Hermann Wagener (who served the Prussian state ministry until 1873 when he had to resign on account of a corruption scandal), also urged Bismarck in the early 1870s to address the problem of social reform. They believed that the lower classes could be won over for a 'social monarchy' if their just demands with respect to working hours, wages and housing were met. Bismarck thus did not suddenly espouse 'state socialism' at the end of the 1870s as part of a dramatic shift towards conservatism. His initiatives in the 1880s had a lengthy gestation period, but they only assumed practical relevance when he was no longer dependent on parliamentary liberalism.

Bismarck thus pursued a twin-pronged policy towards organised labour from the late 1870s. As well as seeking to repress the Social Democrats, he also pioneered social welfare legislation from 1880, focusing on social insurance rather than workers' protection, with the aim of improving the material situation of the lower classes. Bismarck rejected factory legislation or improvements to working conditions as unwarranted interference and incompatible with industrial growth. He angrily dismissed the concerns of the Pomeranian factory inspector, Robert Hertel, about the risks of an explosion at his paper factory at Varzin in 1877, retorting, 'Where is danger ever completely ruled out?'[45] He also rejected restricting the working hours of women and children, arguing that it made no difference if housewives worked at night for 'a really ordered household is not compatible with women working in factories at all'.[46] Instead, he sought to safeguard the workers' material interests by instituting a state-guaranteed welfare system. The system of social insurance he promoted from 1880, which provided for sickness and accident insurance, old age pensions and invalidity insurance, was obligatory and became a model for other states to follow. In 1881 he justified the first accident insurance bill by claiming that it was the duty of the state to protect the members of the community without property and to promote the wellbeing of the weak and needy. If such a policy could be construed as socialist or even communist, this was no argument against it.[47] He also told Busch that socialism was no different from 'practical Christianity',[48] and he described a range of measures, from compulsory schooling to the building of railways and even the emancipation of the peasantry in the early nineteenth century, as socialist.

There is no doubt that Bismarck himself was the architect of the social insurance scheme even if officials such as Theodor Lohmann, the under state secretary in the Ministry of Trade and then in the Reich Office of Interior, played a major role in the drafting of the legislation. His subordinates sometimes contravened his instructions but Bismarck was the driving force behind the laws, which bore his imprint. 'If I am reproached with going ahead too rapidly, so I would liken the task of the leading minister to a locomotive stoker who always ensures the right heat for the engine to work properly,' he told Windthorst. 'Otherwise we would be at a standstill in everything.'[49] Indeed, Lohmann resigned in 1883 because he resented the chancellor's interference in his work and the fact that Bismarck frequently refused to take his advice.[50] The fact that the old age and disability insurance was not passed until 1889 can also largely be attributed to Bismarck's loss of interest in social policy from 1884, presumably because it manifestly failed to bring the political rewards he expected in terms of workers' loyalty to the monarchy.

Bismarck's motives in initiating the social insurance legislation were controversial at the time, arousing mistrust and suspicion inside and outside the Reichstag. Historians, too, have often assessed them critically. While acknowledging the programme's progressive potential and even that it was 'more important in the long run than ... his creation of an empire',[51] they have tended to dismiss Bismarck's motives as cynical. Once again they have appropriated many of the arguments of his contemporary, liberal opponents, suspicious of the fact that a conservative statesman initiated a far-sighted programme of social reform. Heinrich August Winkler has recently acknowledged that what was achieved in the 1880s was 'incomparably more progressive than Bismarck's intentions'. But he has also reiterated the view that it was only achieved as part of a domestic change of course or 'internal foundation of the Reich' that 'set Germany back in other areas'.[52]

Bismarck was undoubtedly motivated by a wide range of considerations, but he had always seen the state as having the obligation to regulate on the social question and mistrusted liberal ideas of self-help. Christian and moral imperatives may have intermeshed with more calculated political and power considerations to encourage his support for state intervention in this sphere. He clearly saw the laws as a way of binding the people to the state and giving those without property a stake in the Reich's future. But other factors may also have influenced him. For example, he wanted to reduce the burden of poor relief on local government and thereby undermine the case for direct taxation. He may too have seen these initiatives as a means of cutting the ground from underneath all the political parties and creating a direct link between the state and the people. Taken together, the anti-socialist legislation and the social welfare legislation were thus less 'carrot and stick' than complementary attempts to enhance the power of the authoritarian state.

Whatever his motives, the fact that the government espoused a form of 'state socialism' at the same time as seeking to repress the political representatives of the working class meant that he reaped few political rewards for his efforts. While helping 'passive workers' unable to work because of illness, accident or old age, the social insurance legislation did little to improve the legal position of 'active workers' who gained no greater degree of protection or representation of their interests in the workplace. Bismarck's policies may in the longer term have provided a basis for more positive contact between the workers' movement and the state. But his desire to hear 'the workers without their leaders and guardians'[53] did not facilitate the integration of the working class into the Reich. Moreover, his unwillingness to agree to significant Reichstag initiatives to limit working hours, improve health and safety controls in factories or provide for arbitration in industrial disputes imposed strict limits on what could be achieved.

Bismarck was not oblivious to the problems created by industrial society but, especially in the climate of economic liberalism in the 1870s, he never developed a coherent economic strategy. His pragmatism shaped his response to most economic issues and, although he often judged conditions realistically and practically, his decisions were often intuitive and based on inconsistent arguments. He understood issues of tariff and trade policy, was never ideologically committed to either free trade or protectionism, and he differentiated between the needs of agriculture and industry. While mindful of his own interests as a large landowner, he also appreciated the growing significance of Germany's industrial development in underwriting German power. His shift to economic protectionism at the end of the 1870s was partly motivated by the desire to promote both industry and agriculture at a time of difficulties in the world market. But by the middle of the 1880s he justified the raising of the agrarian tariffs almost wholly in political terms. He also did not see it as the business of government to develop long-term plans to solve the problems of an increasingly complex economy. He chose to ignore most of the urgent economic and social problems created by the dynamic growth of the German capital city after 1871, displaying more interest in the building of the Kurfürstendamm and the affluent leafy suburb of Berlin-Grunewald than in the acute housing shortage facing Berlin's lower classes. He similarly had little understanding of what motivated the mass migration into the capital, believing that the people involved – including those from Varzin – would have done better to stay at home.[54]

A further important strand in Bismarck's domestic policy which exercised him continuously throughout his chancellorship and which he never satisfactorily resolved was his determination to provide the Reich with financial security and stability. The imperial German constitution envisaged that the Reich would be financed from the income of the *Zollverein* (i.e. customs and tariffs) and that this could be supplemented by the so-called 'matricular contributions' from the states, calculated according to their per capita population. Since the overwhelming majority of the states were now relieved of military expenditure, it appeared reasonable that they should help bear the military cost of the Reich which accounted for over 90 per cent of its budget. Nevertheless, the states were very unenthusiastic about paying these contributions (not least because many of them had benefited previously from *Zollverein* allocations distributed according to the same formula) and the dynamic development of the Reich soon raised the spectre of financial insolvency.

From the early 1870s Bismarck began to consider measures which could raise revenue for the Reich and free it from its dependence on the contributions from the states. Not all his ideas were practicable or reached the statute book, but the slowdown of economic growth from 1873 and the cessation of French reparation payments added new urgency to the task. Above all Bismarck was interested in the nationalisation of the railways as a means of resolving the growing fiscal crisis, and a new Reich Railway Office was created in 1873, albeit justified by national rather than economic arguments. However, the nationalisation of the railways was opposed by the middle states (Bavaria, Saxony and Württemberg defeated a railway bill in the Bundesrat in 1879) and Bismarck was only able to achieve the nationalisation of the Prussian railways.

The financial issue was inextricably linked to the constitutional issue, and this militated against a rational solution to the problem of financing the Reich. The Reich did not have the power to raise direct taxation and the states resisted any solution that might increase power at the centre. Bismarck notoriously preferred indirect taxation to direct taxation, a stance which arose partly from self-interest as a wealthy landowner and which also led him to resist long and hard paying the equivalent of council tax on his rent-free Berlin residence. (He even threatened to move the imperial and Prussian governments from Berlin if he had to pay the 746 marks.[55]) If the nationalisation of the railways could not finance the Reich, Bismarck favoured a lucrative government monopoly on brandy, beer or tobacco. However, the liberal parliamentary majority disliked these alternatives which lessened the Reichstag's control over taxation. Again and again Bismarck's reform proposals were blocked. In 1879 he threatened to abandon the Reich altogether and return to his position as prime minister of a strengthened Prussian unitary state if the monopoly on the import and manufacture of tobacco was rejected.[56] But his bluster achieved little and, although agreement was reached on taxing stock exchange transactions in 1881, his other tax initiatives ended in failure.

It was the protective tariff law of 1879, passed by a new majority of the two conservative parties, a large part of the Centre Party and a group of right-wing National Liberals, that eventually supplied additional revenue to the Reich. While there was no parliamentary majority in the Reichstag in the 1880s for new or increased taxation, there was an acceptance of the need to finance the Reich and a willingness to raise tariffs. Even so, Bismarck opted for economic protectionism opportunistically and he developed no clear conception of what he hoped to achieve in the longer term. Furthermore, he compounded the constitutional conundrum. In 1879 Bismarck agreed to a Conservative–Centre compromise (called the Franckenstein clause after the Centre deputy who proposed it) which ensured that if the revenue from the tariff exceeded 130 million marks a year, the surplus had to be distributed among the states. This arrangement was a concession to federalism and was seen by Bismarck as preferable to a National Liberal proposal that would have strengthened the Reichstag's budgetary control. But, according to its bizarre logic, it meant that in 1890, for example, the states gave 301 million marks to the Reich and received back 379 million marks, a net gain of 78 million marks.[57] Bismarck was thus never able to devise a rational financial structure for the Reich and his successors still faced the problem of the Reich's financial insolvency.

Finally, in the context of consolidating the Reich, mention must also be made of Bismarck's campaigns in the 1880s against the national minorities. Germany was not, of course, the only European state to implement draconian measures against its ethnic communities in the late nineteenth century, but the Germanisation policies pursued above all against the Polish population were an integral part of Bismarck's offensive to consolidate the Reich. Coercive policies were also pursued against the Danes in northern Schleswig from 1888 and considered against the French-speaking population of Alsace-Lorraine after the national elections of 1887. But Bismarck had always had a particular animus against the two million Poles in Prussia's eastern provinces. The size of the Polish community, its rapid demographic growth and its strong adherence to its own culture, traditions and nationality were seen by Bismarck as a major threat to the existence of Prussia even before the unification of Germany. At that time loyalty to the monarchy rather than the principle of nationality formed the basis of Prussian citizenship. After 1871, however, ethnicity, language and cultural uniformity assumed a new significance given the need to consolidate the new state and counter regional, dynastic and confessional particularisms. Just as the *Kulturkampf* reflected the wish to destroy the social and cultural power of the Catholic Church and eliminate alternative sources of institutional loyalty between the citizen and the state, so territorial unification inevitably led to a new relationship between Germans and Poles. National Liberals no longer defended individual Polish rights but, instead, as the promoters of an ethnic–linguistic conception of German nationality and a more centralised and interventionist state, they became the most consistent parliamentary supporters of anti-Polish legislation.

Bismarck's war against the Poles – which Otto Pflanze has likened to a 'final solution' of the Polish problem[58] – was, like the *Kulturkampf*, essentially conducted in Prussia. Its measures were debated and passed in the Prussian Landtag in the face of vigorous opposition from the Centre, although the policies pursued in Prussia inevitably impacted upon relationships in the Reich. The first stage was really an integral part of the *Kulturkampf* when the German language was enforced in elementary and secondary schools in the Polish provinces and became the sole language of public intercourse. Bismarck considered other anti-Polish measures in the 1870s. He talked in the Prussian state ministry about the alliance between the Slavs, Romans and ultramontanism and the need to defend German national interests and the German language against Slavic and ultramontane agitation.[59] But it was undoubtedly the changed economic and ideological climate of the 1880s that prompted and facilitated his more savage initiatives aimed against the Poles as a nationality, not as Catholics. Economic insecurities fuelled xenophobia, racism and anti-Semitism, encouraging attacks on illegal immigrants and fears of 'Polonism'. Moreover the Polish problem was intricately connected with the anxieties created by the transition from an agrarian to an industrial society. Bismarck's policy aimed to reinforce a shrinking rural population as hundreds of thousands of Germans – and Poles – migrated westwards from the East Elbian provinces. Bismarck thus hoped to stabilise what he regarded as an essential pillar of the social and political order. It has further been suggested that Bismarck wanted to weaken the Prussian Poles so that, in the event of a war against Russia, a Polish buffer state could be reconstituted with a minimum impact on the province of Posen. Finally, by the late 1880s Bismarck undoubtedly believed that the campaign against the Poles could serve as a new national task for a younger generation of Germans.

From 1885 some 30,000 Poles and Jews without citizenship began to be expelled from the Reich to Russia and Austrian Galicia. Keen to exploit the bitter and intense public debate, Bismarck actively considered further Germanisation measures from September 1885, including a land purchase programme which would settle Germans on land formerly owned by Poles. In January 1886 in his first major speech in the Prussian Landtag for five years he launched his campaign against the Poles and called for speedy legislation.[60] The settlement law established a commission under the authority of the Prussian Ministry of State and a fund of 100 million marks to buy up Polish properties and strengthen 'Germandom' in Posen and West Prussia. Further repressive measures followed, notably the strengthening of the German character of schools in the eastern provinces, although, as Geoff Eley has pointed out, there was still something improvised about these early Bismarckian initiatives compared to the policies pursued by his successors.[61] It is never easy to gauge how far Bismarck was responding to public pressure and how far he was manipulating it for his own purposes, how far he was leading and how far he was following. Bismarck often had diverse motives. In pursuing his anti-Polish campaign, he may have hoped to detach what he regarded as the loyal Polish peasant from the Polish nationalist movement. Undoubtedly, too, he was influenced by his desire to hold a parliamentary coalition of Conservatives, Free Conservatives and National Liberals together in the late 1880s and pursue strategies which it could endorse. However, the Conservatives were least enthusiastic about the anti-Polish policies and, while there was a majority for anti-Polish measures in the Prussian Landtag, there was a clear majority of parties in the Reichstag which opposed the campaign for humanitarian reasons and effectively passed a first vote of no confidence in the Reich chancellor in 1886.

These Germanisation measures amounted to a bid to change the ethnic composition of the region by imposing the German language and German culture on the Polish population (as distinct from Heinrich Himmler's later concept of Germanisation as the physical eradication of offending minorities). Bismarck claimed he never had anything against the Poles as a people. Nevertheless, as we have seen, the language he employed is particularly brutal, repellent and resonant for the modern reader.[62] However, once again, Bismarck's policy backfired, provoking a violent reaction from the Poles who responded with successful counter-measures of their own. Rather than promote the political and social cohesion of the Reich, the campaign served to politicise and 'nationalise' the Prussian Poles.

Bismarck's domestic policies, especially by the late 1880s, were increasingly seen as devoid of any creative content, divisive in their effects and shaped by a world view which was manifestly outmoded and anachronistic. His efforts to stabilise and consolidate the Reich appeared futile attempts to preserve the status quo at a time of rapid social change. Lothar Gall has argued that Bismarck's dynamic policy of conservative reform evolved into a policy of pure reaction. He even draws a distinction between the conservative interventionist state that developed under Bismarck (which he dismisses as a hybrid) and the modern interventionist state.[63] This may be to let the issue of motives obscure what was genuinely progressive about the outcomes. Moreover, despite the liberal outcry over the abandonment of free trade, there was no inherent reason why the shift to economic protectionism and the 'defence of national work' should have precluded further political or constitutional reforms (which, as we have seen, Bismarck still toyed with in the 1880s). But it is certainly true that Bismarck, who had very little personal contact with the urban population, never developed a coherent response to the problems of industrial society. Ultimately his approach neither eased class antagonisms in the late nineteenth century nor facilitated the consolidation of a nation-state based on social consensus.

Parliaments, parties and the press

Bismarck's attitude to parliament and the political parties raises a number of interesting issues. On the one hand, as we have seen, his political career owed far more to the birth of parliamentarianism than is often assumed and his acceptance of a legitimate role for parliament within a modern constitutional state marked him out from most of his reactionary conservative peers. Nearly half a century ago A.J.P. Taylor described Bismarck as 'a parliamentary statesman exactly like Sir Robert Walpole or the younger Pitt'.[64] In Taylor's view, too, the Bismarckian constitution could have led the way to cabinet government and ultimately parliamentary sovereignty if the German party politicians 'had worked together more and criticised less'.[65] In his support for a national parliament elected by direct, equal and universal male suffrage and acceptance of a secret ballot, Bismarck perhaps did more in the longer term to promote democratic rights and responsibilities in Germany than any other individual in the nineteenth century. As chancellor he was also a compelling parliamentary speaker whose speeches were major public events. He was more than a match for the great parliamentarians of his day such as Ludwig Windthorst, Eduard Lasker and Eugen Richter.

Yet, on the other hand, Bismarck was also the man who wanted to ruin parliamentarianism with parliamentarianism and had an essentially negative conception of what the role of a parliament should be in a modern state. He saw parliament as an arena in which ministers could publicly defend the policies of the crown and as playing a valuable role in preventing bad laws or the waste of public money. But parliament, in his view, could not be allowed to govern, nor could political parties determine state policy. Bismarck presented himself as a non-partisan leader who was above the special interests of the political parties and was thus best able to judge what was most likely to serve the public good. As German chancellor – the only imperial minister – he was not even a member of the German Reichstag. He was only entitled to be present at debates and to speak by virtue of being a Prussian delegate to the Bundesrat, and he preferred to maintain an aloof posture, sitting on the special bench reserved for representatives of the 'united governments'. Especially in the 1880s he consistently used his parliamentary speeches to reinforce the idea that he alone could speak for the German nation as a whole. Indeed, throughout his chancellorship it irked him enormously that even though he identified himself with no political party and maintained an Olympian detachment, the majority of parliamentarians refused to see him as politically neutral. Bismarck was ultimately an authoritarian statesman who was only prepared to allocate to parliaments and political parties a specific and subordinate legislative role within a military monarchy. Recent historiography has also highlighted the calculating and repressive strategies he adopted in order to tame his parliamentary opponents and stifle genuine public debate. His legacy for the development of parliamentary institutions and the political parties in Germany was thus highly ambiguous, containing many negative as well as positive features.

As chancellor and Prussian minister-president Bismarck had to work with two different parliaments which posed quite distinct challenges. The German Reichstag was a single-chamber parliament of 397 deputies elected by universal male suffrage (all men who had reached the age of 25 but not those in active military service). Voting was equal, direct and secret in single-member constituencies, and candidates had to attain an overall majority, so run-off second rounds of voting were often necessary. The constituencies were originally fixed at 100,000 voters but were never redrawn to take into account the effects of urbanisation. Hence the elections increasingly gave disproportionate influence to rural voters, and the share of the vote of a predominantly urban party like the Social Democratic party was much higher than the distribution of seats suggested. Nevertheless, the Reichstag adequately reflected the intentions of German voters. The Prussian Landtag, by contrast, was composed of two chambers, and the *Herrenhaus*, dominated by hereditary ultraconservatives, was as much a brake on the government's plans (as with the local government reform) in the 1870s as the elected Lower House. The Lower House was composed of 433 members and, like the Reichstag, was elected for three-year terms until 1888 when these were extended to five years. As with most municipal elections in Prussia, voting was by means of universal male suffrage but it was not equal, direct or secret. Members were chosen by electors who in turn were selected according to a system whereby the voters were divided into three classes according to the amount of taxes they paid; the comparatively few richest men thus chose as many electors as the great mass of the working class. It is perhaps surprising that in the 1870s this franchise produced a parliament that was not so dissimilar in composition to the national Reichstag, with liberals in a majority over conservatives. But the franchise was essentially plutocratic, thus favouring the emergent bourgeoisie as well as wealthy landowners. Moreover, Bismarck's cooperation with the National Liberals in the Reichstag clearly gave the party an advantage in the Landtag elections, not least because the government had the opportunity to exert pressure through the system of oral voting. By the 1880s, when the government favoured the conservative parties, these were stronger in the Landtag than in the Reichstag. In 1883–84 the left liberals introduced a motion, which had no chance of success, to abolish oral voting in Prussia but the subsequent debate indicated the extent to which all parties anticipated the monarchical succession. The Social Democrats did not manage to get representation in the Prussian parliament at all under Bismarck's chancellorship.

Although key legislation concerning the *Kulturkampf* and the Polish population was passed in the Prussian Landtag, in practice it was the more democratically elected Reichstag that exercised Bismarck most. Indeed, in the 1880s when the elections of October 1882 and November 1885 to the Prussian Lower House produced an increasingly conservative chamber, Bismarck scarcely showed any interest in the Prussian Landtag, and he did not appear in it at all between 1881 and 1885. Throughout his political career as chancellor it was probably his deepest regret that he conceded universal suffrage as the Reichstag franchise, even with the apparent safeguard that deputies would receive no remuneration (and in 1885, when the Social Democratic party paid its deputies allowances, Bismarck successfully sued them for the sums of money involved).[66] Especially in the 1880s Bismarck often toyed with the idea of changing the Reichstag election suffrage, tried various methods of 'bypassing' the parliaments and sought to reduce their budgetary powers.

Bismarck hoped that the Reichstag would have an integrative function after 1871, serving as a focus of national debate, but it must be emphasised that imperial Germany did not have a parliamentary system of government. The powers of the Reichstag looked extensive on paper and included the right to initiate legislation (though the executive was not bound to accept it). But its influence was diminished because there was no system of ministerial responsibility to parliament and the Reichstag could be dissolved at any time by the Bundesrat with the consent of the Kaiser. Indeed, the power of dissolution could be used as a means of breaking down resistance in the Reichstag, and it is perhaps surprising that Bismarck used it only twice, in 1878 when the Reichstag refused to pass the anti-socialist bill and in 1887 when it refused to pass the *Septennat* army bill, which fixed the size of the army for seven years. On both these occasions he was successful, as the new Reichstag then supported the government's plans. Of course the threat of dissolution was almost as persuasive as dissolution itself and the threat was constant, hanging over the Reichstag like the sword of Damocles, whenever it could not reach agreement with the government.

There was no organic relationship between the executive and legislature and thus no party or coalition was obliged to support or oppose the government consistently. Moreover, in the 1870s and even the 1880s the German party system was still in its infancy and there remained considerable fluidity and movement in the relationships within and between the parties. In the 1870s Bismarck relied on the support of the National

Liberals and *Reichspartei* (Free Conservatives) for the passage of legislation to consolidate the new nation-state in the Reichstag. But even the
small, sympathetic *Reichspartei* occasionally voted against his measures
and never followed Bismarck slavishly.[67] The National Liberals, too,
criticised and amended government bills with great freedom, even in
the 1870s, often forcing Bismarck to accept a compromise. In Prussia
they enthusiastically supported the *Kulturkampf* legislation but were also
not infrequently cast in an oppositional role, attacking the activities of
the more reactionary ministers from the constitutional conflict era who
still remained in office. The rise of the two mass parties, the Centre and
the Social Democrats, from 1871 inevitably complicated the party constellation. They were best able to exploit the democratic franchise but
Bismarck's campaigns against them also served to define and radicalise
their constituencies.

Bismarck's collaboration with the liberal majority was never very
smooth, especially since he consistently opposed any extension of parliamentary power after 1871. In retrospect their collaboration was very
much on the chancellor's terms because the liberals never pushed the
issue of parliamentary power to a complete rupture and many were in
awe of Bismarck as the architect of German unity. But ostensibly the
National Liberals were in a strong position – after the elections of March
1871 they had 125 seats and they made further gains in the elections
of January 1874. Bismarck needed their support as the one genuinely
national party, which drew significant support from the non-Prussian
states. He developed a good understanding with National Liberals on the
right of the party, above all Rudolf von Bennigsen, but he resented pressure from the left of the party to augment the role of the Reichstag.
Franz Schenk von Stauffenberg and especially Eduard Lasker, both of
whom Bennigsen also wanted to be offered ministerial positions in 1877,
were committed to further constitutional change and far less willing
collaborators with Bismarck. Lasker, a highly effective and intelligent
Jewish parliamentarian, was largely responsible for uncovering the
corruption scandal in 1873 which forced the resignation of Bismarck's
close associate, Hermann Wagener. When Lasker died in January 1884,
Bismarck forbade five members of the Prussian state ministry from
attending his funeral. Fortified by one and a half bottles of Mosel wine,
he also vilified the dead man for his relentless opposition to his policies
in a Reichstag speech.[68]

The *Kulturkampf* in Prussia cemented Bismarck's collaboration with
the liberals (although it also ultimately compromised German liberalism),
but a key issue that strained their alliance was control over the military

budget. Bismarck succeeded in having the military budget fixed for a further three years in 1871 rather than reviewed annually as the liberals wished. But the likelihood of a compromise was far less evident in 1874 because Stauffenberg and Lasker were inclined to make common cause with the Progressives, led by Eugen Richter, who invariably opposed Bismarck's policies. The Kaiser and his Military Cabinet favoured an 'eternal budget' or *Aeternat*, which would provide a lump sum per capita of the population. Eventually Bismarck was able to negotiate a compromise with Bennigsen which even Lasker was prepared to accept rather than risk splitting their party. The *Septennat* or seven-year budget granted the means to maintain a peacetime army of 402,000 men for seven years. This arrangement was bitterly attacked by the Progressives, for it was highly unlikely that parliamentarians, elected every three years, could build up the expertise to scrutinise such a budget adequately and thus it meant that the army further evaded political controls. Bismarck, however, doubtless welcomed the compromise for, without conceding much to the Reichstag, he had stymied the *Aeternat* which would have rendered the generals even more independent of his own political control. Bismarck's press law in 1874 also produced a crisis with the liberal majority since, although ministers such as Itzenplitz believed it conceded too much to the liberals, they themselves saw it as counter to the liberal principle of free speech. Again a compromise was devised, but the left-wing National Liberals persisted in criticising what they saw as a repressive law and they opposed Bismarck when he later sought to increase the penalties on journalists and editors who, in the chancellor's view, attacked the foundations of the state.

For the duration of his chancellorship, Bismarck needed the support of the majority of the National Liberals, the party most committed to the national idea, if he was to consolidate the Reich. However, he was never satisfied with his dependence on a liberal majority in the Reichstag and the lack of any viable alternative. Bismarck was concerned about the liberals' persistent efforts to weaken the authoritarian aspects of the Reich constitution and he wanted to stabilise the conservative basis of the state. This appeared particularly urgent in view of Wilhelm I's age and the imminent succession of the reputedly liberal crown prince. Bismarck talked about the need to reconstitute the party system in Germany from quite early in the 1870s. By 1875 he was looking for a way of severing the left-wing National Liberals from the party to facilitate its drift to the right and perhaps make possible an alternative right-wing coalition which could support the government on certain issues. Bismarck also contributed to the emergence of the newly constituted German Conservative

Party in July 1876 which, as its name indicated, aspired to appeal beyond Prussia. In February 1876 Bismarck had declared war on the *Kreuzzeitung* after it viciously attacked the liberal era of Bleichröder, Delbrück and Camphausen in a series of articles. Bismarck, however, remained very bitter that some of his former political friends chose to side with the *Kreuzzeitung* against him and many of the so-called *Deklaranten* who had attacked him were members of the new party. Bismarck thus never personally associated himself with the German Conservative Party, but its emergence improved the prospects of forging an alternative conservative majority.

It was not, however, until 1878–79 that Bismarck succeeded in his aim of splitting the National Liberal Party and creating a new parliamentary constellation, and this is often seen as part of a more general change of course in his chancellorship called the *Wende* or 'turning-point'. In 1878 Bismarck seized the opportunity presented by two assassination attempts on the life of Wilhelm I to attack democratic liberalism. The first was by an unemployed plumber's apprentice called Max Hödel on 11 May and the second by Karl Nobiling, a psychopath with a doctorate, on 2 June.[69] After Hödel's attempt, which failed to hit its target, Bismarck pushed an exceptional draft law against social democracy through the Prussian ministry of state and the Bundesrat despite their misgivings (for there was no evidence of socialist involvement in either incident). He anticipated that such a law would place an inordinate strain on liberal unity in the Reichstag, but in the event he was resoundingly defeated for the bill was rejected by 251 votes to 57 votes in May 1878. Whether he was indifferent to this defeat (as Otto Pflanze has argued) or left dangerously exposed and isolated (as Lothar Gall has suggested), Bismarck was rescued from his predicament by the second, far more serious attempt on Wilhelm's life on 2 June. Bismarck was in the park at Friedrichsruh when Tiedemann brought the news of the assassination attempt, and he famously reacted with a shocking degree of ruthlessness and rage, exclaiming, 'Then we'll dissolve the Reichstag!' even before he enquired after the wellbeing of the monarch. Another version of events has Bismarck exclaiming 'Now I've got them!' – by which he meant the National Liberals rather than the Social Democrats – but the chancellor always denied that he said this.[70] At a crown council meeting on 5 June presided over by the crown prince, Bismarck found himself in a minority in wishing to dissolve the Reichstag over the issue. Most of the ministers believed that the Reichstag would now pass a new anti-socialist bill and that fresh elections would not necessarily strengthen the conservatives or lead to greater political stability. But Bismarck appeared to be in a highly irrational and emotional state at this time, suspecting all kinds of liberal intrigues to oust him from power and anxious to undermine the position of any potential political rivals. He made the issue one of confidence in his leadership and used the threat of constitutional changes to force the Bundesrat, too, to agree unanimously to a Reichstag dissolution, despite the misgivings of Baden and Bavaria.[71]

The Reichstag was dissolved on 11 June and the subsequent election campaign was deliberately conducted in an atmosphere of crisis. The government used all the means at its disposal to influence the voters and presented the key issue in the starkest of terms, namely whether one was for or against the *Reichsgründer*. The results were seen as a victory for Bismarck but, although the National Liberals, Progressives and Social Democrats all lost seats, they were perhaps not so politically damaging for liberalism as they first appeared. The liberals still had a small majority over the two conservative parties (both of which made gains) and the National Liberals remained the strongest party. But the Centre, now with 94 seats, occupied a key position and the National Liberals, having enjoyed a pivotal position since 1867, no longer appeared so indispensable. The National Liberals, after much agonising over whether to support such an illiberal law, voted with the conservatives for the revised anti-socialist law in October 1878. Bennigsen, who could never quite jettison his awe of the great man and his achievements for the national cause, was ultimately prepared to compromise with Bismarck. But his decision helped to fracture his party and has been seen as symptomatic of its political and moral decline.[72]

The emergency legislation against Social Democracy helped Bismarck to sow dissension within liberal ranks. But it was the growing political significance of economic issues from 1873, specifically the debate about economic protectionism, that served to undermine German liberalism and expose the cleavage within it. After the right wing of the National Liberals (approximately one-quarter of the party) publicly joined the conservative parties and the Centre in declaring its support for protectionism in October 1878, Bismarck set in motion the change of economic course that he had come to believe was both opportune and necessary. The tariff bill was introduced into the Reichstag in April 1879 and accepted by a majority composed of conservatives, Centre and right-wing National Liberals. Lasker taunted Bismarck for defending the interests of the propertied classes. But the chancellor appealed to the Bible in pouring scorn on the professional politicians without property because 'they sow not, neither do they reap, they do not weave nor spin, and yet they are clothed'.[73] He rejected the efforts of Bennigsen to secure a compromise that might have preserved the unity of his party and instead opted for the Franckenstein clause formulated by the federalist Centre Party. The government, he maintained, needed the support of the political parties but it should not submit to the 'rule of one parliamentary party'.[74]

The significance of this so-called *Wende* or 'turning-point' has been much debated in the historiography of imperial Germany. Liberals, dismayed by the abandonment of *laissez-faire*, branded it a change of system, and many historians have followed Hans-Ulrich Wehler and Helmut Böhme in arguing that Bismarck 're-founded' the Reich on a conservative basis at this juncture.[75] Bismarck, it is claimed, exploited the shift to economic protectionism in 1879 to base the regime on a new coalition of interests (or *Sammlung*) between the large-scale agrarian landowners and the representatives of heavy industry, an alliance which determined the political development of the Reich until its collapse in 1918. Others have questioned the stability and durability of this alliance of 'iron and rye' and seen the contrast between the liberal 1870s and the conservative 1880s as overdrawn.[76] The Reich was conservative and authoritarian from the start, based as it was on the successful power politics of a military monarchy, and much of the legislation supported by the liberals in the 1870s had strengthened the authoritarian state. While its potential to evolve into a liberal constitutional state should not be dismissed out of hand – and Bismarck certainly took the possibility seriously, given that the crown prince and his wife were waiting in the wings – the events of 1878–79 highlighted the weaknesses within German national liberalism. As we have seen, the controversial issue of economic protectionism was not so central to the government's strategy in 1878–79, and the growing fiscal crisis and need to consolidate the financial structure of the Reich preoccupied Bismarck more. Ernst Engelberg has argued that the decisions taken in 1878–79 were significant not because they changed the essence of the state but because they changed nothing at a time when historical and political progress demanded it.[77]

The complex crisis of 1878–79 had a long gestation period but it was also the result of autonomous developments, and Bismarck was as much reacting to events as shaping them himself. The growing mood of economic insecurity after the boom and crash of 1873 provided a significant new context for imperial domestic politics, undermining confidence in liberal economic doctrine and challenging assumptions of sustained economic progress. The economic crisis forged new political and social links between agrarian landowners and a section of heavy industry, both increasingly concerned about the impact of foreign competition and cheap imports and prepared to lobby for the abandonment of economic liberalism. The political parties, unwilling to take unpalatable decisions and thereby risk party unity, preferred not to participate in the flurried organisation of economic interest groups and opted instead to look to the government to deal with the contentious issues which arose from the new economic climate. Bismarck was personally experiencing difficulties selling grain and timber as a landowner in the late 1870s and he followed with interest the growing debate over whether Germany should introduce protective tariffs. But he was more engaged by other schemes to reform the tax system and raise revenue, and in the first half of 1879 he was more concerned about the differential freight rates on Germany's railways, which he saw as favouring foreign producers, than about protective tariffs.[78] For Bismarck, economic protectionism increasingly appeared to be a cause that had strong support outside the Reichstag, could cement a new majority with the otherwise oppositional Centre Party and be used against the liberals. It provided a means of demonstrating to the liberals that they were not indispensable and that they would have to rein back their political aspirations. In February 1878 he took a first step when he proposed a state tobacco monopoly and appeared to declare war on the left wing of the National Liberals who supported free trade. The Grand Duke of Baden immediately recognised that a Reichstag dissolution would have to follow since there was no way that Bismarck could achieve these plans with the current Reichstag.[79]

Bismarck acted with characteristic swiftness and ruthlessness in 1878–79. He caught his opponents by surprise and confused even his own supporters. But he also clearly kept alternative courses of action open until the very last minute. In February 1879 (at a time when, according to Holstein, Bismarck was 'avidly gobbling up economic issues'[80]) he told Moritz Busch that the liberals had turned away from him and that they could have got a lot more out of him if they had not put the existence of their party first.[81] Ultimately the power issue was probably central to Bismarck's manoeuvres in 1878–79. He was prepared to jettison all those, whether ministerial colleagues or former parliamentary allies, who served to constrain his exercise of power, and he saw no future for himself in further cooperation with the National Liberals. Lothar Gall has claimed Bismarck gave up his role as the mediator of compromise in 1878–79 and chose to base his position on the support of the traditional classes, even though he suspected he was entering a blind alley personally and politically.[82] Bismarck, however, betrayed few signs of reluctance or resignation in 1879. Rather, he found new sources of energy and adrenalin as he sought to persuade, cajole and manipulate those around him to do his bidding. Whether sensationally entering into dialogue with Windthorst, whipping the Bundesrat into line, disposing of liberal ministers or re-organising the Reich executive, Bismarck was intent on consolidating his own power position and tightening his grip over all aspects of domestic policy. His essential authoritarianism was given free rein.

Yet Bismarck did not achieve all he wanted from the *Wende* and he failed to exploit all the possibilities created by the developing situation. Just as he could not provide the Reich with a secure financial structure or retard the growth of social democracy, so he could not create pliable majorities for his policies in the Reichstag. The *Wende* did not enable Bismarck to replace the liberal majority that had dominated the Reichstag since 1867 with a conservative parliamentary coalition in the 1880s. In-deed, Bismarck never hoped to replace his dependence on one coalition with dependence on another. If he had a parliamentary strategy, it was always to preserve his freedom of manoeuvre even if he often talked about establishing a stable basis of parliamentary support and professed to envy the British two-party system. Crucially, though, he never expected to be able to govern without the National Liberals, who he continued to see representing the most dynamic and (outside Prussia) the most national forces in German society that had to be harnessed to the Hohenzollern monarchy. The idea of governing on the basis of a coali-tion of conservative, clerical and particularist forces could not be seri-ously entertained. At best Bismarck hoped to encourage the National Liberals to work more closely with the two conservative parties so that the centre of gravity in the parliaments would shift to the right. The possibility of alternative coalitions might serve to tame the political parties and restore his freedom of action.

Bismarck, however, was to be bitterly disappointed in the 1880s, for his relations with the political parties proved to be extremely volatile. The Centre was in no mood to forget its treatment during the *Kulturkampf*, to shift to become a governmental party or allow its Catholic voters to drift back into the (Protestant) political mainstream. Moreover, despite the historical consensus about a shift to conservatism after 1879, this was not reflected in the parliamentary arena in the early 1880s when, on the contrary, liberalism seemed to have emerged from the crisis with renewed vitality. In the early 1880s it appeared to be the Progressives who had gained the most from the split in national liberalism. The Seces-sionists left the National Liberal Party in 1880 (they criticised Bennigsen and the majority for agreeing to the dismantling of the *Kulturkampf* legislation), but Bismarck had to look on while the former left wing slowly restored its links with the Progressives led by Richter. They even-tually merged into a new party, the German Radical (*Freisinnige*) Party, in March 1884. Nor did the left liberals suffer a dent in their popularity at the polls. On the contrary, the results of the Reichstag elections of 1881 and 1884 appeared to indicate that a powerful liberal opposition movement was gathering momentum, a movement which could support and legitimise a radical change of course once Friedrich Wilhelm acceded to the throne. The elections of 1881 decimated the National Liberals and *Reichspartei*. Otto Pflanze has called them 'the greatest reversal in German politics since 1866'.[83] A government analysis contrasted the 'lazy and miserly' conservatives with the left liberal supporters (especially the Jews, responding to anti-Semitic agitation) who were 'active and willing to make sacrifices'. Bismarck's tax reform proposals were also blamed. 'The great reform plans of the Prince have aroused displeasure among the uneducated masses which has been transformed into fear by the self-serving, mendacious Progressive agitation.'[84] Bismarck appeared more isolated and exposed, more out of tune with the public mood, than at any time since becoming chancellor.

Bismarck's efforts to undermine the political parties and to bypass parliamentary processes in the 1880s must be seen in this context. Ending the period of sustained collaboration with the National Liberals meant attempting to govern 'above the parties' with majorities which shifted according to the issue. But Bismarck's attempts to control and manipulate the parties, indeed to construct any majority, met with frustration and failure. Despite its role in the 'Franckenstein coalition', the Centre remained implacably opposed to the government on issues such as the 'iron budget' and colonies, and it was divided over the discriminatory anti-socialist law. In 1881 it joined with the left liberals in defeating Bismarck's tax programme in the Reichstag. The Centre had 100 seats after the elections of 1881 and, although they were divided, the so-called 'enemies of the Reich' – the Centre, left liberals and Social Democrats – commanded over two-thirds of the seats in the Reichstag. A coalition of National Liberals and conservatives was not a viable option and, as Bismarck acknowledged, it would have involved splitting the Conservative Party as well as the National Liberals.[85]

The elections of 1881 thus inaugurated what was perhaps the most difficult period of Bismarck's chancellorship. While he consolidated his grip over the executive, his plans were repeatedly frustrated in the legislature by parties that he regarded as hostile to the state and intent on undermining the process of national consolidation. Otto Pflanze has argued that only in the mid-1880s did Bismarck recover a sense of realism and cease to present the parliaments with bills that had no chance of success.[86] He endeavoured to pursue policies that had no basis of political support in the Reichstag and no broader social support in a country undergoing rapid social and economic transformation. Only the distortions arising from the three-class suffrage in Prussia facilitated his conservative and repressive policies there.

Bismarck could never really believe that the Reichstag elections accurately reflected the views and mood of the electorate. Hence he resorted to increasingly desperate ways of bypassing the Reichstag or eliminating its influence altogether. He supported the creation of a corporatist Prussian economic council (*Wirtschaftsrat*), composed of representatives from industry, trade and agriculture and from professional organisations. The economic council met from January 1881 to advise on economic legislation and Bismarck conceded that, unlike parliamentary deputies, its 75 members should receive daily allowances. But Bismarck's plan to create a German economic council with additional representatives from the Reich was successfully opposed by the political parties in the Reichstag who saw it as a rival 'species of parallel and counter parliament'.[87] He let the Prussian economic council expire after January 1884. Bismarck also considered reforming the Reichstag suffrage, perhaps by introducing indirect election or (since he blamed his defeat in 1881 on a low turn-out) by making voting compulsory. He toyed with the idea of organising the Reichstag's representation on corporatist lines and thus eliminating the parties. 'I believe that political parties and groupings in accordance with high politics and political programmes have outlived their usefulness', he told the Reichstag in 1884. He suggested that they 'will gradually be compelled, if they do not do it voluntarily, to take up a position on economic questions and pursue more than hitherto a policy of interests'. Defeated by the spirit of the age, 'the parties will disappear and melt away in politics like ice and snow'.[88] Bismarck considered preventing parliamentary deputies sitting in more than one parliament, and he also had doubts about the viability of the parliamentary process itself. In June 1882 he threatened that the federal princes, who had created the Reich, could agree on new proposals to change the nature of the union. But there is no real evidence that he seriously considered such a course or that he planned to institute a *Staatsstreich* in the early 1880s.

The parliamentary opposition, although rarely united, sensed in the 1880s that Bismarck was intent on augmenting the power of an authoritarian and increasingly interventionist state. His social policy, tax reforms, preferential treatment of landed interests, anti-socialism and even his colonial ventures all made him suspect. As elections to the Prussian Landtag in the 1880s produced an increasingly conservative chamber, the divergence between the two parliaments Bismarck had to work with became increasingly apparent. A majority in the Reichstag attacked the Landtag majority's support of Germanisation measures in the Polish provinces, but it could do nothing to stop the policies of the Prussian government.

Ultimately there was a sense in which parliamentary politics could never be completely 'normal' under Bismarck. Bismarck was the *Reichsgründer* who had conjured not only the Reich but also the Reichstag into being, and throughout the first twenty years of the Reich's existence, this placed the political parties under massive pressure. Bismarck constantly tinkered with what he had created and saw no arrangement as fixed. He believed he had the right to change the constitution if he saw fit. Moreover, he tended to make every election into a referendum on his policies, past and present. He virtually forced the electorate not to vote in terms of left or right, liberalism or conservatism, ideology or material interests, but to support him or oppose him, with the consequence that they were either patriots or enemies of the Reich.

This was perhaps most apparent in the Reichstag elections of February 1887, sometimes seen as Bismarck's last great coup in domestic policy akin to those of 1866–67 and 1878–79. Bismarck had presented the Reichstag with another *Septennat* army bill in November 1886, one year ahead of schedule, and his intent was clearly provocative. The opposition parties sought a compromise – Windthorst offered a *Quinquennat*, a budget covering five years – but Bismarck sought a dissolution. In January 1887 he made speeches in which he focused attention on the threatening international situation, both with respect to *revanchist* Boulangism in France and the crisis in the Near East.[89] When the Reichstag majority, including the Centre, voted for a three-year military budget that was unacceptable to the government, Bismarck read out Wilhelm I's order that the Reichstag be dissolved. In the elections, which were conducted in an atmosphere of international crisis, Bismarck castigated the unpatriotic opposition parties in the press and used the Prussian Landtag as a forum in which to attack the Reichstag. The turn-out was 77 per cent (it had been 60.5 per cent in 1884) and the result was a resounding victory for the newly formed *Kartell* coalition of the two conservative parties and the National Liberals. The National Liberals almost doubled their representation (from 51 seats to 99 seats) and the chief losers were the Radical Party and Social Democrats (although the socialists' share of the popular vote actually went up). For the last time the voters did what Bismarck asked them to do. The *Septennat* was passed by the new Reichstag in March 1887.

Bismarck's personality and political career undoubtedly cast a deep shadow over German political life and no political party could escape the history of its relationship with him. His relationship with the press and 'public opinion' can also be seen as corrosive of imperial German political culture. He believed that it was possible to manipulate the press and corrupt journalists, to stifle public debate and dictate public opinion. It was well known that Bismarck had at his disposal the Guelph fund, the interest from the property of the deposed Hanoverian monarch, which enabled him to purchase influence in the press by bribing journalists and financing newspapers. The Guelph fund was dubbed his 'reptile fund' after Bismarck asserted in a Landtag speech in 1869 that they needed to pursue 'vicious reptiles right into their hollows to see what they are up to'. As he later acknowledged, however, it was increasingly the Foreign Office spies rather than the subversive journalists who were seen as the vicious reptiles.[90] Notoriously, too, during his long career Bismarck resorted to press decrees and exceptional laws to repress and intimidate independent newspapers and journalists. In 1878 his proposal to create a Reich Office of Censorship and Police was blocked by the states.[91] On numerous occasions he also initiated legal proceedings against editors and journalists whom he accused of libel and slander. In public Bismarck lambasted the press for its 'monstrous mendacity' and he once remarked that 'Every press attack must be smashed, every insult must be avenged.'[92] Fritz Stern has asserted that Bismarck treated the fourth estate 'as he treated all objects of importance: as something to be fought, manipulated, cajoled'.[93]

Nevertheless, as in most spheres of German domestic policy, Bismarck did not have a systematic approach to the government's relations with the press and it is possible to overstate the extent of his press and information policy. Bernd Sösemann has recently argued that many aspects of government press policy cannot be identified with Bismarck personally, for many government departments pursued their own initiatives, quite apart from the contributions made by diplomats, provincial agencies, the police and the courts.[94] Moreover, Bismarck never devised any kind of strategy for the long-term influencing of the press. Far from being autocratically prescriptive in this sphere, he sought to maintain flexibility and freedom of manoeuvre. He never liked to tie himself down to one view or line of action, and preferred to adapt his choices and responses in accordance with an unpredictable course of events. Even the government newspaper, the *Norddeutsche Allgemeine Zeitung*, did not express a consistent or uniform view about foreign policy in the 1870s, and Bismarck also resisted attempts by the minister of interior, Friedrich zu Eulenburg, to politicise the *Reichsanzeiger*, which was used for official announcements.

Bismarck had always recognised the importance of the press and at decisive moments he could use the press with great skill. There is no doubt, too, that during election campaigns and times of crisis, there might be a flood of press articles and leaflets penned by government officials who were essentially articulating Bismarck's views. But the press law of 1874 rendered direct government interference much more difficult than it had been previously. Moreover, the War in Sight crisis of 1875, which was triggered by a government-inspired press article and will be discussed in more detail below, encouraged Bismarck to become more reticent, at least for a time, about all too obvious attempts to manipulate the press which were likely to backfire. Although there is a paucity of evidence, for much of the 1880s Bismarck seems to have preferred to restrict the number of semi-official (offiziös) newspapers to which the government gave information. He relied on a small number of journalists whom he knew to be discreet; and he was very careful about what he gave them – once admitting that he gave them very little – since he did not want to jeopardise his remaining, all too tenuous political links to their liberal readership.

Bismarck lacked the organisational apparatus for a coherent, coordin-ated press policy and he never sought to create one. There was a small press department in the Foreign Office and a literary bureau staffed by unpolitical bureaucrats in the Prussian Ministry of Interior (which mainly served the provincial press). But, as in other areas of policy, Bismarck mistrusted officials and he preferred to give press assignments to his trusted subordinates such as Bucher, Busch and Holstein, who had proven political skills, rather than to work with a press bureau which required clear strategic guidance. In 1877, for example, Bismarck gave Busch material for seven articles (the so-called 'friction articles') which outlined the problems he was encountering in the Berlin executive.[95] In addition, even allowing for the Guelph fund, the amount of money the Berlin government had at its disposal for press purposes was modest by inter-national standards, and Bernd Sösemann has maintained that Bismarck was in no position to corrupt the political press. Berlin's political press, in any case, remained overwhelmingly in liberal hands throughout Bis-marck's chancellorship. If the opposition press practised restraint, this was doubtless as much a consequence of the anti-socialist law as of bribery and manipulation.

Thus, in the press as in the parliaments, the idea that Bismarck singlehandedly poisoned the political culture of imperial Germany for a generation probably belongs in the realms of contemporary fantasy. But, although many developments in German public life were independent of

Bismarck, his public pronouncements and gladiatorial style reinforced perceptions of his despotic and dictatorial regime. His policies often appeared deliberately divisive and provocative, and Holstein likened his procedure in parliament to a sport. 'He introduces an intrinsically sensible proposal, defends it in such an aggressive fashion that Parliament rejects it purely from anger, and then he writes newspaper articles attacking parliamentarianism', he maintained, convinced that Bismarck wanted to make people so indignant that they could not be governed without him.[96] Increasingly by the 1880s there is evidence that parliamentarians, like members of the court, army and higher bureaucracy in Berlin, were marking time and waiting for the inevitable moment in the future when Bismarck would have to leave the political stage. Only then, it was believed, might the business of politics assume some semblance of normality.

Bismarck and German foreign policy

From 1871 to 1890 Bismarck controlled German foreign policy. His diplomatic expertise and successes in the period 1862–71 reinforced the institutional power he wielded as Reich chancellor and Prussian foreign minister, ensuring that there were no significant barriers to the implementation of his will in this sphere. His views were occasionally challenged. Bismarck insisted on the recall of the German ambassador to Paris, Harry Arnim, in 1874 because he had been working on his own initiative to restore the monarchy in France; and in 1879 he had to impose his will on the Kaiser who resisted signing the Dual Alliance with Austria. By the late 1880s, too, there was widespread criticism in Berlin of his policy towards Russia. But Bismarck's will always prevailed and there was no scope for any kind of collective discussion of foreign policy. In effect there was a consensus in Berlin political circles that, however damaging aspects of his domestic policy might be, the chancellor was indispensable in foreign policy.

Bismarck exerted a tight grip over the affairs of the German Foreign Office (which superseded the Prussian Foreign Ministry from 1870) and expected diplomats to 'fall into rank like soldiers'.[97] While many of his officials worked loyally for him for years, Bismarck was an exacting chief who was regarded with adulation, awe and not infrequently terror. Aloof and uncompromising, Bismarck allowed few officials regular access to him apart from the state secretary, whose influence was also circumscribed. The position of state secretary of the Foreign Office was perhaps the most unenviable job in Berlin. The difficulties of working with Bismarck personally, the quantity of work and the meagre salary in comparison to ambassadorships all ensured that most high-level diplomats dreaded being summoned to work in the Wilhelmstrasse. Bismarck enjoyed a smooth and harmonious relationship with Bernhard Ernst von Bülow, who held the state secretaryship from 1873 until his unexpected death in 1879, but the dearth of suitable candidates for the position became all too evident in the early 1880s. After successive provisional arrangements, the Catholic Paul von Hatzfeldt formally took over in October 1882. But Hatzfeldt's dislike of the routine nature of the work, his lack of parliamentary skill, his debts and his ex-wife (an extravagant and flirtatious American whom Bismarck had insisted he divorce before becoming state secretary) all militated against him. Bismarck never appreciated his relaxed style and sent him as ambassador to London in 1885. In May 1886 Bismarck finally achieved his optimum solution when his son, Herbert, had sufficient experience to be promoted from under state secretary to his deputy at the age of 36. Bismarck trusted his son implicitly and as state secretary Herbert was prepared to take upon himself many of the onerous tasks that had burdened his ageing father. But, confronted with the intricacies of Bismarck's diplomacy, even Herbert used to say, 'My father is the only person who can handle this business.'[98]

From 1871 Bismarck's primary concern in foreign policy was to preserve his new Reich and guard against any attempts by the other European powers to undo his work of unification. Much has been written about the famous 'alliance system' that he allegedly devised in order to isolate France, whose implacable enmity towards Germany after the annexation of Alsace-Lorraine he now considered to be a permanent feature in international relations. Bismarck had believed from the 1850s that 'the influence of a power in peacetime ultimately depends on the force it can muster in war and on the alliances with which it can embark on war'.[99] Nevertheless, it was not until the later 1870s that Bismarck fully appreciated the need to create a stable international framework in which Berlin could enjoy good relations with all the major powers with the exception of France. And it was not until the 1880s that the treaties he concluded with the other powers of Europe in any way assumed the character of a 'system', albeit one that he never regarded as permanent or fixed. Recent historians have been more inclined to talk about Bismarck's 'system of stopgaps' than a coherent system of alliances, planned and realised.[100] Bismarck's foreign policy, like his domestic policy, was largely characterised by his predilection for improvisation. Never claiming to be able to predict the future, he always saw diplomatic arrangements as provisional rather than fixed; and unlike his successors in the Foreign Office, he generally preferred elastic, even ambiguous solutions to problems rather than clear and definite outcomes.

Bismarck did not change overnight in 1871 from being a bold and sometimes impetuous foreign policy gambler to a conservative statesman who emphasised Germany's restraint as a 'satiated power' and recommended himself as an impartial 'honest broker' in international disputes. After the Franco-Prussian war, Bismarck knew that it was imperative to keep France weak and internationally isolated. Thus he endorsed the establishment of a republican regime in Paris if that served to ostracise France among the monarchies of Europe, for most of which dynastic relations formed an integral part of diplomacy. He also supported the imposition of a heavy indemnity of 5,000 million francs on France and he was not alone in believing that it would burden France for much longer than proved to be the case. But he was only to learn over time and through bitter experience that the preservation of what he had achieved in Germany was also predicated upon the preservation of peace and stability in Europe. Bismarck had to suffer a major diplomatic reverse in 1875 before he began to come to terms with the international implications of German unification. And he recognised only gradually that, even if Germany was becoming the most powerful and dynamic state on the continent, it could not exercise more than a 'latent hegemony' in Europe. By the late 1880s autonomous pressures already called into question the Reich's future in a stable Europe and Bismarck had to devote more and more effort to ensuring that Berlin remained at the fulcrum of European diplomacy.

The mistrust which had surrounded Bismarck at home in the 1860s was magnified in the foreign offices and chancelleries of Europe in the 1870s. Many foreign diplomats harboured deep suspicions about Bismarck's diplomacy and politics and held him personally responsible for the upheavals in international relations since 1862. Bismarck had sought to justify his pursuit of power politics by appealing to nationalist aspirations, but the annexation of the French provinces appeared to belie the notion that the new German Reich was the legitimate political expression of the German nation. In Britain there were fears that Bismarck might yet turn into another Napoleon, seeking to change the map of Europe more radically in the interests of Prussian aggrandisement.[101] Disraeli famously commented in February 1871 that what they had witnessed amounted to the 'German revolution, a greater political event than the French Revolution of last century'.[102] He claimed the balance of power had been completely destroyed and that the country which suffered most as a result was England. The correspondence between the German crown princess, who was deeply antithetical to the 'adventurer', Bismarck, and her mother, Queen Victoria, also doubtless did little to calm British fears about the direction of German policy.[103]

On the continent of Europe Bismarck had to reassure especially Austria-Hungary and Russia that the new Reich would not seek to extend its borders to include the millions of Germans who remained outside it. The task of convincing Austria that Prussia did not aspire to create a *Großdeutschland* was facilitated by the removal of the anti-Prussian Austrian foreign minister, Beust, in November 1871. Beust's replacement, Count Gyula Andrássy, became a significant partner for Bismarck in helping to foster harmonious Austro-German relations and consolidate the Reich's international position in the 1870s. In October 1873 they both signed a loose and informal agreement with Russia. The Three Emperors' League suited Bismarck's purposes in resurrecting the principle of conservative solidarity, even though it had a precarious quality from the start because of the clash of interests between Austria and Russia in the Balkans. Prussia's good relations with Russia (based not least on their mutual interest in suppressing the Poles) had been placed under strain by the events of German unification, and Russia expected Bismarck now to render counter-services in return for its benevolent neutrality in 1866 and 1870–71. The Reich's rapprochement with Austria eased Russian pressure for compensation a little although it scarcely satisfied it. It indicated that Bismarck wished to maintain good relations with both his eastern neighbours without supporting the interests of either state in the Balkans. In particular, Bismarck was beginning to see Russian designs to gain control over the Straits as incompatible with the Reich's security. But this did not stop him from sending a special envoy, Radowitz, to St Petersburg in February 1875, offering the Russians a free hand in the Near East if in exchange Russia would pledge to remain neutral in another German war against France, a prospective deal that Russia rebuffed.[104] The Three Emperors' League also made it less likely that Russia or Austria would seek a rapprochement with France, a possibility that was considered more seriously in St Petersburg where an anti-German Pan-Slav nationalism was beginning to make its influence felt at the Tsar's court.

Bismarck made efforts in the early 1870s to normalise the Reich's relations with the other European powers and integrate his new creation into the European state system. Yet just as the other powers of Europe felt threatened by a new, dynamic state in their midst, so Bismarck too took time to come to terms with the international implications of his new creation. He saw the Reich threatened by potentially hostile forces and his recurring nightmare from 1871 was that the other powers would form a hostile coalition, intent on undoing his work. If a 'Kaunitz coalition' (the name refers to the anti-Prussian coalition of 1756) of France, Austria and Russia appeared less likely after the Three Emperors' League, Bismarck could not afford to be complacent. Despite a boast to his daughter in 1872 while at Varzin that he could deal with the affairs of Europe in the ten to fifteen minutes before breakfast,[105] his diplomacy in the early 1870s was characterised by the same edgy nervousness and unpredictability that manifested itself in his domestic policy. At home and abroad he was prone to imagining all kinds of conspiracies directed against him. While his aim was essentially conservative – the preservation of the Reich – the methods he chose did not engender confidence or diminish the likelihood of encirclement. Bismarck had not yet learnt that cool, cautious statesmanship elicited a more positive response from the European powers than sudden, dramatic interventions and scaremongering. In the early 1870s Bismarck's diplomacy risked isolating the Reich rather than France. Arguably he was only able to prevent this possibility because external factors, above all the crisis in the Near East and the imperialist rivalries of the other European powers, independently encouraged the major powers to maintain good relations with Germany.

This was amply illustrated in 1875 when Bismarck's diplomacy was surprisingly inept, chiefly because he had not yet realised the extent to which the new Germany enjoyed a position of latent hegemony in Europe. The so-called 'War in Sight crisis' raised the spectre of another war between France and Germany after an article in a Berlin newspaper, the *Post*, on 8 April 1875 aroused fears of France's reorganisation of its army and the introduction of compulsory military service. Although Bismarck later denied all involvement, the article, which was written by a Prussian official, Konstantin Rössler, was the first of several inspired by the Foreign Office's press department and there is little doubt that Bismarck authorised the campaign. Bismarck had been shocked at the speed with which France had paid off the indemnity. France completed the payments in September 1873, thus bringing to an end the period of German occupation of its eastern *départements* and regaining full sovereignty that autumn. Aware of the scale of French resentment over the loss of Alsace-Lorraine, Bismarck was also concerned about the growing influence of monarchist, clerical and Catholic forces in French politics and he blamed the French bishops and the ultramontane press for warmongering. The Radowitz mission to St Petersburg in February 1875 indicates how threatening Bismarck perceived the situation to be, even before the French assembly completed the army reform legislation in March.

In precipitating another crisis in 1875, Bismarck probably wanted to warn France diplomatically and through the press not to consider a war of revenge, and to demonstrate France's isolation in Europe. There is no evidence that he had any serious plans to go to war again in 1875, although his reputation was such that it could not be ruled out that he was preparing German public opinion for such an eventuality. There is also little evidence that he seriously believed that France was contemplating a war against Germany in the near future, although he wrote to Wilhelm I on 5 April that France's excessive rearmament indicated that France was preparing to go to war sooner than they had expected.[106] Bismarck hoped to create a crisis that would intimidate France and benefit the Reich internationally. Three days after the *Post*'s article under the heading 'Is War in Sight?' Bismarck told Robert Lucius von Ballhausen, a leader of the Free Conservatives and later (from 1879) Prussian minister of agriculture, 'I am pleased that it appeared in an independent – not official – newspaper and that I do not have to answer for it. It is quite useful if occasionally a very bright ray of light is thrown on the confused situation. Of war there is no talk whatever.' Bismarck clearly believed that the article 'would have a useful, peaceful effect'.[107]

His move, however, had no such effect as the other European powers were alarmed by Bismarck's posturing, which also shocked Wilhelm I, and they made it quite clear to Berlin that they would not tolerate another French defeat like that of 1871. Even the Russian premier, Gorchakov, who was visiting Berlin in May 1875, supported republican France and, much to Bismarck's annoyance, sought categorical assurances from Bismarck that he had peaceful intentions.[108] Queen Victoria was convinced that Bismarck was intent on achieving continental supremacy and Tsar Alexander II likened him to Napoleon, 'who at the end of each war sought a pretext to begin another one'.[109] Bismarck thus did not emerge personally unscathed from the crisis, which Otto Pflanze has called his 'greatest diplomatic defeat' and attributed to his poor state of health at the time.[110] Apart from conjuring up the spectre of a coalition of Britain, Russia and France to contain German expansionism (presaging the Triple Entente of 1907), Bismarck was now labelled an aggressive disturber of the peace. He submitted his resignation in May 1875 and this was probably the only occasion when he meant it seriously.

Bismarck reformulated his ideas on German foreign policy in the later 1870s. His famous Kissingen Dictate of 15 June 1877 was unusual in its formulation of a clear strategy and it highlighted his fears about an anti-German alliance (his '*cauchemar des coalitions*'). It elevated the principle that in an unstable equilibrium of five great powers in Europe, Germany should always seek to be one of three. Bismarck described his general aim as being to achieve 'an overall political situation in which all the great powers except France have need of us and are as far as possible kept from forming coalitions against us by their relations with one another'.[111] Bismarck's ideas led directly to the formation of a complex series of secret alliances from 1879. They also suggested that the sowing of dissension between the other European powers and the exploitation of conflicts on the periphery of Europe and overseas were significant methods he might use in seeking to preserve the Reich in the centre. Such strategies were not likely to dispel mistrust of Bismarck, taking for granted both that the European powers could be manipulated in this way and that local conflicts could be controlled and contained. Nor was such a foreign policy likely to win over his domestic critics, for liberal, Centre and Social Democrat politicians increasingly urged an unambiguous policy aimed at containing Russia.

It was the situation in the Balkans (the perennial 'Near Eastern Question') rather than his own strategic thinking which ultimately rescued Bismarck from the diplomatic cul-de-sac in which he found himself in 1875. From 1875 a protracted crisis developed in a region that was profoundly affected by the declining position of the Turkish Empire in Europe, the imperialist ambitions of the European powers and the growth of ethnic and religious tensions. A rebellion against Turkish rule in Bosnia and Herzegovina in July 1875 prompted a league of Balkan states (Bulgaria, Serbia and Montenegro) to wage war against Turkey in 1876, eventually precipitating Russian involvement and Turkey's defeat in March 1878. A European conflict loomed as the Russians imposed peace terms on the Turks at San Stefano. The peace took no heed of the interests of the other European powers, above all Austria and Britain, and provided for a drastic weakening of Turkey and the creation of a Greater Bulgaria under Russian protection. Bismarck seized the initiative in a speech delivered in the Reichstag on 19 February 1878 to offer his mediation in the developing crisis.[112] The Congress of Berlin, held between 13 June and 13 July, subsequently allowed Bismarck to put himself forward as an 'honest broker' who was concerned first and foremost to preserve the peace of Europe.

Bismarck's dominating role at the Congress of Berlin, which undoubtedly had a major impact on the German public, has impressed many historians who have judged that he was at the height of his diplomatic powers in 1878. Otto Pflanze has written that the choice of Berlin for the peace congress was 'symbolic of the position to which Bismarck's diplomacy had elevated the Prussian capital in merely fifteen years'. He was presumed to be the only statesman in Europe with the authority and impartiality to preside over the Congress.[113] Bismarck certainly devoted his efforts to achieving a compromise and systematically tackled each issue in turn, albeit impatiently leaving many details to be agreed later. He also impressed his visitors with his powers of persuasion and command of three languages even if they did not completely trust him. Yet Bismarck was not as uninterested in the Balkans as he made out for tactical reasons. Nor was he able or willing to satisfy all the expectations brought to the Congress. Russia, in particular, was aggrieved by the results of the Congress, which, in correcting the terms of the Treaty of San Stefano, seemed to favour Britain, its main imperialist rival, who gained Cyprus, and Austria, its main adversary in the Balkans. Still convinced that they deserved to be rewarded for their reserve in 1870–71, the Tsar and his advisers held Bismarck responsible for the thwarting of their ambitions in 1877–78.[114]

Bismarck's international prestige as a kind of guarantor of the European order was at its height after the Congress of Berlin, and in 1879 he used all his influence and authority over the 82-year-old Kaiser to force him to agree to sign a Dual Alliance with Austria. Wilhelm I was stubbornly opposed to entering into a new kind of relationship with the enemy of 1866. He was conscious, too, that it represented a significant change with respect to Prussia's long friendship with Russia, a relationship that had been fortified by dynastic links (for Wilhelm's sister had married Tsar Nicholas I and Alexander II was his nephew). Bismarck mobilised the crown prince, Moltke, the Prussian ministry of state, ministers from the lesser German states and the later Reich chancellor Chlodwig zu Hohenlohe-Schillingsfürst (then ambassador to Paris) to support his cause. Even then he still had to threaten his own resignation along with that of the entire Prussian government before Wilhelm finally capitulated. The dispute lasted six weeks and Wilhelm ruefully acknowledged at the end of it that Bismarck was 'more necessary than I am'.[115] The treaty was signed in Vienna on 6 October 1879 and the news of the alliance between the two German powers was received enthusiastically in Germany. Its precise terms, promising mutual support in the event of a Russian attack and benevolent neutrality in the event of an attack by a fourth power, remained secret. Seen by some historians as the foreign counterpart of the domestic change of course, the Dual Alliance became the Triple Alliance in May 1882 when the Italians, concerned about the impact of the French occupation of Tunis in 1881, took the initiative to join the Germanic powers. In 1883 both Serbia and Rumania also established links with the Triple Alliance.

Bismarck himself might well have preferred to maintain the looser arrangement secured by the Three Emperors' League, but this had effectively been left in tatters after the Balkan crisis of 1875–78. The tensions between Austria and Russia ultimately forced him to choose between the two powers and from 1876 he gradually became convinced that Austria's vital interests were at stake in the Balkans and that it was more important to bolster Austria's position in Europe than Russia's. The existence of the Austro-Hungarian monarchy served to stabilise Germany's position in Europe and contain Russian expansionism. Cultural links as well as their domestic interests also weighted the odds on the Austrian side. Indeed, Bismarck originally conceived of a much more comprehensive alliance that would be ratified by both countries' parliaments and supplemented by an Austro-German customs union, perhaps even aiming to create a new German Confederation or a central European bloc under Prussian leadership. But Austria-Hungary saw the utility of the alliance merely in terms of German support against Russia. Konrad Canis has concluded from this that Bismarck misunderstood the sense in which Austria-Hungary had become a multinational rather than a German power. He has also argued that Bismarck never saw the Dual Alliance as merely a means of maintaining Germany's security in Europe but, despite his language of peace, compromise and international understanding, always had an alternative strategic conception that involved furthering German hegemony.[116]

Typically, however, Bismarck had tested out the possibility of an alternative alliance with Count Peter Shuvalov, the accommodating Russian ambassador to Berlin who, given that Gorchakov was ill and unwilling to be blamed for an unpopular treaty, became the *de facto* leader of the Russian delegation at the Congress of Berlin. But Bismarck's hopes of seeing Gorchakov replaced by Shuvalov were frustrated. The events of 1876–78 had marked a significant turning-point in Russo-German friendship, and the Pan-Slav nationalists, who had little reason to seek closer relations with Germany and preferred to improve relations with France, had the initiative in St Petersburg. Much to Bismarck's satisfaction, however, the Dual Alliance proved to be no obstacle to the renewal of a more formal Three Emperors' Agreement in June 1881. This was the first in a series of treaties Bismarck promoted in the 1880s, treaties which existed alongside the commitment to Austria and in certain senses qualified and undermined it. The new treaty guaranteed benevolent neutrality in the event of war between one of them and a fourth power, and it also contained provisions about the future of European Turkey, envisaging both the eventual annexation of Bosnia-Herzegovina by Austria and a union between Bulgaria and Eastern Roumelia. It was renewed with some difficulty in 1884. Thus until the middle of the 1880s Bismarck was able to maintain good relations with Russia by resurrecting the eastern alliance of the three imperial monarchies. He thereby ensured that Germany would continue to be one of three in a Europe of five great powers, as he had stipulated in the Kissingen Dictate.

The Triple Alliance was the cornerstone of a complex web of alliances that Bismarck built up in the 1880s that was intended to achieve security for the Reich within a stable European context. If these alliances constituted a 'system', it was never rigid; rather, a series of relationships intermeshed with one another. Moreover it can be seen to have deliberately incorporated elements of instability to ensure that each power within it courted German friendship and support. Bismarck's aim was to make the other powers of Europe feel insecure without German friendship and thus have a vested interest in maintaining their links with Berlin. He wanted to prevent too great a degree of intimacy between the other powers. Bismarck's foreign policy was at its most successful in the early 1880s when Bismarck confessed that it gave him few sleepless nights.[117] Indeed, Otto Pflanze has questioned why he did not exploit Germany's favourable international position at this time to implement a *Staatsstreich*.[118] Confronted with a hostile Reichstag and the prospect of Friedrich Wilhelm's succession to the throne, this was the most propitious time – if he was contemplating it – for Bismarck to sweep away the existing political system and start again.

Yet even in the early 1880s the diplomatic price Bismarck paid for Germany's security was high. Friedrich Scherer has explored how Bismarck used Turkish territory as a bait to divert all the great powers – Russia, Austria, Britain, France and Italy – from Germany and to make anti-German coalitions impossible.[119] He deliberately promoted peripheral conflicts in the expectation that Germany would profit from them. And he forged a new relationship with the Ottoman Empire from 1880 (including the exchange of military officers and advisers and the furtherance of German economic interests in Anatolia) while he rejected a German–Turkish alliance in peacetime as incompatible with his spheres of influence policy in the Balkans. Bismarck's *Orientpolitik* thus developed its own dynamic, embroiling Germany in a potential minefield but offering her little in the future.

Another aspect of Bismarck's foreign policy in the 1880s that has received much scrutiny was his sudden bid to acquire overseas colonies in the period 1884–85. Bismarck had long professed a lack of interest in imperialist ventures overseas and had always appraised Germany's position realistically as a land power in the centre of Europe. In 1881 he remarked, 'As long as I am Reich chancellor, we shall not pursue a colonial policy. We have a fleet that cannot go anywhere, and we must not have any vulnerable points in distant parts of the world that will fall into French hands as soon as anything happens.'[120] Nevertheless from 1883 he actively encouraged German colonial ventures and he surprised the established imperialist powers by sanctioning the creation of German potectorates in Angra Pequena in South-West Africa and Togoland and the Cameroons in 1884, as well as Zanzibar in East Africa and German New Guinea in the Pacific in 1885.

Bismarck's motives have probably exercised historians more than contemporaries or, indeed, Bismarck himself. He may have been responding to domestic pressures. There was a growing popular movement in favour of colonial acquisitions in the 1880s, and the German Colonial Society was founded in 1882 to agitate for a colonial policy. Economic interests also overestimated the value of a colonial empire. It was hoped that a colonial policy might help the German economy to prosper by safeguarding markets and jobs, providing an outlet for emigration and promoting social stability at a time of economic difficulties. But it is unlikely that Bismarck was driven to engage in colonial ventures by any domestic interest group, even though the pressures for an active colonial policy undoubtedly existed independently of Bismarck. Nor is the thesis convincing that Bismarck used the colonial issue as a kind of 'social imperialist' device to distract public attention away from the political problems at home.[121] Bismarck may have believed that a successful colonial policy might be akin to the national issue and serve the consolidation of the Reich, but he certainly did not see colonial acquisitions as some kind of panacea for his domestic problems.

The episode can also be seen as motivated by international considerations. Bismarck may have hoped to use the issue to bring about a rapprochement with France, also supporting French colonial ambitions as a way of deflecting its interest from Alsace-Lorraine. Between November 1884 and February 1885 Bismarck presided over a conference in Berlin to decide on the future of the Congo, and he collaborated with the French prime minister, Jules Ferry, to outmanoeuvre Britain. But there were too many domestic constraints on French foreign policy to allow a genuine rapprochement with Germany, and Ferry was forced out of office in March 1885. Finally, Anglo-German relations and the issue of the succession may have driven Bismarck's policy. It has been suggested that Bismarck's bid for colonies was a manoeuvre to please the crown prince, who, unlike his wife, looked favourably on the establishment of a colonial empire.[122] At a time when Wilhelm I was in poor health, Bismarck may have calculated that colonial expansion would serve as a bridge to the crown prince and his supporters. Moreover, through its potential to cause friction with Britain, it also furnished an ideal means of undermining the anglophile royal couple in the future and served to make the chancellor indispensable. Incensed by the 'ideological' foreign policy of William Gladstone, the Liberal British premier since 1880, Bismarck wanted to forestall a similar experiment in Germany under Friedrich Wilhelm and discredit British influence. As Herbert Bismarck later remarked, colonial policy could be 'conveniently adapted to bring us into conflict with England at any given moment'.[123] Bismarck, too, told the Tsar that colonial policy was a way of driving a wedge between the crown prince and England.[124]

Whatever his motives, the colonial issue proved a highly contentious one for Bismarck. It involved the Reich in a new area that proved very expensive. Bismarck had not anticipated the cost of administering the colonial protectorates and had naively expected that the merchants who traded there could govern. Colonies increased the need for taxation at home. Their acquisition further bolstered the importance of the Reichstag's budgetary powers and gave the parliament a significant new issue over which it could attack the government. It also had unforeseen military and naval implications, and created new enemies for Bismarck at court and in the officer corps. Furthermore, once Germany had staked its claims to territories overseas, it could not abandon them without incurring a loss of international prestige. In 1888 a military expedition had to be dispatched to crush a revolt by Muslim traders in German East Africa. Thus Germany's colonial empire increasingly came to be a financial burden rather than an economic asset and it could not match the expectations invested in it.

Once Bismarck recognised this, he rapidly lost interest in colonies, for he never supported an empty imperialism that did not further Germany's interests. At a time of growing tensions in Europe, the replacement of Gladstone's Liberal government by a more sympathetic Conservative government under Salisbury in June 1885 also encouraged Bismarck to switch priorities and seek to improve Anglo-German relations. Salisbury's remaining in power, he asserted, was 'a hundred times more valuable ... than the whole of East Africa' or 'twenty swamps in Africa'.[125] In December 1888 he famously rebuffed the idea of further colonial ventures in Africa and remarked to the German explorer, Eugen Wolf, 'Your map of Africa is indeed very beautiful, but my map of Africa is in Europe. Here is Russia and here is France and we are in the middle; that is my map of Africa.'[126] Bismarck's brief foray into imperialism had long-term consequences, however, for the colonial empire he established assumed a growing symbolic significance as a manifestation of Germany's claims to be a world power. Even during his last five years in power Bismarck struggled to control the popular forces he had helped to unleash.

Bismarck's attention rapidly shifted back to Europe after 1885, with twin crises developing with respect to both France and the Near East that threatened to jeopardise his careful diplomacy. The Ferry government in France was replaced by one led by Charles de Freycinet in which the *revanchist* General Georges Boulanger was the new war minister. Almost immediately there were rumours that France was seeking to ally with Russia against Germany. The Boulangist crisis proved a formative episode in the development of French nationalism, focusing public attention on the issue of Alsace-Lorraine and culminating in January 1889 when a previously radical and republican *arrondissement* in central Paris elected Boulanger in the general election. In the Near East the crisis of 1885–87 was prompted by a rebellion in Eastern Roumelia, a Turkish province with a Bulgarian population that wanted union with the Russian client state of Bulgaria. When Serbia, which enjoyed Austrian support, sought compensation for the union and declared war on Bulgaria in November 1885, there was a real danger that the latent Austro-Russian conflict in the Balkans might escalate into a major European war. Despite many protestations to the contrary (such as his insistence in 1876 that the Balkans were not 'worth the healthy bones of a single Pomeranian musketeer'[127]), Bismarck was not uninterested in the Near East and had every reason to fear an escalation of the crisis. Moreover, in appraising the Bulgarian crisis, he correctly judged that it was the Russians who felt most vulnerable. They were threatened by internal developments in Bulgaria (specifically the election of a pro-Austrian Coburg prince to the throne in July 1887 after the exile of the former prince, Alexander von Battenberg, who had also been reluctant to toe the Russian line) as well as by aggressive Austrian diplomacy.

The Bulgarian crisis destroyed the Three Emperors' Agreement, but it is difficult not to be impressed by Bismarck's skilful handling of this issue which, more than any other, illustrates how he secured for Berlin a central role in the international state system. Bismarck sought to regulate the Bulgarian crisis in such a way as to maintain a balance of power in the Balkans and allow neither Austria nor Russia to gain the upper hand. Yet the means he adopted to achieve this end demonstrate his almost unparalleled grasp of how the Reich's bilateral relations with another power affected third parties. Despite the Dual Alliance and his basic agreement with Austria's desire to contain Russian expansionism in the Balkans, Bismarck refused to support the Coburg candidacy for the Bulgarian throne and insisted that Austria and Russia should have spheres of influence in the region, with Bulgaria located in the Russian sphere. Concerned that Russia should not be driven into the arms of France for support (and there were powerful voices in St Petersburg advocating this course), Bismarck refused to bow to pressure at home to support Austria unequivocally and pursue an anti-Russian policy. Taking full account of the impact of German policy on the other European powers, he appreciated that the best way to achieve stability in the Near East and the security of Austria was to profess publicly Germany's lack of interest in the Balkans. Behind the scenes, however, he ensured that Austrian interests were safeguarded and that the Russians were reassured of German support.

This policy can be seen as Machiavellian or dishonest but, from Bismarck's point of view, it ensured a satisfactory and peaceful outcome to the Bulgarian crisis. By refusing to support Austria openly and unambiguously in the Balkans, Bismarck served notice to Britain, a power no less concerned about Russian expansionism and the threat to Egypt, that it would have to abandon its 'splendid isolation' and help Austria contain Russian ambitions. He encouraged the cooperation of Britain, Austria and Italy in a Mediterranean entente in early 1887 (reinforced by a more specific agreement in December 1887) which guaranteed the status quo in the region and provided Austria with the support it needed without committing Germany. With Austrian interests secured, Bismarck could thus turn to Russia with confidence and assure St Petersburg that Germany would have no objections in principle if Russia expanded southwards and acquired the Straits of Constantinople. The secret Reinsurance Treaty, concluded between Germany and Russia in 1887, pledged German support of Russian interests in the Balkans and thus conflicted with the terms of the Dual Alliance.

The Reinsurance Treaty with Russia, the existence of which Bismarck only revealed to the German public in 1896, long after his dismissal, has been variously seen as the pinnacle of his diplomatic achievements and as a desperate measure to stave off the consequences of German unification. How long it could have lasted is also a matter of debate. In March 1890 Bismarck's successors 'lost control of the system' by failing to renew the treaty.[128] Bewildered by the complexity of Bismarck's diplomacy and anxious to pursue an unambiguous policy of 'standing up to Russia', they let the treaty lapse despite Russian overtures and, almost immediately,

Russia took steps to bring about a rapprochement with France, resulting in the Franco-Russian alliance of 1894. The treaty arguably flew in the face of the economic realities of the time. In November 1887 Bismarck agreed to the so-called *Lombardverbot*, which largely severed Russia's access to German sources of credit at a time when it urgently needed resources to finance its modernisation programme. Such measures, along with Germany's protective tariffs, might well have driven Russia into the arms of France even if Bismarck had remained longer at the helm. Russo-German relations continued to deteriorate after 1887 despite the Reinsurance Treaty, although Bismarck still attributed this more to Russian perceptions of Germany's role at the Congress of Berlin than to economic tensions between the two countries. But the Reinsurance Treaty did preserve a link between Berlin and St Petersburg that both emperors as well as Bismarck were inclined to preserve. Moreover, Bismarck clearly saw it as diminishing the prospects of German involvement in a disastrous two-front war. Herbert Bismarck called it 'pretty anodyne' and considered that it could only be to Germany's advantage. 'In a serious situation it will keep the Russians from our throats for 6–8 weeks longer than without it.'[129] While this comment is usually cited as evidence of what little importance the Bismarcks attached to the Reinsurance Treaty, Konrad Canis has questioned this interpretation, claiming that the 'serious situation [*Ernstfall*]' to which Herbert Bismarck referred was the future war against France which they deemed increasingly likely. 'We will not shrink from fighting the war against France as we foresee that we cannot avoid it,' Bismarck's son-in-law, Rantzau, noted in a memorandum in October 1887. 'We would not fight a Russian war unless we had to as we have no interests which could thereby be furthered.'[130] Thus, while he sought to avoid war, Bismarck also envisaged the possibility that 'an eastern war of Austria, Italy, probably England and the Balkan states allied against Russia and in western Europe a Franco-German war would be conducted simultaneously'.[131] Bismarck's efforts were primarily directed against a two-front war rather than against war itself, and only by strengthening Britain's ties with Austria did he believe it was possible to keep France and Germany out of a Balkan conflict. If a war developed over the Balkans, he envisaged that 'we would keep still or give the French a good hiding *entre nous*'.[132]

By the late 1880s the international situation appeared to be shifting against Germany. Bismarck, with his complicated manoeuvres and web of secret treaties and alliance partners, was finding it more and more difficult to swim with the tide of events. He found he had to devote his energies not merely to fostering Germany's relations with the other states

of Europe but also to sponsoring and promoting linkages that were independent of Germany. In 1887 he encouraged Austria, Britain, Italy and
Spain to conclude agreements by setting out to each of them in diplomatic dispatches why it was in their interests to do so. His nightmare of
coalitions was certainly as vivid at the end of his long chancellorship as
it was at the beginning. Bismarck struggled to make a general European
war less likely but his arrangements could scarcely carry the burden of
averting one and, since he always allowed for the unpredictability of his
enemies, he also calculated for alternatives. In 1889 he offered Britain a
three-year defensive alliance, a proposal the British rejected. Aimed at
deterring a French attack and pressuring Russia to maintain its links with
Germany, it may also have been conceived as a long-term arrangement.

Bismarck's control of German foreign policy and his multidimensional
grasp of the complexities of international relations once attracted much
admiration from diplomatic historians despite more recent scholarly criticism of his 'crisis management without real prospects'.[133] Nevertheless, if
Germany came to occupy a semi-hegemonial position in Europe after
1871, it is important to emphasise that this was not a result of Bismarck's
diplomacy alone. The other powers of Europe could not fail to be impressed by Germany's economic and demographic growth after unification; and Bismarck himself later emphasised that his efforts to prevent
hostile coalitions would have failed without 'the German military
organisation . . . and without the respect which we instil'.[134] The Reich
was a new entity in Europe, larger than France and with the most efficient army on the continent. The rivalries between the other European
powers in the Balkans, North Africa and central Asia also contributed to
increase the influence of the Reich, encouraging them to turn to Berlin
for support. However, as soon as the Reich took the initiative itself (as in
1875) these rivalries became secondary. The fear that Germany, forged
by war, was still bent on territorial expansion was always likely to resur-
face if the Reich abandoned its position of restraint.

If German 'encirclement' was the ultimate consequence of the unification of Germany, then Bismarck perhaps managed merely to stave off the
inevitable by a series of transitory expedients. Germany's exposed geopolitical location, the impact of its military victories and the annexation
of Alsace-Lorraine all limited Bismarck's freedom of manoeuvre. The
inability to reach any understanding with France after 1871 as well as
the recurring tensions in the Balkans both represented major threats to
the Reich's security that Bismarck, for all his imagination and talent,
could never resolve. Commercial and colonial rivalries further complicated the conduct of diplomacy at a time when new pressures emanating

from an expanded public realm were making themselves felt. New levels of literacy, the growth of the political press, the proliferation of organised interest groups and pressures for democratisation had major implications for the conduct of secret cabinet diplomacy in the style that Bismarck knew best. Bismarck proved adept at exploiting the semi-official press for his purposes; he also fabricated war scares and played to the gallery of public opinion in elections. But, just as in the 1860s the international constellation had favoured his policies, so by the late 1880s Bismarck was increasingly constrained by a very different international environment. It appeared less and less likely that conflicts could be consigned to the periphery of Europe; and a system of checks and balances designed to maintain the status quo in Europe appeared increasingly obsolete and artificial at a time when old multinational and dynastic state formations were being challenged. In seeking to ensnare the powers of Europe in a series of peacetime alliances, Bismarck, perhaps unwittingly, contributed to the long slide towards the First World War. The division of Europe into two, mutually hostile armed camps by 1914 cannot be explained without reference to Bismarck's foreign policy initiatives.

Furthermore, if Bismarck made errors in his conduct of foreign policy, none was so significant as his failure to initiate subordinates into his thinking. Despite often setting out his aims with remarkable clarity and frankness to foreign diplomats, he maintained an aloof distance from most of the officials in the Wilhelmstrasse, unwilling to give them political responsibility and reluctant to engage in genuine debate or discussion about how objectives might best be achieved. Only with Herbert as state secretary was he prepared to enter into any kind of dialogue in the conduct of German foreign policy, but Herbert was a trusted, junior partner rather than the equal of his father. Subordinates schooled in the wisdom of Bismarck's diplomacy thus sometimes took away with them misconceptions about its basic premises or confused appearances with substance. Bernhard von Bülow, the later Reich chancellor, maintained throughout his career that he was Bismarckian in foreign policy, but believed that in essence this meant pushing the powers of Europe about according to Germany's interests as if they were merely pawns on a chessboard. Holstein was not the only subordinate in the Foreign Office who, disillusioned with Bismarck's conduct of affairs, increasingly pursued his own foreign policy in the late 1880s.

Ultimately much of the praise bestowed on the Iron Chancellor's efforts to preserve the peace of Europe between 1871 and 1890 loses sight of the man. Bismarck did not progress smoothly from being a disturber of the international peace in the 1860s, via the role of 'honest broker' at the Congress of Berlin to become a vital pillar of the European order in the 1880s. While there is no doubt that Bismarck's stature and authority increased on the international stage and that by the late 1880s he probably commanded greater respect abroad than at home, his foreign policy was ultimately no less self-serving than his conduct of domestic policy. He sought to perpetuate a creation that only had meaning for him while he was its power centre. He also saw no conflict of interest in exploiting his inside knowledge of foreign relations to protect if not to further his own financial wealth. His desire to deflect attention away from the centre towards the periphery and escalate crises if they served German interests calls into question assumptions that he was intent on preserving the peace of Europe at any price. Bismarck had no sentimental attachment to European peace as an ideal. European peace served the interests of Germany after 1871 just as war had served Prussia's interests in the 1860s. After 1875 Bismarck equated a 'preventive war' with 'committing suicide for fear of death'.[135] It was no longer in his interest to conjure up international crises that could be turned against the Reich.

Bismarck's conduct of foreign policy reinforced his power and made him seem indispensable. The superiority of his diplomatic expertise and skill was widely acknowledged and accepted even among his most hostile parliamentary critics. Moreover the stature he enjoyed abroad as the pre-eminent European statesman instilled respect for his authority at home and further served to bolster his position. Only in the late 1880s were his views and judgements about foreign policy seriously challenged within the ruling elite. Bismarck, who had always sought to avoid a two-front war and understood the importance of Russo-German friendship, faced a growing number of critics who appraised the threat from Russia very differently and believed a preventive war was preferable sooner rather than later. The conduct of foreign policy thus became a significant issue in the struggle for power after the death of Kaiser Wilhelm I and it was eventually subsumed into the general crisis that precipitated Bismarck's dismissal.

Notes

1 Fuchs, I, Gelzer's diary, 15–18 April 1874, p. 160.

2 See H-U. Wehler, 'Bismarck's Imperialism, 1862–1890', *Past and Present*, 48 (1970), p. 123.

3 See especially Wehler, *German Empire*, pp. 55–62, and *Deutsche Gesellschaftsgeschichte*, III, pp. 849–54; see also Edgar Feuchtwanger, *Bismarck* (London, 2002), p. 211.

4 Fuchs, I, Jolly to Hermann Baumgarten, 21 May 1871, p. 18.

5 Ibid., pp. 16–17.

6 The issue concerned a stamp act which was seriously amended by 30 votes to 28 in the Bundesrat because thirteen of the smaller states had delegated their votes to two other states (for reasons of economy). Bismarck insisted that delegates from all the states should be present when important matters were discussed.

7 GW, XII, Reichstag speeches of 21 February 1879, pp. 25–6, and 1 December 1881, pp. 312–13.

8 Pflanze, II, p. 326.

9 GW, XI, speech of 10 March 1877, p. 489.

10 See Robert M. Berdahl, 'Conservative Politics and Aristocratic Landholders in Bismarckian Germany', *Journal of Modern History*, XLIV, 1 (1972), pp. 1–20.

11 See Pflanze, II, pp. 307–9.

12 Schoeps, *Bismarck*, p. 131.

13 See especially Pflanze, II, pp. 143–5.

14 GW, XI, Reichstag speech of 10 March 1877, p. 492. See also Pflanze, II, p. 359.

15 Robert Lucius von Ballhausen, *Bismarck-Erinnerungen* (Stuttgart and Berlin, 1920), 25 September 1876, pp. 90–1; Pflanze, II, pp. 351–2.

16 Fuchs, I, Roggenbach to Grand Duke Friedrich, 5 January 1878, p. 271. See also Pflanze, II, p. 389.

17 GW, XI, Landtag speech of 23 March 1878, p. 584. Cited in Pflanze, II, p. 336.

18 Pflanze, II, pp. 385–6.

19 Ibid., III, p. 35.

20 Cited ibid., p. 37. See also Lucius, *Bismarck-Erinnerungen*, pp. 558–60.

21 Cited in Pflanze, III, p. 38.

22 Cited ibid., p. 75. Rottenburg was a member of the Reich Chancellery staff (1881–90).

23 Lucius, *Bismarck-Erinnerungen*, p. 265.

24 See Pflanze, III, p. 37.

25 Ludwig Bamberger, *Bismarcks grosses Spiel: Die geheimen Tagebücher Ludwig Bambergers*, ed. Ernst Feder (Frankfurt, 1932), 8 May 1873, pp. 302–3.

26 GW, VIII, conversation with Mittnacht, 4/5 December 1883, p. 493.

27 Walther Bußmann (ed.), *Graf Herbert von Bismarck: Aus seiner politischen Privatkorrespondenz* (Göttingen, 1964), Herbert Bismarck to Bernhard von Bülow, 25 June 1885, p. 285.

28 GW, VIII, conversation with Mittnacht, 4/5 December 1883, p. 494.

29 See Axel T. Riehl, *'Der Tanz um den Äquator': Bismarcks antienglischer Kolonialpolitik und die Erwartung des Thronwechsels in Deutschland 1883 bis 1885* (Berlin, 1993), especially pp. 762–70.

30 See below for a discussion of Bismarck's role in foreign policy.

31 See below for a discussion of parliaments. See also Wehler, *German Empire*, especially pp. 71–94.

32 M.L. Anderson and K. Barkin, 'The Myth of the Puttkamer Purge and the Reality of the *Kulturkampf*: Some Reflections on the Historiography of Imperial Germany', *Journal of Modern History*, 54 (1982), p. 673.

33 GW, XII, Reichstag speech of 24 February 1881, pp. 194–5.

34 W.M. Simon (ed.), *Germany in the Age of Bismarck* (London, 1968), p. 222. See also D.G. Williamson, *Bismarck and Germany 1862–1890* (London, 1986), pp. 114–15.

35 Fuchs, I, Gelzer to Grand Duke Friedrich, 28 June 1871, p. 22.

36 Ibid., Gelzer's diary, 16 July 1871, p. 29.

37 Ibid., Turckheim to Jolly, 14 February 1872, p. 49.

38 Pflanze, II, p. 234.

39 Ibid., pp. 234–5; Lucius, *Bismarck-Erinnerungen*, pp. 59–60.

40 GW, XI, Reichstag speech of 17 September 1878, pp. 610–11.

41 Fuchs, I, Grand Duke Friedrich to Crown Prince Friedrich Wilhelm, 15 January 1877, p. 242. See also Riehl, *Tanz um den Äquator*, pp. 772–3.

42 GW, IX, conversation with George G. Smalley, Summer 1893, p. 355. See also Wolfgang Schieder, 'Bismarck und der Sozialismus', in Kunisch, *Bismarck und seine Zeit*, p. 187.

43 Pflanze, II, p. 310.

44 See Fuchs, II, Marschall to Turban, 2 March 1884, p. 238.

45 See *Quellensammlung*, I, vol. 3, *Arbeiterschutz*, ed. Wolfgang Ayass (Stuttgart, 1996), Robert Hertel to Moritz Behrend, 24 July 1877, pp. 450–2 and Bismarck's marginalia on Hertel to Behrend, 31 July 1877, pp. 472–3.

46 Ibid., Bismarck's *Votum* for the State Ministry, 30 September 1876, p. 375.

47 GW, XII, speech of 2 April 1881, p. 241.

48 Busch, *Tagebuchblätter*, III, 26 June 1881, p. 44.

49 *Quellensammlung*, II, vol. 2/1, *Von der Zweiten Unfallversicherungsvorlage bis zum Unfallversicherungsgesetz vom 6 Juli 1884*, ed. Florian Tennstedt and Heidi Winter (Stuttgart, 1995), Adolph Wagner, 'Bismarck und Windthorst', 10 May 1884, p. 578 and pp. xxiv–xxxiii.

50 See especially Florian Tennstedt, 'Sozialreform als Mission: Anmerkungen zum politischen Handeln Theodor Lohmanns', in Jürgen Kocka, Hans-Jürgen Puhle and Klaus Tenfelde (eds), *Von der Arbeiterbewegung zum modernen Sozialstaat: Festschrift für Gerhard A. Ritter zum 65 Geburtstag* (Munich, 1994), pp. 538–59.

51 Theodore S. Hamerow (ed.), *The Age of Bismarck* (New York, 1973), p. 235.

52 H.A. Winkler, *Der lange Weg nach Westen. Bd. I: Deutsche Geschichte vom Ende des alten Reiches bis zum Untergang der Weimarer Republik* (Munich, 2000), pp. 250–1.

53 GW, XIII, speech of 9 May 1885, p. 61.

54 See GW, XIII, speech of 18 May 1889, p. 399, and Werner Hegemann, 'Bismarck als Berliner und als Gegner unserer Hauszinssteuer', in *1930: Das steinerne Berlin*, ed. Ulrich Conrads and Peter Neitzke (Braunschweig and Wiesbaden, 1988) pp. 278–81.

55 See ibid., pp. 280–4.

56 Fuchs, I, Türckheim to Turban, 12 January 1879, p. 335.

57 Dieter Hertz-Eichenrode, *Deutsche Geschichte 1871–1890: Das Kaiserreich in der Ära Bismarck* (Stuttgart, 1992) p. 107.

58 See Pflanze, II, pp. 198–209.

59 William W. Hagen, *Germans, Poles and Jews: The Nationality Conflict in the Prussian East, 1772–1914* (Chicago, 1980) p. 129.

60 GW, XIII, Landtag speech of 28 January 1886, pp. 144–66.

61 Geoff Eley, 'German Politics and Polish Nationality: The Dialectic of Nation-Forming in the East of Prussia', *East European Quarterly*, XVIII, no. 3 (September 1984), p. 343. See also Richard Blanke, *Prussian Poland in the German Empire 1871–1900* (New York, 1981).

62 See Chapter 3 and Rothfels, Bismarck to Malwine, 26/14 March 1861, p. 276.

63 See Gall, II, p. 123.

64 A.J.P. Taylor, *Bismarck: The Man and the Statesman* (London, 1955). Citation from 1985 paperback edition, p. 98.

65 Ibid., p. 99.

66 See A. Lawrence Lowell, *Governments and Parties in Continental Europe*, 2 vols (Boston and New York, 1896) vol. I, p. 254.

67 See Matthias Alexander, *Die Freikonservative Partei 1890–1918: Gemäßigter Konservatismus in der konstitutionellen Monarchie* (Düsseldorf, 2000), pp. 31–5 for a discussion of its relationship to Bismarck.

68 See Pflanze, II, p. 220, and III, p. 111.

69 For more details on these attempts see ibid., II, pp. 392–7.

70 See Gall, II, p. 94.

71 See Pflanze, II, p. 400.

72 For an excellent discussion of German liberalism in English, see Dieter Langewiesche, *Liberalism in Germany* (London, 2000), especially pp. 183–99.

73 GW, XII, speech of 8 May 1879, p. 69. See especially Gall, II, pp. 106–8.

74 GW, XII, speech of 9 July 1879, p. 124.

75 See Wehler, *German Empire*, and Helmut Böhme, *Deutschlands Weg zur Großmacht: Studien zum Verhältnis von Wirtschaft und Staat Während der Reichsgründungszeit 1848–1871*, 2nd edn (Cologne, 1972). Wehler has since modified his view somewhat, see *Deutsche Gesellschaftsgeschichte*, III, pp. 934–6, 990–3.

76 See Otto Pflanze (ed.), *Innenpolitische Probleme des Bismarckreiches* (Munich, 1983); David Blackbourn and Geoff Eley, *The Peculiarities of German History: Bourgeois Society and Politics in Nineteenth Century Germany* (Oxford, 1984).

77 Engelberg, II, pp. 319–20.

78 Pflanze, II, p. 460.

79 Fuchs, I, Grand Duke Friedrich to Gelzer, 3 April 1878, p. 280.

80 Gerhard Ebel (ed.), *Botschafter Graf von Hatzfeldt: Nachgelassene Papiere 1838–1901*, 2 vols (Boppard, 1976), I, Holstein to Hatzfeldt, 15 February 1879, p. 330.

81 Busch, *Tagebuchblätter*, III, 24 February 1879, p. 549.

82 Gall, II, pp. 103, 110.

83 Pflanze, II, p. 54.

84 *Quellensammlung*, I, vol. 1, *Grundfragen staatlicher Sozialpolitik*, ed. Florian Tennstedt and Heidi Winter (Stuttgart, 1994), Rudolf Lindau to Herbert Bismarck, 30 October 1881, p. 686.

85 See Gall, II, p. 122.

86 See Pflanze, III, p. 145.

87 Cited in Gall, II, p. 127.

88 GW, XII, speech of 15 March 1884, pp. 424–5.

89 See GW, XIII, Reichstag speeches of 11 January, 12 January and 13 January 1887, pp. 207–58.

90 GW, XI, speech of 30 January 1869, p. 17; see also Reichstag speech of 9 February 1876, p. 428.

91 Fuchs, I, Grand Duke Friedrich to Turban, 20 August 1878, p. 322.

92 Stern, *Gold and Iron*, p. 263; GW, 12, speech of 12 June 1882, pp. 349–50.

93 Stern, *Gold and Iron*, pp. 263–4.

94 Bernd Sösemann, 'Publizistik in staatlicher Regie: Die Presse- und Informationspolitik der Bismarck-Ära', in Kunisch, *Bismarck und seine Zeit*, p. 307.

95 See Pflanze, II, pp. 363–4.

96 Holstein, II, 12 January 1886, pp. 275–6.

97 Heinrich von Poschinger, *Fürst Bismarck und die Parlamentarier*, 3 vols (Breslau, 1894–96), II, p. 210. See also Lamar Cecil, *The German Diplomatic Service 1871–1914* (Princeton, NJ, 1976), pp. 226–56.

98 Holstein, I, p. 127.

99 GW, II, memorandum to Manteuffel, 18 May 1857, p. 221.

100 See especially Gall, II, pp. 155–9; Klaus Hildebrand, *Das vergangene Reich: Deutsche Außenpolitik von Bismarck zu Hitler 1871–1945* (Stuttgart, 1995), especially pp. 95–146; '"System der Aushilfen"? Chancen und Grenzen deutscher Außenpolitik im Zeitalter Bismarcks (1871–1890)', in Kunisch, *Bismarck und seine Zeit*, p. 126. Cf. Konrad Canis, *Von Bismarck zur Weltpolitik: Deutsche Außenpolitik 1890 bis 1902* (Berlin, 1997), pp. 16–52.

101 See comments of Odo Russell in H. Wolter, *Bismarcks Außenpolitik 1871–1881* (Berlin, 1983), p. 76. See also Karina Urbach, *Bismarck's Favourite Englishman: Lord Odo Russell's Mission to Berlin* (London, 1999), pp. 108–10.

102 Cited in Gall, II, (speech of 9 February 1871), pp. 40–1.

103 Cited in J.C.G. Röhl, *Young Wilhelm: The Kaiser's Early Life 1859–1888* (Cambridge, 1998), p. 96. See also R. Fulford (ed.), *Darling Child: Private Correspondence of Queen Victoria and the Crown Princess of Prussia 1871–1878* (London, 1976). For a discussion of Anglo-German dynastic relations after 1871, see Paul Kennedy, *The Rise of the Anglo-German Antagonism 1860–1914* (London, 1980), paperback edition 1982, pp. 124–32.

104 See Ulrich Lappenküper, *Die Mission Radowitz: Untersuchungen zur Rußlandpolitik Otto von Bismarcks (1871–1875)* (Göttingen, 1990), especially pp. 420–43.

105 GW, XIV/II, Bismarck to Marie, [23 June 1872], p. 834. Cited in Hildebrand, ' "System der Aushilfen"?', p. 126.

106 Lappenküper, *Die Mission Radowitz*, p. 462.

107 Lucius, *Bismarck-Erinnerungen*, p. 72.

108 See Bismarck, *Gedanken und Erinnerungen*, pp. 428–33.

109 Cited in Lappenküper, *Die Mission Radowitz*, p. 506, and Volker Ullrich, *Die nervöse Großmacht 1871–1918: Aufstieg und Untergang des deutschen Kaiserreichs* (Frankfurt am Main, 1999), p. 81.

110 Pflanze, II, p. 272.

111 *Große Politik*, II, 15 June 1877, pp. 153–4.

112 GW, XI, speech of 19 February 1878, pp. 520–34.

113 Pflanze, II, p. 434.

114 See especially Alexander II's 'box on the ears' letter to Wilhelm I, 15 August 1879, *Große Politik*, III, p. 16. See also Gall, II, pp. 117–18.

115 Cited in Pflanze, II, p. 507.

116 Konrad Canis, 'Der Zweibund in der Bismarckschen Außenpolitik', in Helmut Rumpler and Jan Paul Niederkorn (eds), *Der 'Zweibund' 1879: Das deutsch-österreichisch-ungarische Bündnis und die europäische Diplomatie* (Vienna, 1996), pp. 51–3.

117 GW, VIII, conversation with Eduard Cohen, 11 April 1882, p. 446.

118 Pflanze, III, pp. 97–8. Pflanze uses Bismarck's failure to act as evidence against the kind of linkage between Bismarck's foreign and domestic policies that has been suggested by Hans-Ulrich Wehler and others.

119 Friedrich Scherer, *Adler und Halbmond: Bismarck und der Orient 1878–90* (Paderborn, 2001).

120 Poschinger, *Fürst Bismarck und die Parlamentarier*, III, p. 54. See Gall, II, p. 139.

121 See especially Hans-Ulrich Wehler, *Bismarck und der Imperialismus* (Cologne/Berlin, 1969). See also Winfried Baumgart, 'Bismarcks Kolonialpolitik', in Kunisch, *Bismarck und seine Zeit*, pp. 141–53.

122 See Urbach, *Bismarck's Favourite Englishman*, p. 202.

123 Cited in Kennedy, *The Rise of the Anglo-German Antagonism*, p. 171.

124 Holstein, II, 19 September 1884, p. 161. The 'crown prince hypothesis' is put forward by Riehl, *Der Tanz um den Äquator*.

125 Baumgart, 'Bismarcks Kolonialpolitik', p. 152.

126 GW, VIII, conversation with Eugen Wolf, 5 December 1888, p. 646.

127 GW, XI, Reichstag speech of 5 December 1876, p. 476.

128 Paul W. Schroeder, 'World War I as Galloping Gertie: A Reply to Joachim Remak', *Journal of Modern History*, XLIV, 3 (1972), p. 323.

129 Bußmann, *Herbert von Bismarck*, Herbert Bismarck to Bill Bismarck, 19 June 1887, pp. 457–8.

130 Canis, 'Der Zweibund', pp. 59–60.

131 Ibid. See also Herbert Elzer, *Bismarcks Bündnispolitik von 1887: Erfolg und Grenzen einer europäischen Friedensordnung* (Frankfurt am Main, 1991).

132 Bußmann, *Herbert von Bismarck*, Rantzau to Herbert Bismarck, 23 September 1886, p. 376. See Canis, *Von Bismarck zur Weltpolitik*, p. 24.

133 Canis, 'Der Zweibund', p. 67.

134 GW, XII, Reichstag speech of 14 June 1882, p. 379.

135 GW, XI, speech of 9 February 1876, p. 431.

Chapter 6

Corrosive Power

By the autumn of 1887 Bismarck was 72 years old and had wielded power continuously for twenty-five years. He continued to be regarded as a colossus on the international stage, and his achievements, as well as the indefatigable efforts of Bleichröder, had made him a very wealthy man.[1] Under the strict regimen of his young Bavarian doctor, Schweninger, from 1883 (the 'black tyrant' as Bismarck called him[2]), he had lost weight and there was a visible improvement in his appearance by the mid-1880s. His appetite was undiminished and he was observed to consume lobster, goose, sprats, herrings, smoked meat and turkey at one luncheon in 1888.[3] But reports suggest in 1886–87 that he was enjoying better health than he had for years. He relished the challenge of the international crisis in 1886–87, and he was similarly energised by the election campaign of February 1887, which resulted in the victory of the *Kartell*. Despite his frequent complaints that he was tired of office and his resignation threats when he encountered opposition, Bismarck showed no inclination to surrender political power. He continued to mistrust ambitious colleagues and subordinates, seeking to remove potential rivals and anyone whom he suspected of disloyalty or intriguing against him. And despite installing Herbert in the Foreign Office, he made no provision for his eventual successor since this would have signified acceptance of his own political mortality.

Yet by the late 1880s Bismarck was not the man he had once been and this was widely recognised by all those who came into contact with him. He spent less and less time in Berlin, insisting that he needed to rest and recuperate at his estates at Varzin or Friedrichsruh. Indeed, for the last four years of his chancellorship, he was rarely in the capital at all from July until January. He spent most of his time at Friedrichsruh in the Sachsenwald near Hamburg, where he had bought an inn in 1879 which was converted into an unpretentious and homely, some said tasteless, residence. Friedrichsruh was his ideal location since it was possible from there to communicate speedily with Berlin but its distance also absolved him of the need to attend official functions or receive unwanted visitors. Nevertheless, his health permitted him to work only for three or four hours of the day and he spent nearly twelve hours in bed to get seven hours of sleep.[4] He was also increasingly dependent on morphine, which he had been taking at least since the early 1870s to help ease his insomnia and his various ailments. Schweninger later endeavoured rather unconvincingly to quash rumours that the chancellor was addicted to the drug.[5]

The Foreign Office counsellor, Friedrich von Holstein, who continued to work closely with Bismarck in the late 1880s while becoming increasingly critical of his foreign policy, presents a devastating picture of Bismarck's decline in his diary. Bismarck, he wrote in 1885, had an 'increasing sense of power', continuing to use people 'like knives and forks which are changed after each course'.[6] But he now allowed his moods to influence public affairs more than he used to and made contradictory decisions, especially in his marginalia on reports, without consulting the files and without sufficient reflection.[7] He was becoming older, more feeble and spent long periods on the *chaise-longue*. In January 1886 Holstein recorded that Bismarck was losing his grip. 'His Highness is fast shrivelling up: lonely, nervy, suspicious, lacking his former grasp of affairs and thus open to every suggestion coming from his favourite son.'[8] Yet he needed Herbert to correct him, for the chancellor would not tolerate dissent from anyone else. In October 1888 Holstein recorded that Herbert had had to go at short notice to Friedrichsruh 'to reverse one or two of the old man's absurd decisions'.[9] Holstein blamed Bismarck's decline on the success of Schweninger's cure. 'But for Schweninger he might perhaps be dead but he would have died great', he commented acerbically.[10] 'He has become an *old man*', the influential counsellor observed in March 1887.[11] A month later he noted, 'His energy has gone. His cunning, on which he now relies exclusively, spends itself in tortuous exaggeration. His vanity and lust for power have also increased.'[12]

Bismarck's longevity in office had not made him any happier or more satisfied, and he complained that power had consumed all his other interests. He continued to regret the loss of former personal friends, feeling especially embittered about the ultra-conservatives he had formerly associated with, and he never believed he received the recognition or gratitude that he deserved. He intuitively understood that the world he knew best was disappearing and that he no longer had the same energy or vigour to deal with the new challenges. Yet he could not draw the obvious conclusion from this and resign from office gracefully. He rationalised his decision to stay with a panoply of excuses, all grounded in the notion that he was indispensable and that it was his duty to stay on at a time of international or domestic uncertainty. Whether seeing out the reign of his ageing master, Wilhelm I, or 'holding the fort' through the brief, doomed reign of the fatally ill, former Crown Prince Friedrich Wilhelm, or 'steadying the ship' when the young and immature Wilhelm II acceded to the throne, Bismarck justified his insatiable appetite for power in a discourse of selfless and devoted service to the crown. 'He wants to remain at any cost, for the present and in the future,' Roon had written in 1870, 'because he feels that the structure he has begun will collapse as soon as he takes his hand away – making him a laughingstock to the world.'[13] By 1890 Bismarck's long tenure of power had come to be seen by many within the ruling elite as detrimental to the interests of the Reich and the monarchy, corroding the very fabric of national life. As intrigues multiplied to ease him out of office, Bismarck was more willing to see the destruction of his creation than to contemplate surrendering power.

Bismarck and the succession

Throughout his long political career Bismarck depended on the support of Wilhelm I, the Prussian king and later German Kaiser who had appointed him in 1862 and who also had the right to dismiss him. Indeed, if Wilhelm had not lived until the ripe old age of 90 but had instead scarcely outlived his brother, Friedrich Wilhelm IV (who died when he was 66 years old), Bismarck might well not have survived in office long enough even to see the foundation of the Reich. Given the political disposition of the crown prince, the issue of the monarchical succession had cast a permanent shadow over Bismarck's future as Reich chancellor. By the 1880s it seemed scarcely possible that the ageing Wilhelm could live much longer and, especially given the left liberals' electoral victories in 1881 and 1884, Bismarck's chancellorship appeared increasingly conditional. The power of the king and Kaiser could never be merely a necessary monarchical fiction for Bismarck, a convenience behind which he practised his autocratic dictatorship. Even Bismarck's enemy, the quartermaster-general and later successor to Moltke as chief of the general staff, Alfred von Waldersee, acknowledged in February 1887 how 'infinitely difficult' it was 'to conduct policy-making if one has the feeling that the main factor might pass away any day and thus change the situation completely'.[14]

The imminence of the monarchical succession was the crucial context for many of Bismarck's political manoeuvres in the 1880s, as he sought to discipline the executive, remove potential rivals for power and undermine the parliaments through which the liberal supporters of the crown prince could best articulate their sympathy. The elections of 1887, fought in an atmosphere of international crisis over the Reichstag's rejection of the army budget, were clearly designed to secure a stable basis of centre-right parliamentary support and make a political change of course less feasible. Bismarck may, too, have wished to build a bridge to the crown prince via the National Liberals in the new *Kartell*.[15] Bismarck had been anticipating the electoral contest against the left liberals since 1884 and could not fail to be satisfied with the loss of over half their seats and the virtual doubling of National Liberal representation. As the left liberal Ludwig Bamberger concluded, 'The crown prince is now relieved of all embarrassment. He will do what Bismarck wants.'[16]

One of Bismarck's more direct efforts to manipulate dynastic politics to his own advantage in the 1880s famously backfired against him. Bismarck tried to safeguard his position for the event of Friedrich Wilhelm's accession to the throne by encouraging the conservative and autocratic tendencies of Prince Wilhelm, the Kaiser's grandson and future Kaiser Wilhelm II, as a counterbalance to the alleged liberal tendencies of his father. Generational conflict was a common feature of court politics and the Hohenzollern court was no exception in this regard. But Bismarck sought to use it for his own political advantage by setting the son against his father and mobilising the grandfather to support him. Herbert Bismarck, closer to the young prince in age, cultivated Wilhelm's friendship and gained influence over him, although his initially favourable judgement of his character soon underwent a change. Herbert was known for his 'brutal, dark, spiteful nature'and got on well with Wilhelm, in Holstein's view, because they shared 'the same rather crude attitude to life'.[17] Herbert once shot five bullets through a Foreign Office window from the chancellor's garden verandah next door, and he subsequently made light of the suggestion that he might have shot an official. 'Officials have to be kept in a permanent state of irritation and alarm; the moment that ceases they stop working', he maintained.[18] From 1884 the Bismarcks began to involve Wilhelm in foreign policy, much to the vexation of his parents, and from 1887 the prince began to be initiated into details of Reich domestic policy under the uninspired guidance of the minister of finance, Adolf Scholz. Wilhelm's parents deeply resented the role of the Bismarcks in turning their son against them and furthering his connections with what they perceived to be a reactionary and militaristic court culture.

However, even before the death of Wilhelm I, his grandson had demon-strated that he was sufficiently wilful to resist falling completely under the Bismarcks' sway. His association with the anti-Semitic court chaplain, Adolf Stöcker, and his Christian Social movement prompted Bismarck to encourage a major press campaign against the young prince in late 1887 that undoubtedly shattered his confidence in the Bismarcks and preci-pitated their estrangement. Moreover, under the influence of men like Waldersee as well as the diplomat Philipp zu Eulenburg-Hertefeld (who, the Bismarcks believed, was infatuated with the prince), Wilhelm was already developing the view that the position of the Reich chancellor under Bismarck had become too dominant and that what Germany needed was a new, young Kaiser behind whom it could unite. 'He'd better re-member that I shall be his master', Wilhelm retorted angrily after the Stöcker affair. 'I shall not manage without the Chancellor at first. But in due course I hope the German Reich will be sufficiently consolidated to be able to dispense with Prince Bismarck's co-operation.'[19] Bismarck, too, formed a damning impression of Wilhelm's arrogant and superficial char-acter by 1887. Prince Wilhelm, he complained, was 'a hothead who could not *hold his tongue*, allowed himself to be swayed by flatterers, and could lead Germany into a war without realising or wanting it'.[20]

It was the issue of war that highlighted Bismarck's growing isolation in the late 1880s and his dependence on monarchical support in the face of a rising number of domestic critics of his foreign policy. In the late 1880s Berlin ruling circles were awash with rumours and fears of an impending conflict with France, Russia or both, and John Röhl has identified what he calls a 'collective war psychosis' among the nation's ruling elite.[21] In particular, the chancellor faced significant opposition in the Kaiser's mili-tary entourage to what was perceived to be his russophile foreign policy and, for the first time perhaps, Bismarck was justified in suspecting that plots and intrigues were being hatched everywhere in order to oust him from office. In 1887 he had to conduct his foreign policy in the know-ledge that it was opposed by powerful men who had direct access to the throne. Even the chief of the general staff, Moltke, was encouraged by Waldersee and Prince Wilhelm to think in terms of a 'preventive war' against Russia in late 1887 as a means of forestalling the Russian attack they expected in the spring. Bismarck was particularly disturbed by the news of a 'war council' on 17 December 1887 over which the old Kaiser presided and at which Prince Wilhelm was also present. Only the presence of the 90-year-old monarch and the political realism of the 87-year-old Moltke apparently prevented Germany's top military advisers propelling the country into a war with Austria against Russia in late 1887.[22]

Bismarck wanted peace with Russia and he did not believe that Russia wanted a war with Germany. In 1888 he deliberately published the terms of the Dual Alliance with Austria, warning Vienna not to provoke a conflict with Russia since Germany was not bound to support Austria in an offensive war. He also did all he could to bolster the position of the pro-German foreign minister in St Petersburg, Nikolai Karlovich Giers, and neutralise his Pan-Slav critics. Yet the rift over foreign policy gave his domestic opponents a tangible issue on which to attack his leadership and question his judgement. In January 1888 Holstein wrote to Hatzfeldt that everyone in Berlin favoured war except the Reich chancellor, 'who is making the most strenuous efforts to maintain peace'.[23] Some of the chancellor's attackers were opportunists who saw the issue as a means of undermining the chancellor's position and looked to a better future without him; some were men he had slighted or offended over the years, perhaps by failing to promote them. But there was nevertheless a widespread consensus in parliamentary and political circles that his policy towards Russia was misconceived. As the basis for Bismarck's conduct of foreign policy narrowed, Waldersee constituted a particularly serious threat to his power. Waldersee was increasingly seen as a chancellor candidate in the late 1880s, not least because of his personal influence over the 'rising sun', Prince Wilhelm. Not only did the reactionary general advocate a preventive war against Russia, but he also established what was in effect his own private, rival and parallel diplomatic service using the German military attachés posted to German embassies abroad.

Wilhelm I clung tenaciously to life by the standards of the time, and Bismarck, who had often shocked company by being openly disrespectful about his sovereign, found the monarch's support invaluable right up to his death on 9 March 1888. When his end finally came, there is no doubt that it represented a personal as well as a political blow for Bismarck. Bismarck had been elated by the smooth progress of the *Septennat* army bill through the Reichstag. But the news that Wilhelm was ill with a kidney infection and pneumonia prompted him to confess on 7 March, 'What yesterday still appeared the most important thing to me has today been eclipsed by these events.'[24] The chancellor conferred with Wilhelm for the last time on 8 March, when they discussed foreign policy, and he sat at the dying monarch's bedside for several hours later that night. On 9 March Bismarck scarcely concealed his tears of emotion when he had to announce Wilhelm's death officially to the Bundesrat and the Reichstag. Bismarck was never to view the monarchy in the same way after the death of the old Kaiser, whom he had always respected even if he had often imposed his will upon him. Confronted with the prospect of a new generation, Bismarck told Baroness Spitzemberg in April 1888 that monarchs were no longer being born and he even praised Augusta's dignity and sense of duty compared with that of her successor.[25] Almost two years later, ten days after his dismissal at the hands of Wilhelm's grandson (and not three months after the death of Augusta), Bismarck went alone to Charlottenburg and had the mausoleum opened so that he could take final leave of his former king before he departed from Berlin. Still suffering from shock and disbelief, he left roses on Wilhelm's coffin and returned home to the Chancellery with his eyes red from crying.[26] For his own epitaph on his tomb he also chose 'a faithful German servant of Kaiser Wilhelm I'.[27] The deliberate rebuke to the grandson need not detract from his sincere, albeit sentimental attachment to the grandfather.

In 1885, anticipating the monarchical succession, Bismarck told the British ambassador that 'What he should most like would be that some scoundrel should shoot him when the emperor died.'[28] In March 1888, however, the accession of Friedrich Wilhelm to the throne as Kaiser Friedrich III had none of the political significance that it might have had if it had occurred even five years earlier. In early 1887 the crown prince began to complain about a hoarseness that was all too obvious from his voice.[29] While a growth on his larynx was detected in the spring, a succession of German and English doctors disagreed about the diagnosis and it was not until November 1887 that cancer was unequivocally confirmed. Thus even before he ascended to the throne, Friedrich Wilhelm knew that he was terminally ill. In November 1887 Herbert could scarcely conceal his delight, seeing in Friedrich Wilhelm's fate confirmation of Bismarck's earlier view that 'If the Lord means well by Germany, he'll never let the Crown Prince ascend the throne.'[30] The chancellor's reaction betrayed marginally more empathy for his old adversary, or at least some concern for his respect and dignity. Bismarck stepped in to prevent a radical operation being performed on the crown prince in May 1887 without his consent (probably the only means of saving him but also most likely to have killed him). He also quashed the proposal, mooted by some in the ruling elite, to exclude Friedrich from the succession and have the crown pass directly from Wilhelm I to his grandson. And he expressed his deep regret to the crown prince when he was 'caught unawares' and, on the urging of the chief of the Kaiser's Military Cabinet, Emil von Albedyll, Prince Wilhelm was appointed in November 1887 to act as his grandfather's deputy until the old Kaiser's death, should this become necessary.[31] One of Bismarck's first services to the new Kaiser was also to ensure the financial security of his wife and four daughters for whom no provision had been made in Wilhelm I's will. But although

Bismarck may have wept tears when he first heard of Friedrich Wilhelm's illness, he subsequently scorned to indulge in the politics of sentimentality. Days after Kaiser Friedrich's death he spoke disparagingly of his political judgement and understanding, and he also encouraged the slanderous accusations of negligence made against his wife for her role in his care.[32]

From 1887 Friedrich Wilhelm thus no longer constituted a political threat to Bismarck but was instead an object of pity, unable to speak and forced to undergo a tracheotomy in February 1888 to save him from strangulation. On returning to Berlin from San Remo after the death of his father in March 1888, he was politically emasculated and quite unable to liberate himself from a chancellor whom he personally detested. Indeed, he immediately requested that Bismarck remain in office, accepting that he would be able to achieve little during what was to be a mere 99-day reign, let alone appoint a new, more liberal ministry. Bismarck was further able to consolidate his hold over the new monarch and restrain his wife's ambitions by threatening to declare Friedrich unfit to rule and install his son as regent if he failed to comply with his wishes.

All this was a major tragedy for Friedrich III and his wife, and a bitter disappointment to their friends and supporters. But, even if he had remained healthy, there remains some doubt as to whether Friedrich could have fulfilled liberal expectations and stood up to Bismarck. Personally indecisive and inclined to avoid conflicts, he was often reluctant to assume responsibility and his professed liberalism was never put to the test. Moreover, the product of a Prussian military education, he was steeped in the traditions of the Hohenzollern military monarchy and as intransigent as his father on issues such as the army budget. Patricia Kollander has recently emphasised how Friedrich's political views differed from those of his wife, who was far more resolute in her wish to dismantle Bismarck's system of rule and reshape German institutions in accordance with the British model.[33] Friedrich was certainly no supporter of parliamentary government but, rather, was satisfied when Bismarck was willing to cooperate with moderate liberalism within the framework of the existing constitution. It was significant, too, that when he acceded to the throne he bowed to Bismarck's pressure and agreed to call himself Kaiser Friedrich III, accepting the continuity of the Prussian crown. There was no question of the foundation of the Reich marking a new beginning. Rather, Friedrich himself had wanted to be called Friedrich IV, harking back to the old medieval Germanic Reich (which Kaiser Friedrich III had ruled from 1440 to 1493). If Friedrich wanted to reduce Bismarck's power, this was primarily to enhance the prestige of the crown rather than transfer power to the Reichstag. Finally, even if he had managed to jettison Bismarck, it must be doubted whether sufficient political support existed in Germany by the late 1880s for the kind of liberal constitutionalism with which he was associated. The National Liberals never regained the power and influence they had enjoyed in the 1870s before their break with Bismarck and the secession of the party's left wing. And although left liberalism was resurgent in the 1880s, Eugen Richter's new German Radical Party was reduced to a mere thirty-two seats in the elections of 1887. In any case, Friedrich was no more inclined to work with the men in the Radical Party than was Bismarck himself.

Bismarck was certainly buoyant at a state ministry meeting on 13 March 1888, no longer fearing that the new monarch might attempt to institute a change of course. 'He feels relieved of the great concern he had that he would have to fight with a dying man against inappropriate intentions even to the point of demanding his release from office', Lucius recorded Bismarck as saying. 'Everything is going easily and pleasantly with the high gentleman like a *jeu de roulette*.'[34] The relationship between Bismarck and the new royal couple did not remain free of friction, however. The new Kaiserin had been determined for some time to see a marriage between her daughter, Vicky, and Prince Alexander of Battenberg, the former elected ruler of Bulgaria who had been forced to abdicate in 1886 during the Bulgarian crisis. But her plans continued to be crossed by Bismarck, even though his argument that the princess's marriage to Alexander (who was related to the royal family of Hesse) would further complicate Russo-German relations looked increasingly hollow. Bismarck then justified his opposition on the grounds that he wanted to protect Friedrich III from 'martyrdom' at the hands of his dominant wife. His hostility to 'the women who want to have a share in the government' had not ebbed, even if he now judged Augusta more favourably by comparison with her daughter-in-law.[35] Convinced that the new Kaiserin was a 'wild woman', he confessed in April 1888 that he 'often shuddered at the unbroken sensuality that shone from her eyes'. He even believed she was herself in love with Battenberg and 'wants to have him around her . . . who knows with what incestuous(!) intentions'.[36] Massive pressure was brought to bear on Alexander to forgo the marriage (he then married an actress in February 1889) and Bismarck himself threatened to resign if it went ahead. Indeed, Bismarck's determination to prevent the marriage indicates that he saw Alexander (whom Friedrich planned to appoint as governor of Alsace-Lorraine) as a potential Reich chancellor and a direct threat to his own power.

Bismarck also soured his relations with the Kaiser's court by forcing Friedrich to agree to let Prince Wilhelm deputise for him if he was incapacitated. But perhaps the most notable confrontation over domestic politics occurred in May 1888, when Bismarck inexplicably sought to prevent promulgation of a statute extending Prussian Landtag sessions from three years to five, to which Friedrich had already given his consent. The law was published and crisis resolved only after the resignation of the responsible minister, Puttkamer, who was also under parliamentary fire for allegedly using government pressure to influence the outcome of a disputed election. It may be that Bismarck's principal motive in engineering the crisis was to remove the minister of interior since he held him partly responsible for Prince Wilhelm's involvement in the Stöcker affair in November 1887. But Otto Pflanze has called Bismarck's action 'a callous and frivolous deed', creating an unnecessary crisis that plagued the last days of the Kaiser, who died on 15 June 1888.[37]

Bismarck later recalled that he had been 'an absolute *dictator*' during the brief reign of Friedrich III and that never in his entire ministerial career was the conduct of business 'so pleasant or so lacking in friction'.[38] But Bismarck was only willing to stay on good terms with the dying Kaiser if the latter submitted to his wishes, and at no time could the chancellor feel confident about the future because of the new threat looming on the horizon. Bismarck had long become accustomed to living with the ambiguity of his power position. But he undoubtedly dreaded the accession of the 29-year-old prince to the throne, a prince who had been only 3 years old when Bismarck first became Prussian minister-president. In February 1888 Holstein claimed that two factors lay behind Bismarck's behaviour: morphia and Prince Wilhelm.[39] The two men were widely different in terms of age, personality and interests, and even before Wilhelm ascended the throne, Bismarck consciously began to tack with the new wind and seek to please the young crown prince by appearing to favour a war against France. 'With a Kaiser of ninety-one years of age, as well as a Kaiser who is mortally ill, one had to pursue a policy different from that required by a young man craving for action', he acknowledged.[40] The measures the chancellor adopted as a means of provoking France in 1888 (for example, the introduction of irritating passport controls on the Franco-German border) were clearly risible and contrived. But they nevertheless reflected his awareness that he had to adapt to a new style of governance, one that was more suited to the impulsive, impetuous and restless personality of the heir to the throne.

But at 73 years of age Bismarck was too old to consider seriously changing his established patterns of behaviour from June 1888. The chancellor 'is taking the greatest trouble with the young gentleman, gets on well with him', Holstein wrote on 3 July 1888, some two weeks after Wilhelm's accession.[41] But days later the chancellor took off from Berlin as usual, this time for Friedrichsruh, where he stayed until 10 January 1889. The following year was not to be significantly different. Physical distance perhaps facilitated the uneasy coexistence of Kaiser and chancellor for nearly two years, for both of them aspired to command absolute authority and each felt uneasy in the other's presence. On the other hand Bismarck's remoteness has been seen as more significant in precipitating the breakdown of the relationship than all the intrigues of his ambitious foes.[42] Bismarck's long absences slowed down the pace of government business, delayed important decisions and ultimately contributed to the impatience and frustration of the younger man. Bismarck sensed this and he knew that Herbert was not personally or politically able to exert the influence over the young monarch that he could command. But Herbert sought to reassure his father, who, he admitted as early as October 1888, 'is afraid that H.M. is escaping from his grasp'.[43]

'If I was younger and able to be with him every day, as I did with the old emperor, I would twist him around my finger', Bismarck deluded himself in December 1889.[44] But by this time the developing conflict between the two men was apparent to all concerned in Berlin and Bismarck had only three months left in office. The protracted struggle between Kaiser and chancellor was punctuated by temporary compromises and tactical retreats. It was exacerbated by political divergences as well as by personal and generational differences. But ultimately it was a contest over power. 'Beneath the surface there is a strong antagonism between the Kaiser and the chancellor, who has ruled as Kaiser for 10 years and cannot get used to subordination under His Majesty', Holstein observed in November 1889.[45] The eventual outcome was thus never seriously in doubt.

Surrendering power

From June 1888, when Kaiser Wilhelm II succeeded his father, the institutional basis of Bismarck's power slowly crumbled. This was perhaps not so apparent to political outsiders or to the chancelleries of Europe, which continued to see Bismarck as the personification of German power. Nor was Bismarck's style of leadership significantly affected. He was still capable of the 'colossal speech'[46] that intimidated the rest of Europe and his anger, or the fear of it, still instilled discipline and obedience in the executive. But political insiders soon read the signs and drew their inevitable conclusions. The future no longer rested with subservience to the old chancellor, apparently bereft of fresh thinking and positive ideas, but rather with the young monarch who was embarking on what promised to be a long and glorious reign. Wilhelm appeared better able to represent a dynamic new nation with aspirations for world power. 'I am pleased about this event,' Holstein wrote to a friend on 3 July 1888. 'One feels that we have a ruler again, not merely a chancellor.'[47]

A variety of political issues served to underline the growing rift between the two men from 1888, some of which were used tactically in what was essentially a developing power struggle. First, there was the clash over social policy and the related issue of the renewal of the anti-socialist legislation. Wilhelm II had been influenced in his social views above all by his former tutor, Georg Hinzpeter, and he began his reign with ideas of being a 'social Kaiser', hoping to ameliorate the conditions of the working class and effect a reconciliation between German workers and the state. The social question was given additional immediacy from May 1889 by a wave of strikes that began among the miners in Westphalia. Wilhelm insisted on the state's neutrality in the dispute, and he received deputations from both the striking miners and the employers before urging the employers to make concessions. Bismarck was not accustomed to a monarch who took decisions and fired off instructions without consulting his responsible advisers, and it was probably the Kaiser's political activism in this sphere rather than the issue itself that caused the most friction. Indeed, Bismarck even considered expropriating the mine owners and nationalising the mines in 1889, something that was far more radical than anything Wilhelm was proposing.[48] The Kaiser, however, was also in Bismarck's view guilty of 'humanitarian dizziness'.[49] The young monarch endorsed a programme of factory legislation and, unbeknown to Bismarck, an official in the German Foreign Office, Paul Kayser, drafted the detailed proposals that Wilhelm put before a crucial crown council meeting on 24 January 1890. In February 1890 the Kaiser issued two decrees on the social question without the chancellor's countersignature (an unprecedented and probably unconstitutional omission). The first of these instructed Bismarck to organise an international conference on the problem of the working class, while the second was addressed to the Prussian ministers of trade and public works and specified the measures to be adopted in seeking to ameliorate workers' grievances.

Additionally, Wilhelm had no wish to see an intensification of the anti-socialist law, something Bismarck pursued energetically as his position weakened. Bismarck presented a new bill to the Reichstag in October

1889, even though the existing law did not lapse until the end of September 1890. The new bill was subject to no time limit and it now included an expulsion paragraph, permitting the authorities to imprison and deport socialist agitators, powers that were unacceptable to the National Liberals in the *Kartell* coalition. The conflict between Kaiser and chancellor thus seemed to become polarised around the issue of social reform or anti-socialist legislation, but Wilhelm's opposition to the proposed anti-socialist law was also partly tactical. He had always supported the anti-socialist legislation and his hostility to the socialists was constantly expressed throughout his long reign. Nevertheless, it appeared to Wilhelm and the men unofficially advising him that the chancellor wanted to provoke a deliberate confrontation with the Reichstag and thus force one or perhaps several dissolutions. And a *Staatsstreich* would undoubtedly have obliterated Wilhelm's efforts to woo popularity through his workers' protection programme. Contemporaries and historians have suspected that Bismarck wished to create such a dangerous and uncertain domestic situation that his removal would be impossible, and some of his remarks appear to bear this out. 'These questions, such as what to do about social democracy and the relationship between the parliaments and individual states, can no more be solved without bloodshed than could the problem of German unity,' Bismarck told Baroness Spitzemberg in December 1889.[50] A few weeks later he told the Saxon envoy in Berlin, 'The social question cannot be solved with rosewater; for that you need blood and iron.'[51]

The issue of Reichstag strategy thus became a second, crucial element in the crisis that led to Bismarck's dismissal. While the Kaiser nailed his colours to the mast of the *Kartell*, publicly declaring that the parliamentary coalition was as necessary for internal peace as the Triple Alliance was for external peace,[52] Bismarck seemed bent on a course that would destroy the parliamentary coalition he himself had put together in 1887. Unlike the state secretary of the interior and vice-president of the Prussian ministry, Boetticher, the chancellor certainly appeared to place no great importance on a compromise between the *Kartell* parties over the anti-socialist bill in early 1890 before new Reichstag elections took place in February. Rather, he was largely responsible for the disarray in which the *Kartell* parties went into the elections and for the heavy losses they sustained as a result. The *Reichspartei* and National Liberals lost over half their representation while the Social Democrats, with merely 35 seats, received the largest share of the vote of any party. At a state ministry meeting on 2 March 1890 Bismarck discussed with his colleagues the possibility of repeated dissolutions of the Reichstag and a *Staatsstreich* to get rid of universal suffrage. He also sounded out the possibility of

an agreement with the Centre Party that would facilitate a new
Conservative–Centre coalition. Indeed, it was the news that Bismarck
had had a personal meeting with Windthorst on 12 March 1890 that
prompted an outraged Kaiser to have Bismarck summoned from his bed
on 15 March and to demand his resignation. How far Bismarck really
sought to replace the *Kartell* by a Centre–Conservative bloc can be questioned, but there is no doubt that he was considering a parliamentary
majority which included the Centre and that many in the ruling elite
became convinced that a 'Blue–Black' bloc was his intention. At his meeting with Windthorst Bismarck appeared to agree to his terms for the
Centre's support, namely the further dismantling of *Kulturkampf* laws,
but the Centre leader famously remarked afterwards, 'I have just come
from the deathbed of a great man.'[53] Concern was expressed about Bismarck's parliamentary strategy not merely because the Reichstag election
results encouraged an atmosphere of domestic crisis. The implications
of a Blue–Black bloc and a shift away from National Liberalism in the
Reich were expected to have a marked impact on Bavaria, where a belea-
guered pro-Prussian government led by Johann Lutz was only secure if it
had the unequivocal backing of Berlin. If Berlin signalled its willingness
to rely on a Conservative–Centre coalition, it was feared that Lutz would
have to give way to a new ultramontane and particularist government
and that the Reich itself could then unravel.

The power issue itself was a constant bone of contention throughout
the crisis, manifesting itself primarily in a struggle to control the executive and, in particular, the Prussian ministers. The grand duke of Baden
later maintained that 'the cause of the breach between the Emperor and
Bismarck was a question of authority, and that other differences of opinion concerning social legislation and so forth were merely secondary
matters'.[54] The Prussian ministers and imperial state secretaries were
disciplined to accept Bismarck's authority by the late 1880s, but from
1888 the Kaiser began to use his significant powers of patronage and
control of personnel appointments in an attempt to undermine the cohesion of the Prussian government. This placed some ministers in a very
difficult position, torn between loyalty to Bismarck and their desire to
please the young monarch. Even a hitherto docile minister like Scholz
seemed to sense the way the new wind was blowing, however, and in
1889 he devised his Prussian tax reform plans largely independently of
Bismarck. Even after he secured the agreement of the state ministry and
Kaiser to the reform, which included a progressive income tax, Bismarck
successfully blocked it and insisted on prioritising tax relief for landowners
in any reform of direct taxation.[55] Ernst Herrfurth, the newly appointed

minister of interior, also exasperated Bismarck by pursuing an increasingly divergent course in late 1889 because he was confident of the Kaiser's backing. He in effect allowed the Prussian provincial bureaucracy to mediate between the Kaiser and the workers in the miners' strike, and the provincial governors reported directly to the monarch.

However much Bismarck seethed inwardly or voiced his irritation to others, he does appear to have sought to avoid conflicts with Wilhelm over personnel issues, as well as over the bestowal of honours and orders, perhaps calculating that he needed to store up his influence for the big political questions. He did not oppose the appointment of General Julius von Verdy du Vernois as war minister in 1889, for example, even though Verdy was one of the 'demi-gods' with whom he had clashed during the Franco-Prussian War and Bismarck saw him as a personal enemy. More significantly, when Bismarck resigned as minister of trade at the end of January 1890, Wilhelm II secured the appointment of Hans Hermann von Berlepsch as his successor. Berlepsch was the first civilian minister to owe his appointment exclusively to Wilhelm and he was instructed to implement his social reform programme. On 9 March 1890 Wilhelm also ostentatiously bestowed the Order of the Black Eagle (Prussia's highest order) on Boetticher, whom the chancellor was simultaneously accusing of insubordination.

Bismarck was conscious that his control over the executive was slipping and that this was most marked in the sphere of social policy. A conflict appeared inevitable when Wilhelm seized the opportunity at his grandmother's funeral in January 1890 to persuade the king of Saxony to introduce a factory bill into the Bundesrat. At the same time he instructed Boetticher to cast the Prussian votes in its favour.[56] Not only was Bismarck hostile to factory legislation but, as Prussian foreign minister, he alone enjoyed the privilege of instructing the Prussian votes in the Bundesrat. On 24 January 1890 the Kaiser further called a crown council meeting to discuss a variety of measures, including his social policy initiatives, with regard to which he might have expected some support from the Prussian ministers. But, still unable to resist Bismarck, with whom they had met beforehand, the ministers rallied behind the chancellor and Wilhelm was left to retort with frustration that they were not his ministers but Bismarck's. Given the traditional relationship between the monarchy and the Prussian ministers, this was completely unacceptable to Wilhelm, who even took umbrage at press reports that referred to 'the policy of the Reich chancellor'. Wilhelm then endeavoured from late January 1890 to cultivate his relations with ministers and state secretaries on an individual basis and have them make regular presentations

(*Vorträge*) to him on aspects of policy. Bismarck again instinctively moved to stop this invasion of his power sphere. In March 1890 he resurrected a Cabinet Order of 1852 which Manteuffel had instituted and which stipulated that any audiences between individual ministers and the king had to be in the presence of the minister-president. Again, this was highly provocative given the disposition of the young Kaiser and indicated how Bismarck was not prepared to surrender without a fight. Like the news of Bismarck's meeting with Windthorst, the resurrection of the old Cabinet Order infuriated the Kaiser and he demanded its revocation at their final confrontation on 15 March 1890. Bismarck, for his part, was to claim that its revocation would signify a return to absolutism.

Finally, although foreign policy was no longer such an issue of dispute between the summer of 1888 and March 1890, Germany's relations with Russia also surfaced during the chancellor crisis. Throughout 1889 the Kaiser and Waldersee continued to see Bismarck as too russophile, and they attacked the influence of Bleichröder, whose financial transactions were seen as undermining Austria and favouring Russia. Bleichröder's support for the conversion of Russian securities on the Berlin stock exchange in the summer of 1889 particularly angered Wilhelm, who believed the Russians would then be able to undermine the Reich financially as well as prosecute a war against Germany more successfully.[57] Even Herbert Bismarck appeared to side with the Kaiser on this issue, not least because he, too, was very anti-Semitic and saw the Jewish financier as 'a filthy swine' who was dangerous, mendacious and mercenary.[58] Bismarck eventually conciliated the Kaiser rather than his banker, but Wilhelm continued to see the chancellor's policy as determined by 'Jews and Jesuits' (the latter was a reference to Windthorst). In 1889 the Kaiser and Waldersee also made foreign policy independently of the chancellor, giving verbal assurances to the Austrians that Germany would support them even in an offensive war in the Balkans, a commitment which went beyond the stipulations of the Dual Alliance. But by the end of the year there is evidence that the Kaiser was no longer so hostile to Bismarck's foreign policy and that the influence of Waldersee, whom John Röhl has described as playing 'almost the role of a parallel chancellor', was waning.[59] Foreign policy only featured again in the dismissal crisis because Bismarck chose to use it as a way of humiliating Wilhelm and as the pretext for the rupture. On 15 March Wilhelm complained that the chancellor did not keep him informed about all aspects of foreign policy, and Bismarck revealed to him the views of Tsar Alexander III about the immature young Kaiser. When he finally wrote his letter of resignation on 18 March, he deliberately chose to base his decision on an alleged divergence of view over how foreign policy towards Russia should be conducted. The letter was a skilful exercise in public relations, designed for eventual publication (and it was published immediately after Bismarck's death). Bismarck calculated with good reason that a rupture over foreign policy would cast his own role in the best possible light.

Several political issues, then, played a role in the growing rift between Bismarck and Wilhelm II that culminated in the chancellor's dismissal in March 1890. But by far the most important was the power conflict, the struggle for control over the government apparatus and responsibility for decision-making. Wilhelm II was granted enormous powers by the Prussian and imperial German constitutions and he wanted to use them. As a young and inexperienced ruler, he lacked sufficient prestige and authority to assert his authority straight away. But he was encouraged by his circle of informal and 'irresponsible' advisers to seize the initiative where possible and to begin to shift the balance of power within the executive away from the chancellor and towards the crown. It should be emphasised, however, that it was not until the middle of February 1890 that Wilhelm made the decision to seek Bismarck's resignation and throughout most of the protracted manoeuvres he was being advised to act with restraint. Bismarck's abrupt departure was not seen as in the interests of the young Kaiser or the country. Rather, the hope was that Bismarck might relinquish his powers gradually and that he could slowly be eased out of the chancellorship in a way that preserved the dignity and reputation of the *Reichsgründer* and also ensured a successful transition to the rule of Kaiser Wilhelm II. Even after the Kaiser's humiliating defeat at the crown council meeting in January 1890, Wilhelm's advisers praised his restraint and recognised that it was more important that Bismarck stayed on than to secure the Kaiser's social policy.[60] Wilhelm complained about Bismarck's Olympian detachment, his treatment of the monarch 'like a schoolboy' and his domineering behaviour.[61] But even he recognised the damage that might ensue from a complete rupture.

This scenario may have been constructed with a view to ensuring that Wilhelm II gradually acquired the stature and experience necessary to become 'his own chancellor'. But it largely ignored the more irascible and impetuous facets of his personality which made it difficult, though not impossible, to impress on him the need for restraint. More significantly, however, it made no allowances for the personality of the chancellor and his ultimate refusal to surrender power voluntarily. Neither man was thus likely to cooperate in a more gradual and harmonious transfer of power. Bismarck did actively consider devolving his powers in 1890, and at one stage during the crown council meeting on 24 January he stood up and requested his resignation from all his offices. 'I see more and more that I am no longer in my place,' he declared.[62] He stepped down as minister of trade at the end of January, and he contemplated giving up the Prussian minister-presidency and focusing exclusively on foreign policy. In February 1890 he told the Prussian state ministry that he was resigning his Prussian offices because he could not execute Wilhelm II's domestic policy.[63] But crucially he did not honour this commitment. The complicated constitutional structure he had devised may ultimately have defeated even Bismarck's ingenuity, for on reflection he could not tolerate the idea of being merely Reich chancellor if this meant that Boetticher, as the new Prussian minister-president, became his superior. Bismarck also told his family that he intended to resign completely on his seventy-fifth birthday on 1 April 1890.[64] However it seems highly likely that he would have reneged on this decision too if he had not been forced to resign on 18 March.

Bismarck's ultimate refusal to give up his position as Prussian minister-president and foreign minister despite his professed willingness to do so was symptomatic of his behaviour during the last months of his chancellorship and it contributed to what can be seen as a further strand of the crisis. This was the re-surfacing of major anxieties about Bismarck's intentions and actions. Suspicion and mistrust had dogged Bismarck throughout his political career, but in 1889–90 it assumed renewed political significance by precipitating a major shift in attitude among Wilhelm's clique of advisers. During his last year in office the chancellor's political manoeuvres increasingly seemed to indicate that he was resolved to embark on a high-risk strategy that might well prove fatally injurious to the interests of the Reich. Resentment over Bismarck's longevity in office and frustration over the apparent stagnation of Reich policy in the late 1880s thus mutated into real and imagined fears about the dangers likely to ensue if Bismarck remained in power. While a gradual transfer of power continued to be seen as the optimum solution, a complete rupture could be increasingly justified as a necessary defence against violence and bloodshed in the future. The belief that Bismarck was willing to risk civil war by provoking a far more serious constitutional crisis than he had faced in the 1860s alarmed Wilhelm and his advisers, who recognised that it would tarnish the young Kaiser's reign and increase his dependence on Bismarck.

Misgivings about Bismarck's course helped to bring about an unlikely coalition of men who supported the Kaiser but who otherwise had very different political and ideological views. In 1889 the suspicion that Bismarck was planning joint action with Russia to invade Switzerland and flush out the anarchists and terrorists who took refuge there alarmed the grand duke of Baden, who was alerted to this possibility by his representative in Berlin, Adolf Marschall von Bieberstein. The grand duke was to play a key role in the dismissal crisis because of the paternal influence he could bring to bear on his wife's nephew, the Kaiser. From the summer of 1889 his hostility to Bismarck's policies encouraged him and Marschall (who replaced Herbert Bismarck as state secretary of the Foreign Office in 1890) to draw closer not only to Holstein and Philipp Eulenburg but also to Waldersee. Waldersee was close politically to the anti-Semitic and reactionary conservatives, but he was sufficiently realistic to see the tactical necessity of an alliance with the *Kartell* parties. From the middle of 1889 he began to meet regularly with Holstein despite their very different personalities and significant political differences. Some state ministers, notably Boetticher, also expressed their concerns over Bismarck's parliamentary strategy. As we have seen, King Albert of Saxony, Wilhelm II's former tutor, Hinzpeter, and the Foreign Office official, Paul Kayser, were also drawn into the conspiratorial circle. What united these men was their admiration for the Kaiser, their desire to increase his freedom of decision and their hostility to Bismarck's monopoly of power. Partly motivated too by envy and jealousy, they complained about how Bismarck had used his power for material and nepotistic gain. They deliberately sought to break the Bismarcks' control of all political information reaching the Kaiser and encouraged Wilhelm's belief that the chancellor was withholding information from him and not telling him the truth.

Bismarck himself, though he suspected that he was surrounded by spies, had little sense of the intricate web of intrigue that was developing around him or the heterogeneous group of men who were influencing the Kaiser by 1890. Rather, he always saw the ultra-conservatives as the main influence on the Kaiser and his chief threat. He attacked the *Kreuzzeitung* group around its editor, Wilhelm von Hammerstein, and Hans von Kleist-Retzow in the semi-official press as enemies of the Reich, and Hammerstein was arrested in early 1889 for an article that attacked government policy as injurious to the monarchy. The chancellor also worked to counter the influence of the Kaiser's court, relying in particular on the support of the chief of the Kaiser's Civil Cabinet, Hermann von Lucanus, and the chief marshal of the court and household, Eduard von Liebenau. Both these men came to be seen by the anti-Bismarck clique as the chancellor's creatures. Both managed to survive his fall although Liebenau was soon ousted. Bismarck also sought to neutralise the influence of the conservative and religious Kaiserin Auguste Victoria on her husband although she was never guilty of the interest in politics that

Wilhelm's mother or grandmother had shown. However, by the end of 1889 Wilhelm, too, had turned against the *Kreuzzeitung* group, a factor which contributed to the cooling of his relations with Waldersee. By February 1890 Wilhelm was no longer thinking of Waldersee as the next chancellor but ordered General Leo von Caprivi to prepare if necessary to become Bismarck's successor, apparently without consulting anyone although Bismarck subsequently approved the choice.[65] Hohenlohe noted after Bismarck's dismissal on 21 March that the Kaiser 'had already been treating for weeks with Caprivi about his possible nomination as Imperial Chancellor, and since Bismarck had learnt this, things could not continue any longer'.[66]

By early 1890 Bismarck's power base had been seriously undermined and at best he enjoyed a 'dualism of power' with the Kaiser. John Röhl has suggested that a new system of rule was emerging, with the Kaiser determining the broad outlines of domestic policy and making the important personnel decisions while Bismarck was relegated to matters of execution and foreign policy.[67] Bismarck weighed up whether to accept this situation or whether to resign, whether to seek a formal solution to the division of powers or whether to fight to regain the authority he had lost. However, for all the mistrust of his intentions during these weeks and his testing of various options, Bismarck sometimes betrayed no real zeal for a fight. In February 1890 in conversation with the British ambassador to Berlin, he appeared bitter but resigned. The Kaiser 'would only like me to stay so that I can give speeches in the Reichstag and induce the latter to approve money', he complained. He was glad that his seventy-five years lay behind him and that his work was done, but it was sad to see how the edifice he had constructed brick by brick was now in danger of crumbling.[68] Bismarck appeared uncharacteristically unable to make a decision in the crucial weeks of February 1890, and his prevarication was ultimately used against him. The Kaiser was furious when Bismarck withdrew his previous request to resign his Prussian offices and saw it as confirmation of the chancellor's 'unlimited thirst for power'.[69] Many of Bismarck's actions in his last weeks in office suggest a degree of disorientation about the situation in which he now found himself. He made unusual social calls on Moltke, Waldersee and even the Kaiserin Friedrich, perhaps in the hope of receiving support for his remaining in office, although he told the Kaiserin Friedrich, 'I ask only for sympathy.'[70] And on 26 February, while a newly convened, advisory Prussian *Staatsrat* was discussing the Kaiser's social initiatives, Bismarck wandered off through the corridors of the Prussian Ministry of Interior and Foreign Office, opening doors and startling officials.[71] By contrast, on 25 February after a post-election conversation with Wilhelm II that had echoes of his Babelsberg meeting with Wilhelm I in 1862, Bismarck may have believed that he now had the monarch's approval for a *Staatsstreich*. On 2 March he proposed in the Prussian ministry of state that an even more extreme anti-socialist bill should be put before the Reichstag than the one that had been rejected in January. He subsequently, however, bowed to the Kaiser's pressure and abandoned the bill, probably because he recognised that proposed new military increases would suffice on their own to precipitate a confrontation with the parliament.

On 15 March, however, Wilhelm II categorically refused to support a policy of confrontation and insisted that the military bill, too, had to be acceptable to the parliamentary majority. The meeting between the two men in Herbert Bismarck's apartment clearly took a violent turn as they argued over Windthorst, the Cabinet Order of 1852 and Russo-German relations. Bismarck slammed a file of documents down on the table and became so angry that, according to Wilhelm, 'it was all he could do to refrain from throwing the ink-pot at my head'.[72] Bismarck does appear to have come close to hitting the monarch but, even after this altercation, he still refused to resign and Wilhelm sought to avoid the opprobrium of dismissing him. Both Wilhelm von Hahnke and Lucanus, the chiefs of the Kaiser's military and civil cabinets, visited Bismarck on 17 March to enquire why he had not yet submitted his resignation. Only on 18 March did Bismarck finally write his letter of resignation in his office in the Wilhelmstrasse while the new chancellor, Caprivi, was taking charge in the adjoining rooms. Even then Lucius observed that 'The request is drafted in a way calculated to provoke a thorough response and intimates a willingness to stay.'[73] Two days later Wilhelm's reply accepted Bismarck's 'request for release from office' with regret and paid effusive tribute to his former chancellor's personal qualities and achievements. He conferred on Bismarck the title of duke of Lauenburg, a title Bismarck scornfully refused subsequently to use.

To the end Bismarck could not conceive of surrendering his personal responsibility for a political system that he had largely devised. At a time when the authoritarian Reich was facing multiple challenges, he may also have genuinely believed that the state was on the brink of a cataclysmic domestic crisis, that no solution could be found through social consensus and that consequently Germany could not be ruled without him. But, increasingly isolated and criticised within the government, Bismarck clung tenaciously to power and proposed remedies that appeared negative and anachronistic. A growing number of bureaucrats, diplomats, military men and courtiers understandably preferred to look to the future rather than the past and to support the Kaiser's programme for social reconciliation before embarking on further social repression. The anti-Bismarck *fronde* encouraged Wilhelm to bypass a chancellor who was often absent and establish a rival power centre focused on the monarchy. Only in this way could the effects of what they perceived to be Bismarck's obstructive and corrosive power be countered. Holstein, a leading member of the *fronde*, even warned Herbert Bismarck in January 1890 that, 'The idea persists that Prince Bismarck does nothing himself and prevents others from doing anything, and unless this idea is killed at the source it will before long materially alter the prince's position, *inside* Germany at least.'[74] But others, too, who were more sympathetic to the chancellor recognised how his domineering influence over Germany's political development stifled progress and evolution. The astute Baroness Spitzemberg observed that 'a terrible marasmus' had affected Reich domestic politics and that a series of laws had not been passed because they did not suit Bismarck's private material interests or he had no time for them.[75] Thus few in Berlin were to regret the chancellor's fall, even if they were offended by the manner of it. The predominant mood was one of stunned relief and hope that the era of political stagnation was now over. The reaction in the press and parliaments was similarly muted, and the losses on the Berlin stock market were smaller than in November 1887 when the news broke about the crown prince's cancer.[76]

Bismarck in retirement

Bismarck and most of his family departed from Berlin to Friedrichsruh on 29 March. The emotion of the occasion was once again too much for a man who had never really believed that the Kaiser would accept his resignation. Bismarck broke down in tears when he presented his staff at the Reich Chancellery with silver goblets. Along the route to the Lehrter railway station, huge crowds lined the streets, waving and cheering and throwing flowers into the open carriage. At the station the throng spontaneously began to sing the old victory song, '*Die Wacht am Rhein*' and '*Deutschland, Deutschland über alles*'. Bismarck took leave of Caprivi, assembled members of the Reich and Prussian executives, diplomats and officers, and as he boarded the train Baroness Spitzemberg observed tears even on the cheeks of the cuirassiers in the guard of honour.[77] When the hour of departure finally struck, the train steamed out of the station to endless cheers and shouts of 'Auf Wiedersehen!' As one foreign diplomat reported, it bore away 'the great statesman, whose policy has made Prussia so great and powerful, for a long time, if not for ever, from Berlin'.[78]

Bismarck lived for the remaining eight years of his life mainly at Varzin and Friedrichsruh, and he seldom returned to Berlin unless it was to change trains. On one such occasion at the Stettiner railway station in July 1894, he spoke movingly to history students about a city which he had frequently professed to despise.

I was six years old when I first came to Berlin. All the places that I see again here today represent for me my past. Here I was taken for walks as a schoolboy, here I lived as a student, as a *Referendar* [and] as a minister. And now I can say that I have always enjoyed being in Berlin, although I grew up in the countryside and have my roots in country life. But I became comfortable in Berlin through habit . . . Politically I perhaps had my differences in certain respects with the majority of Berliners, but my sense of being at home in Berlin and its surroundings [*mein Heimatgefühl für Berlin und seine Umgebung*] has always remained the same.[79]

Throughout his political career Bismarck had constantly sought refuge and escape from Berlin and it was paradoxical that he only acknowledged his belated affection for the city when he was condemned to rural retirement. But his reflections also suggested how painful and difficult it was for him after twenty-eight years at the centre of German political life to adjust to a life removed from the capital. Bismarck never found the solace he craved in the countryside and he could not retire gracefully from public life.

Embittered at his treatment by Wilhelm II, Bismarck could not disengage from politics after March 1890 but instead he soon became an important focus of opposition to the Kaiser and his 'New Course'. In the weeks after his resignation he conducted numerous interviews with the press and established key contacts, notably with Emil Hartmeyer and Hermann Hofmann, the owner and political editor of the *Hamburger Nachrichten*. This newspaper became in effect Bismarck's mouthpiece, through which he was able to mount his polemical assault on the policies of his successors. The impecunious Hofmann, who had known Bismarck since 1888 and whose debts Bismarck repeatedly settled, became so familiar with the former chancellor's ideas and style of writing that even Herbert was sometimes deceived by his articles and believed they had been written by his father.[80] As early as April 1890 Wilhelm II was expressing his dismay and indignation over articles published in the *Hamburger Nachrichten*.[81] But Bismarck soon had access to a wide variety of talented journalists and to a substantial slice of the German press, especially in south Germany. Holstein claimed Bismarck took 231,000 marks from the 'reptile fund' before leaving Berlin for the purpose of buying influence in the press, but it was understandable that newspapers were interested in publishing his views.[82] Maximilian Harden, who founded and edited the weekly periodical *Die Zukunft* (founded in 1892) and became Wilhelmine, Germany's foremost political and cultural critic, was sympathetic to the fallen chancellor but never allowed himself to be bought by him. Nevertheless, he was able to use his friend, Schweninger, as an intermediary and in the early 1890s he was provided by Bismarck with all kinds of useful information which ensured that his periodical was avidly read in high society. Hugo Jacobi, editor of the *Allgemeine Zeitung* in Munich at the time of Bismarck's dismissal, was another prominent member of what Bismarck referred to as the 'diaspora press'.[83] Bismarck directed his ire above all at Wilhelm II whom he could not forgive for hounding him out of office, but his journalistic campaign soon developed into a massive attack on the New Course. The hostility of the *Reichsgründer* contributed to the political instability of the period after Bismarck's dismissal. Despite attempts to limit the damage and effect a reconciliation, both Caprivi and his successor as chancellor in 1894, Chlodwig zu Hohenlohe-Schillingsfürst, struggled unsuccessfully to command similar authority to the first chancellor, who, all the time, publicly criticised their policies from the sidelines.

Bismarck also devoted time, if not much enthusiasm, in the early years of his retirement to the writing of his memoirs, which were only published after his death and were highly damaging in what they said about Kaiser Wilhelm II. In 1893 he admitted he had had his fill of honours and awards but that he was 'not indifferent to what is said about me after my death'.[84] On another occasion he dismissed what the newspapers wrote about him as 'dust which I can brush off'. 'I only value history, what it will later say about me.'[85] Bismarck started to dictate what eventually became his *Gedanken und Erinnerungen* in the autumn of 1890 and he was assisted by Lothar Bucher, who ceased working in the Foreign Office not long before Bismarck's dismissal. Bucher died in 1892, however, and the project stalled. Bismarck claimed that it was concern for the living and the dead which prevented him telling the truth, but it is clear that a far more significant obstacle was his lack of interest in writing for a time he would not experience himself. He was certainly less motivated by considerations of historical accuracy than by his all-consuming desire for political vengeance. The third volume of Bismarck's memoirs was only published after the First World War, but Bismarck also authorised numerous biographies and other works through which his voice could be heard. These popular and uncritical works of hagiography – dismissed by Max Weber as 'written for the Christmas table of the philistine'[86] – substantially contributed to the hero-worship of Bismarck in the years before 1945.

Bismarck's political activity after 1890 was not confined to the printed word, and through public appearances and speeches he courted publicity and wooed popularity in a way that he had never sought to do in office. Far more accessible than he had been as chancellor, he also lent his name to right-wing organisations such as the Pan-German League and the Agrarian League that attacked government policies in the 1890s. In March 1891 there was much trepidation in Berlin when Bismarck agreed to stand as a National Liberal candidate in a Reichstag by-election in the Hanoverian constituency of Neuhaus, Kehdingen and Geestemünde. Bismarck was forced into a run-off election in April against the Social Democrat candidate but, although he won, he never took up his mandate before the Reichstag was dissolved in May 1893. Frequently contemptuous of party politicians while he held office, he now extolled the virtues of an official opposition and emphasised the legitimate role of parliamentarians within a constitutional monarchy. But ultimately he could not contemplate returning to Berlin as a mere parliamentary deputy, and plans for him to head a new 'National Party' in 1892–93 also came to naught.[87] In March 1893 he told Baroness Spitzemberg that he was 'much too lazy and tired' to put in the hard work necessary to bring himself up to date with affairs and attend the Reichstag.[88] But the prospect of his sudden reappearance in Berlin 'like Banquo's ghost at Macbeth's table' nevertheless terrified the new leadership.[89]

It is often pointed out that there was a strange metamorphosis in the public's view of Bismarck after 1890.[90] Bismarck certainly began to enjoy growing popularity in the 1890s if this is measured in terms of the numbers of people who turned out to see him on his public appearances and who sent him congratulatory messages on his birthdays. In 1892, when Herbert married the Hungarian Countess Marguerite Hoyos in Vienna, the former chancellor's journey to and from Vienna provided further opportunities for him to be fêted like royalty and to receive public ovations in cities such as Dresden, Munich and Bad Kissingen. On his eightieth birthday on 1 April 1895, the widespread celebrations and numerous honours indicated that Bismarck had achieved new heights of popularity. Some 450,000 letters and telegrams were sent to him, most of which no longer survive but which in all probability emanated mainly from public servants, officers, academics, teachers, tradesmen, students, schoolchildren and 'an astonishing number of housewives'.[91] Nevertheless the Reichstag voted not to send him its congratulations, indicating how bitterly the parliament still resented his treatment of it, and many of his former enemies remained aloof. The fact that Bismarck, the founder of the Reich and creator of the Reichstag suffrage, only received 43 per cent of the vote in a turn-out of barely 55 per cent in the first round of the by-election in 1891 also indicates how divided the nation was over his personality and legacy.[92] Moreover, the warmth of feeling among the crowds can be called into question when many may have simply wanted a glimpse of a man who, love him or loathe him, had dwarfed his contemporaries. Finally, there is no doubt that Bismarck's popularity grew as the likelihood of his possible return to office receded and that the new phenomenon of Bismarck adulation developed in a specific political context. The more critical Bismarck was of the New Course and the more Wilhelm II and his government attacked Bismarck, the more his stature grew.

Bismarck, of course, drew great satisfaction from the fact that he appeared to be more popular and respected out of office than he had ever been in power. Celebrated as a national hero, he was already conscious of his role in helping to shape the new idolatry. As the 'chancellor without office', he sought to exert a different kind of power, pitting his moral and intellectual authority against the mediocrities who now ruled in Berlin. Convinced that his historical mission was not yet over, he was less concerned about his place in the history books of the future than about his continuing influence in the 1890s. It was this latter consideration which drove him to insist upon his editorial control of transcripts of his speeches before they were released to the world's press and which also led him to manipulate the new medium of photography to create a starkly simple but potent image of himself.

As at the beginning of his career, Bismarck understood the impact of his physical presence and posed for the camera (usually alongside his dogs) in a way calculated to enhance his individuality. Power and creativity, strength and genius, sovereignty and fearlessness were all exuded from his gaze. The plain black dress he chose to wear in retirement was also designed to emphasise his dignity, suggesting timeless authority and immutability. The young Count Harry Kessler, who met and observed Bismarck for several hours in Kissingen in 1891, wrote that he consciously used the seductive arts and talents of the actor to enhance his public image and present himself to the public as they wanted to see him.[93] He never allowed himself to be filmed, and photographs of the former chancellor had to be approved before they were distributed. Most were retouched so that the withering signs of old age and mortality could be erased. The fact that few unofficial and natural photos of Bismarck in his retirement have survived is testimony to the extent of the manipulation from Friedrichsruh. The growth of amateur photography and the advent of professional paparazzi were already perceived as dangerous to this enterprise. Indeed, even before his dismissal, Bismarck complained about the photographers' intrusions into his private life. 'The fellows lie in wait for you everywhere with their cameras [Knipsapparaten]', he remarked presciently, and when they snapped, you did not know 'whether you were being photographed or shot'.[94] Maintaining the Bismarck myth became a considerable strain for Bismarck the man during the last years of his life. Conscious that his physical decay would undermine his symbolic role and influence, he was ultimately cut off from all but a few selected guests for fear of the impact on the public if he was seen reduced to human proportions.

Bismarck undoubtedly found psychological solace in his new role and sought to maintain the public's interest in his personality. The enthusiastic public receptions and the many demonstrations of gratitude and recognition, if not love, also improved his physical health in the early 1890s after the trauma of his dismissal. His unprecedented criticisms of the reigning monarch and his refusal to withdraw into private life presented his successors, however, with an acute and scarcely solvable dilemma. Unable to ignore 'the old man' at Friedrichsruh who wished to be seen as a sage and a seer and who still sought power and influence even while ousted from high office, the Kaiser's new advisers were often at a loss how to deal with him. Again and again Bismarck's oppositional stance and his growing popularity as a national symbol triggered crises which were highly destabilising for the new regime. In 1892 the Kaiser appealed to Franz Joseph not to receive his 'disobedient subject' in Vienna, and Caprivi (on the advice of Holstein, who had much to lose from a reconciliation between the Kaiser and Bismarck) added fuel to the flames by instructing the German embassy staff there not to attend Herbert's wedding. Such strategies were deeply wounding to the former chancellor and to his loyal public following. Having been informed previously that the Austrian Kaiser would receive him, Bismarck vented his fury in an interview in the Viennese *Neue Freie Presse*.[95]

From 1893 the Kaiser and his court – against the advice of the government – made strenuous efforts to limit the damage by effecting a reconciliation with Bismarck. Such a reconciliation appeared even more urgent when Bismarck fell seriously ill in the late summer of 1893 and it was feared he might die. The former chancellor recovered, however, and after the Kaiser sent him a symbolic bottle of wine (which he apparently drank with Harden) he came to Berlin for a brief, ceremonial visit on 26 January 1894. Wilhelm II then made a return visit to Friedrichsruh on 19 February 1894. But the reconciliation was superficial and neither man had changed his opinion of the other. Moreover, reconciliation carried many risks for the men of the New Course, who feared that the Kaiser might then be persuaded to install a new regime sympathetic to the Bismarcks and the conservatives. Bismarck himself attached little import- ance to being on harmonious terms with the new government or the Kaiser. 'I have never been a courtier, even in relation to the old Kaiser,' he wrote to Lucius in 1892, 'and in my last ten years of office I kept my distance from court affairs.' If he was 'out of favour' with the Kaiser, he could no more change the situation than he could change the weather.[96] In 1896 he exacerbated the rift again when he released to the public via the *Hamburger Nachrichten* details of the secret Reinsurance Treaty of 1887 with Russia, a treaty that the Kaiser had been advised not to renew in March 1890. Wilhelm II was so incensed that he threatened to incar- cerate him in Spandau prison for treason. Earlier, in 1892, he had rejected sending Bismarck to Spandau, declaring, 'I do not intend to make Bis- marck a martyr, to whom the people would make pilgrimages.'[97] On 26 February 1897 it was the Kaiser's turn to aggravate the conflict. In a highly publicised speech to the Brandenburg provincial Landtag, he paid tribute to his grandfather's achievements over and above those of his advisers, whom he dismissed as 'dogsbodies and pygmies'. The public affront to Bismarck was not in doubt, and such was the storm of public indignation that the former chancellor could afford to instruct the *Hamburger Nachrichten* to remain silent.[98]

By this time, of course, Bismarck was growing increasingly frail. He was tended now primarily by the Rantzaus (his daughter and son-in-law), Rudolf Chrysander (a young doctor who was also his private secretary), Schweninger (who came to stay for a few days every fortnight) and a bevy of female nurses and companions. Johanna had died on 27 Novem- ber 1894 at the age of 70 after a protracted period of decline and he never really recovered from her loss. Three weeks later he wrote to his sister how he did not want to leave Varzin to travel to Friedrichsruh for Christmas, where he would feel even lonelier among people. 'What I still had was Johanna, the contact with her, making sure she was con- tent each day, demonstrating the gratitude with which I look back on 48 years. And today everything [is] bleak and empty; the feeling is unjust but *I can not help it*.'[99] His life was now pointless, he complained from Friedrichsruh in January 1895. He was no longer sufficiently sprightly to be a farmer and he could not pursue politics without intervening in a harmful or dishonourable way. 'I see before me the hitherto alien ghost of boredom. I would move to the city, [and] visit theatres and casinos, if hatred and love did not bother me there.' Nor could he summon up his 'manly courage', for he could only do that if he had an enemy and a battlefield.[100] Bismarck never left Friedrichsruh again after Johanna's death. He would have liked to see Varzin again but could not contemplate the journey.

Bismarck's weariness with life never diminished his appetite. Rising at 11 a.m. he was still able to consume three eggs with cognac, then champagne and a glass of grog before lunch began at noon and consisted of several different courses.[101] He continued to eat and drink too much, sometimes lying for most of the day on a sofa and refusing any form of fresh air or exercise. From the spring of 1897 his health deteriorated. Apart from neuralgia, depression and general irritability, severe pain in his left leg and foot gave increasing cause for concern. An amputation was ruled out, however, on account of his age and his name. Privately the 'Iron Chancellor' was mainly confined to a wheelchair and held hot water bottles to his cheek to ease the pain of facial neuralgia. But his family and doctors flinched from any course of action that might change public perceptions of him. The consequence was accelerated decline and greater irritability. Increasingly cut off from the outside world, Bismarck received only the most unavoidable visitors. Hohenlohe and the newly appointed state secretary of the Foreign Office, Bernhard von Bülow, visited him on 28 June 1897 and Bülow was taken aback when Bismarck asked after his father, the state secretary of the Foreign Office who had died in 1879.[102] The new state secretary of the Reich Navy Office, Alfred von Tirpitz, also visited him in August to try to persuade him to go to Kiel the following month for the launch of a battleship named after him. But the former chancellor declined to appear in public 'as a ruin' and sent word to the Kaiser that he only wished to be let alone and to die in peace.[103] By September 1897 Rantzau's exasperation was clearly in evidence. 'Papa complains about everything, demands help and support from everyone, rejects every piece of advice and does not say what he wants', he wrote to Herbert in September 1897.[104]

At the end of October Schweninger revealed to Bismarck's sons that their father's days were numbered. As Bismarck became progressively more dependent on morphine, his household began to conduct a frantic but ultimately successful operation to ensure that the outside world, and especially the Kaiser's government, was kept ignorant of his rapid decline and imminent death. Yet remarkably Bismarck rallied himself for a final, rather sudden visit from Wilhelm II on 16 December, ensuring that the Kaiser left deceived about his true condition. His recurring night-mare was that when his end was near the Kaiser would appear at his deathbed. Wilhelm, however, recognised the symbolic significance of Bismarck's death and ardently wished to be there to hear his final words and to play a glorious role at his funeral. Thus during the last year of Bismarck's life a desperate comedy was played out as the Kaiser took pains to ensure he was informed about his old adversary's state of health, even writing personal letters to Schweninger and offering him financial inducements. The Bismarck household, for their part, plotted to ensure his hopes were frustrated and to keep the detested monarch at arm's length from Friedrichsruh so that the old man could indeed die in peace.

In the end the Bismarcks and, above all, Schweninger succeeded in duping the Kaiser. Schweninger became a master at writing vacuous statements about Bismarck's health, and he spent all day on 27 and 28 July 1898 writing optimistic telegrams and letters with the aim of misleading the press. Wilhelm II, sailing on his annual North Sea cruise, never had the opportunity to race to Bismarck's bedside before he died, gently and peacefully according to Herbert, at 10.57 p.m. on 30 July. And although he immediately returned to Germany, Wilhelm was also frus-trated in his efforts to stage a spectacular funeral in Berlin's cathedral and have the national hero buried in the Hohenzollern crypt. In accord-ance with Bismarck's wishes, a special mausoleum was to be built at Friedrichsruh, to which Johanna's body would also be transferred. By the time the Kaiser and Kaiserin arrived at Friedrichsruh for the funeral service on 2 August, the coffin had even been closed. According to Bülow, who accompanied the Kaiser, Herbert Bismarck confronted Wilhelm with 'manly pride ... courage and spite'.[105] The massive pressure on the Bismarck family during these days ensured that no real grief could be expressed, only relief when it was all over. The Kaiser duly returned to Friedrichsruh seven months later when the coffin was finally moved to the mausoleum on 16 March 1899. Herbert Bismarck, however, had hoped the work on the simple chapel would be completed in November 1898 when the Kaiser was in Palestine and unable to attend.[106]

There was one peculiar postscript to Bismarck's death on 30 July 1898. Almost five hours after Bismarck's death, just before 4 a.m. on 31 July 1898, two paparazzi, Willy Wilcke and Max Priester, broke into Bis-marck's bedroom despite all the security (including a guard of honour sent by the Kaiser) and photographed his corpse.[107] The photograph they took was true to real life, showing Bismarck with his head wrapped in a bandage, slumped in a rather dishevelled bed in a normal, albeit undigni-fied domestic setting. It was then immediately retouched for publication.

The bandage and crockery beside the bed were removed, the bed linen was smoothed and straightened, and the facial features now conveyed a gentle and peaceful passing. On 2 August several Berlin newspapers carried an advert seeking a publisher or purchaser for the photograph, which aroused intense press interest. The Bismarck family, however, moved quickly to prevent its publication and to institute legal proceedings against the photographers, who were subsequently imprisoned. The episode thus highlighted the extraordinary lengths to which two men were prepared to go to satisfy the public's insatiable curiosity about events in Friedrichsruh in the summer of 1898. But it also demonstrated the determination of Bismarck's family to ensure that nothing might damage his image and reputation for posterity. To secure Bismarck's immortality as a national hero, it was incumbent upon his heirs that publication of the first and only authentic photograph of him as a dead man should be suppressed. It was the family's intention that neither of the photographs should ever be published and they languished in the Bismarcks' safe for many years. Even in 1920 Herbert's widow, Marguerite, still saw their publication as sacrilege. The original photograph of Bismarck's deathbed was only published for the first time in a magazine in 1953.

Bismarck's death marked a crucial juncture in his transition from elder statesman to national legend and in the years that followed his family played a vital role in preserving his mythic reputation as the *Reichsgründer*. Nothing that might tarnish his memory was to be permitted. Bill died in 1901, merely two weeks before the unveiling of the great Bismarck statue in Berlin. Herbert, whose devotion to his father had involved such personal sacrifices, died in September 1904. His widow, who was only 33 years old when he died, took it upon herself to oversee the publication of Bismarck's memoirs and act in the interests of the Bismarck family name for the next forty-one years. She died in 1945 not long after her sister-in-law, Sibylle (Malwine's daughter and Bill's widow), shot herself at the age of 81 when the Red Army reached Varzin in March 1945.

There was no great outpouring of national grief or sadness when Bismarck died in 1898. Nevertheless, it was really only the Social Democrat press which thought to criticise the almost inexorable process by which Bismarck became transformed into a national metaphor. After his death Bismarck idolatry quickly assumed massive proportions, and a huge number of monuments and statues were erected across Germany in his honour. Bismarck's personality and achievements were appropriated by nationalists and imperialists, who deified the *Reichsgründer* as the embodiment of German strength and power. But Bismarck's demonisation by his critics was no less significant in serving to shape the myth of his superhuman qualities and abilities. The counter-myth that he almost singlehandedly frustrated the cause of national unity, sowed division and dissension, stymied political progress and emasculated German institutions became part of an alternative national folklore. The demonic view of Bismarck has recurred in the historiography through to the present and ensures his continuing status as the most problematical figure in German history after Hitler.[108]

Notes

1 Herbert Bismarck conservatively estimated Bismarck's estate in 1898 to be about 13 million marks. See Manfred Hank, *Kanzler ohne Amt: Fürst Bismarck nach seiner Entlassung 1890–1898* (Munich, 1977), p. 41.

2 Rothfels, Bismarck to Johanna, 5 June 1885, p. 408.

3 Vierhaus, *Spitzemberg*, 3 December 1888, p. 257.

4 Rothfels, Bismarck to Bernhard, 15 October 1887, pp. 413–14.

5 See Pflanze, III, p. 303. See also Vierhaus, *Spitzemberg*, 1 April 1874, p. 146.

6 Holstein, II, 8 August 1885, p. 228.

7 Ibid., 12 September 1885, pp. 246–7.

8 Ibid., 10 January 1886, p. 274, and 14 February 1886, p. 283.

9 Ibid., 22 October 1888, p. 379.

10 Ibid., 3 October 1886, p. 306.

11 Ibid., 14 March 1887, p. 335.

12 Ibid., 29 April 1887, p. 340.

13 Roon to Blanckenburg, 16 January 1870. Cited in Pflanze, II, p. 66.

14 Cited in Röhl, *Young Wilhelm*, p. 632.

15 See ibid., p. 633, and J. Alden Nichols, *The Year of the Three Kaisers: Bismarck and the German Succession 1887–1888* (Chicago, 1987).

16 Cited in Pflanze, III, p. 234.

17 Vierhaus, *Spitzemberg*, 2 January 1888, p. 238; Holstein, II, 18 June 1885, p. 207.

18 Holstein, II, 25 December 1885, p. 271, and 29 December 1885, p. 273.

19 Ibid., 4 February 1888, p. 363.

20 Cited in Röhl, *Young Wilhelm*, p. 741.

21 See ibid., pp. 627–9.

22 See ibid., pp. 748–51.

23 Gerhard Ebel (ed.), *Botschafter Graf Paul von Hatzfeldt: Nachgelassene Papiere 1838–1901*, 2 vols (Boppard, 1976), I, Holstein to Hatzfeldt, 14 January 1888, p. 657.

24 Vierhaus, *Spitzemberg*, 7 March 1888, p. 241.

25 Ibid., 11 April 1888, p. 249.

26 Ibid., 29 March 1890, p. 275.

27 Hank, *Kanzler ohne Amt*, p. 640.

28 Ebel, *Hatzfeldt*, I, Malet to Granville, 26 February 1885, p. 446.
29 See Lucius, *Bismarck-Erinnerungen*, 17 February 1887, p. 371.
30 Holstein, II, 9 November 1887, p. 356.
31 Röhl, *Young Wilhelm*, pp. 703–5, 709.
32 See Lucius, *Bismarck-Erinnerungen*, 23 June 1888, p. 469; Pflanze, III, p. 294.
33 Kollander, *Frederick III*, especially pp. 195–9.
34 Lucius, *Bismarck-Erinnerungen*, 13 March 1888, p. 433.
35 Citations from Pflanze, III, pp. 284–5.
36 Vierhaus, *Spitzemberg*, 11 April 1888, p. 249. See also Röhl, *Young Wilhelm*, p. 801.
37 See Pflanze, III, p. 287.
38 Cited in Lamar Cecil, *Wilhelm II: Prince and Emperor 1859–1900* (Chapel Hill, 1989), p. 110.
39 Holstein, II, 4 February 1888, p. 362.
40 Ibid., 13 May 1888, p. 374.
41 Helmuth Rogge (ed.), *Friedrich von Holstein: Lebensbekenntnis in Briefen an eine Frau* (Berlin, 1932), Holstein to Ida von Stülpnagel, 3 July 1888, pp. 149–50.
42 See Pflanze, III, p. 307.
43 Holstein, III, Herbert Bismarck to Holstein, 17 October 1888, p. 301.
44 Cited in Pflanze, III, p. 303.
45 Rogge, *Friedrich von Holstein*, Holstein to Ida von Stülpnagel, 13 November 1889, p. 152.
46 Bußmann, *Herbert von Bismarck*, Bernhard von Bülow to Herbert Bismarck, 12 February 1888, p. 508.
47 Rogge, *Friedrich von Holstein*, Holstein to Ida von Stülpnagel, 3 July 1888, p. 149.
48 See Pflanze, III, pp. 333–7.
49 Cited in Cecil, *Wilhelm II*, pp. 135–6; see also pp. 147–59 and Pflanze, III, pp. 359–60.
50 Vierhaus, *Spitzemberg*, 7 December 1889, p. 266.
51 Cited in Pflanze, III, p. 360.
52 See J.C.G. Röhl, *Wilhelm II: Der Aufbau der Persönlichen Monarchie 1888–1900* (Munich, 2001), p. 276.
53 Cited in Pflanze, III, p. 370. See also Margaret Lavinia Anderson, *Windthorst: A Political Biography* (Oxford, 1981), pp. 384–9.
54 Friedrich Curtius (ed.), *Memoirs of Prince Chlodwig of Hohenlohe Schillingsfuerst*, trans. George Chrystal (London, 1906), II, 26 March 1890, p. 411.
55 See Pflanze, III, pp. 321–6.
56 See Röhl, *Wilhelm II*, p. 303.
57 Ibid., p. 250. See also Holstein, III, Holstein to Eisendecher, 5 July 1889, p. 313.
58 Holstein, III, Herbert Bismarck to Holstein, 3 March 1884, p. 107. See Röhl, *Wilhelm II*, p. 253.
59 Röhl, *Wilhelm II*, p. 264.
60 Ibid., p. 310.

61 Cecil, *Wilhelm II*, pp. 160, 169.
62 Cited in Röhl, *Wilhelm II*, p. 308.
63 Ibid., p. 316.
64 Bußmann, *Herbert von Bismarck*, Herbert Bismarck to Bill, 16 February 1890, p. 362.
65 Röhl, *Young Wilhelm*, p. 285.
66 Curtius, *Hohenlohe*, II, 21 March 1890, p. 409.
67 See Röhl, *Wilhelm II*, pp. 311–12.
68 Cited ibid., p. 319.
69 Röhl, *Wilhelm II*, p. 324.
70 Curtius, *Hohenlohe*, II, 21 January 1891, p. 419.
71 See Pflanze, III, pp. 364–6.
72 Curtius, *Hohenlohe*, II, 26 March 1890, p. 412. See also Röhl, *Wilhelm II*, pp. 341–2.
73 Lucius, *Bismarck-Erinnerungen*, 19 March 1890, p. 524.
74 Holstein, III, Holstein to Herbert Bismarck, 24 January 1890, p. 324.
75 Vierhaus, *Spitzemberg*, 10[sic] March 1890, pp. 271–2.
76 See Pflanze, III, p. 375 and Röhl, *Young Wilhelm*, p. 690.
77 Vierhaus, *Spitzemberg*, 29 March 1890, p. 276; Lucius, *Bismarck-Erinnerungen*, 29 March 1890, p. 525. See also Pflanze, III, pp. 375–6.
78 Fuchs, II, Széchényi to Kálnoky, 30 March 1890, p. 760.
79 GW, XIII, speech of 16 July 1894, pp. 536–7.
80 See Hank, *Kanzler ohne Amt*, p. 124.
81 Curtius, *Hohenlohe*, II, 26 April 1890, p. 415.
82 Holstein, I, pp. 150–1.
83 Cited in Hank, *Kanzler ohne Amt*, p. 148.
84 Cited in Lothar Machtan, *Bismarcks Tod und Deutschlands Tränen* (Munich, 1998), p. 77.
85 J. Penzler, *Fürst Bismarck nach seiner Entlassung*, I (Leipzig, 1897), 26 August 1890, p. 217.
86 Max Weber, 'Parliament and Government in Germany under a New Political Order', in P. Lassmann and R. Speirs (eds), *Weber: Political Writings* (Cambridge, 1994), p. 144.
87 See especially Hank, *Kanzler ohne Amt*, pp. 258–70.
88 Vierhaus, *Spitzemberg*, 19 March 1893, p. 307.
89 Cited in Hank, *Kanzler ohne Amt*, p. 268.
90 See for example Ullrich, *Bismarck*, p. 124. See also Werner Pöls, 'Bismarckverehrung und Bismarcklegende als innenpolitisches Problem der wilhelminischen Zeit', *Jahrbuch für die Geschichte Mittel- und Ostdeutschlands*, 20 (1971), pp. 182–201.
91 Hank, *Kanzler ohne Amt*, p. 86.
92 See ibid., p. 263.
93 H. Graf Kessler, *Gesichter und Zeiten: Erinnerungen* (Berlin, 1962), pp. 252–3.
94 Cited in Machtan, *Bismarcks Tod*, p. 152.
95 Curtius, *Hohenlohe*, II, 24 June 1892, p. 432.

96 Rothfels, Bismarck to Lucius, 20 December 1892, p. 427.
97 Curtius, *Hohenlohe*, II, 17 August 1892, p. 435.
98 See Hank, *Kanzler ohne Amt*, p. 613.
99 Rothfels, Bismarck to Malwine, 19 December 1894, p. 430.
100 Rothfels, Bismarck to Mittnacht, 3 January 1895, p. 431.
101 See Machtan, *Bismarcks Tod*, p. 108.
102 Bernhard von Bülow, *Denkwürdigkeiten*, 4 vols (Berlin, 1930–31), I, p. 22.
103 Alfred von Tirpitz, *Erinnerungen* (Leipzig, 1919), pp. 89, 92.
104 Cited in Machtan, *Bismarcks Tod*, p. 18.
105 See Bülow, *Denkwürdigkeiten*, I, p. 230.
106 See Hank, *Kanzler ohne Amt*, p. 640.
107 See Machtan, *Bismarcks Tod* for a full discussion of this episode. Both the touched and untouched photos are reproduced (pp. 73 and 217).
108 See its latest manifestation in Johannes Willms, *Bismarck: Dämon der Deutschen* (Munich, 1997).

Conclusion

Bismarck was in many ways an ideal subject for a 'Profile in Power' because at no point in his political career did he ever lose sight of his own power interests. He instinctively understood how issues of power underpinned the organisation of human society and how they affected all relationships, whether within families or between political parties and social classes. Moreover, even before he sought high office, Bismarck measured power in terms of his ability to impose his will on others and he saw power as guaranteeing his personal autonomy. For Bismarck, power signified a freedom to make decisions and to choose between alternative courses of action and it thus became a means of self-realisation and self-fulfilment.

On the other hand, a focus on Bismarck's power cannot do full justice to the complexity of Bismarck's character and risks reducing his political career to its lowest common denominator. Power consumed his other passions and left him a much less attractive personality at the end of his twenty-eight years in office than he had been when he first became Prussian premier at the age of 47. But, however ambitious Bismarck was for political power, he was never prepared to sacrifice or compromise his individuality in order to achieve it. Nor was he ever interested in political power merely for its own sake or more than momentarily seduced by the external trappings of power. Despite the later accusations of nepotism and his protection of his material wealth, Bismarck never lost an innate sense of self that shielded him against political corruption. Moreover, even when he clung to high office in the last months of his chancellorship, political power remained a means to an end rather than an end in itself. Political power had little meaning for Bismarck if he were not free to create and exploit opportunities, to help shape the contours of historical change or to safeguard his life's work. While determination, energy, skill, ruthlessness, brutality and pugnacity all marked his character, they coexisted alongside a profound intelligence, sensitivity and even humility about his place in history. Bismarck may have defined the meaning of political power for a generation of Germans but he never allowed himself to be defined by it.

Bismarck's power fluctuated over time and his position could never be compared to an absolute monarch or a Napoleon. In the 1860s his position as Prussian premier was scarcely secure and his political career was driven by the needs of political survival as much as by a determination to safeguard the position of the Prussian monarchy and Prussian state in Germany and Europe. After 1871 Bismarck played a central role within the imperial German political system and, with some justification, could claim, 'I am the master of Germany in all but name.'[1] He clearly performed an important integrative function, and contemporaries as well as historians have seen him exercising a 'chancellor dictatorship'. It must be emphasised, however, that Bismarck always worked under constitutional and practical constraints. He operated within a highly complex governmental structure and he contributed to its unwieldiness in no small measure. Bismarck was never satisfied with the distribution of power within the government system, he never saw himself as a dictator and he constantly sought ways of adapting or changing the balance between institutions to augment his personal power. Moreover, Bismarck's power was always conditional, dependent on the confidence vested in him by the king and threatened for most of his political career by the prospect of the succession. If he survived in power for twenty-eight years this was not merely because of ability, achievements or endurance (important though all these may have been) but because three successive monarchs chose to keep him there.

Bismarck's monarchism can perhaps be seen as the fatal flaw in his political thinking, the one area where his great intellect deserted him. If Bismarck concentrated power in his own hands, he also simultaneously concentrated power in the hands of the king and later Kaiser. One of the most problematical areas of his legacy is how he increased the powers of the Prussian military monarchy, through the prosecution of three successful wars, the solution to the constitutional conflict and the provisions of the Reich constitution. He also safeguarded the position of a personal army that was effectively removed from political control. Bismarck perpetuated the myth of divine kingship and successfully deflected criticism of his rule in the executive and in the parliaments by recourse to a language of monarchism. This was not mere verbal camouflage for his own power interests or a convenient fiction. Despite a willingness to utilise popular forces in the pursuit of his aims, Bismarck could not accept the legitimacy of popular sovereignty or countenance a world order that was no longer based on the sovereign rights of kings. When he conceded in 1888 that monarchs were no longer being born, he appeared belatedly to acknowledge that monarchy was an anachronism and that hereditary kingship was an inadequate basis for the government of a modern state. But he could never concede that his democratic liberal enemies had been right and that there was no alternative to government by and for the people.

In this sense 'the crisis of government in the Second Reich' began well before Bismarck's dismissal.[2] The clash of interest between monarchical authority and parliamentary pretension, implicit in the constitutional conflict, created tensions during Bismarck's tenure of office that were visible at every turn. Bismarck denigrated parliamentarians but he also constantly complained about the arbitrariness and fickleness of the monarchical system that ensnared him. He expressed exasperation at crown council meetings at which ministers had to wear military uniform and the king, reserving the ultimate right of decision, took aside the minister in whom he personally had the most confidence and allowed himself to be influenced by him. Yet it was paradoxical that Bismarck did so much to create the power that eventually destroyed his political career. His rejection of consensual politics and his claim to be politically neutral, above party political squabbles, furthered his dependence on traditional monarchical authority and increased his political isolation. Denied a cohesive cabinet and a stable basis of parliamentary support, by some measures Bismarck wielded less power than a contemporary British prime minister.

Bismarck's physical presence, his unique blend of personal qualities and his achievements in founding the Reich can all be seen as contributing to what can be described as his charismatic authority within the imperial German political system. Within the executive and in the parliaments, among political opponents as well as supporters, Bismarck was widely seen to tower above his contemporaries and to inspire awe if not admiration. Even his bitter opponent, August Bebel, later confessed to admire Bismarck, 'for he was a man who knew what he wanted'.[3] Nevertheless, this recognition of the impact of Bismarck's prestige, his personality and even perhaps his embodiment of a new ideal of masculinity on his exercise of power is quite different from accepting the idea, recently put forward by Hans-Ulrich Wehler, that Bismarck was 'the first man in Germany to practise charismatic rule'.[4] This assertion implicitly links Bismarck to Adolf Hitler, whose dictatorship has been cogently analysed by Ian Kershaw in this series using Max Weber's concept of charismatic authority. According to Wehler, who attempted to apply the same Weberian category, Bismarck inspired 'an extreme measure of acclaim and loyalty' through his ability to master domestic and international crises. Thus a 'charismatic community' of passionate Bismarck worshippers played a key role in the executive (or 'power cartel'), in the pro-government parties and in most of the election campaigns that were turned into vehicles of plebiscitary acclaim. But Weber identified three kinds of political rule – traditional (monarchical), rational or legal (parliamentary or bureaucratic), and charismatic (legitimised by personal results and, in its purest form, outside history and unable to be foreseen) – and the first two categories are at least as important in explaining the origins and basis of Bismarck's power as is the third.[5] Bismarck's power combined elements of all three of Weber's categories (which is surely no accident given that Weber formulated his theories in a political culture that Bismarck had done so much to shape) but he was never dependent on popular acclaim or achieving political results. As Richard Evans has countered, the basis of Bismarck's rule was institutional rather than charismatic.[6] He wielded power through controlling key offices within the state and combining the roles of Prussian minister-president, Prussian foreign minister, Reich chancellor, president of the Bundesrat and Prussian trade minister. Moreover all of these were the gift of the traditional monarch who appointed him.

The idea that Bismarck practised a Bonapartist dictatorship, combining charismatic, plebiscitary and traditional elements in a socially conservative authoritarian regime, is also no longer convincing as an explanatory model. Even contemporaries discussed the extent to which Bismarck used Bonapartist or 'Caesarist' methods of rule borrowed from the example of Napoleon III in France, although the role of the parliaments in Germany and the nature of elections were clearly very different. Recent research has undermined the once prevalent view that Bismarck shored up the traditional power structure at a specific juncture of capitalist development, becoming the 'saviour' of the middle classes by allowing them a limited degree of political influence but thereby imposing 'a massive burden on Germany's internal social and political development'.[7] Bismarck can no longer be seen as politically responsible for a 'peculiar path' that Germany took on the road to modernisation. The social, economic and cultural influence of the German middle classes was not markedly different from that of their western neighbours, nor were the political decisions made in 1866–67 or 1870–71 or 1878–79 so fateful for the future development of the German political system. One of Bismarck's great strengths was that he could live with political ambiguity, and the solutions he devised to problems were never fixed or immutable but always capable of evolution and amendment. Bismarck was energised by conflict but also prepared to compromise if it suited his political purposes. The potentialities of such compromises were never in the hands of Bismarck alone.

Bismarck chafed against the constitutional and institutional constraints on his exercise of power. In addition, he was largely dependent on circumstances, and many of his successes depended on autonomous forces or factors that were beyond his capacity to manipulate or control. Bismarck has often been accused of an unprincipled opportunism since he was prepared to ally with parties, forces and interests whose aims he only partially shared and often discarded them when they no longer suited his political purposes. Nevertheless it was precisely when he entered into such partnerships that he was most effective for they served to broaden the basis of his rule and gave him a leverage, for example within the executive or *vis-à-vis* the monarch, which he otherwise lacked. Bismarck was adept at exploiting favourable opportunities, but the circumstances and forces that he utilised were also rarely of his own making. The apparent discrepancy between the dynamic and dramatic period of unification and the era of consolidation from 1871 was as much the result of changed political and economic circumstances as the consequence of a shift in Bismarck's mentality. After 1871 domestic and international factors robbed him of his earlier freedom of manoeuvre and encouraged the perception that flexibility had given way to rigidity in his thinking.

Bismarck set new standards of political leadership in Germany and his methods always attracted more controversy than his aims or his achievements. Even those most impressed by his charismatic qualities often harboured a deep malaise about the means he used to achieve his political ends. Members of the political opposition resented how Bismarck turned the Reich into 'a hunting ground in which we are the hunted game', while disaffected officials decried his regime as an 'orgy of scorn and abuse of mankind, collectively and individually'.[8] In 1917 Max Weber wrote a far more pertinent article on Bismarck's legacy than his influential writings on the nature of charismatic domination.[9] Weber perceived that much of the adulation that surrounded Bismarck was 'not for the grandeur of his subtle, sovereign mind, but exclusively for the element of violence and cunning in his statesmanship, the real or imagined brutality in his methods'. Fatefully, he argued, Bismarck left no kind of political tradition in Germany, no strong or independent political party that could further his aims. 'He did not recruit, nor could he even tolerate, men with an independent cast of mind, to say nothing of men of character.' In Weber's view Bismarck thus left behind a nation accustomed to passivity and compliance, unable to articulate a political will of its own.

Bismarck's legacy is controversial and contradictory. Militarism, intolerant nationalism, the glorification of war and political authoritarianism can all be seen as the consequences of his policies, and it is perhaps not surprising that most of his recent German biographers have sought to distance themselves from his creation. The Reich, they insist, was a highly unstable and short-lived construct, which has nothing in common with the second, reunified nation-state and should now be consigned to history.[10] Bismarck's efforts to balance monarchical, federal and democratic institutions or his pioneering of social insurance legislation count for little when they were simultaneously calculated to augment his own power and defeat a succession of enemies. His legacy is inevitably mired in the catastrophes of the first half of the twentieth century, inextricably linked to the omissions, failures and crimes of his successors. Yet it is remarkable how quickly even his contemporary opponents accepted the geopolitical legitimacy of the Reich and, to this outsider at least, it appears impossible to discuss the origins of modern Germany without him. It seems self-evident that Bismarck's policies contributed to create a new German entity, separate from Austria, and that, for all their social divisiveness, they helped shape a national identity that proved beyond the capacity of two world wars and forty years of division to obliterate.

Bismarck's power was exceptional in imperial Germany. As the founder of the Reich and the creator of its institutions, he could never play a 'normal' role within its constitutional framework. 'A German Reich, a Wilhelmstrasse 77 without Bismarck – our nation [*Geschlecht*] cannot conceive of that', Baroness Spitzemberg wrote the day after his dismissal.[11] It was always apparent that his rule represented a kind of interregnum, an unavoidable and necessary concentration of power at the centre while the new Reich was consolidated. It was also evident to all that many political choices had to be deferred until he left office when the real political struggles, not least the contest between monarchical authority and its challengers, could be resumed under more normal conditions. For most of those who had to work with Bismarck, the first chancellor outstayed his welcome, outlived his political usefulness long before 1890. His power became an oppressive and stultifying burden and, whatever remnants of charismatic authority he still enjoyed, whatever the trepidation about the future, his departure signified a welcome, emotional release after nearly thirty years of his political dominance. Bismarck had once favoured putting Germany into the saddle and letting it ride. By the 1880s he had lost confidence in its ability to do so and had to be coerced to hand over the reins. But he could no more singlehandedly determine Germany's course than he could predict the future. The choices of the future would be made by his successors.

Notes

1 Wehler, *German Empire*, p. 56.

2 The reference is to the subtitle of John C.G. Röhl, *Germany without Bismarck: The Crisis of Government in the Second Reich, 1890–1900* (London, 1967).

3 Francis L. Carsten, 'Die deutsche Sozialdemokratie und Bismarcks Werk', in Kunisch, *Bismarck und seine Zeit*, p. 218.

4 Wehler, *Deutsche Gesellschaftsgeschichte*, p. 376.

5 See Max Weber, 'The Nature of Charismatic Domination', in W.G. Runciman, *Max Weber: Selections in Translation* (Cambridge, 1978), pp. 226–50.

6 Richard J. Evans, 'Bürgerliche Gesellschaft und charismatische Herrschaft: Gab es einen deutschen Sonderweg in die Moderne?', *Die Zeit*, No. 42 (13 October 1995), pp. 32–3.

7 Wehler, *German Empire*, pp. 58, 61.

8 Cited in Christian von Krockow, *Die Deutschen in ihrem Jahrhundert 1890–1990* (Reinbek bei Hamburg, 1990), p. 46; Holstein, I, p. 118.

9 The article, 'Bismarck's Legacy', was originally published in the *Frankfurter Zeitung*. See Max Weber, 'Parliament and Government in Germany under a New Political Order', in Weber, *Political Writings*, pp. 135–45.

10 See Gall, II, p. 233, and Ullrich, *Bismarck*, p. 135; cf. Krockow, *Bismarck,* who argued that German reunification in 1990 gave 'Bismarck and his work a new, almost haunting significance' (pp. 8–9).

11 Vierhaus, *Spitzemberg*, 19 March 1890, p. 271.

Chronology

1815   (1 April) Otto von Bismarck is born at Schönhausen in Brandenburg

Reorganisation of Europe at the Congress of Vienna; General Act confirms the creation of the German Confederation and Prussian acquisition of the Rhineland and Westphalia, northern Saxony and Swedish Pomerania (8 June)

(18 June) Defeat of Napoleon at Waterloo

1816   The Bismarck family moves to Kniephof in Pomerania

1822–27   Bismarck attends the Plamann Institute in Berlin

1827   Birth of Malwine, Bismarck's sister

1827–30   Bismarck attends the Friedrich-Wilhelm Gymnasium

1830–32   Bismarck attends the Gymnasium zum Grauen Kloster and completes his Abitur

1832–35   Bismarck is a student in Göttingen and Berlin

1834   Creation of *Zollverein*

1836–38   Bismarck is a *Regierungsreferendar* in Aachen and Berlin

1838   Bismarck does military service at Potsdam and Greifswald

1839   (January) Death of Bismarck's mother

Bismarck leaves state service to farm paternal estate at Kniephof

1842   Bismarck travels to England, France and Switzerland

1843   Bismarck is introduced to Trieglaff circle of pietists and Marie von Thadden

1844   Bismarck's second attempt at career in state service

Marie von Thadden marries Moritz von Blanckenburg

Bismarck is introduced to Johanna von Puttkamer

1845   Death of Bismarck's father

1846   Bismarck moves to Schönhausen

(November) Death of Marie von Thadden

1847   (May and June) Bismarck is a member of the United Landtag

(28 July) Bismarck marries Johanna von Puttkamer

1848   Revolution breaks out in Berlin (March), and Bismarck plays an active role in the counter-revolutionary struggle

(April) Bismarck is member of the second United Landtag

(April) Schleswig-Holstein crisis leads to war between Prussia and Denmark

(May) Elections to Frankfurt Parliament

(21 August) Birth of Bismarck's daughter, Marie, in Schönhausen

(December) Government of Wilhelm von Brandenburg imposes a new constitution

1849   Bismarck is elected to the new parliamentary Landtag

(April) Friedrich Wilhelm IV rejects the imperial crown of a lesser Germany offered by Frankfurt parliament

(28 December) Birth of Bismarck's son, Herbert, in Berlin

1850   (March) Bismarck takes up seat in Erfurt parliament

(July) Peace is agreed between Prussia and Denmark

(November) Otto von Manteuffel forms a new government

(November) Olmütz agreement; Prussia abandons the Erfurt Union project for a lesser Germany

(3 December) Bismarck's speech defending Olmütz agreement

1851   (Spring) Restoration of German Confederation

Bismarck is appointed Prussian envoy to Bundestag at Frankfurt

(December) Louis Napoleon establishes French Second Empire

1852   (25 March) Bismarck's duel with Georg von Vincke

(May) Treaty of London defines relationship of Schleswig-Holstein to Denmark and subjects the duchies to international regulation

(1 August) Birth of Bismarck's son, Wilhelm ('Bill'), in Frankfurt

1853–56   Crimean War

1854   (July) Bismarck is appointed member of *Staatsrat*

1855   Bismarck first visits Napoleon III

Bismarck becomes a member of the new *Herrenhaus*

1857   Bismarck's second visit to France under Napoleon III

1857–58   Bismarck's debate with Leopold von Gerlach

1858   Moltke becomes chief of the general staff

(October) Friedrich Wilhelm IV suffers a stroke and Prince Wilhelm becomes prince regent

Dismissal of Manteuffel government; new ministry under Prince Karl Anton von Hohenzollern-Sigmaringen

(November) Liberal gains in Landtag elections

1859   (March) Bismarck is appointed ambassador to St Petersburg

(April–July) France and Piedmont fight Austria in Italian War

	(September) Creation of *Nationalverein* (National Association)
	(December) Roon becomes war minister
1861	(January) Death of Friedrich Wilhelm IV and accession of Wilhelm I
	(June) Foundation of Progressive Party
	(December) Prussian foreign minister, Albrecht von Bernstorff, attempts to revive lesser German Union policy
	(December) Progressives become largest party in Landtag in elections
1862	(March) Prussian Landtag votes in favour of free trade treaty with France
	Landtag dissolution in March and elections in May exacerbate constitutional conflict
	(March) Government of Prince Adolf zu Hohenlohe-Ingelfingen; Queen Augusta opposes Bismarck's appointment
	(May) Bismarck is appointed ambassador to Paris
	(August–September) Holiday with Katharina Orlov in Biarritz
	(17 September) Crown council meeting at which Wilhelm I rejects compromise over army reform; he then drafts his abdication
	(18 September) Roon's *'periculum in mora'* telegram to Bismarck
	(22 September) Bismarck's interview with Wilhelm I at Babelsberg
	(23 September) Bismarck is appointed Prussian minister-president
	(30 September) 'Blood and iron' speech to Landtag's budget committee
	(8 October) Bismarck is appointed Prussian foreign minister
1863–64	Bismarck's conversations with Ferdinand Lassalle, leader of the General German Workers' Association
1863	(February) Polish uprising in Russian Poland
	(8 February) Alvensleben convention with Russia
	(May) Landtag is dissolved after its rejection of revised army reform proposals
	(1 June) Press decree
	(5 June) Crown Prince Friedrich Wilhelm makes speech at Danzig criticising the Bismarck government
	(August) Bismarck prevents Wilhelm attending the 'princes' congress' in Frankfurt to discuss Austrian proposals to reform German Confederation

(August and September) Prussian counter-proposals to reform German Confederation include establishment of national, elected parliament

(15 November) Death of Frederick VII of Denmark and accession of Christian IX

(18 November) Christian IX signs new constitution which affects the status of Schleswig and Holstein

(24 December) German Confederation troops occupy Holstein and Lauenburg

Friedrich von Augustenburg proclaims himself Duke Friedrich VIII of Schleswig-Holstein

1864   Austro-Prussian alliance; occupation of Holstein (January) and Schleswig (February) lead to war against Denmark

(3–4 February) Prussian crown council discusses annexation of duchies

Landtag rejects war credits bill

(18 April) Austro-Prussian forces storm Danish fortifications at Düppel

(20 April–25 June) London conference on Schleswig-Holstein problem

(26 June) Austria and Prussia resume war against Denmark

(1 August) Preliminary peace with Denmark

(August) Negotiations between Bismarck and Rechberg in Schönbrunn lead to draft treaty (Schönbrunn convention)

(October) Bismarck holidays with the Orlovs in Biarritz

(30 October) Treaty of Vienna confirms Austrian and Prussian control of Schleswig, Holstein and Lauenburg

1865   Constitutional conflict worsens after failure of further compromise plan over army reform and Landtag's rejection of navy bill

Manteuffel is appointed governor of Schleswig

(August) Gastein convention with Austria

(15 September) Bismarck is elevated to status of hereditary count

1866   Prussian protests over Austrian pro-Augustenburg policy in Holstein

(28 February) Crown council discusses war against Austria

(April) Prussian alliance with Italy

(9 April) Prussian proposal to German Confederation for national, democratically elected parliament to consider reform

(May) Resignation of finance minister, Karl von Bodelschwingh
(7 May) Ferdinand Cohen-Blind attempts to assassinate Bismarck
(8 May) Gerlach's article 'War and Reform' published in the *Kreuzzeitung*
(May) Gablenz proposals for Schleswig-Holstein
(1 June) Austria refers problem of duchies to the Confederation
(14 June–26 July) Prussian Seven Weeks' War against Austria and other states of German Confederation
(27/28 June) Prussians defeat Hanoverians at Langensalza
(3 July) Prussians defeat Austrians at Königgrätz (Sadowa)
(3 July) Elections to Prussian Landtag
(16 July) Prussian occupation of Frankfurt
(26 July) Preliminary peace of Nikolsburg
(18 August) Prussia concludes treaty of federation with allied North German states
(23 August) Peace of Prague
(August) Creation of North German Confederation and Prussian annexation of Schleswig-Holstein, Hanover, Hesse-Kassel and Frankfurt
(August) Prussia concludes alliance treaties with Bavaria, Württemberg and Baden
(3 September) Indemnity bill passed by Prussian Landtag
(October–November) Bismarck drafts 'Putbus dictates' on new constitutional structure
(15 December) Draft constitution is presented to a conference of German governments

1867 Constituent Reichstag elected (12 February) and passes constitution of North German Confederation (16 April)
Bismarck is appointed *Bundeskanzler* of North German Confederation
(April) Bismarck purchases estate of Varzin in Pomerania with endowment granted by Prussian Landtag
(April–May) Luxemburg crisis; London conference confirms the grand duchy's independent status and its continuing membership of *Zollverein*
(12 June) Formal foundation of National Liberal Party
(1 July) Constitution of North German Confederation comes into operation
(August) First legislative Reichstag elected
(August) *Bundeskanzleramt* set up under Rudolf Delbrück

1868	(February and March) Elections to *Zollparlament* mobilise anti-Prussian forces in south German states
	(September) Deposition of Spanish Queen Isabella by Spanish military opens question of Spanish succession
1869	(May) Landtag elections in Bavaria give absolute majority to the anti-Prussian Patriotic Party
1870	(June) Bismarck secures consent of Wilhelm I and Prince Leopold of Hohenzollern-Sigmaringen to latter's candidacy for Spanish throne
	(13 July) Bismarck releases edited version of Ems dispatch
	(19 July) French declaration of war
	(14 August) Prussian war council at Herny in Lorraine
	Battle of Sedan (1/2 September), and capture of Napoleon III
	(31 October) Russia denounces Black Sea clauses of Treaty of Paris (1856)
	(October and November) Negotiations with south German states at Versailles
	(9 December) Reichstag of North German Confederation accepts constitutional changes
1871	(18 January) Proclamation of German Empire from Versailles Bismarck is created a hereditary prince and becomes Reich chancellor; he receives the Sachsenwald near Hamburg (which becomes his estate of Friedrichsruh) as a gift from Wilhelm I
	(February) Provisional peace with France provides for annexation of Alsace-Lorraine
	(March) Elections to national Reichstag; new Centre Party becomes second largest party
	(10 May) Peace of Frankfurt
	(July) Abolition of Catholic Section of *Kultusministerium* marks beginning of *Kulturkampf*
1872	(January) Adalbert Falk replaces Heinrich von Mühler as *Kultusminister*
	(December) Local government bill is passed in the *Herrenhaus* after the creation of new peers
	(December) Bismarck resigns as minister-president and is replaced by Roon (with effect from 1 January 1873)
1873	'Great Crash' marks end of economic boom
	(May) Laws increase state control over education and the clergy
	(October) Resignation of Roon
	(October) Three Emperors' League formed

1874	Bismarck secures the recall of the German ambassador to Paris, Harry von Arnim (February), and has him tried and convicted for treason
	(13 July) Eduard Kullmann attempts to assassinate Bismarck at Bad Kissingen
1875	War in Sight crisis (April/May), and Bismarck offers his resignation
	(July) Rebellion against Turkish rule in Bosnia-Herzegovina
	Death of Kathy Orlov
1876	(April) Resignation of Rudolf Delbrück
	(June) Balkan League declares war on Turkey
	(July) Foundation of German Conservative Party
1877	(1 January) First Reich offices (Justice and Alsace-Lorraine) set up, subordinated to the Reich chancellor
	(24 April) Russia declares war on Turkey
	Bismarck offers ministerial position and vice-chancellorship to the National Liberal leader, Rudolf von Bennigsen
	(15 June) Kissingen Dictate
	(July) Bismarck's paper factories at Varzin are inspected
1878	(March) Ministerial reshuffle (Finance, Trade and Interior)
	(March) Deputisation law facilitates dissolution of *Reichskanzleramt* and reorganisation of Reich executive
	(3 March) Treaty of San Stefano
	(11 May) Attempted assassination of Wilhelm I by Max Hödel
	(2 June) Attempted assassination of Wilhelm I by Karl Nobiling
	(24 May) Anti-socialist bill is rejected by Reichstag
	(June) Otto zu Stolberg-Wernigerode becomes vice-president of Prussian ministry of state and deputy chancellor
	(11 June) Dissolution of Reichstag
	(13 June–13 July) Congress of Berlin
	(October) Revised anti-socialist law is passed
	(6 November) Marie von Bismarck marries Count Kuno zu Rantzau
1879	Bismarck threatens to resign over reform of Bundesrat's procedures
	(12 July) Tariff law passed by Reichstag
	(6 October) Dual Alliance is signed in Vienna
1880	(September) Bismarck becomes minister of trade
	Secessionists leave National Liberal Party
1881	(January) First meeting of Prussian economic council

(Spring) Bismarck prevents marriage between Herbert and Elisabeth von Carolath-Beuthen

(March) First accident insurance bill is introduced to Reichstag

(18 June) Three Emperors' Agreement is signed

Reichstag elections (October) lead to major gains for the left liberals

1882   (20 May) Triple Alliance formed when Italy joins Dual Alliance

1883   (May) Ernst Schweninger becomes Bismarck's doctor

(15 June) Medical insurance law passed by Reichstag

1884   Revival of Prussian *Staatsrat*

(March) German Radical (*Freisinnige*) Party founded

(April) Bismarck agrees to establishment of German protectorate at Angra Pequena (South-West Africa)

(6 July) Extended accident insurance law is passed by Reichstag

(September) Renewal of Three Emperors' Agreement

(November) Congo Conference opens in Berlin

1885   Bismarck purchases former ancestral land at Schönhausen

(March) Bismarck's government authorises expulsion of Polish and Jewish aliens from Prussian eastern provinces

Kulturkampf legislation starts to be dismantled

(September) Revolution in Eastern Roumelia triggers Bulgarian crisis

(13 November) Serbia declares war on Bulgaria

1886   (7 April) Settlement law funding German land purchases in Polish provinces is passed in Prussian Landtag

(May) Herbert von Bismarck becomes state secretary of the Foreign Office

(14 July) General Boulanger is appointed minister of war in France

1887   (14 January) Reichstag is dissolved over rejection of *Septennat*

(February) Reichstag elections lead to majority for *Kartell*

(11 March) *Kartell* passes *Septennat*

(24 March) Mediterranean entente between Austria, Britain and Italy

(16 May) General Boulanger is dismissed from French cabinet

(18 June) Secret Reinsurance Treaty with Russia

(12 November) Crown prince's cancer is officially confirmed

(17 December) War council (without Bismarck) discusses war against Russia

1888   (9 March) Death of Wilhelm I and accession of Friedrich III

(15 June) Death of Friedrich III and accession of Wilhelm II

1889   (27 January) Boulanger crisis culminates in his election in Paris

Old age and disability insurance law passed by Reichstag

Miners' strike in Westphalia (May) spreads to Saxony, Silesia and the Saar basin

1890   (24 January) Crown council meeting discusses Kaiser's social plans

(25 January) Reichstag rejects anti-socialist bill

(27 January) Bismarck resigns as minister of trade

Wilhelm II's 'February decrees' on social reform

(February) *Kartell* loses its majority in the Reichstag elections

(12 March) Bismarck's meeting with Windthorst

(15 March) Confrontation between Bismarck and Wilhelm II

Bismarck writes letter of resignation (18 March), which is formally accepted on 20 March

(26 March) Resignation of Herbert as state secretary of the Foreign Office is officially accepted

(29 March) Bismarck leaves Berlin

1891   (April) Bismarck is elected to the Reichstag in a by-election

1892   Herbert Bismarck marries Marguerite Hoyos in Vienna (21 June), and Wilhelm II's government advises Austrian emperor Franz Joseph not to receive Bismarck

1894   (26 January) Bismarck pays a ceremonial visit to Berlin

(19 February) Wilhelm II visits Friedrichsruh

(27 November) Death of Johanna

1895   (1 April) Bismarck's 80th birthday

1896   (October) Bismarck reveals details of secret Reinsurance Treaty of 1887 in the *Hamburger Nachrichten*

1897   (26 February) Wilhelm II's 'dogsbodies and pygmies' speech

(28 June) Hohenlohe and Bülow visit Friedrichsruh

(16 December) Kaiser Wilhelm II visits Friedrichsruh

1898   (30 July) Bismarck dies

Further Reading in English

The best biographies of Bismarck available in English are Lothar Gall, *Bismarck: The White Revolutionary*, 2 vols, I: *1815–1871* and II: *1871–1898* (London, 1986) and Otto Pflanze, *Bismarck and the Development of Modern Germany*, 3 vols, I: *The Period of Unification 1815–1871*, II: *The Period of Consolidation 1871–1880*, III: *The Period of Fortification 1880–1898* (Princeton, NJ, 1990). Pflanze's is the more comprehensive and the two volumes on the politics of the Reich are particularly impressive. Gall's work is highly interpretative and thought-provoking but perhaps less accessible to the general reader. Unfortunately the two-volume biography of Bismarck by Ernst Engelberg has not been translated into English. The first volume, *Bismarck: Urpreuße und Reichsgründer* (Berlin, 1985), paints a vivid and sympathetic portrait of Bismarck's family and early life and is superior to the second volume, *Bismarck: Das Reich in der Mitte Europas* (Berlin, 1990), which emphasises the Bonapartist features of Bismarck's rule and focuses in particular on the state's relationship with the working class.

Those who are daunted by the prospect of multi-volume biographies can turn to Edgar Feuchtwanger, *Bismarck* (London, 2002), which is readable and concise, and synthesises much recent research. Some of the older, single-volume biographies of Bismarck are now rather dated. A.J.P. Taylor, *Bismarck: The Man and the Statesman* (London, 1955) is stimulating and typically provocative but too often the views expressed are unsubstantiated and it is no longer completely reliable. Edward Crankshaw's highly critical, often vituperative *Bismarck* (London, 1981) presents him as cynical, unscrupulous and wantonly devious, destructive rather than constructive, and driven by his own power ambitions. George O. Kent, *Bismarck and his Times* (Carbondale and Edwardsville, Ill., 1978) provides a more measured life and times and W.N. Medlicott, *Bismarck and Modern Germany* (London, 1965) is still well worth reading. Erich Eyck, *Bismarck and the German Empire* (London, 1948) is written from the standpoint of one of Germany's leading liberal historians. Fritz Stern, *Gold and Iron: Bismarck, Bleichröder and the Building of the German Empire* (London, 1977) is flawed in construction but contains much valuable material about Bismarck's private wealth and his relationship with his Jewish banker. A useful survey of the Bismarck historiography is provided by Karina Urbach, 'Between Saviour and Villain: 100 Years of Bismarck Biographies' in *The Historical Journal*, vol. 41 (December 1998). Theodore S. Hamerow (ed.), *Otto von Bismarck and Imperial Germany: A Historical Assessment* (Lexington, Mass., 1994) is a compilation of different historians' views of Bismarck.

Most of the sources used for this book are only available in German but anglophone historians interested in Bismarckian Germany can continue to find many fresh insights in the first three volumes of Norman Rich and M.H. Fisher (eds), *The Holstein Papers*, 4 vols (Cambridge, 1955–63). Some of the diplomatic documents can be found in the first volume of E.T.S. Dugdale (ed.), *German Diplomatic Documents 1871–1914*, 4 vols (London, 1928–31). Bismarck's (rather embellished) reflections and reminiscences were translated into English as *Bismarck: The Man and the Statesman*, 2 vols (London, 1898). Charles Lowe (ed.), *Bismarck's Table Talk* (London, 1895) is a distillation into one volume of conversations that were originally published in three. Herbert Bismarck (ed.), *The Love Letters of Prince Bismarck*, 2 vols (London, 1901) includes many of the early letters from Bismarck to Johanna. Further correspondence can be found in W. Littlefield (ed.), *Bismarck's Letters to his Wife from the Seat of War, 1870–1871* (New York, 1903) and J. Penzler (ed.), *Correspondence of William I and Bismarck with other Letters*, 2 vols (London, 1898). Documents on the period up to German unification can be found in John Breuilly, *Austria, Prussia and Germany 1806–1871* (London, 2002) and H. Böhme (ed.), *The Foundation of the German Empire* (Oxford, 1970). Additional material is provided in W.M. Simon, *Germany in the Age of Bismarck* (London and New York, 1968), W.N. Medlicott and D.K. Coveney (eds), *Bismarck and Europe* (London, 1971) and Theodore S. Hamerow (ed.), *The Age of Bismarck: Documents and Interpretations* (New York, 1973). Louis Snyder, *The Blood and Iron Chancellor: A Documentary Biography of Otto von Bismarck* (Princeton, NJ, 1967) uses a variety of source materials including cartoons. David Hargreaves, *Bismarck and German Unification* (London, 1991) and D.G. Williamson, *Bismarck and Germany 1862–1890* (London, 1986) both contain documents and provide useful introductions for students.

An excellent and up-to-date general introduction to nineteenth-century Germany is provided by David Blackbourn's *History of Germany 1780–1918: The Long Nineteenth Century* (London, 2nd edn 2003). James J. Sheehan, *German History 1770–1866* (Oxford, 1989), Paul W. Schroeder, *The Transformation of European Politics, 1763–1848* (Oxford, 1994) and

Thomas Nipperdey, *Germany from Napoleon to Bismarck* (Princeton, NJ, 1996) are also indispensable. John Breuilly (ed.), *Nineteenth Century Germany: Politics, Culture and Society 1780–1918* (London, 2001) is a useful collection of essays. Wolfram Siemann, *The German Revolution of 1848* (London, 1998) is the best account of the revolution and it can be supplemented with older classics such as Theodore S. Hamerow's *Restoration, Revolution, Reaction* (Princeton, NJ, 1958) and *The Social Foundations of German Unification*, 2 vols (Princeton, NJ, 1969–72). Another important work on the period before unification which sets the problem of Austro-Prussian dualism in perspective is Brendan Simms, *The Struggle for Mastery in Germany, 1779–1850* (London, 1998). David E. Barclay, *Frederick William IV and the Prussian Monarchy 1840–1860* (Oxford, 1995) offers a penetrating account of the monarchical system before the accession of Wilhelm I. Robert M. Berdahl, *The Politics of the Prussian Nobility: The Development of a Conservative Ideology 1770–1848* (Princeton, NJ, 1988) helps to place Bismarck's political views within the wider evolution of conservative thinking. John R. Gillis, *The Prussian Bureuacracy in Crisis 1840–1860* (Stanford, Calif., 1971) explores the implications of the shift from bureaucratic absolutism to constitutional monarchy for the Prussian civil service. Hermann Beck, *The Origins of the Authoritarian Welfare State in Prussia: Conservatives, Bureaucracy and the Social Question, 1815–70* (Ann Arbor, 1995) is an important analysis of the origins of social conservatism.

The process of German unification and the role of German nationalism is discussed by John Breuilly, *The Formation of the First German Nation State, 1800–1871* (London, 1996). The nature and development of German nationalism is also analysed by Hagen Schulze, *The Course of German Nationalism: From Frederick the Great to Bismarck 1763–1867* (Cambridge, 1991). Nicholas Hope, *The Alternative to German Unification: The Anti-Prussian Party, Frankfurt, Nassau and the two Hessen 1859–1867* (Wiesbaden, 1973) explores the *großdeutsch* perspective. F.R. Bridge, *The Habsburg Monarchy among the Great Powers 1815–1918* (Oxford, 1918) is excellent on Austrian foreign policy. E.N. Anderson, *The Social and Political Conflict in Prussia 1858–1864* (Lincoln, Nebr., 1954) is still the most detailed account of the constitutional conflict. The wars of German unification are addressed by William Carr, *The Origins of the Wars of German Unification* (London, 1991). W.E. Mosse, *The European Powers and the German Question 1848–1871* (Cambridge, 1958) remains indispensable for an understanding of the wider international context. Geoffrey Wawro, *The Austro-Prussian War: Austria's War with Prussia and Italy in 1866* (Cambridge, 1996) scrutinises the military campaign. Denis

Showalter, *Railroads and Rifles: Soldiers, Technology and the Unification of Germany* (Hamden, Conn., 1986) and Arden Bucholz, *Moltke and the German Wars 1864–1871* (Basingstoke, 2001) are also concerned with the origins of the Prussian victories. Lawrence D. Steefel, *Bismarck, the Hohenzollern Candidacy and the Origins of the Franco-German War of 1870* (Cambridge, Mass., 1962) remains a reliable account of the diplomatic background despite newer research into German decision-making in 1870. Gordon Craig, *The Battle of Königgrätz* (London, 1965) and Michael Howard, *The Franco-Prussian War: The German Invasion of France 1870–1871* (London, 1961) are classic accounts of the two wars. Stimulating essays on the wider implications of the wars can be found in S. Förster and J. Nagler (eds), *On the Road to Total War: The American Civil War and the German Wars of Unification 1861–1871* (Cambridge, 1997).

There has been an enormous growth of interest in imperial Germany in the last forty years and there is now a broad range of literature available in English on the period between 1871 and 1914. It is fair to say, however, that since the Fischer controversy of the 1960s, research has focused more on the Wilhelmine period and the origins of the First World War than on Bismarckian Germany, and this emphasis is also reflected in the historiography. Volker Berghahn, *Imperial Germany, 1871–1914: Economy, Society, Culture and Politics* (Oxford, 1994) is reliable and authoritative although it has little to say about Bismarck or Bismarckian high politics. Wolfgang J. Mommsen, *Imperial Germany 1867–1918: Politics, Culture and Society in an Authoritarian State* (London, 1995) is a collection of thought-provoking essays on some of the key problems in interpreting the imperial German state and its relationship to German society. Another important collection of essays is James J. Sheehan (ed.), *Imperial Germany* (New York, 1975). Gordon A. Craig includes substantial chapters on Bismarckian Germany in his textbook, *German History 1866–1945* (Oxford, 1978). Roderick McClean and Matthew S. Seligmann, *Germany from Reich to Republic 1871–1918* (London, 2000) is a useful, brief introduction for students, as is Lynn Abrams, *Bismarck and the German Empire 1871–1918* (London, 1995). Hans-Ulrich Wehler's highly influential and systematised analysis, *The German Empire 1871–1918* (Leamington Spa, 1985) could never be recommended as a textbook to students, and many of its judgements and assumptions, not least about the nature of Bismarck's rule, have now been refined or superseded by more recent research. Important aspects of the imperial German military monarchy are addressed in John C.G. Röhl, *The Kaiser and his Court* (Cambridge, 1994) and in Gordon Craig's classic study, *The Politics of the Prussian Army 1640–1945* (Oxford, 1955). By contrast, George Steinmetz,

Regulating the Social: The Welfare State and Local Politics in Imperial Germany (Princeton, NJ, 1993) explores the state bureaucracy's role in promoting modern, bourgeois and industrial interests. David Blackbourn and Geoff Eley also focus on imperial Germany's dynamic economic and social development and its political implications in *The Peculiarities of German History: Bourgeois Society and Politics in Nineteenth-Century Germany* (Oxford, 1984).

On the national minorities, William W. Hagen, *Germans, Poles and Jews: The Nationality Conflict in the Prussian East 1772–1914* (Chicago, 1980), Richard Blanke, *Prussian Poland in the German Empire, 1871–1900* (New York, 1981) and Lech Trzeciakowski, *The Kulturkampf in Prussian Poland* (New York, 1990) all explore the troubled relationship between the national state and its Polish minority. Dan P. Silverman, *Reluctant Union: Alsace-Lorraine and Imperial Germany 1871–1918* (Harrisburg, Pa., 1972) discusses the consequences of the annexation of the two French provinces.

The political parties and electoral politics are particularly well served. The best account of German liberalism is Dieter Langewiesche, *Liberalism in Germany* (London, 2000), which can be supplemented by James J. Sheehan, *German Liberalism in the Nineteenth Century* (Chicago, 1978) and Dan S. White, *The Splintered Party: National Liberalism in Hessen and the Reich* (Cambridge, Mass., 1976). The Centre Party and the confessional divide are discussed in Helmut Walser Smith, *German Nationalism and Religious Conflict: Culture, Ideology, Politics, 1870–1914* (Princeton, NJ, 1995), Ellen E. Evans, *The Center Party 1870–1933: A Study in Political Catholicism* (Carbondale, Ill., 1981) and R.J. Ross, *The Failure of Bismarck's Kulturkampf* (Washington, DC, 1998). Jonathan Sperber's *Popular Catholicism in Nineteenth-Century Germany* (Princeton, NJ, 1984) sets the *Kulturkampf* in the wider context of how the Catholic milieu became cohesive and politicised from 1850. Margaret Lavinia Anderson's *Windthorst: A Political Biography* (Oxford, 1981) is an informative and readable biography of the Centre Party leader. James Retallack, *Notables of the Right: The Conservative Party and Political Mobilization in Germany, 1876–1918* (London, 1988) explores the evolution of the German Conservative Party. Larry E. Jones and James Retallack (eds), *Between Reform, Reaction and Resistance: Studies in the History of German Conservatism from 1789 to 1945* (Providence, 1993) is a useful collection of essays. For students interested in German Social Democracy, Roger Fletcher (ed.), *Bernstein to Brandt: A Short History of German Social Democracy* (London 1987), Susanne Miller and Heinrich Potthoff, *A History of German Social Democracy: From 1848 to the Present* (Leamington Spa, 1986) and

W.L. Guttsmann, *The German Social Democratic Party 1875–1933* (London, 1981) can serve as introductions, while Vernon L. Lidtke, *The Outlawed Party: Social Democracy 1878–1890* (Princeton, NJ, 1966) covers the period of the anti-socialist law. Both David Crew, *Town in the Ruhr: A Social History of Bochum 1860–1914* (New York, 1979) and Lynn Abrams, *Workers' Culture in Imperial Germany: Leisure and Recreation in the Rhineland and Westphalia* (London, 1992) explore the impact of social and economic change on local communities. Jonathan Sperber, *The Kaiser's Voters: Electors and Elections in Imperial Germany* (Cambridge, 1997) uses new, advanced mathematical methods to analyse the Reichstag election results and to challenge previous assumptions about the electoral support of the political parties. The impact of universal suffrage and its role in forging an increasingly democratic political culture before 1914 is the subject of Margaret Lavinia Anderson's fine study, *Practicing Democracy: Elections and Political Culture in Imperial Germany* (Princeton, NJ, 2000). The collection of articles in Geoff Eley (ed.), *Society, Culture and the State in Germany 1870–1930* (Ann Arbor, 1996) seeks to open up new perspectives on imperial Germany.

On foreign policy, students are referred to Imanuel Geiss, *German Foreign Policy 1871–1914* (London, 1976), F.R. Bridge and Roger Bullen, *The Great Powers and the European State System 1815–1914* (London, 1980) and John Lowe, *The Great Powers: Imperialism and the German Problem 1865–1925* (London, 1994). The first volume of Norman Rich's two-volume biography, *Friedrich von Holstein: Politics and Diplomacy in the Era of Bismarck and Wilhelm II* (Cambridge, 1965) provides a detailed analysis of German foreign policy decision-making from the 1870s. Lamar Cecil, *The German Diplomatic Service 1871–1918* (Princeton, NJ, 1976) explores conditions in the German Foreign Office, and Paul Kennedy, *The Rise of the Anglo-German Antagonism* (London, 1980) is far more than a diplomatic history. Older works such as W.N. Medlicott's *The Congress of Berlin and After* (London, 1938) and *Bismarck, Gladstone and the Concert of Europe* (London, 1956) still have much to recommend them. Klaus Hildebrand is one of the foremost experts on German foreign policy and his contribution, 'Opportunities and Limits of German Foreign Policy in the Bismarck Era, 1879–1890: "A System of Stopgaps"?' in Gregor Schöllgen (ed.), *Escape into War? The Foreign Policy of Imperial Germany* (Oxford, 1990) gives English readers a taste of the recent debate about Bismarck's foreign policy. W.O. Henderson, *The German Colonial Empire 1884–1919* (London, 1993) is a useful overview of Germany's colonial experience, while S. Förster, W.J. Mommsen and R. Robinson (eds), *Bismarck, Europe and Africa: The Berlin Africa Conference 1884–1885 and* the *Onset of Partition* (Oxford, 1988) provides a detailed analysis of one aspect of Bismarck's colonial policy. Karina Urbach, *Bismarck's Favourite Englishman: Lord Odo Russell's Mission to Berlin* (London, 1999) offers insights into Bismarck and his policy from the perspective of the British ambassador.

Bismarck's position after the death of Wilhelm I and his eventual dismissal are amply covered in the available literature. Leading the field must be John C.G. Röhl's monumental biography of Wilhelm II. The first volume, *Young Wilhelm: The Kaiser's Early Life 1859–1888* (Cambridge, 1998), provides an unparalleled account of Bismarckian high politics and life at the Prussian court. The second volume, *Wilhelm II, 1888–1900: The Kaiser's Personal Monarchy* (Cambridge, forthcoming 2004), provides the definitive account of the events leading to Bismarck's dismissal and highlights the difficulties the former chancellor posed for the new regime once he was ousted from office. J. Alden Nichols, *The Year of the Three Kaisers: Bismarck and the German Succession 1887–1888* (Chicago, 1987), Patricia Kollander, *Frederick III: Germany's Liberal Emperor* (Westport, Conn., 1995) and Lamar Cecil, *Wilhelm II: Prince and Emperor 1859– 1900* (Chapel Hill, 1989) also capture the period of Bismarck's decline.

Index